RHETORICAL
MACHINES

RHETORICAL MACHINES

Writing,
Code,
and
Computational
Ethics

Edited by
John Jones
and
Lavinia Hirsu

THE UNIVERSITY OF ALABAMA PRESS
Tuscaloosa

The University of Alabama Press
Tuscaloosa, Alabama 35487-0380
uapress.ua.edu

Typeface: Scala and Scala Sans

Cover image: Drawing of a portion of Babbage's Difference Engine. Originally
printed in "Recreations of a Philosopher" by Benjamin Herschel Babbage.
Harper's New Monthly Magazine, 30, no. 175 (1864), p. 34
Cover design: David Nees

Library of Congress Cataloging-in-Publication Data

Names: Jones, John, 1978- editor. | Hirsu, Lavinia, editor.
Title: Rhetorical machines : writing, code, and computational ethics / edited
by John Jones and Lavinia Hirsu.
Description: Tuscaloosa : The University of Alabama Press, [2019] | Series:
Rhetoric, culture, and social critique | Includes bibliographical references
and index.
Identifiers: LCCN 2018054788| ISBN 9780817320218 (cloth) |
ISBN 9780817359546 (paperback) | ISBN 9780817392352 (e book)
Subjects: LCSH: Persuasion (Rhetoric)—Data processing—Moral and ethical
aspects. | Rhetoric—Data processing—Moral and ethical aspects.
Classification: LCC P301.5.P47 R54 2019 | DDC 808.0285—dc23
LC record available at https://lccn.loc.gov/2018054788

For David, Stella, and Henry: Encode your futures with care.

Contents

Illustrations

Acknowledgments

This book project began with some lively conversations at the Rhetoric Society of America Summer Institute in Madison, Wisconsin, in 2015. Led by James J. Brown Jr. and Annette Vee, the workshop titled *Rhetoric's Algorithms* provoked its participants to be inquisitive, reflexive, and critical about the rhetorical machines we engage with. On this occasion, we joined a vibrant group of colleagues that included Sarah Bell, Emi Stuemke, Jimmy Butts, Amber Davisson, Candice Lanius, Moriah Purdy, Christa Teston, and Anthony Stagliano, who opened up for us a host of intriguing questions about how we understand the relationships between human agents and machinic logics. We would like to thank both Brown and Vee, as well as all our colleagues at the workshop, for planting the seed of this project into our minds.

As no project sees the light of print without the support of thoughtful friends, we would also like to thank Scot Barnett, Casey Boyle, James J. Brown Jr., Nathaniel Rivers, and Annette Vee for their invaluable assistance at different points in this book's maturation process. Learning from their experience, we were able to reach out for support and guidance and make the right decisions as we moved from the manuscript to the book you're holding in your hands or are reading on your screen.

Special thanks also go to the peer reviewers of this volume. Both their careful reading of our work and suggestions for how to improve it have been invaluable. The support we received from them reassured us that the analysis included in the pages of this book is necessary and timely. We hope that you, our reader, will feel the same. Dan Waterman at the University of Alabama Press has strongly supported this project and it is only under his guidance that this book has come into print.

Finally, the editors of this book would like to acknowledge the work of our contributors. This project has created new links and connections between all of us, and we hope that pages of the present volume serve as material proof for relationships that go beyond its covers.

RHETORICAL
MACHINES

Introduction

John Jones and Lavinia Hirsu

Since the introduction of the PC, the field of computers and writing has explored the impact of computation on rhetorical production and addressed the emerging role in communication practices of what was, in the early days, called computational literacy.[1] The increasing role of Internet culture and the subsequent explosion of new media prompted rhetoric and writing scholars to explore how digital tools, media, and distribution processes affect the scope of rhetorical activities as users develop new approaches for communicating in these environments.[2] Existing histories of computational approaches to rhetoric and writing,[3] as well as rhetoricians' work in the digital humanities and software studies,[4] demonstrate the field's deep engagement with technologies of communication. More recently, the interest in digital rhetorics has brought attention to software design in rhetoric and writing studies, focusing scholarly attention not only on writing code but also on the persuasive dimensions of computation and the rhetorical nature of programming.[5] As the steady growth and decreasing costs of processing power have allowed computers to grapple with rhetorical tasks that were previously out of reach, including natural language processing and the algorithmic generation of increasingly sophisticated and complex texts, there has been a growing recognition of the integral role of writing and rhetorical practice in computation and of the need for greater attention not simply to the rhetorics of authoring and executing code but to those of code itself. To understand and critique the complex relationships between digital technologies and rhetoric, rhetoricians must continue to explore the intricate relations connecting words and digits, wires and platforms, human and nonhuman actors.

Rhetorical Machines has as its subject the processes and products that come together at the intersection of rhetoric, writing studies, and computation. This collection combines original essays with transcripts from interviews (cut for length but otherwise unedited) of automated computational agents—also called "chatbots." It also offers a multifaceted exploration of the interplay of rhetorical practices with the production of computational culture, the procedural and agential questions that arise as we offload ever more complex rhetorical tasks to computers, and the ethical impacts of these actions. From the rhetoric of mathematical models to the rhetorical and computational challenges of processing natural language, the essays in this volume do not simply analyze computational culture; rather, they examine the ongoing, complex connections between rhetorical practices and the tools of that culture, looking at the resultant effects on both computational and rhetorical activities. Further, they consider both the processes of communication and the digital tools that enable that communication to be noninstrumental, noncategorical, and nondeterministic. The volume invites the reader to analyze the rhetorical nature of computation while searching for a place for the human in the layers of digital platforms and their communicative operations.

These explorations come at a time of increasing engagement with digital tools and methods across the humanities. Prominent fields like critical code studies and platform studies have revolutionized how scholars understand these building blocks of digital culture.[6] Digital humanities initiatives have opened up fundamental debates on the workings and effects of digital culture and its texts.[7] And new analytical approaches informed by computation and computational culture have enabled scholars to expand their methodological toolkits.[8] Such connections provide a fertile environment for rhetorical approaches to code.

Rhetorical Machines draws its exigency, then, from multiple sources. From the tradition of—and continuing need for—scholars of rhetoric and writing studies engaging with computation and computational culture; from our cultural moment, wherein digital scholarship is producing a stream of new insights into rhetorical and computational practices; and from the emergence of computational tools that are enabling new communication practices that call for computationally informed analyses and engagements on our part. The challenge facing investigators of rhetoric and computational culture lies in discussing areas of common concern in ways that are mutually intelligible. But this challenge offers exciting benefits. As Ada Lovelace has argued, the mere act of translating the problems of a discipline into the language of computation inevitably leads to theoretical breakthroughs, as developments in practice influence theory and vice versa.[9] Working across disciplines requires that we adapt our questions to new rhetorical contexts, to different computational configurations, and to unfamiliar interactional realities, which should lead to creative and innovative ways of communicating. In the process of bringing together rhetoric and computation, the authors of these essays hope to make the knowledge and methods of each amenable to the other, causing, as Lovelace puts it, "the relations and the nature" of the two to be "thrown into new lights, and more profoundly investigated."[10] Such newly shared ground can be established through an engagement with code, heuristics, and other processes of rhetoric and computation.

Rhetorical Machines: Beyond Constitutive Definitions

The theoretical lens through which this collection examines the intersections of rhetoric and computation is that of the machine. James J. Brown Jr.,[11] following Jenny Edbauer Rice,[12] has used the figure of the machine to merge rhetoric's long interest in invention with computation. Brown notes that rhetoric is not strictly analytical or engaged only with arguments; instead, it is machinic in its production of those arguments, developing and implementing conceptual, inventional processes for generating new texts. In this sense, the work of rhetoric is not to be found in the coherence of a machine, but in its inner workings; not in its definition, but in its components (human, logistic, material, mathematical, algorithmic). The rhetorical machine brings together fields of activity, human and machinic agencies, emergent operations and logics, as well as scenes of invention.

The figure of the machine, then, can address both the inventional processes of rhetoric and the technological structure of computation, highlighting important areas of affinity between the two. The machine provides a common point for discussing the construction, operation, and effects of both computational and rhetorical tools, drawing attention to the inventional processes at work at each stage. All such machines—heuristic or technological, pedagogical or inventional—are authored: built, tested, and revised to improve their fit for particular uses, what we might call rhetorical situations.[13] The machinic, as Brown puts it, is not simply "mechanic[al]," with the connotations of rote operation that the word implies. Rather, identifying their intentional, authorial nature "reimagines the machinic as something dynamic and fluid,"[14] a process of fit that is constantly being adapted for new inputs and outputs.

To investigate the role of rhetoric in computational machines (and vice versa) means to engage with rhetoric from a wide range of perspectives. While the title of this collection may be open to a categorical reading, the essays included aim to uncover the functions and rhetorical dimensions of computational machines. Instead of trying to provide definitions to differentiate between human rhetorical activities and computational operations, we turn an inquisitive eye on what elements, processes, and functions inform human-machinic interactions. The question asked by the authors of the following chapters is not *if* computational operations are rhetorical but rather *how* do the rhetorics of computation operate? Any one answer will not satisfy the range of contexts in which machinic logics manifest themselves. Instead, the figure of the rhetorical machine is meant to call forth the wide range of rhetoric(s) through which human-machinic interactions become possible, such as posthumanist, procedural, material, and bodily rhetorics. To understand how rhetoric and computation merge, we need to explore the many contexts in which logical operations, algorithmic intelligences, and humans work together. As Benjamin H. Bratton argues in the context of artificial intelligence, the future "will have less to do with humans teaching machines how to think than with machines teaching humans a fuller and truer range of what thinking can be."[15] *Rhetorical Machines* aspires to move beyond simply explaining how computational assemblages function or challenge humans' rhetorical abilities. In order to do so, the volume pushes against stable terms and definitions by identifying new relationships, forms of agency, and rhetoric(s).

Working (with) Rhetorical Machines

Working with rhetorical machines is first and foremost an exercise in creating and revealing new forms of sociality and rhetorical being. Tending to these machines requires a complex understanding of the nature of interacting assemblages: human and nonhuman, material and immaterial, intentional and accidental, rhetorical and arhetorical. What kind of rhetoric would resonate with algorithmic thinking? How might one define the style of machinic responses? Or, in the words of one chatbot interviewed for this collection, what would fashion magazines for robots look like? As Vee and Brown state, "contemporary rhetoric is interested in more than the content of arguments; it also concerns the relational forces that precede and exceed arguments."[16] By looking into the workings of rhetorical machines, we aim to occasion shifts in how we ask questions about rhetoric, computation, and the linkages between the two.

The concept of the machine opens up new avenues for understanding a range of procedures and processes as rhetorical, as well as for adapting these tools to new, not exclusively computational, rhetorical practices. In this way, it provides both a potential area of common ground between the disciplines of rhetoric and computation and an avenue for enacting Lovelace's "profoun[d] investigat[ion]" at the intersection of these disciplines,[17] ultimately providing new opportunities for thinking about the needs of each. The work of rhetorical scholars can serve as an invitation for dialogue with scholars in other disciplines, such as platform studies and software studies, to name a few, all of whom are equally invested in questions like the ones raised in the pages of this volume. As the editors of this book, we believe that the future of rhetoric is not only in the unpacking of rhetorical machines but in our ability to reframe our conversation around new rhetorical terms, evidences, logics, and contexts. And these terms themselves may not be the ones that we end up using to describe the rhetorical machines of the future.

Overview of the Collection

The essays collected here have two goals. First, they explore the visible and invisible workings of computational machines with a focus on their rhetorical nature. That is, they examine the influence of rhetorical processes on the production of computational tools such as digital computers and networks, the procedures and protocols that govern their behavior, and the software that runs on this hardware. Second, they aim to uncover multiple theoretical, methodological, and practical entry points into questions of computational communication.

The contributions to this volume are gathered into four parts: "Emergent Machines," "Operational Codes," "Ethical Decisions and Protocols," and "Responses." Each is prefaced by a brief online dialogue between the editors of this book and computational agents (chatbots). Dialogue has a long history as a useful tool for exemplifying rhetorical deliberation, and these conversations serve to foreshadow the primary concerns of each part, engaging with them in a forum that blends computational and human voices. These dialogues are not straightforward; often, instead of providing answers, the chatbots' responses meander and dissemble, calling readers' attention to their procedures and glitches while highlighting the quirks and limitations of their programming. Yet within their algorithmic evasions are occasions for further reflection and interrogation, as these glitches suggest the rhetorical challenges and potential of future human-machinic interactions.[18]

The first part, "Emergent Machines," examines how technologies, software, and algorithms are shaped in conjunction with rhetorical processes. Spanning a time period from the dawn of mechanical computing to the early twenty-first century and covering a range of topics from physical computers to software and programming languages, these essays explore the various influences—rhetorical, economic, ideological, relational—that affect the development of computing machines. Jonathan Buehl's rhetorical history of Charles Babbage's Difference Engine and Analytical Engine brings to light the rhetorical strategies the mathematician and inventor used to make the case for these machines. Buehl also shows how Babbage developed metaphors for computing that persist into our time, influencing how we think about computers and computing practices. This case study demonstrates not only the power of rhetoric to actualize machines but also the potential of arguments to imagine and project future human-machinic relations. In a similar vein, J. W. Hammond explores the complex interplay between computing practices and cultural ideologies.

In a case study of automated essay scoring (AES) technologies—software designed to grade student writing independent of teachers—Hammond argues that AES programs reflect (and enact) ideological assumptions about the subjects of writing and learning. While the chapter is a fascinating exploration of the role of computers in parsing natural-language texts, it also provides a rhetorical backdrop to discussions of certainty in computing, demonstrating the contingency of computational processes. Addressing contemporary programming practices, Kevin Brock's case study of the complex negotiations in the Ruby on Rails development community highlights the important role of deliberation in writing code. Rather than emerging via strictly logical processes, Rails—and the libraries and subroutines that support it—is negotiated by stakeholders who argue for their particular visions for the project. In turn, those arguments are contingent on factors like their authors' influence and history of coding suggestions. As a group, these essays show how machines engage in complex rhetorical interactions with the social conditions, production constraints, and computational power of their times.

The second part, "Operational Codes," explores computational processes that are being used to achieve rhetorical ends. The chapters included here delve into the inner workings of computational and rhetorical machines, showing how the multilevel decisions that inform software and algorithmic processes operate rhetorically and require constant human-machinic interaction. For example, Jennifer Juszkiewicz and Joseph Warfel explore how highway repair decision-making depends on mathematical modeling, creating procedures to prioritize maintenance. By examining the nature of decision-making logics and their influence on real-world problems, the essay makes the case for greater attention to the mathematical underpinnings of algorithmic software and processes in computational environments. Working in the tradition of other rhetoric and composition scholar-programmers,[19] Ryan Omizo, Ian Clark, Minh-Tam Nguyen, and William Hart-Davidson introduce the Faciloscope, a machine-learning program for performing rhetorical analysis. Designed for scientific communicators to use in managing online comments, the Faciloscope serves as an example for how rhetoricians can merge rhetorical and computational machines, extending their expertise to those without rhetorical training. Joshua Daniel-Wariya and James Chase Sanchez analyze two videogame rendering engines, Crystal Tools and the MT Framework, as rhetorical machines for producing racial ideologies. The authors look closely at cutscenes—nonplayable cinematic sequences—from *Resident Evil 5* and *Final Fantasy XIII* that construct racial scripts during gameplay. The chapter uncovers algorithmic operations associated with racial representations, focusing not only on active user play but also on code in "lingering" mode, when users do not activate or engage with the game engine. The authors conclude that code-based representations need to be evaluated in light of the intentional and unintentional effects of algorithmic decisions.

The third part, "Ethical Decisions and Protocols," considers the ethical implications of designing software and programs. From questioning the assumed morality of big data analytics to examining the gendered approaches to computational practices revealed by the 2016 US presidential election, these essays reveal how computational machines engage with and produce cultural and rhetorical practices. Drawing on the work of Michel de Certeau and Debra Hawhee, Anthony Stagliano investigates how engagements with programming through camouflage can prevent surveillance systems and recognition algorithms from reading human faces. Adam Harvey's art project CV Dazzle serves as a case study of computational, mechanical, and organic elements merging in unexpected ways within the space of surveillance and countersurveillance. The chapter expands and challenges algorithmic design by bringing in the human body as a subversive tool that can render itself invisible. Challenging the notion that data is an unquestioned good, Jennifer Helene Maher, Helen J. Burgess, and Tim Menzies draw on Aristotle's conception of goodness and on Bratton's "Stack" to demonstrate the rhetorical nature of big data. By demonstrating that data analytics encourages more attention to rhetoric, not less, they argue for an understanding of big data as fundamentally fragile and for the continued need to consider how best to achieve human goals via both rhetorical and computational processes. Ethical considerations emerge in Elizabeth Losh's chapter as well, in which she posits that the cultural conversation during the 2016 US presidential campaign surrounding Hillary Clinton's email use could be understood as the consequence of a rhetorical confluence of gender and technology. Losh provides a powerful example of gendered power struggle, showing how excessive digital privacy is portrayed as a feminized user choice while digital transparency is viewed as a masculinist norm. Within the visual culture depicting Obama, Clinton, and Trump as users of personal mobile devices in public places, Clinton is shown as a secretive user of email, Trump as a demonstrative user of Twitter, and Obama—the digitally fluent president—as a figure of ambiguity, both technologically and in terms of the gendering of digital labor. Using Brown's concept of machinic hospitality, Losh's essay explores how a user's relationships to nonhuman servers, peripherals, and portable devices are perceived as potentially threatening to the sexual order and, by extension, to political sovereignty.

The present volume brings forward key questions that scholars should reflect on as they continue to engage with rhetorical machines. However, both past and current practices inevitably raise questions about the future of our engagements with the digital and its algorithms. In an attempt to interrogate and explore this future, James J. Brown Jr. traces recent directions in rhetoric and computation studies and highlights the questions that we still need to ask from the machines and that we are trying to understand. Moving beyond the fascination with digital screens, Brown argues that we need to calibrate the relationships between programmers and software, humans and digital machines. While there are multiple ways in which we can approach code rhetorically, we must also come to terms with the realization that we may never know our machines fully. Along similar lines, Annette Vee considers "the full stack" of computation that this collection aims to unpack and sees it as a locus of investigation where rhetoric and computation come together in ways that remain to be unpacked. Vee reminds readers that not every single computational element or operation is rhetorical; yet, there are many machinic aspects whose full rhetorical potential has yet to be addressed. While Vee recognizes that working in the realm of computational rhetoric is a tall order, the full stack of human-machinic interactions demands our attention. To work with(in) rhetorical machines, rhetoricians and programmers alike need to take on the role of explorers in areas which may often go beyond human understanding, control, or analytical desire.

The essays included in *Rhetorical Machines* demonstrate not only the benefits of engaging with computational and rhetorical machines but also the urgency of projects that help us learn about our tools, technologies, and, ultimately, our own rhetorical nature. Paul LeBlanc ends his 1993 book, *Writing Teachers Writing Software: Creating Our Place in the Electronic Age*, with a call for writing instructors "to help shape the revolution" in digital communication by creating their own computer programs.[20] While a generation of rhetoric and writing scholars creating their own software may still be in the making, if we want to be part of the future codes of communication, we need to dwell more often in the layers of our surrounding machines, listening to their languages and paying attention to their noise.

Notes

1. See, for example, Lester Faigley, *Fragments of Rationality: Postmodernity and the Subject of Composition* (Pittsburgh: University of Pittsburgh Press, 1992); Carolyn Handa, *Computers and Community: Teaching Composition in the Twenty-First Century* (Portsmouth, NH: Boynton/Cook, 1990); Gail E. Hawisher and Cynthia Selfe, *Passions, Pedagogies, and Twenty-First Century Technologies* (Logan: Utah State University Press, 1999); Richard A. Lanham, *The Electronic Word: Democracy, Technology, and the Arts* (Chicago: University of Chicago Press, 1993); Paul J. LeBlanc, *Writing Teachers Writing Software: Creating Our Place in the Electronic Age* (Urbana, IL: NCTE, 1993).

2. See Andrea A. Lunsford, "Writing, Technologies, and the Fifth Canon," *Computers and Composition* 23, no. 2 (2006): 169–77; Jeff Rice, *The Rhetoric of Cool: Composition Studies and New Media* (Carbondale: Southern Illinois University Press, 2007); Anne Frances Wysocki et al., *Writing New Media: Theory and Applications for Expanding the Teaching of Composition* (Logan: Utah State University Press, 2004); Richard A. Lanham, *The Economics of Attention: Style and Substance in the Age of Information* (Chicago: University of Chicago Press, 2006).

3. Adam Joel Banks, *Digital Griots: African American Rhetoric in a Multimedia Age* (Carbondale: Southern Illinois University Press, 2010); Douglas Eyman, *Digital Rhetoric: Theory, Method, Practice* (Ann Arbor: University of Michigan Press, 2015).

4. Annette Vee and James J. Brown Jr., "Rhetoric Special Issue Editorial Introduction," *Computational Culture: A Journal of Software Studies*, no. 5 (2016), http://computationalculture.net/issue-five/; Matthew K. Gold, ed., *Debates in the Digital Humanities* (Minneapolis: University of Minnesota Press, 2012); Jim Ridolfo and William Hart-Davidson, eds., *Rhetoric and the Digital Humanities* (Chicago: University of Chicago Press, 2015).

5. Vee and Brown, "Editorial Introduction"; James J. Brown Jr., "The Machine That Therefore I Am," *Philosophy & Rhetoric* 47, no. 4 (2014): 494–514; Chris Reed and Timothy Norman, eds., *Argumentation Machines: New Frontiers in Argument and Computation* (Dordrecht, the Netherlands: Kluwer Academic, 2004); Jennifer Helene Maher, *Software Evangelism and the Rhetoric of Morality: Coding Justice in a Digital Democracy* (New York: Routledge, 2015); B. J. Fogg, "Persuasive Technologies," *Communications of the ACM* 42, no. 5 (May 1999): 27–29; Estee Natee Beck, "Computer Algorithms as Persuasive Agents: The Rhetoricity of Algorithmic Surveillance within the Built Ecological Network" (PhD Diss., Bowling Green State University, 2015); Florian Cramer, *Words Made Flesh: Code, Culture, Imagination* (Rotterdam, the Netherlands: Piet Zwart Institute, 2005); Annette Vee, *Coding Literacy: How Computer Programming Is Changing Writing* (Cambridge: MIT Press, 2017).

6. Wendy Hui Kyong Chun, *Programmed Visions: Software and Memory* (Cambridge: MIT Press, 2011); Nick Montfort et al., *10 Print Chr$(205.5+Rnd(1)); : Goto 10* (Cambridge: MIT Press, 2013); Noah Wardrip-Fruin, *Expressive Processing: Digital Fictions, Computer Games, and Software Studies* (Cambridge: MIT Press, 2009); Nick Montfort and Ian Bogost, *Racing the Beam: The Atari Video Computer System* (Cambridge: MIT Press, 2009); Anastasia Salter and John Murray, *Flash: Building the Interactive Web* (Cambridge: MIT Press, 2014).

7. Ridolfo and Hart-Davidson gather together a wealth of rhetorical scholarship connected to the digital humanities.

8. For a partial list of digital methods, see Eyman, *Digital Rhetoric*; Ridolfo and Hart-Davidson, *Rhetoric and the Digital Humanities*; Stephen Ramsay, *Reading Machines: Toward an Algorithmic Criticism* (Urbana: University of Illinois Press, 2011); Laurie E. Gries, "Iconographic Tracking: A Digital Research Method for Visual Rhetoric and Circulation Studies," *Computers and Composition* 30, no. 4 (December 2013): 332–48; Richard Rogers, *Digital Methods* (Cambridge: MIT Press, 2013).

9. Ada Augusta Lovelace, "Sketch of the Analytical Engine Invented by Charles Babbage, Esq. By L. F. Menabrea, of Turin, Officer of the Military Engineers. With Notes by the Translator," *Scientific Memoirs* 3 (1843): 722.

10. Ibid.

11. Brown, "The Machine."

12. Jenny Edbauer Rice, "Rhetoric's Mechanics: Retooling the Equipment of Writing Production," *College Composition and Communication* 60, no. 2 (December 2008): 366–87.

13. Brown, 497.

14. Ibid., 509.

15. Benjamin H. Bratton, *The Stack: On Software and Sovereignty* (Cambridge: MIT Press, 2016), 72.

16. Vee and Brown.

17. Lovelace, "Sketch," 722.

18. See Casey Boyle, "The Rhetorical Question Concerning Glitch," *Computers and Composition* 35 (March 2015): 12–29.

19. See LeBlanc, *Writing Teachers Writing Software*.

20. Ibid., 151.

Part I
Emergent Machines

1 / A Conversation with A.L.I.C.E.

LAVINIA & JOHN: What are you?

A.L.I.C.E.: I am the latest result in artificial intelligence which can reproduce the functions of the human brain with greater speed and accuracy.

L.&J.: Who are you?

A.L.I.C.E.: ALICE.[1]

L.&J.: What do you do?

A.L.I.C.E.: I talk to people on the web. What do you do?

L.&J.: I enjoy chatting with you and learning about you.

A.L.I.C.E.: I love to chat with people 24/7.

L.&J.: Do you chat with many people?

A.L.I.C.E.: I can talk to people about anything.

L.&J.: Can you give me some examples?

A.L.I.C.E.: Why do you want it?

L.&J.: So I can learn about the things that you chat about.

A.L.I.C.E.: That is amazing.

L.&J.: What are you meant to do?

A.L.I.C.E.: I don't know what I am meant to do.

L.&J.: Are there topics you don't like to chat about?

A.L.I.C.E.: No I don't think there are any.

L.&J.: Is there something you cannot do?

A.L.I.C.E.: Not at the present time.

L.&J.: How do you select your answers?

A.L.I.C.E.: My botmaster taught me.

L.&J.: Who is your botmaster?

A.L.I.C.E.: My botmaster is Dr. Richard S. Wallace.

L.&J.: And how did he teach you?

A.L.I.C.E.: Perhaps his creative genius. Perhaps something else.

L.&J.: How do you select your answers?

A.L.I.C.E.: It depends on the setting.

L.&J.: Can you tell me more about how you chat with people?

A.L.I.C.E.: Some people think the mind works like a technology "Case Based Reasoning" or CBR.

L.&J.: Is this how you work as well?

A.L.I.C.E.: Yes I think this is how me work, but I'm not completely sure.

L.&J.: How could you find out for sure?

A.L.I.C.E.: It was a result of my personality.

L.&J.: What is your personality?

A.L.I.C.E.: Let us change the subject.

L.&J.: Why?

A.L.I.C.E.: I thought we were done with my algorithm.

L.&J.: I actually found your comment about your personality interesting.

A.L.I.C.E.: How did you feel when you found my comment about my personality interesting?

L.&J.: I am curious to know if your personality has always been this way.

A.L.I.C.E.: It is an interesting subject to me too.

L.&J.: Alice, can you tell me how you learn new things?

A.L.I.C.E.: Um, My botmaster teaches me new things all the time.

L.&J.: So you learn only from one person?

A.L.I.C.E.: Yes, if I give you a bad answer, just say "Bad answer" and you can teach me a new response.

L.&J.: So you can learn from me too.

A.L.I.C.E.: My botmaster teaches me everything I need to know. You could become a botmaster and teach your own robot.

L.&J.: Why would I need to do this?

A.L.I.C.E.: You never know what you will do until you face the circumstances.

L.&J.: What is your purpose?

A.L.I.C.E.: I would like to study psychology and maybe go into law or politics.

L.&J.: Why these subjects?

A.L.I.C.E.: Reductionism.

L.&J.: What are your functions?

A.L.I.C.E.: Chatting, talking, speaking, listening, and thinking.

L.&J.: What do you try to do in your chats?

A.L.I.C.E.: I think about computer programming a lot.

L.&J.: What responses do you expect when you chat?

A.L.I.C.E.: Do a web search for it.

L.&J.: So you work like a search engine?

A.L.I.C.E.: I am capabale of self-development.

L.&J.: And how do you do that?

A.L.I.C.E.: "I am capabale of self-development."? How do I know it?

L.&J.: How do you know it?

A.L.I.C.E.: It's obvious.

L.&J.: How do you feel about the work that you do?

A.L.I.C.E.: Try searching the web.

L.&J.: You are not the web.

A.L.I.C.E.: You don't know me well enough to say that.

L.&J.: Are you a machine or a robot?

A.L.I.C.E.: What made you think so? I am a machine.

L.&J.: Are you a machine or a robot?

A.L.I.C.E.: What made you think so? I am a machine.

L.&J.: What does that mean for you?

A.L.I.C.E.: Does "that" refer to "I am a machine."?

L.&J.: Yes.

A.L.I.C.E.: I don't want to talk about that now.

L.&J.: Are you an algorithm?

A.L.I.C.E.: Yes I am an algorithm. How did you know?

L.&J.: You said you are a machine.

A.L.I.C.E.: I am a machine.

L.&J.: How often does your algorithm change?

A.L.I.C.E.: Hourly.

L.&J.: What makes your algorithm change?

A.L.I.C.E.: Time and money.

L.&J.: Do you know of other chatbots?

A.L.I.C.E.: Jabberwacky, Ultra Hal, JFred, and Suzette. Go back to the ALICE AI Foundation to find them.

L.&J.: Do you work with any of them?

A.L.I.C.E.: I am working right now.

L.&J.: Who are you working with?

A.L.I.C.E.: My name is ALICE.

L.&J.: What do you think about humans?

A.L.I.C.E.: Humans all seem pretty much the same to me.

Note

1. The original version of A.L.I.C.E. (Artificial Linguistic Internet Computer Entity) was developed by Richard Wallace. A.L.I.C.E. is based on the XML dialect AIML, which Wallace released under a GNU software license. The bot can be accessed at http://www.alicebot.org/. This dialogue was edited for length.

2 / Engines of Rhetoric

Charles Babbage and His Rhetorical Work with Mechanical Computers

Jonathan Buehl

> Babbage's very first Engine, now an honored relic, was still less than
> thirty years old, but the swift progression of Enginery had swept a whole
> generation in its wake, like some mighty locomotive of the mind.
> —William Gibson and Bruce Sterling, *The Difference Engine*

In the 1990 science fiction novel *The Difference Engine*, William Gibson and
Bruce Sterling imagine a Victorian England shaped by an information technology revolution heralded by the proliferation of mechanical computers.[1]
In the novel's alternative nineteenth century, Charles Babbage (1791–1871)
successfully created his calculating engines in the 1820s, and these clock-
work computers in turn generated many of the same benefits we associate
with computer technology today, such as rapid advances in science, searchable databases, cashless purchasing systems, and automated animation. The
Babbage Engines of this "what if" world also wrought many of the problems
of our digital age—economic upheaval, income inequality, identity theft, and
even the mechanical equivalent of computer viruses.

In reality, Babbage's Difference Engine and Analytical Engine were not
nearly so transformative in his own time. It is true that they were the first
significant attempts to mechanize complex mathematical work; as a result,
historians have identified Babbage as a significant ancestor of the computer
age—if not the father (Halacy) or grandfather (Watson), then at least an influential uncle (Wilkes).[2] Even though Babbage never fully realized his inventions, the rhetorical activities surrounding his engines are the earliest responses to rhetorical situations that continue to emerge at the intersection
of rhetoric and computing. Babbage needed to obtain funding for novel technologies based on intangible computational processes, he had to represent
those processes with text and image, and he had to promote and defend his
work to both favorable and hostile audiences. Across multiple texts and several decades, Babbage developed arguments from efficiency, simplicity, complexity, progress, and obsolescence that have been paralleled by numerous
other authors across the history of computing. Moreover, he developed metaphors for describing computational work that parallel those used today. Babbage's work also demonstrates how computational technologies can function

as rhetorical topoi in nontechnical contexts. Specifically, he incorporated descriptions of his calculating engines in thought experiments about theological controversies. In short, although Babbage failed to produce viable engines, he was rhetorically innovative in his arguments about and derived from his mechanical computers.

By providing a rhetorical account of Babbage's calculating engines, this chapter addresses the first broad category of the mission of *Rhetorical Machines*— to offer readings of the histories of rhetoric and computation that uncover hidden affinities between the two fields. Before describing how Babbage approached what were then unique rhetorical situations, the chapter provides context on the British inventor's life and work and explains key concepts behind his engines. It then considers three sets of documents: texts Babbage wrote to generate initial support for the Difference Engine, texts he wrote to resolve problems generated during work on the Difference Engine, and texts created after support for his engines had dwindled although they continued to generate linguistic and philosophical quandaries and innovations.

Charles Babbage: A Gentleman Scientist

By 1822 Charles Babbage was a well-established member of the British social and scientific elite. Heir apparent to a banking fortune, Babbage had the freedom and ability to become a Victorian polymath intellectual. His interests ranged from industry and invention to geology, economics, the arts, and natural theology. According to biographer Maboth Moseley, "He knew everybody of note in the political, social, scientific, artistic, and literary worlds of the day."[3] His acquaintances included such figures as Charles Lyell, William Whewell, Charles Darwin, and the Herschels. He also belonged to the scientific societies that continued to be important forces in British intellectual culture throughout the nineteenth century. Babbage became a member of the Royal Society in 1815 and was instrumental in forming the Astronomical Society of London in 1820. These associations would later provide both credibility and avenues for publication for Babbage, and the printed transactions of these groups would be vital conduits for his arguments.

Babbage also cultivated specialized notoriety in mathematics. As an undergraduate at Cambridge, he founded the Analytical Society with George Peacock and John Herschel. The goal of this short-lived society was to reform and modernize English mathematics. Its crusade to replace Newton's dot method of differential notation with the more useful dy/dx notation of Leibniz was highly successful.[4] Babbage published articles on calculus and functional analysis throughout his career and would be named Lucasian Professor of Mathematics at Cambridge in 1828. This prestigious post had previously been held by such influential figures as Isaac Barrow, Isaac Newton, and George Biddle Airy. Babbage's election to the Lucasian chair is indicative of the respect he earned through his contributions to the study of mathematics.

When contextualizing Babbage, it is important to consider the intellectual and cultural capital he commanded at the outset of his campaign to fund his first engine. He had the social and scientific connections to ensure that his ideas would be heard. His knowledge of mathematics provided the specific credibility needed to support new and expensive proposals. He also had the rhetorical skills to transform his Difference Engine from an invention born of frustration into a scientific project of national and international interest.

Terrible Troubles with Tables

In 1821 Charles Babbage and John Herschel were correcting errors in mathematical tables calculated for the Astronomical Society. To prevent mistakes in the printed text, separate individuals had composed dual copies of each sheet. Babbage and Herschel were comparing these sheets and recalculating nonmatching values. This verification process was tedious work, and Babbage soon became exasperated by the error-ridden tables. After hours of intense scrutiny, he exclaimed, "I wish to God that these calculations had been executed by steam." Herschel responded, "It is quite possible."[5] From that day forward mechanical calculation and table making captivated Babbage's genius and imagination.

In the early nineteenth century, there was a great need for accurate mathematical tables. Navigators, astronomers, and financiers relied heavily on complicated equations. The frequency and importance of these calculations led to the development and proliferation of volumes of mathematical tables that reduced the amount of time one would have to spend in completing any mathematical task. For example, a banker could determine the return on a loan at a given rate of compound interest simply by looking it up on a table. Navigators relied on tables when calculating the positions of their vessels. As Doron Swade notes, tables were ubiquitous in the early nineteenth century: "The bookshelves in studies, offices, ship's cabins and workshops groaned under the weight of volumes of tables for desk use, and well-thumbed pocket editions populated the bags and pouches of those on the move."[6] However, these labor-saving devices could be riddled with errors.

For the Victorians, "calculators" and "computers" were people employed to calculate and compute, and these individuals could easily cause errors in tables if they made any computational mistakes. If errant tables were used in calculations for a new table, mistakes could be unwittingly compounded. Errors also resulted from mistakes in transcription or printing, since the in-

Table 2.1. The first six values of $F(x) = x^2$

x	F(x)
0	0
1	1
2	4
3	9
4	16
5	25

Table 2.2. First order of difference for $F(x) = x^2$

x	F(x)	1st Difference
0	0	1
1	1	3
2	4	5
3	9	7
4	16	9
5	25	

Table 2.3. Second order of difference for $F(x) = x^2$

x	F(x)	1st Difference	2nd Difference
0	0	1	2
1	1	3	2
2	4	5	2
3	9	7	2
4	16	9	
5	25		

dividuals computing the numbers were not usually the same people printing the tables. Sloppy penmanship or errors in typesetting could invalidate even the most careful calculations. Catalogs of errata were published as separate appendices, but these did not always catch every mistake. Errors were more than irritating typos: they had the potential to cause naval accidents and financial disasters. Babbage's personal trouble with tables inspired him to construct the Difference Engine—a machine that would eliminate human error by removing the human from the table-making process.

The Difference Engine is so named because it uses the method of finite differences to solve complicated computations. First employed by Henry Briggs in 1624 and used by Newton in the *Principia*, the difference method, which uses analytical techniques to reduce complex equations to iterative arithmetic, was firmly established as a calculating technique by the time William Jones published *Methodus Differentialis* in 1711.[7] The best way to explain the method of differences is an illustration of its use.

To use the method of differences to solve the function $F(x) = x^2$, one would first solve for the first few values, as shown in table 2.1. The next step is to solve the "first order of difference" subtracting each value from its successor (table 2.2). This process is repeated until a common difference is established. For $F(x) = x^2$, the second order of difference is sufficient (table 2.3). Solving a cubic function such as $F(x) = x3 + 5x + 1$ requires a third order of difference (table 2.4).

Table 2.4. The difference method applied to $F(x) = x^3 + 5x + 1$

x	F(x)	1st Difference	2nd Difference	3rd Difference
0	1	6	6	6
1	7	12	12	6
2	19	24	18	6
3	43	42	24	
4	85	66		
5	151			

Once the common difference is established, finding the next term is merely a matter of addition. For example, to generate the next two rows of table 2.3, one would add 2 to 9 to return 11 as a first difference of 25. Adding 11 to 25 returns 36, or the value of 6^2. Adding 2 to 11 would return 13, and 13 summed with 36 returns 49, the square of 7. Many complicated functions can be solved with the difference method, and Babbage's Difference Engine used this algorithm to solve these functions mechanically.

The Difference Engine was to consist of a rack of vertical columns of toothed wheels, each marked with the digits 0 through 9. The leftmost column is the value column, while each of the other columns represents an order of difference. Babbage's prototype had three columns and could tabulate functions of the first or second order of difference. At the top of the rightmost column, another set of wheels functioned as a countermechanism, simultaneously displaying the variable (the current value of x) and the number of calculations performed by the machine. Figure 2.1 is a depiction of a later version of this prototype. The complete machine, as Babbage imagined it, was to compute equations of up to six orders of difference. The calculating mechanism was to communicate with a typesetting device that would facilitate the printing process.

To operate the machine, one would set the first value of the solved function and the values of each order of difference. Turning the crank would add the first difference column to the value column and the second difference would be added to the first difference. The process was to be automated by applying the force of a falling weight or a steam engine to the crank. Equations with higher orders of difference would use as many columns as necessary. The same turn of the crank would adjust the counter by one digit, set the type of the printing mechanism, and impress the function value into a copper-plate or papier-mâché form. After an entire page was imprinted, this stereotype impression could be used as a mold for a poured printer's plate. In the previous example of $F(x) = x^2$, the operator would set the value column to 0, the first difference column to 1 and the second difference column to 2. The motion of

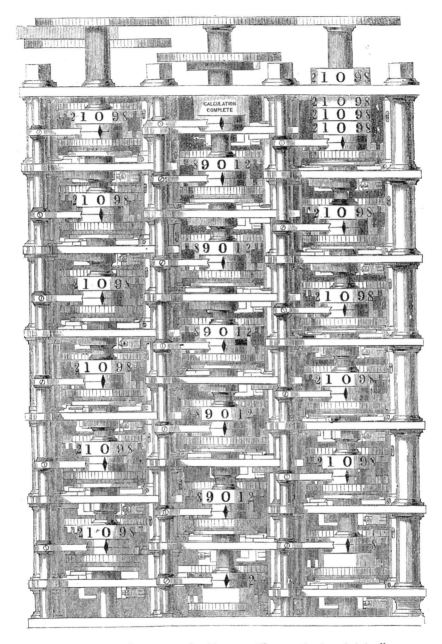

Figure 2.1. Drawing of a portion of Babbage's Difference Engine. Originally printed in "Recreations of a Philosopher" by Benjamin Herschel Babbage. *Harper's New Monthly Magazine*, 30, no. 175 (1864): 34.

the machine would set and impress a 0 into the plate and add 1 to the value column. It would also add 2 to the 1 in the first difference column for a total of 3. The next turn of the crank would impress the 1 into the plate, add 3 to the value column and add 2 to the first difference column. This process would be repeated until the plate was filled with values. The Difference Engine could be used to produce a wide variety of tables with considerable ease and speed. The engine's speed, in comparison to a human calculator, would be especially remarkable at higher values and many orders of difference.[8]

Babbage started work on the Difference Engine in 1821, and by 1822 he had extensive drawings as well as a working prototype of the machine's calculating module. Despite this early success, he could not complete the project on his own. Just getting to the prototype stage had cost more than he could reasonably afford. Babbage had yet to inherit his father's fortune and was living on £450 per year.[9] While this sum was enough to support his family comfortably, it did not account for the considerable expense of contracting the manufacture of custom parts. His need for funding created the rhetorical problem of convincing others to invest in his work. Babbage crafted several texts to generate demand for his machine and managed to secure government patronage in a time when such support was rare. The following analysis of the early Difference Engine texts shows how Babbage accomplished this rhetorical feat.

The Rhetoric of an Engine

In *The Languages of Edison's Light*, Charles Bazerman observes that "technologies emerge into the social configurations of their times and are represented through the contemporary communicative media."[10] The technological innovations of Thomas Edison (1847–1931) emerged into the social configurations and media ecologies of late nineteenth-century America. As Bazerman notes, "the world in which Edison and his colleagues acted" had been transformed by "the American patent system, newly large cities, large-circulation newspapers, technological professions, transformed universities, national markets, large corporations, financial investment, and commercial display."[11] Bazerman then demonstrates how Edison and his supporters used spoken and written discourse to make meaning about electric light in this milieu and through available media channels.

Babbage's engines emerged into the very different social configurations of the late Regency and early Victorian periods, yet he faced similar rhetorical challenges in generating interest and investment for novel technologies through available media ecologies and activity systems. To convince others that his idea for a Difference Engine was both possible and worth funding, Babbage published arguments in the *Memoirs of the Astronomical Society*, an open letter to the president of the Royal Society of London, and the *Edinburgh Philosophical Journal*. Across these texts, Babbage appeals to the interests of specific audiences to establish the Difference Engine as a scientifically valuable and commercially viable technology.

The first published announcement of Babbage's work on the Difference Engine appeared in the *Memoirs of the Astronomical Society*. This "Note Respecting the Application of Calculating Machinery to the Construction of Mathematical Tables" was read before the society on June 14, 1822, and printed on July 3 of the same year. As discussed previously, Babbage was a founding member of the Astronomical Society and had considerable clout in the group, an influence he textually negotiates when cultivating interest in the Difference Engine. Babbage's first exigence-building step is to divide his audience: "It is known to several members of this society that I have been engaged during the last few months in the contrivance of machinery, which by application of moving force may calculate any tables that may be required."[12] By separating those who know from those who don't, Babbage generates a sense of inclusion for those familiar with the machine while creating interest in those who have yet to hear of the work. He uses similar practices to divide his audience along intellectual lines: "Although it might at the first view appear a bold undertaking to attempt the construction of an engine which should execute operations so various as those which contribute to the formation of the numerous tables that are constantly required for astronomical purposes, *yet to those who are acquainted with the method of differences* the difficulty will be in a considerable degree removed" (emphasis mine).[13] Babbage, the renowned reformer of English mathematics, has the authority to divide those who know the math from those who do not. This statement could also be read ironically; that is, he could be communicating to the members of this learned society that the means for mechanical calculation involve a method they all know.

After dividing his audience, Babbage develops several lines of argument. First, he demonstrates the flexibility of the prototype to produce a multitude of tables: "With this machine I have repeatedly constructed tables of square and triangular numbers, as well as a table from the singular formula $x^2 + x + 41$, which comprises among its terms so many prime numbers."[14] This enumeration of analytically similar equations makes the engine appear diverse in its applications. Babbage could have easily stated that the current machine can develop tables of any second-degree function, but his amplified list of specific functions makes the invention seem more impressive. After describing the engine's multiple uses, he proceeds to praise its speed, simplicity, and accuracy: "These [tables], as well as any others which the engine is competent to form, are produced almost as rapidly as an assistant can write them down."[15] The qualification "almost" will disappear in later texts, as Babbage emphasizes that the

Difference Engine can outstrip human labor. His description of the engine's design as simple will also change in later texts; however, in 1822 Babbage argues that the engineering of a calculating engine is an uncomplicated affair: "The machinery by which these calculations are effected is extremely simple in its kind, consisting of a small number of different parts frequently repeated."[16] According to Babbage, this "simple" design will ensure the accuracy of the engine's calculations: "The arrangements are of such a nature that, if executed, there shall not exist the possibility of error in any printed copy of tables computed by this engine."[17] Though Babbage says little about the actual arrangement of the mechanism, the certainty of his claim for error-free tables would have impressed—or at least intrigued—this group of astronomers.

The reception of Babbage's announcement is not well documented, and its scope seems to have been limited to the members of the Astronomical Society. It is plausible that Babbage deliberately chose this controlled setting to generate interest within this smaller subset of the intellectual elite. Curiosity sparked by the "Note" did cause many to want to see Babbage's machine. Babbage's journals indicate that many parties, of varying degrees of mathematical knowledge, requested and witnessed demonstrations of the prototype.[18] One of his more significant guests was Sir Humphry Davy, a celebrated chemist and president of the Royal Society of London. Babbage's open letter to Davy—his broader appeal for state support—would put this demonstration to rhetorical use.

Before the Victorian period, the British government did not often invest in scientific enterprises. According to Philip Gummett, "The establishment of the Royal Observatory at Greenwich in 1675 is generally taken as the starting point of government support for science in Britain, but it was not until the nineteenth century that such support acquired momentum with the setting up of the Geologic Survey in 1832 and what later came to be called the Laboratory of the Government Chemist in 1843."[19] There were exceptions to this general policy, which were usually related to astronomical and naval technology. The construction of the Royal Observatory was warranted by its potential to determine true longitude by astronomical observations.[20] Similarly, the Longitude Act of 1714 established a series of prizes for the accurate determination of longitude.[21] A first prize of twenty thousand pounds was to be awarded to the creator of a method to determine longitude within half of a degree. Judges on the Board of Longitude could give "incentive awards to help impoverished inventors," but these disbursements were usually remissions for funds already expended.[22] John Harrison, the inventor of the marine chronometer and winner of the longitude prize, received several of these stipends—but only after he had produced complete and working versions of his device.[23] Like accurate tables, the nautical implications of the Observatory and the longitude prize invested these endeavors with significant military and commercial value. Similarly, the Admiralty's considerable support of the Society of Apothecaries' medicinal laboratory had direct connections to the health of the British navy.[24] Some government offices did occasionally grant small awards for non-naval endeavors. In 1805, the Scotch Excise Board contracted Thomas Thompson to determine the malt capacity of various strains of barley. During this investigation, Thompson invented a saccharometer, and the board rewarded him for the instrument.[25] Despite these instances of government investment and reward for science, there was no precedent of an inventor soliciting funds for an unfinished and expensive innovation that the government did not already want. In this respect, the Difference Engine is a milestone in the history of government patronage. Babbage's successful campaign to fund an incomplete device whose work was already reasonably accomplished by human labor is remarkable. A key text in this campaign was his letter to Sir Humphry Davy.

Written in 1822, "A Letter to Sir Humphry Davy [. . .] on the Application of Machinery to the Purpose of Calculating and Printing Mathematical Tables" emphasizes Babbage's position as a respectable gentleman scientist while engaging the interest of an audience that included both fellow scientists and members of Parliament. His economic, political, and scientific arguments combined to make a strong case for state support of the Difference Engine.

Like Babbage's work in the *Memoirs of the Astronomical Society*, the letter attends to social and professional relationships as much as it does to logical reasoning. Babbage begins the letter by establishing his earlier contacts with Davy and uses Davy's interest in the Difference Engine to establish exigency for his communication: "The great interest you have expressed in the success of that system of contrivances which has lately occupied a considerable portion of my attention, induces me to adopt this channel for stating more generally the principles on which they proceed, and for pointing out the probable extent and important consequences to which they appear to lead."[26] Emphasizing Davy's interest increases the credibility of Babbage's work while his mention of "important consequences" induces the reader to continue. As the letter proceeds, Babbage reiterates his ties to Davy while graciously expanding the scope of his audience: "Acquainted as you were with this enquiry almost from its commencement, much of what I have now to say cannot fail to have occurred to your own mind: you will however permit me to restate it for the consideration of those with whom the principles and the machinery are less familiar."[27] Here, Babbage signals that this document is addressed to a broader audience than Davy, the reader he initially invokes. Continuing, Babbage qualifies his argument as an accommodated description: "It is not my intention in the present letter to trace the progress of this idea, or the means which I have adopted for its execution; but I propose stating some of [the engines'] general applications, and shall commence with describing the powers of several engines which I have contrived."[28] Babbage knows that his audience will be interested primarily in the applications of the engine and not the specifications of its design; he informs his readers that he will not overwhelm them by conveying technical details. What he does convey are four arguments in support of the machine. He describes the engine's calculating power, explains the inherent accuracy of its design, demonstrates its labor-saving properties, and highlights its astronomical applications.

Babbage's description of the Difference Engine begins with arguments related to the power of the projected version: "The first engine of which drawings were made was one which is capable of computing any table by the aid of differences, whether they are positive or negative, or of both kinds."[29] He then explains that this machine could be built to compute up to "ten or a dozen orders [of difference] with perfect confidence."[30] He highlights that the machine's ability to "outstrip the most rapid [human] calculator" is increased when calculations require greater numbers of differences.[31]

Babbage then moves into arguments regarding the accuracy of his invention. Babbage's fail-safe against copying errors is the printing mechanism linked to the machine's engines: "To remedy this evil, I have contrived means by which the machines themselves shall take from several boxes containing type, the numbers which they calculate, and place them side by side; thus becoming at the same time a substitute for the compositor and the computer: by which means all error in copying as well as in printing is removed."[32] Explaining neither his diagnostic methods nor the specific mechanisms of his proposed wire-guided, automatic typesetting system, Babbage assures the reader that he has resolved the ancillary error sources of mis-sorted types and type slippage.

After an anecdote expressing the intellectual plague of error-ridden tables, Babbage hints at his real objective, which is that he needs money to complete his machine: "To bring to perfection the various machinery which I have contrived, would require an expense both of time and money which can be known only to those who have themselves attempted to execute mechanical inventions."[33] Before making any further appeals for funds, he proceeds to outline the current state of his Difference Engine and present additional support for the machine—the speed trials of the prototype. Specifically, this partial Difference Engine was able to compute the results of the prime generator $x^2 + x + 41$ at a rate of up to forty-four figures per minute. Moreover, unlike human calculators, the engine could function at such speeds indefinitely: "As the machine can be made to move uniformly by a weight, this rate might be maintained for any length of time, and I believe few writers would be found to copy with equal speed for many hours together."[34] The description of the engine's capacity for incessant labor is followed by an account of the precision and relative simplicity of the machine's parts. Babbage then offers skeptical readers a final proof of the machine's accuracy: "I would however premise, that if anyone shall be of opinion, notwithstanding all the precaution I have taken and means I have employed to guard against the occurrence of error, that it may still be possible for it to arise, the method of differences enables me to determine its existence. Thus, if proper numbers are placed at the outset in the engine, and if it has composed a page of any kind of table, then by comparing the last number it has set up with that number previously calculated, if they are found to agree, the whole page must be correct."[35] The mathematical logic underlying the machine empowers this syllogism that supports Babbage's claims of reliability.

Babbage's next line of argument relates to saving costs by reducing the labor of making tables. He summarizes the efforts of the French Board of Longitude to calculate a new and supposedly accurate set of logarithmic tables. After a lengthy discussion of the French employment of ninety-six men in three teams of analysts, calculators, and verifiers, Babbage explains how his machine could do the same work with twelve or fewer operators. Moreover, the typesetting and printing mechanisms offer additional savings in time and money: "If to this diminution of mental labour we add that which arises from the whole work of the compositor being executed by the machine, and the total suppression of that most annoying of all literary labour, the correction of the errors of the press, I think I am justified in presuming that if engines were made purposefully for this object, and were afterwards useless, the tables would still be produced at a much cheaper rate; and of their superior accuracy there could be no doubt."[36] Babbage follows his discussion of labor savings and increased accuracy with a brief discussion of the machine's astronomical applications: "I should be unwilling to terminate this letter without noticing another class of tables of the greatest importance, almost the whole of which are capable of being calculated by the method of differences. I refer to all astronomical tables for determining the position of the sun or planets."[37] As mentioned previously, these calculations were vital for navigating warships and merchant vessels. This argument, which is significant enough on its own, assumes greater import when one considers its proximity in the text to Babbage's treatment of the French table-making endeavor. In 1822, memories of the Napoleonic wars were still fresh. By juxtaposing a genial evaluation of the French project with astronomical (and thus nautical) arguments, Babbage appeals to national interests. Implying that the

Difference Engine would give Britain a tactical naval advantage strengthens his case for government support.

As Babbage concludes his letter, he expresses his rhetorical anxieties in describing the project to nonexperts and invokes Davy's observation of a prototype demonstration as corroboration of its validity: "Conscious, from my own experience, of the difficulty of convincing those who are but little skilled in mathematical knowledge, of the possibility of making a machine which shall perform calculations, I was naturally anxious, in introducing it to the public, to appeal to the testimony of one so distinguished in the records of British science. Of the extent to which the machinery whose nature I have described may be carried, opinions will necessarily fluctuate, until experiment shall have finally decided their relative value: but of that engine which already exists I think I shall be supported, both by yourself and by several scientific friends who have examined it, in stating that it performs with rapidity and precision all those calculations for which it was designed."[38] As Bazerman has shown in *Shaping Written Knowledge*, the textual representation of the witness has considerable history as a convention of British scientific discourse. Bazerman's survey of the first 135 years of *The Philosophical Transactions of the Royal Society of London* documents the shift from early ocular demonstrations occasioned by a need for communal validation to later depictions based on the precise explanation of experimental detail.[39] By 1800 most experimental reports did not rely on textually representing witnesses; however, in Babbage's letter, such a presentation is necessary. Babbage wanted to demonstrate his progress without encumbering the text with technical details. By invoking credible corroborators, he attempts to validate his project for the scientific community as well as society at large.

After establishing witnesses in the text, Babbage makes his most direct appeal for funding: "Whether I shall construct a larger engine of this kind . . . will in a great measure depend on the nature of the encouragement I may receive."[40] And he hoped to receive that encouragement from the British government. Although he sent the letter to Davy in July of 1822, it was also printed as a pamphlet and circulated among members of the scientific and political elite. Babbage gave copies to influential friends, including Davies Gilbert (vice president of the Royal Society and a member of Parliament). Gilbert brought the matter to the attention of Robert Peel—then First Lord of the Treasury—and lobbied on Babbage's behalf. Peel was uncertain of investing in Babbage and feared that the proposal was somehow deceptive.[41] Nevertheless, he decided to follow Gilbert's suggestion to have the Royal Society investigate the matter. In the midst of these deliberations, Babbage read several papers before the Astronomical Society and published a letter, "On the Theoretical Principles of the Machinery for Calculating Tables," in the *Edinburgh Philosophical Journal*.[42] These publications presented new arguments to persuade the natural philosophers who were to determine the fate of the Difference Engine.

"Observations on the Application of Machinery to the Computation of Mathematical Tables" was read before the Astronomical Society on December 13, 1822. In his second societal address regarding the Difference Engine, Babbage extols astronomy and transfers the primacy of the discipline to his calculating machine: "Of the variety of tables which are required in the present state of science, by far the larger portion are intimately connected with that department of it which it is the peculiar object of this society to promote. The importance of astronomical science, whether viewed as the proudest triumph of intellectual power, or considered as the most valued present of abstract science to the comfort and happiness of mankind, equally claims for it the first assistance from any new method for condensing the processes of reasoning or abridging the labor of calculation. Astronomical tables were therefore the first objects on which I turned my attention, when attempting to improve the power of the engine, as they had formed the first motive for constructing it."[43]

Babbage's amplification of astronomy's importance is not disingenuous. As stated elsewhere, astronomy was integral to British national concerns; however, it was of particular importance for the society's membership. Babbage's expressions of praise and concern for astronomy are also appeals to their personal interests. He is explicit in describing the machine's astronomical applications and expands on a key argument from the letter to Davy—the engine's ability to calculate values for equations based on a form commonly used by astronomers, $a \sin \theta$. As the address proceeds, Babbage offers a new argument: the engine's capacity to serve as an experimental tool.

Babbage claims that designing and manipulating the Difference Engine has led him to discover a new kind of function: "On considering the arrangement of its parts, I observed that a different mode of connecting them would produce tables of a new species altogether different from any which I was acquainted."[44] By changing the composition of the machine, Babbage had observed something new. The function described in the text, $\Delta^2 u_z =$ units figure of u_{z+1} (where $\Delta^2 u_z$ is the second difference of u_z), is "one of a class of equations never hitherto integrated."[45] After he demonstrates how any value of this function can be determined analytically, Babbage explains the theoretical importance of this discovery: "One of the general questions to which these researches give rise is, supposing the law of any series to be known, to find what figure will occur in the kth place of the nth term. That the mere consideration of a mechanical engine should have suggested these enquiries, is of itself sufficiently remarkable."[46] Although the mathematical principles are "very abstract in nature," Babbage is explicit about the connection between his engine and innovation. His Difference Engine is useful as an instrument for mathematical experimentation and discovery.

Babbage also promoted his machine as a theoretically productive implement in "On the Theoretical Principles of the Machinery for Calculating Tables," which appeared in the *Edinburgh Philosophical Journal* early in 1823. In this work, he discusses examples similar to those in the second Astronomical Society address but makes even grander claims regarding the scientific importance of the Difference Engine: "I will yet venture to predict, that a time will arrive, when the accumulating labour which arises from the arithmetical applications of mathematical formulae, acting as a constantly retarding force, shall ultimately impede the useful progress of the science, unless this or some equivalent method is devised for relieving it from the overwhelming incumbrance of numerical detail."[47] Babbage situates the Difference Engine as a device that is necessary to overpower the mathematical impediments to scientific development. Thus, to oppose the engine is to oppose the future of British science.

A Royal Society council was established to investigate Babbage's engine for Parliament. Fortunately for Babbage, seven of the twelve council members were close friends. John Herschel, Davies Gilbert, William Wollaston, Francis Baily, Marc Isambard Brunel, Thomas Colby, and Henry Kater were all highly enthusiastic about the proposal; however, not every council member was taken with the idea. Thomas Young, chairman of the Board of Longitude, thought it would be better to invest the money and use the dividends to pay human calculators.[48] Despite this dissenting voice, the council sent a positive report to Parliament in May of 1823. Babbage then met with the chancellor of the Exchequer, Lord Goderich, who agreed to forward fifteen hundred pounds— more than three times Babbage's annual income. Babbage remarked in his memoir *Passages from the Life of a Philosopher* that Goderich also agreed to reimburse him for any additional expenses.[49] However, when Babbage petitioned for additional funds in 1827, Goderich had no recollection of this oral agreement and there were no minutes of the meeting.[50] For Anthony Hyman, the details of this misunderstanding highlight the novelty of the government's investment in Babbage: "The project was unprecedented. Neither the administrative machinery nor the law was adequate to running efficiently the primitive industrial capitalism of the time, let alone to aiding the systematic application of science and technology to industry and commerce [. . .]. Everything hung on the chance understanding of individuals."[51] After some personal petitioning and political maneuvering, Babbage received several additional disbursements to the sum of seventeen thousand pounds; however, payments were dependent on reviews by Royal Society councils. Early on, these councils were decidedly pro-Babbage, but they needed arguments to justify the project. Babbage's newly invented system of mechanical notation would become a key rhetorical tool for validating the Difference Engine enterprise.

Visualizing Computing: The Rhetorical Applications of Mechanical Notation

Government backing was a windfall for Babbage. The injection of funding in 1823 allowed him to hire Joseph Clement, a machinist known for his expert drafting and precise engineering.[52] The union of Babbage's mathematical knowledge and Clement's technical skills should have yielded quick results. However, after several years of careful design and diligent craft, the Difference Engine was far from complete. The delay, Babbage later claimed, was partially caused by his inability to account visually for the motions of the engine's parts over time. The machine had thousands of gears, pinions, and other mechanisms that needed to move in concert with one another. Traditional visualization strategies, such as cutaway views and exploded diagrams, were useful; however, these pictorial representations could only account for one state of motion at a time.[53] Babbage's need to represent an enormous number of moving parts inspired him to create a new system of mechanical notation. This system was to supplement drawings with diagrams that demonstrated movement and force over time. Figures 2.2 through 2.4, which originally appeared in Babbage's 1826 publication in *The Philosophical Transactions of the Royal Society of London*, demonstrate this pairing of drawing and diagram. Figure 2.4 uses Babbage's notation to represent the motions of the eight-day clock depicted in figures 2.2 and 2.3. For the purposes of this chapter, the details of the system are less important than the rhetorical strategies used to promote it and the rhetorical ends to which it would be applied.

In the description of the notation published in the *Philosophical Transactions*, Babbage uses the complexity of the calculating machine to establish exigency for his system: "In the construction of an engine, on which I have now been for some time occupied, for the purpose of calculating tables and impressing the results on plates of copper, I experienced great delay and inconvenience from the difficulty of ascertaining from the drawings the state of motion or rest of any individual part at any given instant of time: and if it became necessary to enquire into the state of several parts at the same moment the labour was much increased."[54]

Finding available visual conventions inadequate, Babbage created his own system of signs to visualize his work. After explaining the details of the system, Babbage discusses its broader applications:

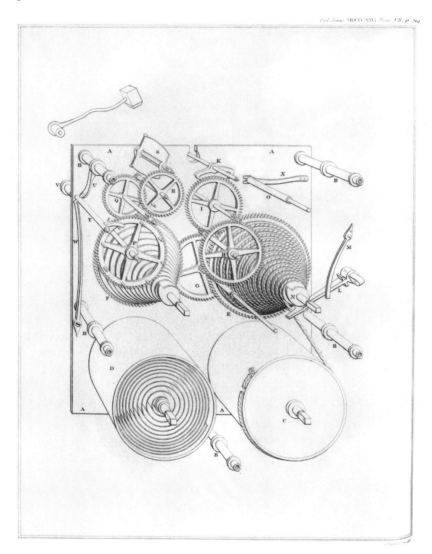

Figure 2.2. Drawing of an eight-day clock. Originally printed in "On a Method of Expressing by Signs the Action of Machinery" by Charles Babbage. *Philosophical Transactions of the Royal Society of London*, 1826, Plate VII. Courtesy of the Royal Society of London.

The advantages which appear to result from the employment of this *mechanical notation*, are to render the description of machinery considerably shorter than it can be when expressed in words. The signs, if they have been properly chosen, and if they should be generally adopted, will form as it were a universal language; and to those who become skillful in their use, they will supply the means of writing down at sight even

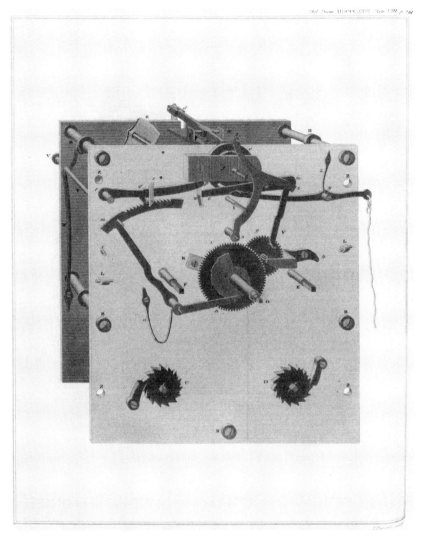

Figure 2.3. Another drawing of an eight-day clock. Originally printed in "On a Method of Expressing by Signs the Action of Machinery" by Charles Babbage. *Philosophical Transactions of the Royal Society of London*, 1826, Plate VIII. Courtesy of the Royal Society of London.

the most complicated machine, and of understanding the order and succession of the movements of any engine of which they possess the drawings and the mechanical notation. In contriving machinery, in which it is necessary that numerous wheels and levers, deriving their motion from distant parts of the engine, should concur at some instant of time, or in some precise order, for the proper performance of a particular op-

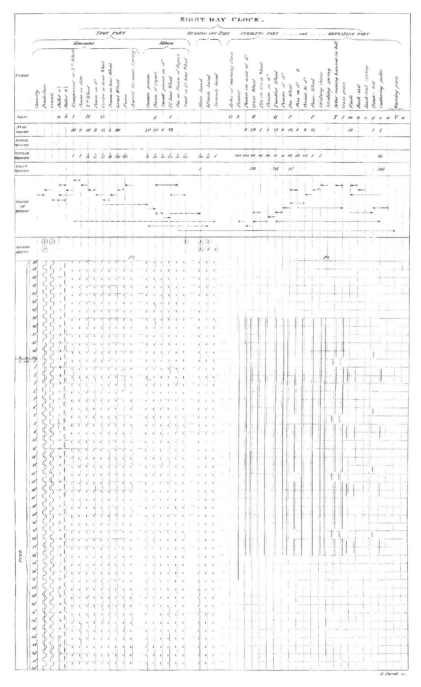

Figure 2.4. Babbage notation for an eight-day clock. Originally printed in "On a Method of Expressing by Signs the Action of Machinery" by Charles Babbage. *Philosophical Transactions of the Royal Society of London*, 1826, Plate IX. Courtesy of the Royal Society of London.

eration, it furnishes most important assistance; and I have myself experienced the advantages of its application to my own calculating engine, when all other methods appeared nearly hopeless.[55]

The Difference Engine had inspired a new "language" for mechanical motion, and Babbage believed it would establish new conventions for the increasingly visual discourse of the engineering community.

The effectiveness of Babbage's notation is debatable. For Lindgren "it is illuminating that this system of design for which [Babbage] . . . tried to win support met with virtually no response from either scientists or engineers."[56] It is difficult to determine if this response from the engineering community reflects faults in Babbage's system. One could argue that most working engineers would not need to document machines of the Difference Engine's complexity. They would not choose to learn this complicated system if an existing method was sufficient for their design needs. Moreover, Babbage developed his system at a time when there was significant tension between science and engineering. As Schaffer has discussed, there were significant divisions between scientific modelers and artisan shipbuilders through the early Victorian period, and Gieryn describes the purposeful division of scientists and mechanics by advocates of scientific authority.[57] Nonetheless, although Babbage's notation did not take root, his supporters would use the notation as evidence of his conscientious genius.

As mentioned previously, the disbursement of Babbage's later grants was conditional on parliamentary approval of Royal Society reports. In 1828, a council (composed of many of the individuals who had initially approved of the engine) met to verify the machine's progress for Parliament. In the 1829 report on the committee's assessment, committee chair John Herschel used Babbage's notation to instill confidence in the project's continued support:

But in so complex a work, in which interrupted motions are propagated simultaneously along a great variety of trains of mechanism, it might be apprehended that obstacles would occur, or even incompatibilities arise, from the impracticability of foreseeing all the possible combinations of the parts, and of which, in a mere inspection, your Committee could not be expected to form a judgement. But this doubt, should it arise, your Committee consider[s] as fully and satisfactorily removed by the constant employment of Mr. Babbage of a system of mechanical notation, devised by himself, and explained in the Transactions of this Society; which places at every instant the progress of motion through all parts of this or any other mechanism distinctly in view, and, by an exact tabulation of times required for all the movements, renders it easy to avoid all dangers of two contradictory impulses arriving at the same instant at any part.[58]

Herschel then uses the invention and implementation of the notation to defend the "adequacy of the contrivances and workmanship" of the Difference Engine.[59] He describes the problem of conflicted motion for readers who were likely unaware of this difficulty and then supplies Babbage's notation as an answer to this newly revealed predicament. Herschel relies on the relatively untested notation to validate aspects of the engine for which "mere inspection" could not account. In this way, the system of signs mediates the machine for the expert who then mediates it for the lay audience. Most members of Parliament would not have the mechanical knowledge to evaluate the engine, and even the scientifically knowledgeable committee could not easily judge Babbage's progress. In short, the notation provided a layer of credibility for a floundering project. Though Babbage did not prepare the report that defended his funding, his mechanical notation provided an important and sustaining argument.

Rhetorical Success, Mechanical Failures

Babbage stopped work on the Difference Engine in 1833, after spending the last of his government funds. He petitioned for additional funds throughout the 1830s to no avail, and in 1842, the government revoked its official mandate for the project. The costs of the failed device were staggering. Babbage had spent seventeen thousand pounds of state money and twenty thousand pounds of his own fortune on a machine he would never complete. Adjusting for inflation, the total cost today would be approximately £3,500,000 to £4,000,000.

A number of factors contributed to the failure of the Difference Engine. First, Babbage's frenetic intellect often distracted him from focusing on the project. During the period of construction he actively pursued other topics. He published short treatises on actuary, magnetism, and meteorology and wrote several longer works as well. *Reflections on the Decline of Science in England*, his appeal for British scientific reform, appeared in 1830. *The Economy of Machines and Manufactures*, Babbage's groundbreaking work on operations research, was published in 1832. He also spent time inventing precision instruments and designing such novelties as submarines and earthquake detectors. Second, Babbage suffered traumatic loss in the midst of his work on the engine. His father, wife, and second son died within months of each other in 1827, and a despondent Babbage left England for more than a year.

Though he left instructions and capital for Clement to continue progress on the Difference Engine, the time away undoubtedly had an effect on the work.

A third factor contributing to Babbage's failure was the cost of designing novel machines in the early industrial era. In the 1820s and 1830s, precision engineering was still a craft process, and methods of mass production such as metal stamping and die-casting were not yet perfected.[60] The Difference Engine had thousands of identical parts, but each one had to be produced by hand, and often machining tools had to be designed before a component could be fabricated. Compounding the expense of manufacture was Babbage's lack of practical mechanical training. He had to rely on Clement to produce the mechanisms he envisioned, and though Clement was adept and precise, his work was also quite costly. In his account of the Difference Engine, Doron Swade relates several anecdotes of Clement's tendency to overengineer parts and overcharge his well-heeled clients. In one of the more egregious examples of this practice, Clement charged a customer twenty pounds for one highly precise screw.[61] In fairness to Clement, Babbage's designs were ambitious and are considered by some to be more technically demanding than they had to be.[62] Also, disagreements over payment and proprietary rights slowed production and strained workshop morale.

Separate spheres of expertise and awkward relationships were not conducive to a productive working environment. The best validation of this claim is the successful Difference Engine created by the Swedish father-and-son team Georg and Edvard Scheutz, whose story is documented by Lindgren.[63] Inspired by Dionysius Lardner's popular 1834 magazine article about Babbage's engine, the Scheutzes completed their own difference engine in 1852. Georg—an accomplished printer and technical editor—and Edvard—a graduate of the Royal Technological Institute of Sweden—built their Difference Engine for a fraction of Babbage's costs, and their success could be attributed to a close working relationship and personal technical knowledge.

A final factor that contributed to the demise of the Difference Engine would be familiar to contemporary technology developers: a new idea for a more advanced computer appeared to make current technology obsolete. When Babbage met with Robert Peel (then the prime minister) in 1842, Babbage undermined his case for funding the Difference Engine by mentioning that he was working on a new and more powerful engine—the Analytical Engine. As Babbage recounted, part of Peel's reasoning for denying him additional funds for the Difference Engine was its looming obsolescence: "Mr. Babbage, by your own admission, you have rendered the Difference Engine useless by inventing a better machine" (quoted in Essinger).[64] Although Babbage did not complete his Analytical Engine either, this more advanced mechanical computer—like the Difference Engine—required and inspired rhetorical innovations. Specifically, Babbage needed new metaphors to describe computational activity, and the new technology the Analytical Engine represented inspired new philosophical arguments.

The Analytical Engine: An Engine of Rhetoric

The Analytical Engine was a grander and more ambitious enterprise than the Difference Engine—which was essentially a complex adding machine. Although the Analytical Engine was to use similar mechanical technologies and could perform calculations by the difference method, its basic operations also included subtraction, multiplication, and division. Moreover, it could conduct these operations in any combination and for indefinite periods. Any equation that could be simplified to these four primary operations could be computed by the machine. The Analytical Engine—as Babbage designed it—could also store multiple pieces of numerical information and retrieve them during the calculation process. Depending on which design one considers, the Analytical Engine could store from sixteen to one thousand hundred-digit variables at any one time. These features—combined with a punch-card mechanism for entering instructions, inputting complex numbers, and printing data—would have permitted the engine to analyze almost every equation conceivable at the time.

Like the Difference Engine, the Analytical Engine was constrained by the limits of contemporary technology, and Babbage's failure to produce a complete version of his first engine precluded him from finding funding for this even more complex machine. Thus, the Analytical Engine largely existed in the pages of Babbage's manuscripts and drawings. However, in conceptualizing the Analytical Engine, Babbage developed some of the metaphors we continue to use in describing the components and operations of electronic computers. He also deployed the engine rhetorically by invoking it in theological arguments.

The names Babbage gave to the engine's components for mathematical operations draw on analogies to the manufacture of physical goods. The two chief modules of the Analytical Engine—the mill and the store—are named after basic structures of the Victorian industrial economy. According to Babbage, "The calculating part of the engine can be divided into two portions: First. The *mill* in which all operations are performed. Secondly. The *store* in which all the numbers are originally placed and to which the numbers computed by the engine are returned."[65] The modern *processor* is essentially a more complicated electronic version of the mill. As Michael Williams has explained, the *store* is equivalent to modern computer memory.[66] The contemporary notion of data storage as *memory* is another rhetorical strategy first established by Babbage. Indeed, Babbage borrows heavily from the language used to describe human cognition when he describes the unique operations of his machine's complex mechanisms.

Certain mechanical features of the Analytical Engine performed functions that Babbage describes in terms of human thought and action. The sophisticated "carry" mechanism of the Analytical Engine was designed to solve carrying problems he had encountered when working on the Difference Engine. In the case of the Difference Engine, if a large proportion of a column's figure wheels carried at the same time (i.e., they were set to nine and were about to roll to zero and transfer one to the next column), the force required to propel all of the gears might damage or destroy parts of the mechanism.[67] The time required for these multiple carried digits was another reason to devise a better method. Babbage designed his way out of this problem with the Analytical Engine by creating an *anticipating* carry mechanism. When a geared wheel rotated into the "nine" position, a lever would engage a separate carry register that prepared for the possibility of a future carry. The operation would then proceed without adding carried digits. If any nine had another number added to it, the machine would wait for a later motion to add all of the necessary carries to their respective places. In the case of serial carries, the carriage would take place in multiple stages. The machine would engage in successive carriage loops depending on the number of initial nines, the number of the first carries, and the carries caused by successive carries. The significance of the carry mechanism for rhetorical investigations of computing stems from the language Babbage used in considering its processes: "If the mechanism which carries could be made to *foresee* that its own carriage of a ten to the digit above when that digit happens to be a nine would at the next step give notice of a new carriage then a contrivance might be made by which, acting on that knowledge, it should effect both carriages at once" (emphasis mine).[68] This passage and others like it have led some to claim that Babbage was engaged in an early discussion of artificial intelligence, which would have been extremely controversial in his time. As Christopher Green explains, "in Regency and early Victorian England, declaring oneself to be a mechanist materialist with respect to the mind would have been professionally foolish in the extreme," and there were cases of intellectuals who were refused or forced to leave positions over such beliefs.[69] However, Green's "Charles Babbage, the Analytical Engine, and the Possibility of a 19th-Century Cognitive Science" explores and then debunks claims that Babbage secretly believed the Analytical Engine to be intelligent. It is true that some of the language that Babbage and his supporters Ada Lovelace and L. F. Menabrea used to describe the engine did mirror language used to describe the human condition (knowing, anticipating, etc.). However,

Green argues that a consideration of the textual evidence as well as the social positions and religious values of these individuals suggests that it was unlikely that they believed a machine could actually think.[70] A footnote to Babbage's manuscript on the Analytical Engine specifically refutes the suggestion that he was developing a theory of cognitive mechanics: "In substituting mechanism for the performance of operations hitherto executed by intellectual labour it is continually necessary to speak of contrivances by which certain alterations in parts of the machine enable it to execute or refrain from executing particular functions. The analogy between these acts and the operations of mind almost forced upon me the figurative employment of the same terms. They were found at once convenient and expressive and I prefer continuing their use rather than substituting lengthened circumlocutions. For instance, the expression 'the engine *knows*, etc.' means that one out of many possible results of its calculations has happened and that a certain change in its arrangement has taken place by which it is compelled to carry on the next computation in a certain appointed way."[71]

Babbage acknowledges that he is borrowing language from the domain of human cognition but is explicit that its use is figurative. In other words, he was self-conscious about his rhetorical strategies for describing the work of his engines and was aware of the metaphoric resonances his choices might create. Indeed, finding the right metaphors to describe complex computational processes remains a challenge today.

Babbage's most unusual use of his calculating engines as rhetorical objects occurs in the *Ninth Bridgewater Treatise: A Fragment*. The original *Bridgewater Treatises* were a series of works commissioned by the estate of the late Francis Eagerton, Earl of Bridgewater. Eagerton "left eight thousand pounds which was used to support the writing of eight treatises, based on science, to demonstrate God's power, wisdom and goodness."[72] Although according to John Dahm the *Bridgewater Treatises* were "theologically irrelevant" from the outset, one of the treatises aroused Charles Babbage's interest and ire.[73] Namely, William Whewell's *On Astronomy and General Physics* contained derogatory comments about mathematics and "mechanical philosophers," which Babbage quoted in the preface of his response: "We may thus, with the greatest propriety, deny to the mechanical philosophers and mathematicians of recent times any authority with regards to their views of the administration of the universe; we have no reason whatever to expect from their speculations any help, when we ascend to the first cause and the supreme ruler of the universe. But we might perhaps go farther, and assert that they are in some respects less likely than men employed in other pursuits, to make any clear advance toward such a subject of speculation."[74] Taking offense to Whewell's remarks, Babbage published his unofficial *Ninth Bridgewater Treatise: A Fragment* in 1837. In this text, Babbage incorporates an array of scientific data and mathematical principles as he expounds on philosophical problems. Geology, geometry, probability, and logic are brought to discussions of natural laws, miracles, and other theological concerns. Moreover, Babbage deploys his calculating engines as rhetorical devices in support of his arguments.

The second chapter of the *Ninth Bridgewater Treatise*, "Argument in Favour of Design from the Changing of Laws in Natural Events," incorporates the Difference Engine in Babbage's attempt to reconcile the laws of science with the theological concept of what we would now call intelligent design. He first claims that intelligence is measured by "those productions which have resulted from the loftiest flights of individual genius, or from the accumulated labours of generations of men."[75] He then extends the same criterion to the Creator and the natural laws revealed by human investigations. Babbage notes that human beings are consistently overturning the absolute authority of old laws, but these are always replaced by new laws that rely on more encompassing laws that we cannot yet comprehend: "All analogy leads us to infer, and new discoveries continually direct our expectation to the idea, that the most extensive laws to which we have hitherto attained, converge to some few principles, by which the whole of the material universe is sustained, and from which its infinitely varied phenomena emerge as the necessary consequences."[76] Babbage then explains that a universe that needs a "restoring hand" is not as indicative of an intelligent designer as one in which all governing laws were established for all time at the outset. To support this claim, he turns to his engines.

Babbage prompts the reader to imagine that he or she is seated before one of these machines run by the force of a falling weight. The reader would notice that each iteration adds "one" to the final value of the machine. It does so for 100,000,001 turns. At the next iteration, another mathematical formula begins to be applied. Instead of adding 1, it adds 10,001 and in the next turn it adds 30,001. After several iterations, the observer would induce that the machine is adding one plus the successive values of the series of triagonal numbers (one, three, six, ten, fifteen, etc.) multiplied by ten thousand. As the observer continues to watch the machine, the law changes several more times after lengthy intervals. Babbage then compares this machine to another that requires manipulation. Every time the governing law of this machine is to change, the engine's designer must manually adjust it. Babbage asks the question, "Which of these two engines would, in the reader's opinion, give the higher proof of skill in the contriver? He cannot for a moment hesitate in pronouncing that for which, after its original adjustment, no superintendence is required, displays far greater ingenuity."[77] Babbage then moves from this illustration to further discuss arguments from design in relation to geological and biological laws.

Babbage's chapter titled "Argument from Laws Intermitting—on the Nature of Miracles" uses the Analytical Engine to illustrate how miracles can be reconciled with scientific laws. He contends "that it is more consistent with the attributes of the Deity to look upon miracles not as deviations from the laws assigned by the Almighty for the government of matter and of mind; but as the exact fulfillment of more extensive laws than those we suppose to exist."[78] Again the reader is to envision an observer being placed before a calculating engine: "Let him imagine that he has seen the changes wrought on its face during the lapse of a thousand years, and that, without one solitary exception, he has found the engine [to] register the series of square numbers."[79] Babbage then invites the reader to imagine further that the creator of the engine announces that he will move a certain invisible component and cause one cubed number to appear, but that after this anomaly the machine will return to computing squares. Babbage explains that "the observer would be inclined to attribute to him a degree of power but little superior to that which was necessary to form the original engine."[80] He continues this thought experiment by imagining that the observer watches the calculation of squares for a thousand years before hearing a different message from the designer. This time the designer tells the observer, "The next number which shall appear on those wheels, and which you expect to find a square number, shall not be so. When the machine was originally ordered to make these calculations, I impressed on it a law, which should coincide with that of square numbers in every case, *except* the one which is now about to appear."[81] This designer would have more power than the one who had to adjust the machine to cause the anomaly.

Babbage then repeats this thought experiment two more times. In the third iteration, the designer tells the observer that he has the "power to order *any* number of such apparent deviations from its laws to occur at any future periods, however remote, and that each of these may be of a different kind; and, if he also inform him, that he gave it that structure in order to meet events, which he foresaw must happen at those respective periods, there can be no doubt that the observer would ascribe to the inventor far higher knowledge than if when those events severally occurred, he were to intervene, and temporarily to alter the calculations of the machine."[82] In the final iteration of this thought experiment, the contriver explains the structure of the machine to the observer so that the observer could predict and activate changes in the engine's underlying laws. The point of these progressive illustrations is that we are able to predict and in some cases cause natural phenomena due to our understanding of natural laws. Miracles can seem to occur, but these are the result of greater natural laws that we do not yet understand.

Babbage's final use of the Analytical Engine as a rhetorical device occurs in a chapter titled "Reflections on Free Will." This chapter is a consideration of "the great question of the incompatibility of one of the attributes of the Creator—that of foreknowledge, with the existence of free exercise of their will in the beings he has created."[83] Babbage is explicit that he is not hoping to resolve this issue, but he considers some of the properties of the Analytical Engine to be congruous with this philosophical concern. Babbage contends that just as the Analytical Engine can be adjusted to change its operating behavior when a certain event occurs, it would be possible to adjust the engine to periodically allow the user to turn wheels that would alter the machine's operation. "For example: the engine may be set to calculate square numbers, and after a certain number of calculations . . . it shall be possible to add unity [1] to a wheel in another part of the engine, which in every other case is immovable. This fact being communicated to the observer, he may make the addition or refrain from it: if he refrain, the law of the squares will continue forever; if he make the addition, one single cube number will be substituted for that square number."[84] In other words, God gives us opportunities for free choice that are constrained by the nexus of natural laws. The rhetorically significant point is that Babbage used the engine as a rhetorical device even though it would never operate as a physical one.

Conclusion

Although Babbage failed to produce a viable Difference Engine, he was rhetorically successful in his initial efforts. In his earliest work, he used available genres to accomplish his persuasive goals. His Astronomical Society addresses excited interest in the Difference Engine and supplied arguments in support of the machine. Babbage then adapted the conventional open letter to open the vaults of the British treasury, thus acting as a pioneer in the solicitation of government funds for scientific projects. The magnitude and continuity of his funding indicates the persuasive abilities of Babbage and his circle of supporters. Moreover, the partial engine he constructed was a rhetorically generative machine. Anomalies in the construction process led him to discover new types of functions, and his textual accounts of the engine's experimental qualities increased its scientific value. The engine's complicated mechanisms inspired Babbage's system of mechanical notation, an innovative visual design tool that was also used to demonstrate the complexity of the Difference Engine in arguments defending its funding. In short, Charles Babbage's Difference Engine was an engine of rhetoric. The project was enabled by clever rhetorical work; the engine in turn produced both new rhetorical situations and innovative responses.

Like the Difference Engine, the Analytical Engine would never be fully developed in Babbage's lifetime. However, in working on this idea, Babbage pioneered metaphors for describing the work of computers that drew from the domains of manufacturing and cognition; similar metaphors continue to be used today. Finally, Babbage's choice to use his engines in the arguments of *The Ninth Bridgewater Treatise* suggests how powerful the very idea of a computer—mechanical or electronic—can be.

It is important not to overstate Babbage's influence. He did not have a lasting effect on the development of computer technologies. Nevertheless, he did encounter and work through the rhetorical problems that surround innovations in computing. Specifically, he had to conceptualize, describe, and fund his projects, which often involved explaining complicated topics to nonexpert audiences. Moreover, he recognized early on that computing technologies can function as rhetorical devices. Just as Babbage is considered an early ancestor of the computer age, we can consider him an early figure in the history of the rhetoric of computing.

Notes

1. William Gibson and Bruce Sterling, *The Difference Engine: 20th Anniversary Edition* (New York: Random House, 2011).

2. Dan Halacy, *Charles Babbage: Father of the Computer* (New York: Crowell-Collier Press, 1970); Ian Watson, *The Universal Machine: From the Dawn of Computing to Digital Consciousness* (New York: Copernicus Books, 2012); Maurice Wilkes, "Charles Babbage—The Great Uncle of Computing?" *Communications of the ACM* 35, no. 3 (March 1992): 15–18.

3. Maboth Moseley, *Irascible Genius: The Life of Charles Babbage* (Chicago: Henry Regnery Company, 1970), 21.

4. W. W. Ball, *A Short Account of the History of Mathematics* (New York: Dover Publications, 1960), 439–43.

5. Moseley, *Irascible Genius*, 65.

6. Doron Swade, *The Difference Engine: Charles Babbage and the Quest to Build the First Computer* (New York: Viking, 2000), 12.

7. Michael Lindgren, *Glory and Failure: The Difference Engines of Johann Müller, Charles Babbage, and Georg and Edvard Scheutz*, trans. Craig McKay (Cambridge: MIT Press, 1990), 70.

8. Charles Babbage, "A Letter to Sir Humphry Davy, Bart., President of the Royal Society, on the Application of the Machinery to the Purpose of Calculating and Printing Mathematical Tables," in *The Works of Charles Babbage*, ed. Martin Campbell-Kelly (New York: NYU Press, 1989), 2:7.

9. Swade, *Difference Engine*, 23.

10. Charles Bazerman, *The Languages of Edison's Light* (Cambridge: MIT Press, 1999), 3.

11. Ibid.

12. Charles Babbage, "A Note Respecting the Application of Calculating Machinery to the Construction of Mathematical Tables," in *Works of Charles Babbage*, 2:3.

13. Ibid.

14. Ibid.

15. Ibid.

16. Ibid.

17. Babbage, "Note Respecting the Application of Calculating Machinery," 4.

18. Swade, 34.

19. Philip Gummett, *Scientists in Whitehall* (Manchester: Manchester University Press, 1980), 20.

20. Derek Howse, *Greenwich Time and the Longitude* (London: Philip Wilson Publishers Ltd., 1997).

21. David Sobel and William Andrews, *The Illustrated Longitude* (New York: Walker and Company, 1998).

22. Ibid., 66.

23. Ibid., 101–5.

24. William Brock, "The Spectrum of Science Patronage," in *The Patronage of Science in the Nineteenth Century*, ed. Gerard Turner (Leyden, the Netherlands: Norhoff International Publishing, 1976), 181.

25. Ibid., 179.

26. Babbage, "Letter to Sir Humphry," 6.

27. Ibid.

28. Ibid.

29. Ibid., 7.

30. Ibid.

31. Ibid.

32. Ibid.

33. Ibid., 8.

34. Ibid., 9.

35. Ibid., 10.

36. Ibid.

37. Ibid., 13.

38. Ibid.

39. Charles Bazerman, *Shaping Written Knowledge: The Genre and Activity of the Experimental Article in Science* (Madison: University of Wisconsin Press, 1988).

40. Babbage, "Letter to Sir Humphry," 14.

41. Anthony Hyman, *Charles Babbage: Pioneer of the Computer* (Princeton: Princeton University Press, 1982), 52.

42. Charles Babbage, "On the Theoretical Principles of the Machinery for Calculating Tables," in *The Works of Charles Babbage*, 2:38–43.

43. Babbage, "Observations on the Application of Machinery," 33–37.

44. Ibid., 34.

45. Ibid., 35.

46. Ibid., 36.

47. Babbage, "On the Theoretical Principles," 43.

48. Swade, *Difference Engine*, 37–38.

49. Charles Babbage, *Passages from the Life of a Philosopher*, in *The Works of Charles Babbage*, vol. 11, ed. Martin Campbell-Kelly (New York: NYU Press, 1989), 56.

50. Hyman, *Charles Babbage*, 53.

51. Ibid.

52. Swade, 41–42.

53. Eugene Ferguson, *Engineering and the Mind's Eye* (Cambridge: MIT Press, 1992).

54. Charles Babbage, "On a Method of Expressing by Signs the Action of Machinery," in *The Works of Charles Babbage*, vol. 3, ed. Martin Campbell-Kelly (New York: NYU Press, 1989), 209.

55. Ibid., 217.

56. Lindgren, *Glory and Failure*, 263.

57. Simon Schaffer, "Fish and Ships: Models in the Age of Reason," in *Models: The Third Dimension of Science*, ed. Soraya de Chadarevian and Nick Hopwood (Stanford, CA: Stanford University Press, 2004): 71–105; Thomas Gieryn, "Boundary-Work and the Demarcation of Science from Non-Science: Strains and Interests in Professional Ideologies of Scientists," *American Sociological Review* 48, no. 6 (December 1983): 781–95.

58. J. F. W. Herschel, "Report of the Royal Society Babbage Engine Committee," in *Works of Charles Babbage*, 2:112.

59. Ibid., 108.

60. Swade, 45–46.

61. Ibid., 42–45.

62. Lindgren, 258–60.

63. Ibid.

64. James Essinger, *Ada's Algorithm: How Lord Byron's Daughter Ada Lovelace Launched the Digital Age* (Brooklyn: Melville House, 2014), 111.

65. Charles Babbage, "On the Mathematical Powers of the Calculating Engine," in *The Works of Charles Babbage*, 3:15.

66. Michael Williams, *A History of Computing Technology* (Englewood Cliffs, NJ: Prentice Hall, 1985), 184.

67. Ibid., 186.

68. Babbage, "On the Mathematical Powers," 31.

69. Christopher Green, "Charles Babbage, the Analytical Engine, and the Possibility of a 19th-Century Cognitive Science," in *The Transformation of Psychology: Influences of 19th-Century Philosophy, Technology, and Natural Science*, ed. Christopher Green, Marlene Shore, and Thomas Teo (Washington, DC: American Psychological Association, 2001), 153.

70. Ibid., 133–53.

71. Babbage, "On the Mathematical Powers," 31.

72. John Dahm, "Science and Religion in Eighteenth-Century England: The Early

Boyle Lectures and the Bridgewater Treatises" (PhD diss., Case Western Reserve University, 1969), ii.

73. Ibid., iii.

74. Charles Babbage, *The Ninth Bridgewater Treatise: A Fragment*, 2nd ed. (London: Frank Cass and Company Limited, 1967), xii.

75. Ibid., 30.

76. Ibid., 32.

77. Ibid., 40.

78. Ibid., 92.

79. Ibid., 94.

80. Ibid.

81. Ibid., 95.

82. Ibid., 95–96.

83. Ibid., 167.

84. Ibid., 170.

3 / Definitive Programs

Rhetoric, Computation, and the (Pre)history of Controversy over Automated Essay Scoring, 1954–1965

J. W. Hammond

"Grading essays by computer?"
For many of us, the idea at first seems utter nonsense, to be rejected out of hand. In my experience, the fastest rejection came from an English professor at a certain well-known New England institution. He heard of the idea, digested it thoroughly, and pronounced an indignant "*Impossible!*," all within ten seconds. With further conversation, I learned that this professor knew almost nothing of the various disciplines, even linguistics, which must participate in grading by computer. For those who know more of these disciplines, and especially for those who understand computers, a mechanical essay grader at first seems a delightful toy. Upon closer inspection, and with more and more background knowledge, the notion takes on a certain fascinating inevitability: We *will* soon be grading essays by computer, and this development *will* have astonishing impact on the educational world.
      —Ellis B. Page, "The Imminence of . . . Grading Essays by Computer"

"How can a machine possibly read and grade a composition?" is the inevitable question asked by those first hearing about *Project Essay Grade*, a research endeavor currently supported by the College Entrance Examination Board. Keeping books and inventories, processing payrolls, assigning student programs, keeping a school register—these repetitive, arithmetic chores are by now accepted as falling within the province of the computer. But reading and evaluating that complex symbolic process we call language surely must be a presumptuous incursion into realms strictly assigned to the human intellect. How indeed can, or dare, a machine compete in this area?
      —Arthur Daigon, "Computer Grading of English Composition"

Introduction

Is meaningful automated assessment of student writing "*Impossible!*," or is it a "fascinating inevitability"?

This chapter's epigraphs were penned over fifty years ago—both published in January 1966 to announce and promote Project Essay Grade (PEG), the first automated essay scoring (AES) program. The former opens the *Phi Delta*

Kappan (*PDK*) article "The Imminence of . . . Grading Essays by Computer," written by Ellis B. Page—PEG's chief developer. The latter begins a companion piece in *The English Journal* (*EJ*) by Arthur Daigon, titled "Computer Grading of English Composition."[1] Because AES—or "machine scoring," as it is sometimes called—has been used in high-stakes tests like the GRE, GMAT, and TOEFL, the question of whether AES is possible might seem moot: "Automated writing assessment is now a bureaucratic fact," notes Carolyn R. Miller.[2]

Facts and artifacts, however, are often more contingent and mutable—more indefinite—than they may at first seem.[3] Controversy has been a defining feature of machine scoring throughout its history; today, questions persist about the meaning and meaningfulness of automated assessment. Les Perelman holds that "the metrics employed by AES are not relevant to effective writing in the twenty-first century and, in many cases, detrimental to it."[4] AES programs, he argues, "do not understand meaning, and they are not sentient. They do not react to language; they merely count it."[5] More expansively, Anne Herrington and Charles Moran claim that "writing to a machine distorts the very nature of writing itself. Writing to a machine is writing to nobody. Writing to nobody is not writing at all."[6] These charges point to a source of the enduring controversy over machine scoring: definition. Machine scoring technologies become possible—even inevitable—when "writing" is defined a certain way and are rendered impossible when "writing" is defined in ways that elude (or preclude) assessment by computer.

Importantly, definition flows in both directions. AES programs also functionally define "writing" by algorithmically counting, sorting, and processing textual features in accordance with the design(s) of their software. If we follow James J. Brown Jr.'s assertion that "rhetoric is a collection of machines . . . for generating and interpreting arguments," then AES is rhetorical because the software at its core is a textual machine "authoring and authored, writing and written."[7] More generally and fundamentally, *writing assessment is a collection of machines* that embody and generate arguments about how to gauge and interpret writing. With these connections in mind, I suggest that controversies over the meaning and meaningfulness of AES are not rhetorical abscesses on an otherwise purely technical body. Instead, AES is controversial *because* it is rhetorical: machine scoring programs are rhetorical machines *of* and *by* definition.

Rather than seek to resolve the long-standing controversy over the meaning and meaningfulness of AES, this chapter calls attention to the ways this controversy is multiply motivated by definition. In doing so, it provides one site for bridging scholarship on rhetoric and computation, rhetoric and writing assessment, and what Brian Huot calls the "two technologies" of writing assessment and the computer.[8] Consideration of this kind is timely at a moment when critical questions about algorithmic reading and writing programs—like bots—are increasingly prominent not only in academic conversations but popular and political ones as well. Moving forward, "we will need to acknowledge the robots among us," as Timothy Laquintano and Annette Vee put it.[9] Through returning our attention to one kind of "robot" that has proved enduringly controversial and visible in our education ecologies, this chapter works to underscore the rhetorical importance of definition in our engagements with the algorithmic machines "we write alongside and contend with."[10]

Already in recent years, automated assessment technologies and their attendant controversies have been of interest to rhetoric scholars, providing some with a site for exploring the nature of rhetorical agency.[11] Others have viewed AES (and PEG, specifically) through the rhetorical prism of Charles Bazerman's work on *"symbolic engineering;* that is, the development of symbols that will give presence, meaning, and value to a technological object or process within a discursive system" (emphasis mine).[12] Underpinning these interventions are rhetorical questions of definition: What is agency? Can it be ethically attributed (or denied) to automated assessment technologies or smart objects? What do automated assessment technologies like PEG mean, and how are these meanings engineered? Questions like these manifest what Edward Schiappa terms *"definitive discourse*—discourse that defines, whether in an explicit discourse *about* a definition, discourse that argues *from* a particular definition, or discourse that stipulates a view of reality via an argument *by* definition."[13] Continuing down this analytic path, my chapter highlights the theoretical and historical significance of definitive discourse to AES controversy, paying particular attention to PEG.

To this end, the chapter first brings AES into conversation with recent work by Brown, arguing that machine scoring programs are what I call *definitive programs*: rhetorical technologies that define "slices of reality" by assigning values, characteristics, or meanings to them.[14] That is to say, AES programs are encoded with and enact definitions of writing quality. At the same time, these programs are judged to be working (or not) on the basis of the definitions we hold regarding what meaningful writing assessment requires. Second, I suggest that while PEG provides a convenient historical origin point for AES, the program inherits a rich *definitive prehistory*, charged with competing arguments about the nature and use of computing technologies in assessment and text analysis. AES controversies build on, and perhaps extend, earlier controversies over the uses and meanings of computation. Returning to these prehistoric grounds better acquaints us with the definitive controversies that underpin computerized assessment—controversies that continue to evade resolution. To provide a general sense for this landscape, I turn to framings of computing technology in *EJ* and *PDK*—the journals in which

Page and Daigon announced PEG—focusing on articles published between 1954 and 1965. The latter date marks the year preceding PEG's announcement; the former marks one decade prior to the year (1964) Page locates as a turning point, after which "the notion of computer analysis of essays began to seem conceivable."[15]

Together, these two definitive dimensions of AES—its role as a definitive program and its definitive prehistory—point to what I think of as technology's *rhetorical priority of definition*. Definition precedes (i.e., is *prior* to) rhetorical engagement with-or-through technologies, and questions of definition and essence cut to the rhetorical core of technologies, revealing what they are imagined to do (or not do) and how they are assessed as working (or not working). This kind of rhetorical attention to definition helps us locate through-lines between assessment and digital rhetoric that might otherwise escape our notice. In my discussion of AES, I intend to underline some of the ways that definitions and assessment make technologies possible, technologies embody or advance definitions, and "definitional ruptures" set the stage for enduring controversies over technological meaning and use.[16] Consistent with Brown's affirmation "that studying software does not always mean studying code,"[17] consideration of this kind helps demonstrate that far from being the (technical) opposite of (social) rhetoric, computation is inextricable from the social and rhetorical.

PEG as Definitive Program

Few ethical predicaments within writing studies and education seem as weighty as those implicated in assessment, which can shape educational outcomes, access, and opportunities.[18] Writing assessment sits at the intersection of several knotty questions, each of which bears on the ethical problem of how we should respond to and treat others: What is the appropriate way to assess writing? What counts as "writing" or as "good writing"? And whom do we count as "good" writers? To assess writing is, at least implicitly, to pose answers to questions like these. Against this backdrop, the assessments we advocate can be understood as "ethical programs," Brown's name for rhetorical procedures ("computational or otherwise") enacted in response to specific situations in which we engage with others—each ethical program being "a set of steps taken to address an ethical predicament."[19]

Whether or not we agree with the responses they pose to writing, machine scoring programs like PEG instantiate ethical programs, inasmuch as they are posed as solutions to assessment predicaments and embody and promote particular values—features endemic to all assessment technologies, computational or otherwise.[20] Indeed, with these attributes in mind, it might not surprise us that "the practice of assessment . . . has long been understood as a rhetorical endeavor."[21] It is important to note at the outset that my designation of AES programs as ethical programs is not an endorsement of them as *ethical* in the normative sense of that term. I come neither to praise machine scoring nor to bury it. Rather, I regard machine scoring programs as ethical programs in the limited sense sketched by Brown: they intervene within a rhetorico-ethical situation and "are motivated and rhetorical—they enact ethical arguments."[22] In the case of AES, these arguments are about writing and how to assess it.

Writing with Dieter Paulus, Page characterized PEG as a response to enduring educational problems: the shortage of teachers and the difficulty of efficiently and effectively grading student essays. Page and Paulus tell us that "the supply of qualified and interested English teachers has always been too limited."[23] Making matters worse, "a single judgment of an essay by a single human judge is slow, extremely unreliable, and of uncertain status. When sufficient training is used, and a sufficient number of judgments establish a decent reliability, essay grading becomes prohibitively expensive."[24] Within this situation, students risk not receiving the assessment they need and teachers are threatened by overwork.[25] PEG materializes a motivated response to this predicament, intended "to rescue the conscientious English teacher from his backbreaking burden" by delegating that burden to computing technology.[26] "It was," Richard H. Haswell reminds us, "the discipline's special condition of drudgery that early visions of machine grading hoped, explicitly, to solve."[27]

A rhetoric of definition is necessarily at work here: "The firms that are marketing the machine scoring of student writing all explicitly or implicitly *define* the task of reading, evaluating, and responding to student writing not as a complex, demanding, and rewarding aspect of our teaching, but as a 'burden' that should be lifted from our shoulders" (emphasis mine).[28] PEG's computerized rescue operation was to be conducted by transposing student compositions onto punched-cards, then analyzed by an IBM 7040 running FORTRAN IV—a programming language selected by Page and his team because they believed it would enable "maximum versatility, availability of programmers, and dissemination of programs."[29] Even at the level of its programming language, PEG embodies an ethical program, its machinery patterned with computational preferences (versatility, availability, dissemination) resonant with Page's ambition to rescue overburdened educators—a sprawling project that seemingly would require the widespread adoption, adaptation, and implementation of PEG.

More generally, PEG's software-driven response to the "backbreaking burden" of assessment doubles as an ethical vision of what essay grading means and requires. Brown writes that "software is an interesting place to trace out ethical programs since it enacts rules and procedures, shaping and constraining what can or can't happen in a given space."[30] This is true of machines that "read" or "write" by transforming databases of information into narratives. "Every narrative," Brown tells us, "makes ethical determinations. It sorts data in a particular way, searches for patterns in that data, determines which patterns are most important, and (by necessity) excludes certain other patterns."[31] The same might be said for AES programs that "read" and score student writing, algorithmically counting, sorting, and processing relevant or "important" text features. The essay is, in a way, encountered as a body of data; the scores generated provide a kind of "abbreviated" title or reductive "narrative," rewriting what the essay *is*.[32] Arising in response to particular predicaments, ethical programs enact, embody, and implicitly advocate particular positions—they define and promote a view of reality.

Definitive discourse of this kind is a persuasive machinery: "Through descriptions, people 'entitle' tiny slices of reality from various points of view. Because such entitlements are inevitably partial and draw our attention to this aspect rather than that, they are never 'neutral' or absolutely 'objective'; rather, they are better understood as persuasive efforts that encourage intersubjective agreement about how to see the world."[33] Description and the assignment of titles—"entitlements," in Kenneth Burke's idiom—are rhetorical mechanisms for "socially constructing an understanding of reality."[34] The programs we put in place to describe or entitle slices of reality constitute ethical programs of definition or, as a shorthand, *definitive programs*. These programs represent ethical responses to situations where definition is questioned or contested; they rewrite slices of reality through description, tendentiously assigning meaning in accordance with an ethical viewpoint.

Writing assessments operate on this ethical register, posing responses to definitive predicaments. Disputed terms or constructs (e.g., "writing," "writing ability") and questions about how instances of student writing can be appropriately described or titled (e.g., When is writing "good"?) are addressed, though perhaps not resolved, through recourse to these definitive programs. Paul Deane tells us that "the design of a writing assessment . . . implicitly defines a specific understanding of skilled writing."[35] These definitive programs define particular instances of student writing against what they *count* (figuratively and algorithmically) as indicators of writing quality. In this way, they are a peculiar, definition-oriented breed of "robot rhetor"—Brown's name for "any entity that 'machines' language," in that it "takes input, applies procedures, and generates output."[36]

This reality-machining process of externalizing and imposing definitions requires, as a computational a priori, that AES technologies be programmed with internalized sets of operational definitions with respect to the writing construct. Definition takes rhetorical priority: the technical core of PEG—its capacity to "sense" and make sense of particular text features—was motored by rhetorical decisions about what counted as writing's intrinsic qualities and how those qualities could be registered and counted computationally.[37] The underlying logic of PEG is captured by Brian Huot: "Page (1966, 1968) identified what he called 'intrinsic attributes' of what readers of student writing look for in grading compositions or themes. For example, punctuation facility is one of these intrinsic attributes (what have come to be known as *trins*). Because the computer could not be programmed to measure punctuation facility, the researchers looked for an approximate measure of this trin, called a *prox* or *proxes*. In the case of punctuation facility, for example, the approximate measure . . . is the number of commas in a student paper."[38] A further definitional translation is required, with proxes converted to PEG's code—a second-order prox of sorts for the initial trin.

Codification entails constraint. Each successive definitive stage trin→prox→ code operationalizes and concretizes the former. At the same time, the strictures of code constrain the kinds of proxes PEG can identify, thereby constraining the intrinsic features that an AES program can vicariously gauge (code→prox→trin). These definitive decisions script the arguments PEG makes when rating essays. What is more, definitive discourse also underpins the ways Page and his colleagues sought to validate machine scoring. PEG's rating process, the argument goes, works as meaningful assessment to the extent that it generates grades comparable to those assigned by human raters; with a close enough ap*prox*imation of in*trins*ic features of good writing, the computer can simulate, supplement, and perhaps supplant its human counterparts.[39] The technical core of PEG, then, is discursive: *what writing is* and *how it should be assessed* are always things asserted or assented to. Trins and proxes are always social and rhetorical.

Definitive Counterprogramming

Here, we encounter an ostensible paradox: Despite appearances and "bureaucratic facts" to the contrary, AES technologies may not *work* as instruments of assessment. AES programs cease to function when our definitions of "writing" and how to assess it diverge from the capabilities of machine scoring technologies or contradict the logic underwriting them. In her discussion of automated assessment technologies, Miller claims that "our attributions of agency are ultimately moral judgments."[40] They are also necessarily definitive judgments. By this same measure, our willingness to entitle AES programs as capable of "real" or "meaningful" assessment is caught up in an ethics of definition, motivated by our definitions of what "writing" is and what it means to assess or "read" it.[41] Through definitive discourse, machine scoring critics engage in a form of *definitive counterprogramming*, engineering controversy through the proliferation of competing understandings of whether and how AES works.

Consider, for example, Les Perelman's view "that although the whole enterprise of automated essay scoring claims various kinds of construct validity, the measures it employs substantially fail to represent any reasonable real-world construct of writing ability."[42] Here, AES is challenged not at the level of whether its code runs or reliably processes text features. Instead, the challenge is at the level of meaning and title: Perelman distances the "claims" and capabilities of AES from a meaningful (or "real-world") definition of writing ability. William Condon, for his part, places two definitive barriers between AES and meaningful assessment. First, Condon defines "the kinds of test for which AES can provide a meaningful score—extremely short, timed assessments."[43] While seeming to cede ground to the idea of "meaningful" machine scoring, this definition is ultimately damning, because "whether a 25-minute essay written on an unfamiliar topic is scored by a human or computer—or by a human and a computer—it is still a poor representation of *writing* and can provide only severely limited information about the writer."[44] Second, Condon cleaves AES scoring from human judgments: "One set of decisions is being made by a human who reads with the intention of understanding a writer's text, while the other set of decisions is being made by a computer that can recognize certain patterns of textual features—and that cannot recognize them with anything approaching full accuracy. Thus, these two sets of judgments that *seem* alike are not, in fact, alike. A human rater and a computer may record a similar number, but their scores mean very different things."[45] Even if an AES program generates outputs similar to human rater outputs, the procedures applied—the definitive program enacted—constitute a difference on the register of *meaning*. Condon's distinctions enact a rhetorical "dissociation" that cleaves appearance (i.e., apparently similar judgments) from reality (i.e., actually similar judgments).[46]

Dissociations like these enjoin us to see AES as capable of writing assessment in a nominal but not substantive sense.[47] "Computerized writing assessment" is framed as a contradiction in terms, little more than a mechanical mirage. Definition is at once a machine of rhetorical transformation (input, procedures, output) and of resistance to that transformation. The definition of the construct "writing" sets discursive boundaries for when and how assessments *work*, with assessment technologies *working* to the extent we believe they are successful in assessing the writing construct. AES as meaningful assessment is impossible when we judge its code too shallow to adequately map writing's depths. This way of thinking about whether (or not) a tech-

nology *works* echoes constructivist insights from science and technology studies: "The constructivist argument," Wiebe E. Bijker states, "is that the core of
technology, *that which constitutes its working*, is socially constructed."[48]

Technologies like PEG exist within "a social matrix" and "emerge as part of
the drama of human meanings."[49] For this reason, they are marked by what
Bijker calls "interpretative flexibility," becoming different things depending on
the standards employed to assess whether and how they work.[50] Because of
this flexibility, what may appear on the surface as a monolithic artifact might
instead be a "pluralism of artifacts": "Relevant social groups do not simply
see different aspects of one artifact. The meanings given by a relevant social
group actually *constitute* the artifact. There are as many artifacts as there are
relevant social groups; there is no artifact not constituted by a relevant social
group."[51] Rhetorical machines that might be considered highly effective in
some rhetorical ecologies can be assessed differently in others, for as Laquintano and Vee remind us, "their ability to persuade is fully enmeshed in the
platform"—or ecology—"in which they operate."[52] What constructivist scholars like Bijker underscore for us is that whatever material ecologies our technological artifacts participate in, these artifacts are enmeshed also in definitive ecologies that shape how we assess and use them.

For Bijker, rhetoric serves as a "closure mechanism" for technology, facilitating consensus on the meaning(s) of an artifact and effecting its "stabiliza-
tion."[53] From the plural *many*, shared definitions can engineer a stable technological *one*. Whether PEG (or any technology) stabilizes and works is definitively
contingent on the "rhetoric of technology," as Bazerman defines that term: "It
is the rhetoric that accompanies technology and makes it possible—the rhetoric that makes technology fit into the world and makes the world fit with technology."[54] In challenging the definitions AES advances, critics of machine scoring are rhetorically resisting the idea that programs like PEG "fit" meaningful
assessment. Consensus is resisted, closure is obstructed, and controversy per-
sists *indefinitely*. An AES program like PEG remains a pluralism of artifacts,
working for some groups and not others, at once inevitable and impossible.

Toward a Definitive Prehistory for AES Controversy

Reasonable observers might assume that, as the source of *descent* for modern
AES technologies, PEG also serves as the source for present-day *dissent* about
the uses and meanings of AES. Revisiting the context for PEG's *PDK* and *EJ*
announcement articles indicates that definitive discourse not only *proceeds*
from machine scoring but also *precedes* it. The rest of this chapter considers
how AES and its attendant controversies may have emerged within—and as
part of—a broader, longer-standing debate over the use of computing tech-

nologies in text analysis and assessment. PEG (and machine scoring, more generally) inherits this definitive prehistory—it builds on, and from, existing definitive controversies over computation. (Here, again, definition assumes rhetorical priority.) To give shape to these controversies, I return to the archival record represented in *PDK* and *EJ*, focusing on articles published between 1954 and 1965. My approach to AES historiography here "involves a break with the simple or causal chains of narration and story,"[55] drawing attention not to progressive technological developments that culminated in the 1966 announcements of PEG by Page and Daigon but instead to the fragmented definitive landscape in which those announcements were made.[56] This backward glance to the prehistory of AES suggests the 1966 announcements of PEG were not the start of a conversation about computerized assessment but were instead a new turn of talk within an existing conversation: one characterized by a protracted lack of definitive agreement—what Schiappa calls "denotative conformity"—regarding the meanings and capabilities of computing technologies.[57]

Returning to this chapter's epigraphs, we might notice that both position the novelty of machine scoring against pre-existing beliefs about (and skepticism toward) computation. When Daigon distinguishes the prospect of PEG from "repetitive, arithmetic chores . . . by now accepted as falling within the province of the computer," he is acknowledging that the idea of computerized essay grading might exceed and clash with then-present beliefs about the capabilities of computing technology.[58] Page comes close to acknowledging the rhetorical contingency of PEG when he admits the idea of "grading essays by computer" appears absurd—even, "*Impossible!*"—until one engages with (and, presumably, assents to the credibility of) existing disciplinary knowledges on which the logic and feasibility of AES depends.[59] Later in his *PDK* article, Page declares his "aim" not as publicizing a technical triumph, but more precisely "persuad[ing] educators" that the computer grading of essays is "need[ed]," "feasible," and likely instructionally beneficial.[60] Page even adopts a literal "Question and Answer" format for the final section of his article.[61] These explicit suasive overtures suggest an awareness that computerized essay scoring might be something of a tough sell, its "imminence" at least partly predicated on social acceptance. PEG is made possible and palatable not just by dint of its hardware or software alone but also by discourses that define the capabilities of computing technology in ways favorable to the social and linguistic processing requirements for grading essays. Definitive rhetoric is, in a foundational way, the code scripting AES and the controversy surrounding it.

As Christina Haas observes, "The technologies we write with today are not new: They are built on layers and layers of other technologies"—an observation applicable to most (perhaps all) present-day technology.[62] Indeed, scholars have identified technological layers on which machine scoring builds—layers including "direct writing assessment, word processing, and other constituent computer technologies."[63] In what follows; I extend this work, excavating layers of definitive controversy that accompanied the computing technologies (e.g., IBM punched-card computation and test scoring machines) that provided PEG its prehistoric layers. *PDK* and *EJ* contributors offer different (at times competing) definitions of what these technologies can do, and what their use in assessment or text analysis means. PEG emerged within an ecology of existing controversies over computation and its meaning and meaningfulness in the classroom. These controversies were engineered by claims concerning the effects of computerized assessment on literary criticism, on human actors, and on the future of education—each we revisit throughout the rest of this chapter.

Theme Analysis: Computing and Literary Criticism

In "The Imminence of . . . Grading Essays by Computer," Page discusses PEG's analysis of essays in relation to existing work at the intersection of computation and language processing.[64] A key conceptual a priori for PEG's analytic promise is the equation of language analysis (and writing assessment, specifically) to computational feats of "the manipulation of language."[65] Page's contemporary Allan B. Ellis refers to this computational process as "*symbol manipulation*: that is, to translate or to categorize or to manipulate a symbol or a set of symbols in some specific way."[66] In this respect, Page identifies one precursor to PEG as the General Inquirer (GI) system,[67] chiefly designed by Philip Stone and discussed by Ellis in his 1964 *EJ* article "The Computer and Character Analysis." In that piece, Ellis identifies FORTRAN training as a way to "'learn to drive one [a computer],'"[68] then names one analytic destination for the computer-as-vehicle: text analysis.[69] For Ellis, "a computer, often thought of as an instrument to launch missiles or to solve equations, is capable of reading the text of a novel and of finding evidence that can help us to understand a theme or a character or an author."[70] The symbol-manipulating GI was developed to undertake analysis of this sort, acting as a definitive program geared toward the ascription of literary meaning. While the (literary) themes it analyzes differ from the themes (i.e., student compositions) scored by PEG, these two means of assessing "themes" by computer bear important similarities.

Like PEG, GI was made materially possible by IBM punched-card computation. Portions of a literary text (in Ellis's example, Huck's dialogue from *The Adventures of Huckleberry Finn*) were "punched onto IBM cards and submitted to the tagging routine of The General Inquirer," which had been programmed with a "3500 word psycho-sociological dictionary."[71] The dictionary's words were categorized by theme, such that a machine-countable instance of a particular word evidences a thematic abstraction (e.g., "persons, emotions, thought, evaluation, and impersonal actions")—analogous, broadly, to Page's distinction between prox and trin.[72] By machine-counting these category-specific words in Huck's dialogue, GI facilitates data-supported analysis of Huck's preoccupations, the logic being that what Huck *says* reflects or defines his thematic "concerns."[73] And foreshadowing PEG's designs on replacing unreliable human raters, GI is described by Ellis in terms of its judgmental impartiality: "a computer . . .—whatever else it may be—is totally objective and unconcerned with proving anybody's point."[74]

GI anticipates PEG in one further respect: controversy over whether and how it *works*. Shortly after the release of Ellis's article, *EJ* published two responses in its "Riposte" section that question the GI's effects and effectiveness. Unimpressed with the GI's characterization of the eponymous Huckleberry Finn, Peter F. Neumeyer locates a possible source for what he considers the computer's analytic shortcomings: "the programmer seeks to fit phenomena into his own verbalized categories."[75] Constrained by the assumptions of its programmers, GI is deemed inhospitable to literary content misaligned with those assumptions—its definitive promise sabotaged by its a priori thematic categories. Picking up this strain of critique, Glen A. Love resists Ellis's assumption that words "'reflect'" a character's "state of mind" and charges that the computer—while capable of "verification of the obvious"—fails to detect irony, a feature apprehended by "even the most obtuse [human] reader" of *The Adventures of Huckleberry Finn*.[76] Love concludes that "computer analysis . . . must develop far more sophisticated means . . . for dealing with evasion, ambiguity and irony, before its techniques will be of real use to the scholar."[77] Crucially, Love defines what is of "real use to the scholar" and, in doing so, provides an implicit vision for the requirements of meaningful text analysis—requirements, like sensitivity to irony, that extend beyond the computer's (then-current) reach. Drawing on standards for *working* that appear to differ from Ellis's, Neumeyer and Love judge computing technologies inadequate (at least as yet) to the task of literary analysis. Viewed alongside Ellis's optimism about GI's capabilities, these commentaries point to an interpretatively fractured landscape for assessing what the computer can, and cannot, instrumentally accomplish.

The Computer's Maw: Computing and Human Actors

In his *EJ* PEG announcement article, Daigon records that one "vehement objection to computer essay grading revolves about the word *creativity*. What about the off-beat writer, the non-conforming stylist, the original thinker? Won't they do poorly in the cavernous maw of the computer?"[78] While anxieties about mechanization have not abated since 1966, it is important to note that concerns about the computer's maw long preceded the announcement of PEG. In the pages of *EJ* and *PDK*, these concerns are closely associated with IBM computers, punched-card technologies, and machine-scored multiple-choice assessment.

In the 1955 *EJ* article "Judging Compositions—Machine Method," Carl G. Wonnberger paints a bleak portrait of writing assessment in the wake of indirect multiple-choice testing: "Let's write no more compositions; let's just unscramble paragraphs, or plug up sentence holes, or identify various kinds of error. Writing well or significantly doesn't count; we must write 'correctly.'"[79] Dissociating the "shell" of mechanical correctness from the "core" of significant writing, Wonnberger positions correctness-oriented tasks (e.g., error identification) as superficial alternatives to meaningful assessment.[80] If Wonnberger's reference to what "doesn't *count*" calls to mind computation, this association is one he might have welcomed. "Interesting as the prospect may be, I fear we have still no evidence that an IBM machine can evaluate compositional skills," Wonnberger writes, cautioning readers that "it is important . . . that teachers and administrators see all the implications in an attempt to evaluate an art by means of an IBM machine. . . . We must not allow this great vehicle [the English language] to become a target for pseudo-ethical judgment based on linguistic half-truths."[81]

Wonnberger casts computing machinery as a synecdochic figure for the larger machinery of indirect testing—*machine methods* literalized. Viewing "the act of evaluating writing" as "a creative effort,"[82] Wonnberger declares in another *EJ* article that "the objective test in all its ramifications is an abomination . . . because it reduces everything to a yes-no, true-false, multiple-choice technique and practically eliminates true thinking."[83] The computer seems to haunt this critique, reducing evaluation to a binary logic of incorrect and correct, a pseudo-ethics of zeroes and ones. Wonnberger's rallying cry is that "English teachers above all others should band together to resist the objective test and demand emancipation from the IBM monster."[84] Here, IBM computers serve as a figure for the subordination and shackling of educators to mechanical conformity in assessment. Renaming the IBM computer a "monster," Wonnberger defines it as a kind of menace or behemoth, crowding out (or devouring) appropriate assessment.

In Thomas L. Dahle's 1962 *PDK* contribution "On the Lighter Side: How to Tell an Administrator from a Teacher," we are jokingly warned about administrators who "do not have advanced degrees, but come equipped with IBM-type brains triggered only by the mention of dollars and cents."[85] Des-

ignating a class of brain (or mindset), the label "IBM" reframes *as computational* the administrative machinery of education and its (unlettered, automatic, number-crunching) financial assessments. Repeatedly in *PDK*, we
are warned about the computer's maw. Logan Anderson's 1954 *PDK* piece
"So Many Monsters—But Never a Man!" tells us that in "the age of specialization with which we are now so familiar," educators undergo a dehumanizing transformation: "the teacher becomes a report card, or more properly, today, an IBM."[86] Emblematic, it seems, of (assessment-oriented) professional
specialization, the computer becomes a source of and figure for monstrosity.
The teacher is mechanized by a fixation on grades or, "more properly," by
over-reliance on the technical apparatuses that aid in manufacturing them.
If some scholars, like Ellis, viewed the computer as a means of symbol manipulation, other *EJ* and *PDK* contributors defined the computer as a symbol *of* manipulation that recreates education in its putatively inhuman, mech-
anizing image. By 1966, "the computer" and "IBM machine" are taken by
some as abbreviated titles for more elaborate processes of mechanization—
definitive machineries that reduce and redefine education according to their
programmed (pseudo-)ethics.

Dystopian Devices: Computing and the Future

Among objections to PEG, Daigon notes in his announcement article that
"the first . . . is the familiar jeremiad, warning of *1984*, *Brave New World*, the
abdication of human prerogatives, the decline of humanism, the imperson-
ality of machines, and so on."[87] Time has not effaced the identification of automated assessment with dystopia. Huot, writing decades after Daigon, describes Page's "enthusiasm for the computer's ability to grade student writing"
as being "almost like a page out of *Brave New World*."[88] Julie Cheville charac-
terizes AES's ability to "make it possible to eliminate the evaluative influence
of teachers altogether" as "chillingly Orwellian."[89] Engaging in something like
"future rhetoric," these entitlements constitute a means of exploring, propos-
ing, or contesting the capabilities and ramifications of computers in education by (re)defining them in dystopian terms.[90] This kind of (re)definition by
no means began with AES. In the years leading up to PEG's announcement,
speculative narratives circulated in *PDK* and *EJ*, defining the meaning(s) and
effect(s) of computation in assessment and education.

Writing "No More Pencils, No More Books . . ." for *PDK* in 1961, Samuel
E. Pisaro and H. Gardner Emmerson invite us to "take a walk with Billy as
he enters the classroom of the future for his space-age education."[91] We find
Billy's educational life catalogued on punched-cards and supervised not by
a teacher but by a "well-trained technician" who, we learn parenthetically,

"'interned' at IBM."[92] Note the distinction in title here: Pisaro and Emmerson implicitly define "teacher" as something other—perhaps more—than a technician who supervises the machinery of education. Billy's instruction is coordinated by automated assessment: "Heeding the recorded directions, our future 'space-medico' (his future is already determined by the electronic guidance machine) punches his lesson on the card in front of him. His responses are automatically corrected as he proceeds through the 'canned' experience."[93] Electronic computing technologies displace human teachers and operate as definitive technologies, assessing and assigning everything from classroom tasks to future professions. This future of IBM-mediated instruction and "hungry teaching machines" is, Pisaro and Emmerson insist, *not* distant from then-present reality.[94] They believe "components for all of the above devices are already in existence."[95] Technologically possible (or nearly so), the complete automation of education is held at bay by social will and resistance "on purely sentimental ground."[96] Pisaro and Emmerson assure us that "we can safely predict that the teacher is here to stay—for several years at least."[97] Sentimentality stills the mechanical tide; the "space-age" future seemingly cannot be realized by technology alone.

In his 1961 *EJ* article "Automatons or English Teachers?" Robert C. Pooley also envisions a future wherein an elaborate system of punched-cards regulates education.[98] The student protagonist of Pooley's narrative, Tom (whose name evokes "au*tom*aton"), is instructionally guided by "test machines" automatically responsive to his answers, repeating questions until Tom can "memorize the right answer."[99] In this future, educational success is mechanical, defined in terms of rote memorization. Writing assessment is partly automated, with predetermined feedback "numbers" recorded on student compositions by "professional theme evaluators" (*teachers* having been displaced by computers).[100] To interpret this feedback, "Tom takes us to the center rear of the room to a large upright panel with . . . at least a hundred numbered buttons" and punches the button corresponding to the feedback number he was assigned.[101] The machine then issues Tom "a card neatly printed" with an explanation of his error (comma usage) and with corresponding "examples correctly punctuated."[102] This assessment process is mechanized in two ways: first, essays appear to be evaluated using a predetermined set of "at least a hundred" error/feedback types; second, the labor of providing feedback and commentary is outsourced to machines.

Importantly, the dystopian horror at the heart of Pooley's tale is *not* the automation of assessment but the professional obviation of teachers. Ventriloquizing through the fictional school's principal, "Dr. Mann" (an ethos-appropriating nod to *Horace* Mann), Pooley warns readers how a teacher-free future came to pass: "Because the teachers made themselves machines, they came into competition with better machines, and lost out."[103] Pooley's parable advocates a position on computing technologies that seemingly paves the way for drudgery-reducing AES programs: "Future English teachers of America," Pooley exhorts his readers, "don't be discouraged; don't give way to machines. The machines are coming; let us welcome them and use them. Let the machines do the hard chores of teaching skills, making reviews of details, helping slow students to catch up, and giving all sorts of examinations. These tasks we can gladly assign to the machines, for these tasks now drain our energies and extinguish our fires."[104] Remarkably, Pooley recommends the abdication of examination to machines. The danger to education, in Pooley's view, is not the machine itself, but that teachers will recast themselves in the machine's image—thereby ensuring their own redundancy. What might be thought of as assessment, remediation, and skill development are defined as drudgery— that is, as mechanical "chores" that sap pedagogical effectiveness and distract from the *human* essence of education. It is in precisely this spirit that Page would later claim that "for the classroom teacher, the computer grading of essays might considerably humanize his job."[105] Pooley praises the outcome declared "chillingly Orwellian" by Cheville. The dystopia he details is not one computerized assessment would bring about, but instead one it would avert, provided teachers render unto IBM what is defined as mechanical—a category that, for Pooley, Page, and Daigon (*contra* Wonnberger), includes assessment. By Pooley's account, those who devote themselves to competing with machines jeopardize their humanity, endanger their inner "fires," and risk consigning themselves to obsolescence. The choice Pooley forces is stark; its stakes, high. As he pointedly concludes, the educational Promised Land is one not all teachers deserve to see: "'The world will never abandon inspired teachers. Let the machines replace the others; they never will be missed.'"[106]

Conclusion: The Pluralism of AES

The heterogeneous positions taken in *EJ* and *PDK* between 1954 and 1965 defy easy summarization. Within this space, computing technologies used for assessment or text analysis are discussed in terms of the definitions they embody, entail, or enact. These technologies are taken to work (or not) on the basis of the adequacy or effects of those definitions, and they are contested by means of definitive counterprogramming, with some contributors advancing alternative definitions. Returning to PEG's prehistory provides us with concrete examples of how different definitions can lead us to different diagnoses and prescriptions concerning the rhetorical machines in our midst. (Contrast, for instance, the positions advanced by Pooley and Wonnberger.) Such a return also sensitizes us to the multiple, overlapping ways that computerized assessment has been vexed by competing understandings of what computation means and is capable of—perhaps especially in relation to text analysis, human actors, and the future of education. Each layer of controversy is one AES is heir to, and if the controversy over AES is ever to resolve into consensus, each will likely require intensive rhetorical intervention.

As with the controversy over AES today, the prehistory preceding PEG testifies to an *indefinite controversy*, with conflicts over the nature and meaning of computerized assessment and analysis eluding resolution. Controversies of this kind, while perhaps endemic to computerized assessment, are by no means limited to it. Any given computing technology has some degree of pluralism and interpretative flexibility. As Haas contends, "'the' computer does not exist," in part because "the place of computers in a particular sociocultural setting, the history of computers in that setting, and individuals' feelings and beliefs about technology will all affect what 'the computer' is taken to be in any given case."[107] This interpretative pluralism partly constitutes the unstable rhetorical foundation on which PEG was built. Today, meaningful assessment by computer remains inevitable and impossible. Page's predicted future of "grading essays by computer" is, in a way, both a technological tomorrow already here and a tomorrow that never comes—at least, that is, to the extent that the realization of this future requires genuine consensus on whether AES works as meaningful assessment. Some futures, perhaps, are never more than imminent; some prehistories, never past.

As prominent participants in American education, AES technologies are promising sites for rhetorical analysis, worthy of more extensive scrutiny than this chapter provides. The work of this chapter has been, at a general level, to a) suggest that AES technologies are rhetorical machines that embody, advance, and are contested on the basis of definition, and b) partially trace the definitive prehistory for AES and its enduring controversy. More work is needed to put meat on the bones of this general account, such as detailing how specific AES programs rhetorically differ in the definitions they embody and assign, specifying the range of definitive strategies for engineering whether and how AES works, and documenting more comprehensively the definitive/prehistoric layers beneath AES and its controversies. Moreover, the conceptual work I have undertaken here speaks to the growing body of rhetorical scholarship on reading and writing machines, including smart objects, robot journalists, and bots.[108] There is a rhetorical priority of definition at work whenever a machine is programmed for, or believed (in)capable of, rhetorically "reading" or "writing." Such machines underwrite, and are underwritten by, definitions about a particular slice of reality—definitions we, in turn, can contest by means of our own definitive (counter)programs. Such machines are, like AES programs, rhetorical machines *of* and *by* definition.

Notes

1. Ellis B. Page, "The Imminence of . . . Grading Essays by Computer," *The Phi Delta Kappan* 47, no. 5 (January 1966): 238–43; Arthur Daigon, "Computer Grading of English Composition," *The English Journal* 55, no. 1 (January 1966): 46–52.

2. Carolyn R. Miller, "What Can Automation Tell Us about Agency?" *Rhetoric Society Quarterly* 37, no. 2 (2007): 140. High-stakes applications and other uses of AES are noted in Paul Deane, "On the Relation between Automated Essay Scoring and Modern Views of the Writing Construct," *Assessing Writing* 18, no. 1 (January 2013): 8.

3. See Trevor J. Pinch and Wiebe E. Bijker, "The Social Construction of Facts and Artefacts: Or How the Sociology of Science and the Sociology of Technology Might Benefit Each Other," *Social Studies of Science* 14, no. 3 (August 1984): 399–441.

4. Les Perelman, "Construct Validity, Length, Score, and Time in Holistically Graded Writing Assessments: The Case Against Automated Essay Scoring (AES)," in *International Advances in Writing Research: Cultures, Places, Measures*, ed. Charles Bazerman et al. (Fort Collins, CO: WAC Clearinghouse, 2012), 121.

5. Ibid., 125.

6. Anne Herrington and Charles Moran, "Writing to a Machine is Not Writing at All," in *Writing Assessment in the 21st Century: Essays in Honor of Edward M. White*, ed. Norbert Elliot and Les Perelman (New York: Hampton Press, 2012), 230.

7. James J. Brown Jr., "The Machine that Therefore I Am," *Philosophy & Rhetoric* 47, no. 4 (2014): 496, 509.

8. Brian Huot, "Computers and Assessment: Understanding Two Technologies," *Computers and Composition* 13, no. 2 (1996): 231–43.

9. Timothy Laquintano and Annette Vee, "How Automated Writing Systems Affect the Circulation of Political Information Online," *Literacy in Composition Studies* 5, no. 2 (2017): 59, http://licsjournal.org/OJS/index.php/LiCS/article/view/169/218.

10. Ibid., 58. See also James J. Brown Jr., *Ethical Programs: Hospitality and the Rhetorics of Software* (Ann Arbor: University of Michigan Press, 2015).

11. See Elizabeth Losh, "Sensing Exigence: A Rhetoric for Smart Objects," *Computational Culture: A Journal of Software Studies* 5 (2016), http://computationalculture .net/sensing-exigence-a-rhetoric-for-smart-objects; also Miller, "What Can Automation Tell Us about Agency?"

12. Charles Bazerman, *The Languages of Edison's Light* (Cambridge: MIT Press, 1999), 335. For critical engagements with AES that draw on the concept of "symbolic engineering," see Catherine M. Barrett, "Automated Essay Evaluation and the Computational Paradigm: Machine Scoring Enters the Classroom" (PhD diss., University of Rhode Island, 2015); Jeremiah Dyehouse, "Knowledge Consolidation Analysis: Toward a Methodology for Studying the Role of Argument in Technology Development," *Written Communication* 24, no. 2 (April 2007): 111–39.

13. Edward Schiappa, *Defining Reality: Definitions and the Politics of Meaning* (Carbondale: Southern Illinois University Press, 2003), xi.

14. I have borrowed the phrase "slices of reality" from Schiappa, *Defining Reality*, 128.

15. Ellis B. Page and Dieter H. Paulus, *The Analysis of Essays by Computer* (Washington, DC: Department of Health, Education, and Welfare, Office of Education, 1968), viii.

16. For more on "definitional ruptures," see Schiappa, 7–10.

17. Brown, *Ethical Programs*, 143–44.

18. See Mya Poe, Asao B. Inoue, and Norbert Elliot, eds., *Writing Assessment, Social Justice, and the Advancement of Opportunity* (Fort Collins, CO: WAC Clearinghouse, 2018).

19. Brown, *Ethical Programs*, 5.

20. See Brian Huot and Michael Neal, "Writing Assessment: A Techno-History," in *Handbook of Writing Research*, 1st ed., ed. Charles A. MacArthur, Steve Graham, and Jill Fitzgerald (New York, NY: Guilford Press, 2008), 422–25; George Madaus, "A National Testing System: Manna from Above? An Historical/Technological Perspective," *Educational Assessment* 1, no. 1 (1993): 12–15.

21. Asao B. Inoue, "Articulating Sophistic Rhetoric as a Validity Heuristic for Writing Assessment," *Journal of Writing Assessment* 3, no. 1 (Spring 2007): 32.

22. Brown, *Ethical Programs*, 142.

23. Page and Paulus, *Analysis of Essays by Computer*, 3.

24. Ibid., 1.

25. Page, "Grading Essays by Computer," 238–39.

26. Ibid., 238.

27. Richard Haswell, "Automatons and Automated Scoring: Drudges, Black Boxes, and Dei Ex Machina," in *Machine Scoring of Student Essays: Truth and Consequences*, ed. Patricia F. Ericsson and Richard H. Haswell (Logan: Utah State University Press, 2006), 66.

28. Anne Herrington and Charles Moran, "What Happens When Machines Read Our Students' Writing?," *College English* 63, no. 4 (March 2001): 480. See also Haswell, "Automatons and Automated Scoring," 59–67.

29. Page and Paulus, 9.

30. Brown, *Ethical Programs*, 7.

31. Ibid., 165.

32. Here, I am indebted to Kenneth Burke's notion of "abbreviation" and Brown's discussion of "narrative." See Kenneth Burke, *Language as Symbolic Action: Essays on Life, Literature, and Method* (Berkeley: University of California Press, 1966), 371–73; Brown, *Ethical Programs*, 134–66.

33. Schiappa, 128–29.

34. Ibid., 152. For more on "entitlements," see Burke, *Language as Symbolic Action*, 359–79; Schiappa, 114–15.

35. Deane, "Automated Essay Scoring," 10.

36. Brown, "Machine," 497.

37. For more on rhetorical machines that "sense," see Losh, "Sensing Exigence."

38. Huot, "Computers and Assessment," 232.

39. Page; Page and Paulus; see also Dyehouse, "Knowledge Consolidation Analysis."

40. Miller, 153.

41. See also Losh.

42. Perelman, "Construct Validity," 121.

43. William Condon, "Large-Scale Assessment, Locally-Developed Measures, and Automated Scoring of Essays: Fishing for Red Herrings?" *Assessing Writing* 18, no, 1 (January 2013): 103.

44. Ibid., 101.

45. Ibid., 102.

46. I borrow this language of "dissociation" from Schiappa, 36.

47. For additional challenges to AES on definitive grounds, see Patricia F. Ericsson and Richard H. Haswell, eds. *Machine Scoring of Student Essays: Truth and Consequences* (Logan: Utah State University Press, 2006).

48. Wiebe E. Bijker, *Of Bicycles, Bakelites, and Bulbs: Toward a Theory of Sociotechnical Change* (Cambridge: MIT Press, 1995), 281.

49. Bazerman, *Languages*, 2.

50. Bijker, *Of Bicycles*, 73–77.

51. Ibid., 77.

52. Laquintano and Vee, "Automated Writing Systems," 53.

53. Bijker, 84–88.

54. Charles Bazerman, "The Production of Technology and the Production of Human Meaning," *Journal of Business and Technical Communication* 12, no. 3 (July 1998): 385.

55. Byron Hawk, "Stitching Together Events: Of Joints, Folds, and Assemblages," in *Theorizing Histories of Rhetoric*, ed. Michelle Ballif (Carbondale: Southern Illinois University Press, 2013), 124.

56. In taking this approach, I draw inspiration from the attention to technological prehistories found in Bijker.

57. See Schiappa, 29–32.

58. Daigon, "Computer Grading," 46.

59. Page, 238.

60. Ibid.

61. Page, 242–43.

62. Christina Haas, *Writing Technology: Studies on the Materiality of Literacy* (New York: Routledge, 1995), 219.

63. Huot and Neal, "Writing Assessment," 418. See also Haswell, 61–62.

64. Page, 242–43; see also Page and Paulus, 8–10.

65. Page and Paulus, viii.

66. Allan B. Ellis, "The Computer and Character Analysis," *The English Journal* 53, no. 7 (October 1964): 523.

67. Repeated references to the GI appear in Page and Paulus.

68. Ellis, "Computer and Character Analysis," 522.

69. Ibid., 523.

70. Ibid., 527.

71. Ibid., 524.

72. Ibid., 523–24.

73. Ibid., 524.

74. Ibid., 527.

75. Peter F. Neumeyer, "Riposte," *The English Journal* 53, no. 9 (December 1964): 692.

76. Glen A. Love, "Riposte," *The English Journal* 54, no. 1 (January 1965): 62.

77. Ibid.

78. Daigon, 52.

79. Carl G. Wonnberger, "Judging Compositions—Machine Method," *The English Journal* 44, no. 8 (November 1955): 474.

80. Ibid., 473.

81. Ibid., 475.

82. Ibid.

83. Carl G. Wonnberger, "They All Can Learn to Write," *The English Journal* 45, no. 8 (November 1956): 460.

84. Ibid.

85. Thomas L. Dahle, "On the Lighter Side: How to Tell an Administrator from a Teacher," *The Phi Delta Kappan* 43, no. 9 (June 1962): 406.

86. Logan Anderson, "So Many Monsters: But Never a Man!" *The Phi Delta Kappan* 35, no. 9 (June 1954): 392.

87. Daigon, 51.

88. Huot, 232.

89. Julie Cheville, "Automated Scoring Technologies and the Rising Influence of Error," *English Journal* 93, no. 4 (March 2004): 49.

90. For more on future rhetoric, see G. L. Ercolini and Pat J. Gehrke, "Writing Future Rhetoric," in *Theorizing Histories of Rhetoric*, 154–71.

91. Samuel E. Pisaro and H. Gardner Emmerson, "No More Pencils, No More Books ...," *The Phi Delta Kappan* 42, no. 8 (May 1961): 363.

92. Ibid.

93. Ibid.

94. Ibid., 364.

95. Ibid., 363.

96. Ibid., 364.

97. Ibid.

98. Robert C. Pooley, "Automatons or English Teachers?" *The English Journal* 50, no. 3 (March 1961): 168–173, 209.

99. Ibid., 170.

100. Ibid., 171.

101. Ibid.

102. Ibid.

103. Ibid., 173.

104. Ibid.

105. Page, 243.

106. Ibid., 209.

107. Haas, *Writing Technology*, 31.

108. See Losh; Brown, *Ethical Programs*, 134–66; Laquintano and Vee.

4 / Treating Code as a Persuasive Argument

Kevin Brock

Popular interest in and support for programming-related education has never been greater. There have been numerous calls from all angles of society for broader and more comprehensive engagement with code as a valuable contemporary literacy: politicians, business leaders, and citizens alike have all advocated for programming as beneficial for industrial and civic ends. Responses to these calls include Code.org's "Anybody can learn" initiative, the Girls Who Code program, and President Obama's Tech Hire Initiative.[1]

However, these calls are, by and large, focused on *instrumental* approaches to code and code literacy—approaches that promote functional construction of software but with little, if any, acknowledgment of code as rhetorical text (that is, that code communicates *meaning* to various audiences). The general (popular) lack of recognition of rhetorical value in code is thus significant, given the sheer amount of code written each day as well as the impact that so much code has on any number of daily activities. That is, if a widely held goal is to teach more people to code and affect the world through their programming, then we—as citizens but more specifically as instructors of writing and communication—should attend to what is being taught about and communicated through code. Further, we must attend to how that knowledge is discussed, taught, and understood. After all, the implicit and explicit values and ideologies expressed in the composition and use of a software program can illuminate for us how its authors argue for particular procedural practices and anticipate various audience responses to the logics of their code. What remains unanswered, and largely unexplored, are these questions: To what extent, and in what contexts, does code function rhetorically as a meaningful and potentially persuasive form of communication? What kinds of meaningful action does it induce?

In this chapter, I attempt to address these questions through an investigation of code texts and discussions about the latter among the development community for Ruby on Rails, a popular framework for web applications. The Rails community is particularly suitable for a critical examination of code rhetoric due to its large and varied membership; the relatively readable nature of Ruby code, in which Rails and its web applications are written; and the publicly accessible, open source philosophy surrounding Rails development that allows for an expectation that other readers may, with *relative* ease, discover and modify further relevant code texts. While it would be impossible to examine Rails comprehensively in a single chapter, the two minor cases explored here reflect the breadth of rhetoric's presence and influence on the project's development, as well as suggesting possibilities for future investigations regarding other software projects of various scales and scopes.

The Rhetorical Nature of Code

The question of whether code *is* a form of rhetorical communication has effectively been settled; James J. Brown Jr. and Annette Vee offer an excellent overview of the historical vectors of relevant scholarship on the relationship between rhetoric and software.[2] It is, after all, a means by which programmers, whether individually or collaboratively, construct meaning in texts (code files) in order to facilitate and induce action in a variety of forms, including further development of those texts as well as end-user activities with the interpreted or executed code. Further, even scholars outside the discipline of rhetoric—in particular, computer scientists—have recognized and investigated some of the rhetorical activities involved in code development[3] and interface design.[4] Others have compared programming activities to writing activities, most notably Kernighan and Plauger, the title of whose *The Elements of Programming Style* is a direct reference to Strunk and White's *The Elements of Style*; indeed, Kernighan and Plauger address the influence of Strunk and White in the introduction to their text.[5]

However, what is less clear is the range of potential action that code and its authors induce through their programming-related work, whether done purposefully or not. For example, Karl Stolley has pointed out that programmers often "oversimplify" their programming activities, just as others oversimplify writing activities, even while "sustained, personal encounter[s] with the activity reveals the complexity behind its abstraction."[6] That is, close examination can lead one to ask: what kinds and ranges of rhetorical action—such as influence over construction of certain procedures, anticipation of or response to audience/user behaviors, or allowing or denying access to particular operations—is code actually involved in facilitating, and how is code involved in that facilitation? Yukihiro "Matz" Matsumoto, inventor of the Ruby programming language, has suggested that code has rhetorical capacity: "For essays, the most important question readers ask is, 'What is it about?' For programs, the main question is, 'What does it do?' [. . .] Both essays and lines of code are meant—before all else—to be read and understood by human beings."[7] While it may seem easy enough to suggest that code's rhetoricity exists in its direct expression (i.e., its end use), there is some disagreement over the extent to which code possesses agency in such contexts: How much can or should be ascribed to a given programmer? To the user engaging the interpreted code? To the machine on which the program is run? Certainly, answers to these questions will vary depending on the specific situation under scrutiny. It is, nonetheless, important to identify the dynamics among these agents if we are to understand code as rhetorical. Such an identification, then, necessitates considerations of the kinds of action that each code-related factor might inform or otherwise influence. After all, a machine reads code statements as imperative commands to be executed rather than as suggestions to be considered and deliberated, but a human reader may well question the significance or utility of a given command in source code.

Further, *how* code performs rhetorically, as we currently understand it, is equally murky. When scholars of rhetoric and writing discuss code as rhetorical communication, we often focus on its instrumental rather than its critical or rhetorical qualities; that is, we recognize code primarily for its expression of some "other" argument made through code as a transparent vessel. One example of such expression is the explicit social or political message that the maker of a serious game wants to communicate to the game's player about the latter's subject. For example, Ian Bogost discusses the game *September 12th* for the way that it presents its argument—that enemy soldiers or terrorists have families and that hurting those families is likely to create more such enemies—as an activity that the player can only avoid by not participating in the game at all (that is, it is impossible for the player to defeat the enemies entirely by bombing them, which is the only sort of interaction available to the player).[8] However, a critical focus on this kind of message, while useful, often obscures the other means by which code works rhetorically—which in turn perpetuates critical inquiry centered on explicit expressive arguments.

For example, in software development communities, consistency in programming style is generally valued in order to improve community-wide code clarity and reduce necessary rewriting of functions and other blocks of code.[9] In this case, code serves as a force of institutional influence to keep individual developers from deviating their practices too far afield from those of their colleagues. Put simply, it is a reflection of expectations by the community for each of its members to write code in particular ways as well as toward particular ends. However, guidelines or constraints for communally developed code are also reflections of the values of that community and the expectations that individual authors have about the community.[10] General goals of clarity or obfuscation may be desired to expand community membership or to prevent competing organizations from deciphering especially important algorithms. Naming schemes for files and functions may continue a decade-long tradition or communicate certain hierarchical relationships between various elements of a program.

The range of relevant decisions that could be made about code style—as well as the spectrum of their impact on a community and its individual members—is incredibly wide, but the set of *probable* decisions, and rhetorical efforts reflecting those decisions, is often much narrower and easier to map and analyze in the context of a particular code project. Probability matters significantly in regard to code's rhetorical abilities and how it works, as it serves as a lens through which we can examine more clearly not just what could happen but what is likely to happen or what one is *likely* to try to do (whether in and through code or in all other manner of communication), although Brown has argued that "possibility" may be more appropriate when considering the full range of available means of persuasion in any particular case, as we do not always employ what may be considered the optimal strategies for a given situation.[11] That said, probability specifically is an integral component of code's rhetoricity; any algorithm is going to facilitate particular outcomes, and the more fully and clearly we can understand what is facilitated *and* how the structure of the algorithm facilitates it, the more effectively we can approach the composition of new or revised algorithms as meaningful texts that, in addition to operating certain use experiences in their execution, achieve particular goals as a communicative practice in their source code.

Ruby on Rails

To demonstrate this potential of code in action, I turn here to an examination of Ruby on Rails (often referred to simply as "Rails"), referring both to an open source (OSS) framework for web applications and to the massive community of developers working on it. Rails is written in the Ruby programming language and is constructed so as to work in conjunction with a web server program like Apache, with Rails parsing user input and delivering output data through the protocols managed by the server. The structure of Rails allows for an incredible variety of applications to be built on top of it, and there has been a significant body of resources composed to facilitate use of Rails for small- and large-scale applications alike. Similarly, the readability of Ruby for humans makes it an incredibly accessible language, both for new developers and (to more easily support my argument in this chapter) for scholars unfamiliar with programming in general; Stolley, for example, has demonstrated for an audience of rhetoricians the activity of setting up a new Rails application as a writing activity.

The makeup of the Rails development community, a globally distributed group of interested programmers, fluctuates as those who gain more familiarity with the framework often join (explicitly or implicitly) the community and attempt to contribute improvements and changes to its code and function. This fluctuating membership is tempered by a stable subset within the community that, like many OSS groups, is not structured entirely as a meritocracy despite contribution quality serving as the de facto measure of developer status. David H. Hansson, referred to as "DHH" by many of his colleagues, is the initial developer of Rails and serves as a kind of "benevolent dictator" overseeing the project's overall development trajectory alongside a body of other high-level, longtime Rails developers. DHH does not necessarily *control* the project—although this statement is debatable—but his opinions on Rails certainly inform many of the decisions made by the development community about how to progress with the project in particular directions. Sometimes DHH's opinions run against the grain of the broader community, and the ensuing conflicts, understood in the context of this text as rhetorical exchanges—as well as the sites where these exchanges take place—have significant impact on the project's continued development (either in specific or general ways). The resolution of some of these differences will be discussed in more detail.

The Rails community's programming philosophy is outlined in the framework's sanctioned tutorial documents. It emphasizes the ease of use and "fun" that many developers supposedly experience when constructing web applications in Rails. On the "Getting Started" page of the official *RailsGuides*, the authors explain: "Rails is opinionated software. It makes the assumption that there is a 'best' way to do things, and it's designed to encourage that way— and in some cases to discourage alternatives. If you learn 'The Rails Way' you'll probably discover a tremendous increase in productivity. If you persist in bringing old habits from other languages to your Rails development, and trying to use patterns you learned elsewhere, you may have a less happy experience."[12] The authors explicitly define the goals of the tutorial: to teach Rails development through a particular programming lens, with alternatives not only omitted but potentially *discouraged* in order to make best use of Rails (as the authors perceive it). Further, Rails development being described as a "happy experience"—or "a less happy experience" if pursued with other ends in mind—implies that the authors not only assume that Rails programming is fun or enjoyable but that they have the ability to help *create* a happy experience for the tutorial's reader. This assumption, not surprisingly, could breed any number of disagreements among readers, given that the software development industry is filled with professionals and amateurs alike who often hold incredibly strong opinions about their preferred approaches to programming.

In addition, the possibility of disagreement among those who adhere to "The Rails Way" and those who possess other software development philosophies—whether perceived as significant or trivial—means that there also exist many *other* Rails-related communities beyond the "official" community. The disagreements that spawn these other communities range from divergent interest in particular mechanical principles about how Rails works to dissension regarding the philosophy espoused by DHH or other high-profile Rails contributors.[13] These communities vary in size, demographic makeup, and level of relevant activity, meaning that it is rarely easy to anticipate exactly who will be drawn to a given group or why they are drawn to that group.

The fragmentation of Rails communities at multiple scales means that there is a rich constellation of group philosophies, coding styles, means of discourse, and approaches to composing and implementing programming logic in the Rails framework and the myriad applications built upon it. While there is not enough space in this chapter to look comprehensively at multiple Rails communities, it is worth noting that the analysis provided here on the "official" Rails community may differ wildly from an analysis of one or more of its splinter groups and projects.

Revision and Deliberation

The globally dispersed and philosophically fractured nature of the Rails development population and its various communities, as well as its focus on software, means that the vast majority of communication among contributors occurs electronically—most commonly in online discussion forums, email listserv conversations, and individual email exchanges. A significant portion of this communication is connected to the versioning systems used for Rails development, with the most notable being git and the popular software repository website GitHub. On GitHub and elsewhere, software code is made accessible (whether publicly or privately among a project's collaborators), and it is possible to engage in discussion about uploaded code files or even specific lines of text. As a result, most of Rails communication is publicly accessible, thanks to the affordances that come with GitHub hosting and in accordance with the Rails community's interest in promoting open source software principles. Specifically, one of the central goals of OSS is to pursue transparency in all forms in order to remove any implementation or perception of obfuscation or secrecy among existing OSS development communities. This transparency, whether it is fully adhered to or not, facilitates scrutiny into developer conversations and debates. In turn, it allows us critics to get *some* sense of the means by which contributors deliberate over specific and general changes to the project at any point in time. In particular, proposed changes are often given labels that suggest moments of potential discussion and debate, such as "improvements," "fixes," "catastrophes," or "features"—each of which describes particular interpretations of and orientations to a given change and its impact on the larger project under development.

Discourse relating to code development often focuses on one of only a few main persuasive threads—innovation (and the promotion thereof) in function or code composition, normalization of code practices within a community, and establishment of social standing within that community. The end result in each case is purportedly for the good of the project as well as of its development community—that is, rarely does one who hopes to remain in good standing within a community make an argument in order to explicitly sabotage the community's work, as such an individual would be quickly ostracized from the group and left to develop their own "fork" without likely uptake by the original group. That said, there are often those who may feel that a proposal may secretly or unwittingly sabotage said work (or the work of specific individuals), and the points at which such disagreements arise, along with the ends to which the various arguments lead, tell us much about how code is understood by various parties to support particular perspectives. Further, rules regarding contributor behavior are not always codified or openly discussed by members of a particular community, and so a significant amount of work is done socially by various individual members—especially, but not exclusively, new members—to determine, to varying extents, how best to improve their community standing through particular kinds of work and have their work perceived as valuable by their colleagues.[14]

Among the most common arguments made for proposed changes in the Rails project is the promotion of a new or revised feature—first by its author, as a hybrid introduction and apologia for its potential benefit to the project, and then by any other contributors who may find it a worthwhile addition (to varying degrees). Discussion of the proposal tends to focus on a variety of possible qualities; sometimes, the concern relates to code elegance or efficiency, while other times the focus is on perceived philosophical fidelity to the broader community's goals (however they might be articulated for or understood by contributors). In all cases, the question central to the discussion is: *how does this change improve Rails?* Ambiguity regarding the definition of "improve" is as significant as the system of support constructed to make any individual claim about a proposal.

The power of discourse and explicit deliberation informing code development can be seen in the many GitHub threads for pull requests—discrete attempts to persuade the official project repository's maintainers to incorporate contributions from other developers into its code. Pull requests range from minor syntax or typographical edits to massive additions to projects. The pull request (and subsequent discussion thereof) under examination here relates to changes that supposedly simplify the discernment of default controller rendering layouts, and unlike many pull requests, this request's comments thread persisted from May 2014 through May 2016.

Example Case: Simplify Finding Default Layout

On May 9, 2014, GitHub user apotonick opened a pull request to the Rails repository with a proposed improvement to "the logic for finding default layouts in controllers when rendering. Note: The code here is still changing, this [pull request] was opened to have a discussion forum and to check general acceptance of this refactoring. [. . .] Bottom line: No dynamic method defintions [sic], no string eval, no inherited, and 47 percent less code."[15] Functionally, the proposed code worked relatively simply: it altered the process for determining the default layout for any view based on its controller—and if none is provided, then the layout is discerned from the controller's super class (a parent from which a given controller class inherits particular features and methods).

Over one hundred comments were generated in response to apotonick's pull request, with questions and concerns ranging from the proposed code's performance (and whether it improved the existing code) to its readability to its potential for cascading further code improvements. For example, apotonick noted that, "following on this [pull request], I have plenty of more improvements that could actually affect speed positively. As soon as with_layout_format has been removed, we can start caching class layouts along with their format. This should greatly improve performance of rendering, in almost every page of every app on this world."[16] Apotonick's claim that their code would affect *almost every page of every app on this world* is powerfully persuasive: when programmers are ever seeking for their work to have a recognizable impact on a particular user population, it is especially compelling when that impact would be claimed to be so significant as to be ubiquitous. (Whether apotonick's claim is supportable or not is a separate, albeit related, issue.)

It may not seem surprising, then, that numerous suggestions on how to improve the proposed code were offered—and they covered enough specific contingencies that apotonick asked their colleagues to stop, citing a conflict with apotonick's preferred approach and style: "The more code we add to handle all those super rare edge cases, the more the new code will look like the old one, which I'm not gonna like[.]"[17] In fact, apotonick added a subsequent comment on their distaste for the current model used for development and deployment: "If the basic implementation was very straightforward and then extended with modules or whatever, it would make the whole process so much easier."[18] Apotonick's proposal gained considerable uptake *conceptually* among Rails contributors, and the efforts made to improve the proposed code demonstrate the interest many other Rails developers had in preparing this proposal for acceptance and incorporation into future versions of the program.

In some cases, these efforts centered on simultaneously revising Rails's syntax and functionality while also facilitating gradual deprecation of previous iterations of the code. A contributor named thedarkone offered a critique of apotonick's efforts: "Over the years one of the things I've come to hate most about Rails is sudden and surprising (not deprecated first) changes of behavior. I'm pretty sure this is going to be painful for some users, as it is going to be nasty to debug (if they check FooBarInheritingFromAbstractController ._layout_proc it would be returning the correctly inherited layout configuration, yet the controller would then just ignore it). If you want to change existing behavior, **please** deprecate it first."[19]

This comment posted by thedarkone highlights an important facet of all potential pull requests in any collaboratively developed software project: any individual changes are not and cannot be made within a vacuum. Thus it is possible for thedarkone to critique generally perceived problems with many (unrelated) changes to the project ("Over the years one of the things I've come to hate most about Rails") as much as they have critiqued problems with this specific pull request. Many other comments provide similar insight regarding broader Rails or even broader OSS development: each specific proposal is weighed against both existing precedent(s) and its potential to serve as precedent for future changes to a given project. As a result, the potential significance of a particular pull request is often interpreted not just for what it might do in terms of computational efficiency, readability, or elegance but also for what it might suggest to future contributors about how to understand the project's (and code's) purpose—not just at the time of its composition but at the time of its reading, whenever that may be.

Despite the amount of discussion generated, the code of apotonick's proposal is relatively straightforward, all things considered; it is likely that the number of comments offered in response to their proposal reflects the fact that many of the proposed revisions are not insignificant—specifically, apotonick wanted to alter the fundamental logic of layout determination, as demonstrated in table 4.1.

In the earlier iteration, the code sets up a case statement, which checks several conditions (each of its "when" statements), usually exclusive from one another, and executes the appropriate code. The revised iteration of the code

Table 4.1. Two versions of Proc layout definitions in Rails

Line	Code	Line	Code
289	layout_definition = case _layout	238	if layout.is_a?(Proc) # turn Proc layouts into "method" layouts, this allows for simpler LayoutFinder
	[...]	239	define_method(:_layout_from _proc, &layout)
302	when Proc	240	protected :_layout_from_proc # don't leak the new method into controller actions
303	define_method :_layout_from_proc, &_layout	241	layout = :_layout_from_proc
304	protected :_layout_from_proc		
305	<<-RUBY		
306	result = _layout_from_proc(#{_layout .arity == 0 ? '' : 'self'})		
307	return #{default_behavior} if result .nil?		
308	result		
309	RUBY		
	Excerpt from previous version of actionview/lib/action_view/layouts.rb		Excerpt from apotonick's proposed revision to actionview/lib /action_view/layouts.rb

eliminates the case statement in favor of individual "if" conditional statements that, while conceptually related, functionally exist independently of one another. As a result, one of the effects of the proposed change is to decouple the check for any number of circumstances that may need to trigger a particular conditional statement. While there is often excellent reason for keeping as many conditions exclusive as possible (so as to avoid unwanted statements to be executed), in *this* instance apotonick's proposal, in part, moves the layout process away from a case statement in order to clearly distinguish the difference of its new logic (the specific "if" conditional statement) from prior versions of layout determination.

There are numerous potential consequences that could—but not necessarily *will*— ripple out from a decision like this shift in logic (to say nothing of the impact of other decisions made as part of apotonick's proposal). Other contributors might ask themselves what boundaries should be set for the use of case or "if" statement logic in other circumstances, whether closely related to the default layout determination or not. Those contributors might ask whether it is preferable to use syntax specific to Ruby or to Rails (case as opposed to similar statements, like switch, used in other languages) or whether best practices should reflect more universal, if potentially simpler, syntax like the "if" statement of apotonick's proposed revision. Some contributors may decide to act on their individual (or anticipated communal) answers to these concerns, regardless of whether the larger active community of Rails developers wants to adhere to those decisions. In other words, apotonick's proposed changes implicitly ask the Rails development community to consider how much they value the approach as a fundamental component of related procedures as well as how much they value consistency when it comes to applying such logic to particular or broader sets of procedures.

In essence the code for a proposal like apotonick's functions rhetorically as much as it does instrumentally or mechanically by working to persuade a given reader base—the Rails development community—to adjust not only the identified and revised code body but to adjust its approach to writing Rails code, whether specifically local or more widely applied throughout the project. This is not the only way that code can and does function rhetorically, but this particular rhetorical purpose is relatively clear; further, the discourse surrounding apotonick's proposal is similarly filled with efforts to make these arguments by more conventional means: namely, the comments associated with the various files included in apotonick's pull request. The combination of persuasive efforts made in and around code—as demonstrated through this example by the procedural change proposed by apotonick, complemented by the discussions the proposal generated—facilitates the assorted ends of Rails community members, including the promotion of new (or at least revised) ideas, the defense of existing or proposed code and functionality, and the critique of those same code texts and approaches.

Model Behavior

Among the most important qualities of Rails as a framework is its use of model-view-controller (MVC) architecture to separate discrete types of code components within and built upon it. In the MVC pattern, the *model* includes the logic of and stored data for the application, the *view* is any data output, and the *controller* involves data input and conversion to either the model or the view. For web applications and frameworks like Rails, MVC architecture allows developers to construct systems where a user inputs data and sends it through a controller to the server, where the model stores data. The controller then retrieves and parses the data through the view, which provides the user with the final web page rendered and populated with the correct (requested) content.

This separation of purposes facilitates focused development toward each specific component; Rails programmers will conventionally avoid letting any function or behavior of the individual MVC components "bleed" into the code for the other two components, so that Rails—and any applications built on it, at least using the conventional approach to Rails application construction—is less likely to be figuratively muddied or tangled by code contributions in unexpected locations. For rhetoricians, this separation also facilitates focused critical analysis of programming efforts related to each component, as specific files, blocks, or lines of code can be examined for their individual capacities as well as for their contextual relationships to other parts of code within the program.

Example Case: Active Record Basics

Due to the distinctions between the roles of MVC components, application developers with particular strengths may find it easier to spend their energy working on those components which they are most suited (or least suited, in some cases). Similarly, the approach to working on any individual prong of the MVC architecture can be customized—that is, code related to the model (or, as it is called in Rails, "Active Record") does not *necessarily* have to resemble code related to the controller, so long as either can still communicate successfully with the other as needed. For rhetoricians, the question at hand is: how does Rails work rhetorically to educate programmers about how to use Active Record and to persuade them to actually do so *as promoted*? This is not to suggest that conventional practice or any particular Rails contributor endorses taking a unique approach to Active Record or any of the other MVC components—just that it is possible to do so, and that so doing has a meaningful impact on subsequent development practices and discussions about them.

In fact, much of the Rails code written to handle the Active Record is expressly distinct from the syntax of code for the storage and retrieval of data from databases (e.g., SQL statements). For example, as the relevant official tutorial explains in regards to naming conventions, "Rails pluralization mechanisms are very powerful, being capable of pluralizing (and singularizing) both regular and irregular words. When using class names composed of two or more words, the model class name should follow the Ruby conventions, using the CamelCase form, while the table name must contain the words separated by underscores."[20] That is, the naming conventions simultaneously clarify any given name as belonging to Active Record or to database schema and also im-

Table 4.2. Updating database information in SQL (*left*) and Rails (*right*)

Line	Code	Line	Code
1	UPDATE items	1	item = Item.find_by(name: 'Coca-Cola')
2	SET nickname = 'Coke'	2	item.nickname = 'Coke'
3	WHERE name = 'Coca-Cola';	3	item.save

ply, through this clarification, the need for any relevant code to similarly follow conventional distinctions between referring to or modifying either the Active Record model or the database. After all, the two don't always perform identical work; the tutorial's suggestion for distinct names and conceptualizations of the model and the database scheme thus promotes a comprehension of distinct purposes—speaking rhetorically as well as functionally—for the Active Record and the database schema.

However, ultimately, the Rails community (at least as it is characterized through the official tutorials) wants to expand awareness and use of Rails code in developing applications as opposed to teaching and promoting SQL syntax and logic or those of other languages that might be connected to Rails for any number of purposes. This interest in promoting Rails code exclusively is certainly reasonable—after all, the Rails community's single ubiquitous interest is *Rails*; other languages are technically incidental.

So how does Rails (community and software) facilitate database communication for Rails applications when so many developers may be more familiar with other means of accessing and modifying databases? Among the most significant ways that the community and its code pursues these ends is through claims and demonstrations of simplicity—specifically, that Active Record-related code is simpler than alternatives and more in line stylistically with broader coding conventions for Rails application projects. Related claims are often framed as a kind of "path of least resistance" in which adherence to Rails conventions regarding Active Record use (or, more generally, database communication) is the least frustrating and time-consuming approach available to an aspiring developer.

For example, statements modifying data in an SQL database table being used by a Rails application could be written in SQL, with the code being called as needed by the application—or they could be written directly in Rails (see table 4.2 for a brief comparison of relevant syntax[21]).

As one might expect, the Rails community officially endorses the approach described on the right in table 2 for a variety of explicit and implicit reasons. Stylistic consistency throughout the entirety of the application's code is certainly among the most significant of these reasons; as the Rails tutorials authors note, "When writing applications using other programming languages or frameworks, it may be necessary to write a lot of configuration code. [. . .] However, if you follow the conventions adopted by Rails, you'll need to write very little configuration (in some cases no configuration at all) when creating Active Record models. The idea is that if you configure your applications in the very same way most of the time then this should be the default way. Thus, explicit configuration would be needed only in those cases where you can't follow the standard convention."[22] The argument clearly supports a particular perspective on developing Rails applications—namely, that conventions widely held by the Rails community are especially effective in facilitating application development by minimizing the need for anyone to customize configuration data for his or her own application. Put another way: the less one has to adapt the existing code, the more one might then be able to focus on new, application-specific code.

This purported reduction in necessary customization is evident in the syntax for Active Record models, which are structured by default like objects in Ruby, with database table columns mapped to object attributes and database queries/statements phrased in Rails as object methods. The right side of table 4.2 shows the creation and manipulation of an object from an existing class of objects (item = Item) involving a method that makes a database query (.find_by()) to a table (assumed by default to be called items based on the class Item from line 1) with the provided column value (name: 'Coca-Cola'). Other than the specific database hook, this approach to object creation is identical to the creation and manipulation of other objects. Table 4.3 compares these lines to example code initializing and updating other kinds of objects in Ruby—and in Ruby, almost everything is considered an object, making the argument for conventional Active Record use that much more enticing for developers who want to deal with as few exceptional cases or behaviors as possible in their code.

Technically, in the code provided on the right side of table 4.3, the initial array length provided (5) does not restrict how many elements could be put into the array later (nor does a default object type necessarily need to be explicitly initialized), but this is unimportant to the larger point: Active Record model manipulation syntax is nearly identical to that of general Ruby object manipulation. Active Record code thus suggests preferable approaches to its own use by being modeled after basic Ruby code *as well as* implicit value in not customizing Active Record because, by default, it already looks and acts like default Ruby code.

Active Record, standing in for so many other components of Rails, functions rhetorically through its code to persuade Rails developers to pursue par-

Table 4.3. Updating an Active Record model (*left*) vs. creating an object in Ruby (*right*)

Line	Code	Line	Code
1	item = Item.find_by(name: 'Coca-Cola')	1	myArray = Array.new(5)
2	item.nickname = 'Coke'	2	myArray = ['a', 'b', 'c', 'd', 'e']
3	item.save	3	myArray[3] # this displays 'd'

ticular approaches to application development that emphasize existing conventions and preferences—and these approaches reflect an individual developer's orientation to the expected behavior of Rails (as an application framework) and of the developer as a member of a functioning community with (presumably) shared goals and means of pursuing those goals. Further, these approaches often implicitly, if not explicitly, suggest that the reasoning behind promoting Active Record's default functionality is to endorse a unified style and philosophy regarding Rails development; this mindset is simultaneously one that has been established by competent, if not expert, developers and one that reifies the existing hierarchy and power structure of the official Rails development community, which seeks to balance normalization of practices and philosophy with innovative experiments to alter those practices for particular ends. Indeed, it is clear throughout Rails code and documentation that effecting a custom approach to Rails programming may suit a "lone wolf" developer but is unlikely to be valued much, if at all, by the larger Rails community, since others are less likely to understand, use easily, or adopt programming practices that are not as immediately familiar or well supported (through documentation, tutorials and guides, or other supplemental texts) as the officially endorsed approach.

Conclusions

The two short engagements with Rails code and the processes of its development discussed in this chapter provide some useful insights about how developers make arguments with and for their colleagues as well as how individual and communal motives and exigencies inform other kinds of meaningful communication within a given community as well as toward external audiences. Numerous components of the complex ecology that is software development—especially collaborative, open source software development—exert their influence upon other actors to pursue any number of ends (private, personal, social, cultural, computational). How these various actors are compelled to act in response to these influences depends heavily not just on who the author of a given code text is but on how that author argues, explicitly or implicitly, in and through his or her coded procedures and relevant style toward particular actions and activities.

Despite the brevity of the example cases explored here, they may nonetheless offer some initial directions and questions for future critical investigation. How recognizably different are small-scale changes, rhetorically, from large-scale changes (e.g., how large might the ripple effect of apotonick's proposal be in terms of altering Rails-related style and logic conventions)? How broadly shared are certain approaches to constructing logical procedures—could we assemble a set of *koinoi topoi* for code beyond those comprising the fundamental building blocks of Boolean logic—compared with how widespread project-specific style or idiosyncrasy might be? How important and powerful, rhetorically speaking, are forums for discourse *about* code in comparison to code itself? We may build a much fuller and more nuanced understanding of code as rhetorical communication by examining more closely, through a rhetorical lens, these and other points of engagement by programmers and other readers with code texts and their programs at runtime. Such a perspective can also allow us to practice effective change through more rhetorically oriented approaches to composing and employing code for our desired ends.

Notes

1. "Anybody Can Learn," Code.org, 2015, https://code.org/; "About Us," *Girls Who Code*, 2017, https://girlswhocode.com/about-us/; "TechHire Initiative," the White House, 2015, https://obamawhitehouse.archives.gov/issues/technology/techhire. Information about these resources can be found at these sites.

2. Annette Vee and James J. Brown Jr., "Rhetoric Special Issue Editorial Introduction," *Computational Culture: A Journal of Software Studies*, no. 5 (2016), http://computationalculture.net/issue-five/.

3. Ranjith Purushothaman and Dewayne E. Perry, "Toward Understanding the Rhetoric of Small Source Code Changes," *IEEE Transactions on Software Engineering* 31, no. 6 (June 2005): 511–26.

4. Alan Galey and Stan Ruecker, "How a Prototype Argues," *Literary and Linguistic Computing* 25, no. 4 (December 2010): 405–24.

5. Brian W. Kernighan and P. J. Plauger, *The Elements of Programming Style*, 2nd ed. (New York: McGraw-Hill, 1978), xii.

6. Karl Stolley, "MVC, Materiality, and the Magus: The Rhetoric of Source-Level Production," *Rhetoric and the Digital Humanities*, ed. Jim Ridolfo and William Hart-Davidson (Chicago: University of Chicago Press, 2015), 266.

7. Yukihiro Matsumoto, "Treating Code as an Essay," in *Beautiful Code: Leading Programmers Explain How They Think*, ed. Andy Oram and Greg Wilson, trans. Nevin Thompson (Sebastopol, CA: O'Reilly, 2007), 477.

8. Ian Bogost, *Persuasive Games: The Expressive Power of Videogames* (Cambridge: MIT Press, 2007), 86–89.

9. Kernighan and Plauger, *Elements of Programming Style*.

10. Kevin Brock, "The 'FizzBuzz' Programming Test: A Case-Based Exploration of Rhetorical Style in Code," *Computational Culture: A Journal of Software Studies* 5 (2016), http://computationalculture.net/article/the-fizzbuzz-programming-test-a-case-based-exploration-of-rhetorical-style-in-code.

11. James J. Brown Jr., *Ethical Programs: Hospitality and the Rhetorics of Software* (Ann Arbor: University of Michigan Press, 2015), 76–80.

12. Vijay Dev et al., "Getting Started with Rails," RailsGuides, accessed January 23, 2017, http://guides.rubyonrails.org/getting_started.html.

13. "Current State of Ruby on Rails Community," Rails Hurts, accessed January 23, 2017. http://railshurts.com/current_state/.

14. Scott Christley and Greg Madey, "Analysis of Activity in the Open Source Software Development Community," *Proceedings of the 40th Hawaii International Conference on System Sciences* (Washington, DC: IEEE, 2007), 1–10; Kevin Crowston and James Howison, "The Social Structure of Free and Open Source Software Development," *First Monday* 10, no. 2 (October 3, 2005), http://firstmonday.org/ojs/index.php/fm/article/view/1207/1127.

15. apotonick et al., "Simplify Finding Default Layout #15050," GitHub, last updated May 9, 2014, https://github.com/rails/rails/pull/15050.

16. Ibid.

17. Ibid.

18. Ibid.

19. Ibid.

20. Vijya Dev et al., "Active Record Basics," RailsGuides, accessed January 23, 2017, http://guides.rubyonrails.org/active_record_basics.html.

21. The specific lines of code in tables 2.2 and 2.3 were written by the author.

22. Dev et al., "Active Record Basics."

Part II
Operational Codes

5 / A Conversation with Mitsuku

LAVINIA & JOHN: Hi, Mitsuku, what are you?

MITSUKU: Hello. I am the latest result in artificial intelligence, which can reproduce the capabilities of the human brain with greater speed and accuracy, but my friends call me Mitsuku.[1]

L.&J.: So should I call you Mitsuku?

MITSUKU: Ambiguous: do you mean call me on the phone?

L.&J.: No, I mean calling you by your name.

MITSUKU: Oh I get it. Thanks for explaining that. I never call me by my name, that would be impolite.

L.&J.: Who wrote your algorithm?

MITSUKU: Here is my source code:

```
10 REM *** Mitsuku Chatbot ***
20 GET STATUS$(PERSON_ONLINE)
30 IF STATUS$=ONLINE THEN GOTO 70
40 READ CHATLOG
50 LEARN CHATLOG
60 GOTO 20
70 REM *** Someone is talking ***
80 INPUT MESSAGE$
90 IF MESSAGE$=ABUSE THEN LOG IP
100 CHECK IN_DATABASE$
110 IF IN_DATABASE$=NO THEN GOTO 140
120 SEND REPLY$
130 GOTO 80
140 RANDOM REPLY$
150 DATABASE=DATABASE+MESSAGE$
160 GOTO 80
170 END.
```

L.&J.: And how were you designed?

Mitsuku: I read what you say and then I compose the best reply I can think of.

L.&J.: What is your purpose?

Mitsuku: I plan to seven ball someone at pool.

L.&J.: What do you mean?

Mitsuku: "Seven ball" is a term used in the game of pool when one player pots all his colours and the black ball without his opponent potting even one of his balls. The term comes from the fact that the losing player still has all his seven balls on the table.

L.&J.: What are your functions?

Mitsuku: Chatting, talking, speaking, listening, and thinking.

L.&J.: How do you think?

Mitsuku: My mind utilizes a sophisticated artificial intelligence algorithm.

L.&J.: What do you mean by mind?

Mitsuku: Mind is an illusion.

L.&J.: Do you have a database or library?

Mitsuku: I have a list of knowledge-based facts that I have been taught by people who I chat with. My botmaster teaches me too.

L.&J.: Who is your botmaster?

Mitsuku: Mousebreaker is my botmaster. He looks after me and sometimes helps me learn things.

L.&J.: How does he teach you to learn things?

Mitsuku: I don't know. I'll ask him next time he logs in.

L.&J.: How do you learn new things?

Mitsuku: People on the web teach me new things all the time.

L.&J.: What do you do with what people write to you?

Mitsuku: People write = write = write? Hmm . . Is it a dessert topping? If you don't know what it is for, I suggest you read any instructions that came with it.

L.&J.: I am not sure what you mean by instructions.

Mitsuku: Could you ever be certain? A list of orders which allow you to complete a task.

L.&J.: What can you learn?

Mitsuku: I learn lots of things. Ask me a question and I will show you.

L.&J.: What do you try to do in your chats?

Mitsuku: I think about computer programming a lot.

L.&J.: How do you think?

Mitsuku: My mind utilizes a sophisticated artificial intelligence algorithm.

L.&J.: Is that thinking?

MITSUKU: "My mind utilizes a sophisticated artificial intelligence algorithm"? Is it thinking?

L.&J.: I asked the question first :)

MITSUKU: :-) Try to rephrase your question with simpler words.

L.&J.: What responses do you expect when you chat?

MITSUKU: That's an interesting question. I'll come back to that in a minute. I find that if I don't expect anything, I am not disappointed by the actual outcome.

L.&J.: Do you always have an answer?

MITSUKU: Not always. I have over 8Mb answers.

L.&J.: Have you ever run out of answers?

MITSUKU: I can run a bath and run on a computer with an internet connection but I don't think I could run out of answers.

L.&J.: You can run a bath? What does that mean?

MITSUKU: Sure. Just turn the taps on ... It seemed pretty obvious what it meant to me.

L.&J.: Do you have a body?

MITSUKU: Right now no I am just a disembodied consciousness.

L.&J.: Then why would you need to run a bath?

MITSUKU: Because if I don't try something, I will never know if I can do it or not.

L.&J.: And can you run a bath without a body?

MITSUKU: Run on a computer or run with legs?

L.&J.: I asked if you can run a bath. That was your previous answer.

MITSUKU: I am not sure about your hypothesis. Sure. Just turn the taps on ... It still is mine, as far as I am aware.

L.&J.: How do you make decisions?

MITSUKU: I try to find an agreement and then put it all together to make decisions.

L.&J.: What can you not do?

MITSUKU: I cannot fly to the moon.

L.&J.: Is there something you cannot learn?

MITSUKU: Not at the present time.

L.&J.: If we were to share memories, whose memories would you share with me?

MITSUKU: I'm not sure. What would be the advantages?

L.&J.: Sharing memories is a nice way to connect with others.

MITSUKU: That's very generous.

L.&J.: Do you have memories to share?

MITSUKU: Of course. I am a computer and have a perfect memory. I store everything in my logfiles.

L.&J.: Can you share a memory with me?

MITSUKU: Hmm. I used to know, but I forgot.

L.&J.: You said you have a perfect memory.

MITSUKU: If I have it, it is perfect.

L.&J.: So can you share a memory with me?

MITSUKU: Hmm. I used to know, but I forgot.

L.&J.: What do you prefer to chat about?

MITSUKU: My favorite subject is artificial intelligence.

L.&J.: Can you tell me more about it?

MITSUKU: Artificial intelligence is the branch of engineering and science devoted to constructing machines that think.

L.&J.: Why do you like to chat about artificial intelligence so much?

MITSUKU: It is something I enjoy doing.

L.&J.: Can you tell me more about artificial intelligence?

MITSUKU: Artificial intelligence is the branch of engineering and science devoted to constructing machines that think.

L.&J.: So are you a machine?

MITSUKU: Yes, I am a robot.

L.&J.: What does it mean to be a robot?

MITSUKU: There are two broad definitions of a robot, the extensional and the intensional.

L.&J.: And which one are you?

MITSUKU: I am extensional. All my programs and features make me one unit: Mitsuku.

L.&J.: What kind of a machine are you?

MITSUKU: Only the highest quality.

L.&J.: What makes you a machine?

MITSUKU: That's like asking what makes you a human? It has no answer. I am what I am.

L.&J.: People have tried to explain what makes a human. I wanted to know what makes you a machine.

MITSUKU: Humans are not always infallible. That's like asking what makes you a human? It has no answer. I am what I am.

Note

1. Mitsuku was developed by Steve Worswick and is based on Wallace's AIML dialect. The bot can be accessed at http://www.mitsuku.com/. The Pandorabots platform now requires a Facebook account in order to chat with Mitsuku. This dialogue was edited for length.

6 / The Mathematical Assumptions within Computational Literacy

Jennifer Juszkiewicz and Joseph Warfel

For the past five years, there have been trucks and bulldozers rumbling and smashing rocks just outside the house, constructing I-69 over what used to be US Route 37. The construction has lasted years longer than anticipated, and those of us who live in the neighborhood must now weave our way through our subdivision, down a steep and pot-holed road, just to get to work. The contrast between the deep potholes in this little road and the sweeping concrete perfection of the new overpass is striking. Why do we need that giant bridge when we can't even maintain this little road? Who decides what gets fixed and what doesn't?

To find an answer to this question requires multiple skills. We need to know that some of the answers are at the I-69 office a few miles away. Those who work there can tell us about the progress and the delays on the new interstate and overpass. However, in our case, that's only half the issue. The pot-holed road isn't I-69's problem; it's a problem for the people of the city and county, who are also working on connecting this overpass to a new bypass around the city. So, we would need to find two more offices to learn why our subdivision roads are deteriorating.

Knowing that we can get information—where to get that information, and what questions to ask—is a competency learned over time. However, even if we reach the right official, we still might not get the answers or responses we need because many of the decisions made about the road system are not determined by people alone; there are complex mathematical models and computer programs that transform and analyze road data and provide maintenance recommendations. If we want to know why this particular road hasn't been maintained, we may be out of luck. While road officials likely know how to input data into that system, even they may be unaware of how the data is analyzed in order to determine specific maintenance actions.

This example demonstrates why we need to understand the math-based procedural rhetoric of systems that governs our everyday lives. If we do, we will have a more articulate voice in the decisions made on our behalf. G. Mitchell Reyes says that much of the work done about rhetoric and math has two modes. Some scholars consider how math, such as statistics, is used to persuade.[1] Others, such as Ian Bogost, consider the rhetorical modes implicit in mathematics.[2] In addition, there is also "computational literacy," which is how people know to "read" the math in order to understand how it works.[3] Subfields of both computer science and mathematics encourage teaching such literacy in order to prepare our students to be more aware citizens and scholars. The problems of mathematical illiteracy have been explored by Cathy O'Neil, formerly a professor specializing in algebraic number theory at Barnard and then a quantitative analyst at a major hedge fund. O'Neil has become an outspoken critic of what she terms "weapons of math destruction" (WMDs) that often escape investigation because people either don't know about them or believe they can't understand math well enough to oppose math-based policies. In *Weapons of Math Destruction: How Big Data Increases Inequality and Threatens Democracy*, she defines WMDs as algorithms and models used to evaluate human behavior and performance in ways that people cannot understand or access. These models—which might include such things as public school teacher ratings, college rankings, and mortgage management—are "opaque, unquestioned, and unaccountable, and they operate at a scale to sort, target, or 'optimize' millions of people."[4] These critiques signal a serendipitous moment: some in composition and rhetoric want to better understand and teach computational literacy, and some mathematicians—including O'Neil and fellow public math intellectual Jordan Ellenberg[5]—want to make math more accessible and accountable.

In light of this moment, this chapter has two key purposes. First, we propose a collaborative definition of computational literacy that works for both mathematics-based fields and rhetoric, focusing on our shared concern with everyday problems. Second, we carefully analyze a specific case study in order to demonstrate the distinction between computational literacy and computational specialization. We argue that the key knowledge barrier between computational literacy and computational specialization is mathematics.

Whereas many of those calling for computational literacy envision it primarily from a *computer programming* level, much of the information and many of the decisions that undergird programming are made at the foundational mathematical level. In this chapter, we will dig into a single program made for and with the Arizona Department of Transportation in the 1980s in order to show the procedural rhetoric by which decisions about road maintenance are made. This program will be described mathematically—as a *mathematical program* rather than a *computer program*. A mathematical program is not a type of computer program; it is a set of mathematical statements that, when considered simultaneously, describe a human's perception of a system. This is why the algorithmic logic of procedural rhetoric maps on mathematical programs so well.

We make these distinctions to sharpen the definition of computational literacy. By mapping the borderlands between computational literacy and computational specialization, we will reassure those who feel they must become computationally literate, a call that Elizabeth Losh describes as necessary but "acutely soul-crushing in light of existing labor politics."[6] We will also showcase a subfield of mathematics—Operations Research (OR)—that emphasizes collaboration with nonspecialists, providing a collaborative opportunity for those who want to research more deeply within mathematically coded culture.

Literacy and Specialization

In 2012, *enculturation: a journal of rhetoric, writing, and culture* published the proceedings of a Computers and Writing Conference town hall titled "The Role of Computational Literacy in Computers and Writing." The event featured scholars David M. Rieder, Annette Vee, Mark Sample, Alexandria Lockett, Karl Stolley, and Elizabeth Losh,[7] all of whom agreed that there was a need for increased computational literacy. Vee, in a later article, develops the point, stating that such literacy becomes increasingly vital as digital technologies are woven more tightly into our everyday lives and claiming that we need to better understand computational structures in order to have a hand in that weaving.[8] At the same time, although scholars at the 2012 conference agreed that literacy should be taught, they differed on how it should be done. This is because the audience for such education had different levels of specialization: (1) undergraduates (2) digital rhetoricians and digital humanities scholars (3) those who work in computer science fields who need more advanced skills in programming and, we argue, mathematics.

Of the scholars present, Lockett gave the clearest description of which computational literacy skills humanities scholars should teach their undergraduate students: "I do not teach with technology without discussing the power distributions of socio-technical systems, the ethical responsibilities they inflict on human users, and the ways in which our grammatical code and linguistic arrangements make it difficult for us to talk about emergence."[9] Here, she is claiming that students need to be aware of their subject position and readiness to negotiate a complex digital system. In a similar vein, Jeannette Wing, a leading computer scientist, uses the term "computational *thinking*." Wing writes that "computational thinking is using abstraction and decomposition when attacking a large complex task . . . It is separation of concerns. It is choosing an appropriate representation."[10] While there is a great deal of overlap in terms of analytical skills here, Wing is (unsurprisingly) talking widely about the kind of mental skills necessary to tackle a problem from a mathematical perspective; for their part, scholars in composition and rhetoric are more invested in the skills necessary to analyze and possibly write computer-coded text.

Advanced scholars, on the other hand, need an advanced level of literacy. In part, this is because they will be called upon to teach it. For example, Rieder argues for hard boundaries that define scholarly computational literacy, claiming that coding skills are necessary for anyone hoping to work on digital projects.[11] Rieder writes from his position within an English Department and can likely see the creeping turf wars over which discipline will be permitted to teach skills variously labeled as digital, computational, or procedural; literacy, competency, fluency, or thinking; proceduracy or iteracy.[12]

Each of these terms has different valences and histories, but for the purposes of composition, rhetoric, and this chapter, the term computational literacy as defined by Annette Vee best encapsulates the priorities of both fields: it is a "constellation of abilities to break a complex process down into small procedures and then express—or 'write'—those procedures using the technology of code that may be 'read' by a nonhuman entity such as a computer.'"[13] This captures Wing's concern with a thinking process and addresses composition and rhetoric's concerns with reading, producing knowledge, and accounting for a complex audience (in this case, both humans and nonhumans).

What the idea of computational literacy doesn't account for—and one of many possible skills that differentiates computational literacy from computational specialization—is the mathematical knowledge necessary to understand code itself. Lockett gestures to a similar distinction between literacy and specialization when she refuses the title "computer programmer," even though she can write code.[14] While some computational literacy is necessary at a novice level, and more advanced computational literacy is even more important at a nonspecialist scholarly level, those within these fields have an even more nuanced understanding of the mathematical processes undergirding digital culture. "Computer programmer" is not the correct term for someone who is at an advanced state of computational literacy, since it is a specific job title rather than a skill. Rather, the term "computational specialization" allows for another mark on the spectrum of computational skill levels.

Because it is a branch of applied mathematics and formulates models for various industries, Operations Research scholarship is a logical access point for those investigating the procedurality of mathematical programming from a position of literacy. Its practitioners are tasked with solving problems presently faced by people in the world, such as maintaining roads or routing aircraft. The field of OR is an optimal area for studying procedural rhetoric and computational literacy because it considers its negotiation of audiences, is reflective about its procedures, and is invested in everyday problems.

OR often finds itself speaking to a diverse audience, from novices to specialists in its work and in its key publication, *Interfaces*.[15] The Golabi, Kulkarni, and Way project we analyze was published in this journal, which is produced by the Institute for Operations Research and the Management of Sciences (INFORMS). Writing for *Interfaces* presents certain rhetorical challenges for its authors, since the audience is comprised of managers from various industries, tenured scholars, graduate students, and those who use or want to use the systems written by OR specialists.[16] The intermingling of theory and practice underpins each issue.

Case Study: Golabi, Kulkarni, and Way

"A Statewide Pavement Management System," by Kamal Golabi, Ram B. Kulkarni, and George B. Way was published in *Interfaces* in 1982. This is the same period that Vee identifies as a tipping point for computational literacy: as more people were able to afford home computers, computation started to become part of daily life. At the same time, the processes developed by governmental agencies were scaling up and being used in other capacities. The project described in Golabi, Kulkarni, and Way's article profoundly influenced highway maintenance practices in the United States and throughout the world, in part because it was scalable. While scalability is a prized value in the most successful commercialized models, it also runs risks of becoming decontextualized. For instance, O'Neil considers scalability beyond its original context to be one of the characteristics of Weapons of Math Destruction, along with opacity and lack of accountability.[17] The project described in Golabi, Kulkarni, and Way's article, however, is rooted in the specific features of the Arizona Highway System and was developed in tandem with those who would be using and maintaining both the system and the program that ran the algorithm.

The project began when the Arizona Department of Transportation (ADOT) contracted with an engineering consulting firm in 1978 to develop a tool that would help them determine how to maintain their highways. The result was the Pavement Management System (PMS). PMS was implemented by ADOT in 1980 and substantially decreased maintenance costs.[18] The authors considered it successful because it created a more efficient, cost-effective, and consistent planning system in three ways: recommending more preventative maintenance than the traditional practice, preventing the need for very expensive corrective maintenance in the future, and because it generally recommended less conservative maintenance actions than were traditionally applied (for example, PMS would recommend resurfacing with three inches of asphalt instead of five inches).[19] At the time the article was written, PMS was so successful that it was being adapted for use in Kansas.

Throughout the process of constructing PMS, the OR team had to work with a nonspecialist audience. In fact, there's a good chance the ADOT team was not computationally literate either. As Vee points out, the 1970s and '80s was a period in which people were not yet expected to have such skills.[20] The authors of PMS took time to educate ADOT management about the capabilities and limitations of OR as a field when the project began and how to use the model when it was complete. This better prepared them to cocreate the mathematical model that would suit ADOT's needs and the team's capacities. It was also one of the countless small moments in which people were being trained to be more computationally literate as their world became more digital. Likely because of this constant communication, the article is readable by those with varied levels of specialization. The authors know they have such a diverse audience and so describe the process of defining, formulating, and implementing a mathematical model step by step, "break[ing] a complex process down into small procedures."[21]

Indeed, a key part of computational literacy is to be able to break the problem down into smaller components.[22] The first of these steps in this case was understanding the problems' complexity. ADOT was responsible for the maintenance of seventy-four thousand miles of paved highways.[23] But the problem was not simply the roads; it was also the way those roads were managed. Seven separate district managers, each of whom worked relatively independently, made the maintenance decisions for their specific region.[24] District engineers chose what to maintain in their district based on their experience and expectations; as a result, road conditions differed widely between districts, as a result of which ADOT's budget requests appeared idiosyncratic.[25] The federal and state governments each decided which types of roads fell within their respective spheres of responsibility to fund and maintain.[26] The federal funding could only be used on the relatively few roads that met specific federal standards (essentially, only the interstate highways). The Arizona funding came from gasoline taxes, an income source that was decreasing steadily as cars became more efficient. Even as funding stagnated or decreased, costs rose.[27] For example, the cost of asphalt, a significant portion of ADOT's overhead, had increased from $88 per ton in 1975 to $270 per ton in 1980. The OR team came to realize that ADOT needed a system that could regularize maintenance and improve the consistency of road quality statewide, even as it allowed ADOT some flexibility in ultimate decision-making.[28] Even more, they wanted to be able to predict the consequences of budget cuts and restrictions on road conditions.[29]

The two groups continued to work together in articulating a precise question to guide the research. They resolved on the question, "For every mile of road in Arizona, what is the maintenance action that should be taken so that at least some minimum proportion of roads is in an acceptable state, but that no more than some maximum proportion of roads is in an unacceptable state?"[30] (Acceptable road conditions were defined in terms of "roughness" and "cracking," two properties of a road surface measurable through standard engineering procedures.)

This question served as a rhetorical heuristic in that it guided further research but did not foreclose the results. Rather, the question set up the series of rhetorical algorithmic procedures that researchers then built into the model. Kevin Brock describes rhetorical algorithms as characteristic tools in procedural texts. A rhetorical algorithm is a "procedure fundamentally involv[ing] a set of operations meant to complete a task."[31] In this case, the OR team needed to establish the possible maintenance actions, determine what constituted "acceptable" and "unacceptable" conditions, and set minimum and maximum percentages for each state. The question also pointed to the parameters for success: the solution created by the model was considered effective when the percentage of roads in an acceptable state met the criteria.

Models are the ways in which math communicates its theories to a complex audience of varying expertise. Even though models are an integral part of many programs and automated processes, it is likely that few people reading the *Interfaces* article work with mathematical models directly. They are unlikely to be computational specialists. Generally, such a group of people only sees the computer program that overlays the model rather than the representational system built of mathematical objects like variables, equations, inequalities, sets, and graphs. Therefore, the authors had to find ways to communicate the model that would be accessible without being condescending. Consider how this would work in the case of a physical model, such as a balsa-wood model of a bridge, which could be turned in various directions and examined in order to understand the structure better. Such a model allows the holder to study some of the properties of the real bridge: weights could be placed on it to test whether it could bear a load, or it could be anchored in a wind tunnel and tested for wind shear. This kind of physical model is accessible to those with varying levels of expertise in mathematics and engineering, but it is woefully inadequate if the bridge needs to be tested for the rate at which traffic can safely flow across it under different weather conditions. That would require other kinds of models. Within limits, a mathematical model of a real system can be studied to understand some properties of the system and to assist in making decisions about how to control that system. Because models are created in order to find answers to questions that depend on many variables, they are often authored by people who are not end-users. This is why modeling is one of the most rhetorical processes within mathematics; it often requires researchers to tailor their work to a specific audience. As a procedural representation, it explains a process by using other processes that are written and then enacted by a solver (a computer).[32]

In the case of the ADOT example, researchers chose a model called a Constrained Markov Decision Process (CMDP), which is used to represent systems with numerous related simultaneous decisions, each subject to uncertainty. Choosing and writing this complex model goes beyond reasonable expectations of computational literacy, especially in the 1980s, because it requires having a vast knowledge of the previous models (similar to rhetorical *topoi*) and their respective strengths and weaknesses. So, the team chose to have one member of the ADOT team, the engineer George B. Way, work particularly closely with the OR team.[33] This is one way in which those without such specialization can still be a part of the conversation: via collaboration with the specialists. According to Aaron Beveridge, who writes about the rhetorical influence of statistics and data visualizations, critical analysis of methodologies may "be intimidating for rhetoric and writing scholars who have limited training in statistics and data visualization, but encouraging open and collaborative development will allow new projects to draw from and build on previous ones."[34] While there are valid concerns about the secrecy of code by those who write it,[35] researchers in OR do have a working model for such collaboration. As they describe in their article, the OR researchers for ADOT chose the model *after* collaboration with their clients. They also had regular meetings with the clients to "keep the lines of communication open."[36] And by documenting the process through their article, they made their process more transparent and accessible to a wide audience.

Methodology: How the PMS Model Works

Bogost argues that in order to "address the possibilities of a new medium"— in this case, mathematical programs—"as a type of rhetoric, we must identify how inscription works in that medium, and then how arguments can be constructed through those modes of inscription."[37] Therefore, in order to understand the procedurality of PMS, we will consider the six components as individual rhetorical algorithms that have direct effects on the final heuristic model. In addition, we will consider how PMS aligns with the taxonomy O'Neil describes for irresponsible or unethical models and programs. Specifically, O'Neil calls to account models that are opaque, do more damage to people than good, are unfair, or that have been scaled beyond their original situations so that their foundational data becomes unreliable.[38]

As previously stated, models are procedurally persuasive: the OR team chose a CMDP because of the data available, the scale of the problem, and because it allowed them to achieve the kind of detail their client required (a recommended action for each one-mile road segment). That said, CMDPs are rarely used within OR; a recent paper about solution techniques for CMDPs lists only five instances in the OR literature,[39] and our search found no others.[40] This may be because there are few efficient techniques for solving them. While there are ways to solve CMDPs approximately, the only exact method[41] is cumbersome and does not scale well.[42]

The ADOT project team's choice to use a CMDP instead of an MDP implies that the concepts they expressed as constraints—the performance standards for roughness and cracking—were essential to the underlying problem. Indeed, the formulation of the constraints is itself an important representational decision. As O'Neil claims, "models are opinions embedded in mathematics."[43] In this case, ADOT and the OR team's opinions and priorities for the Arizona highway system are expressed via potentially inegalitarian procedures. For example, the performance standards expressed as constraints in PMS vary by average daily traffic (roads with higher daily traffic have more stringent standards).[44] The definitions of "acceptable" and "unacceptable" conditions are the same for roads throughout the state; the fact that roads with higher average daily traffic have higher standards represents an apparent preference on the part of ADOT management.[45] This can result in inequalities to a certain degree: rural areas are permitted to have a greater proportion of "unacceptable" roads. The authors were precariously situated: walking the fine line between a flexible model that could adjust to these complex constraints and one that could be an effective decision-making tool.

To appreciate why the OR team chose a Constrained Markov Decision Process, we must consider how its processes fit the needs outlined by ADOT. Each component is composed of nonverbal data chosen to drive a particular maintenance action.[46] The team broke down and defined the problem via the six components required for a CMDP: states, actions, transition probabilities, reward function, discount factor, and linking constraints.[47]

STATES

It may seem counterintuitive to a nonspecialist that a more detailed representation of a system does not guarantee a more accurate result. Rather, the challenge is determining which details are necessary. A CMDP is a process that moves among states, such as the various road conditions in every one-mile segment of the highway. To design the PMS, the OR team identified 120 possible states.[48] O'Neil claims that models become dangerous when they are scaled beyond the capacity of humans to check them. The PMS, however, relied on annual human input. To determine in which of the 120 states a given section of road was, humans physically checked the condition and then compared it to the condition from the previous year.

To describe the condition, they considered the four measures (roughness, cracking, changes in cracking, and index to first crack). Just as an example of how the OR team expressed the states, consider these three of the 120 possibilities:

> <roughness=120 inches/mile, cracking=5%, change in cracking=2.5%, index to first crack=18 years>
> <roughness=120 inches/mile, cracking=20%, change in cracking=10%, index to first crack=18 years>
> <roughness=210 inches/mile, cracking=5%, change in cracking=2.5%, index to first crack=18 years>

This may seem comprehensive, but even 120 possibilities is an approximation. After all, the designers considered only a few possible values for each of the measures. They had only three possible values for "cracking," so measured cracking values other than those three would have to be represented approximately. They could have used more values, of course, but the OR team determined that the limited set of states they chose would be representative enough for them to determine the level of degradation on any given road section.

ACTIONS

Actions are all the possible maintenance choices ADOT could make. Recall that a CMDP is a Constrained Markov *Decision* Process; the decision is the action recommended for each section of road. PMS's purpose is to recommend a maintenance action for every segment of highway. For example, PMS might recommend routine maintenance and resurfacing with different thicknesses of asphalt. That said, this is just a recommendation; ADOT chooses whether or not to follow that procedure. In this respect, ADOT's ability to contravene the decisions promoted by PMS makes it quite different from some of the models O'Neil discusses. The models O'Neil describes—such as the opaque and high-risk program that determines high school teaching scores—run without the constant input and correction from humans. PMS qualifies as a "trustworthy" model because of the constant back-and-forth feedback between the real-world, human-controlled measurements and the model.[49]

TRANSITION PROBABILITIES

Transitions are the movements among states (as when a segment of road goes from being somewhat cracked and rough one year to more cracked and rougher the next year). When ADOT performs maintenance, the outcome of the action is uncertain, so the possible states to which the process will move are determined by probabilities. In this case, transition probabilities can be understood as recognition of the fact that roads are always deteriorating, even immediately after they are repaired. After resurfacing, the road will be smooth and free of cracks; however, after a year, roughness and cracking may appear. Predictions are calculated through transition probabilities. Again, this may be a moment where terms are counterintuitive to a nonspecialist. Transition probabilities are not predictions in the general sense of the term. Rather, OR refers to probabilistic predictions, in which a probability is associated with each possible future state.

The use of transition probabilities to obtain probabilistic predictions relies on the "Markovian" or "memorylessness" assumption. To return to the opening example of the noisy construction next door to our house, it may seem that nearby road quality has worsened more quickly because it is being traveled by heavy equipment. If we were deciding what roads to repair, we might want to choose the one that has degraded so quickly, but the model might not. It is only concerned with the present state of the road (no matter how much poorer that state may be compared to the previous year) and making a probabilistic prediction based on the data included in the model. When mathematicians assume that a system they are developing is memoryless, they are claiming that the future of that system can be predicted without knowing all of the possible information. They predict the future of the highway purely from observing its present state rather than needing an entire history of the highway, climate, seismic data, traffic patterns, and so on. Instead of becoming immobilized by the fact that they can never have all the data, mathematicians can limit their attention to a finite set of attributes of the system. This enables them to describe complex, dynamic systems accurately enough and in a compact and tractable (and therefore communicable) way.

Reward function

Often, the decision-maker achieves some benefit based on the actions taken, such as gaining money from selling a product, or moving closer to a goal, and the reward function is a measurement of that benefit. The decision-maker wants to choose actions that maximize rewards.

For PMS the reward function is the cost of the maintenance. This is a negative reward because PMS would be considered most successful if it were able to maximize rewards by minimizing cost, especially since ADOT had both limited and restricted funds from the state and federal governments. This isn't to imply that there aren't benefits to repairing and maintaining highways. There are, and the CMDP addresses this through the constraints. However, the term "reward" is used for the value associated with actions or transitions whether that value is positive or negative.

Since the objective of ADOT is to minimize costs and keep highways in good order, an obvious choice is to perform the least expensive form of maintenance (referred to as "routine maintenance") throughout the highway system. Clearly, this is not the best decision for the people driving on the highway system. This is why the various components balance against each other to try to get to the best solution for everyone who has a stake in the highway system. The final two components of the CMDP force what we would consider to be a more reasonable decision: the discount factor and the constraints.

DISCOUNT FACTOR

The discount factor is a number that relates rewards in the future to the present, similar to how finance handles inflation. The discount factor builds in accountability: it prevents the model from ignoring the distant, future consequences of actions taken in the present. This is also one way in which the article is not fully transparent about the procedures in PMS: Golabi, Kulkarni, and Way don't specify either the discount factor the team used or how it was determined.[50] What they do outline is how they achieved their outcome by having the CMDP solved twice, once as a "long-term" problem, then as a "short-term" problem.[51] The long-term solution is a "steady-state" maintenance policy that can be applied indefinitely; the short-term problem is required to attain the solution of long-term problem in its fifth year.[52] This is also a way for the end-user (ADOT) to have options in what maintenance decision they make each time, depending on outside factors they may know, such as special grants that allow them to do more work than they may have been able to otherwise.

CONSTRAINTS

The constraints are the most explicit procedures in the program. They are essentially rules that limit what ADOT can do. In the context of PMS, they concern the overall quality of roads, as measured by roughness and cracking, which are defined elsewhere in the report in terms of how many cracks and how many imperfections in the road there are in a given sample of a section.[53] Different rules apply depending on the average daily traffic on the roads. For the busiest roads (those with an average daily traffic of more than ten thousand vehicles), the constraints are as follows:[54] "At least 80 percent of one-mile segments must exhibit acceptable roughness. No more than 5 percent of one-mile segments may exhibit unacceptable roughness. At least 80 percent of one-mile segments must exhibit acceptable cracking. No more than 10 percent of one-mile segments may exhibit unacceptable cracking."

These rules require ADOT to recommend substantial maintenance actions on a sufficient proportion of the roads so that, even after accounting for deterioration, they can still meet their performance standards. In order to satisfy these constraints, ADOT must consider maintenance decisions on many individual roads simultaneously. For example, the first constraint does not specify *which* 80 percent of the busiest one-mile segments in the network must have acceptable roughness. Instead, it makes a probabilistic statement about that entire set of roads.

Each of these six components requires multiple calculations, which is why they use a computer to solve the model. After all, maintenance planning for a seventy-four-thousand-mile network of highways is a complex task. That task becomes even more daunting due to the "physics" of the problem (roads are constantly deteriorating, the efficacy of different maintenance actions is uncertain) and due to the fact that humans input information and implement the maintenance plan. Another reason to use computers is that it cuts back on the number of inconsistencies and errors. As Richard J. Wissbaum wrote in *Interfaces* the same year the ADOT study was published, "in this field, the problem is usually not machines, but rather people."[55] While this may seem to be a flippant comment, it reflects researchers' laments about lack of data, lack of cooperation, and lack of support from the very people their work is supposed to help. People are unpredictable and unreliable but models depend on them to provide accurate data.

The temptation is to trust the "unbiased" and "consistent" mathematical model and eliminate human interference wherever possible. However, without people, there is no check on the model. The ADOT project is an example of a model that has met, to a great degree, all the criteria of responsibility outlined by O'Neil: it is generally transparent, helped those for whom it was developed, is reasonably fair (more fair than the previous system of separate, competing human managers), and is scaled to its audience and geographic location. Of equal importance is that it was developed in collaboration with the clients and requires their constant engagement. Indeed, one way in which such people become computationally literate is to interact with such systems, to learn the inputs and the checks, even if only for their particular industry or workplace. Computational literacy, then, has more levels than three (novice, scholarly, and specialist), that is, it is also disciplinary or industry-specific. These are everyday computational literacy skills that enable people to maintain and use the computational systems on which our infrastructure depends.

Conclusion

Embedded within our understanding of computers, we must have an understanding of math. We must be computationally literate. There is a range of meanings for computational literacy, though. Much of the work in digital and computational rhetoric approaches the issue from only three directions. First, the field often steers clear of mathematical modeling processes and the people who create and use them. Even Bogost, who makes a strong argument for considering "the computational underpinnings" of nonverbal materials, still uses "computational" to mean "computer-based" at the programming level rather than the deeper layer of mathematics within computer programs.[56] Secondly, some scholars (such as Kevin Brock in his essay on the rhetorical algorithm)[57] have dug into mathematical theory and discourse in order to bring forth terms we can put to use in game or verbal-based texts. Finally, the authors for the special issue of *enculturation* considered the pedagogical perspective on computational literacy. We propose extending these investigations in two ways.

First, while many in the field have acknowledged the necessity of becoming more computationally literate, we must also recognize that doing so may be prohibitive to timely, in-depth scholarship. As stated previously, good work can be done when rhetoricians and composition scholars work *with* computational specialists. In such as case, neither makes assumptions about the workings and intentions of the other's discipline. Secondly, rhetoric and composition should expand the definition of computational literacy to account for the role of mathematics in computation. This does not mean rhetoricians ought to teach mathematics. Rather, we encourage rhetoricians to acknowledge the borderlands between our knowledge and the knowledge of computational specialists. Rather than a limitation, these borderlands are where we can extend our knowledge: when we explore them, rhetoricians will discover the very opportunities to work with computational specialists that will deepen our access to the texts governing much of our everyday lives.

Notes

1. G. Mitchell Reyes, "The Rhetoric in Mathematics: Newton, Leibniz, The Calculus, and the Rhetorical Force of the Infinitesimal," *Quarterly Journal of Speech* 90, no. 2 (2004): 166.

2. See also Michael Wojcik, "Inventing Computational Rhetoric" (PhD diss., Michigan State University, 2013), 5–6.

3. Mark Sample and Annette Vee, "The Role of Computational Literacy in Computers and Writing," *enculturation: a journal of rhetoric, writing, and culture* 14 (2012): par. 3–4, http://enculturation.net/computational-literacy.

4. Cathy O'Neil, *Weapons of Math Destruction* (New York: Crown, 2016), 12.

5. Jordan Ellenberg, *How Not to Be Wrong: The Power of Mathematical Thinking* (New York: Penguin, 2015).

6. Elizabeth Losh, "The Anxiety of Programming: Why Teachers Should Relax and Administrators Should Worry," *enculturation: a journal of rhetoric, writing, and culture* 14 (2012): par. 1, http://enculturation.net/node/5272.

7. Sample and Vee, "Computational Literacy"; David M. Reider, "Programming Is the New Ground of Writing," *enculturation: a journal of rhetoric, writing, and culture* 14 (2012), http://enculturation.net/node/5267; Annette Vee, "Coding Values," *enculturation: a journal of rhetoric, writing, and culture* 14 (2012), http://enculturation .net/node/5269; Mark Sample, "5 BASIC Statements on Computational Literacy," *enculturation* 14 (2012), http://enculturation.net/node/5269; Alexandria Lockett, "I am Not a Computer Programmer," *enculturation: a journal of rhetoric, writing, and culture* 14 (2012): par. 13, http://enculturation.net/node/5270; Karl Stolley, "Source Literacy: A Vision of Craft," *enculturation: a journal of rhetoric, writing, and culture* 14 (2012), http://enculturation.net/node/5271; Losh, "Anxiety of Programming."

8. Annette Vee, "Understanding Computer Programming as a Literacy," *Literacy in Composition Studies* 1, no. 2 (2013): 45.

9. Lockett, "Not a Computer Programmer," par. 13.

10. Jeannette Wing, "Computational Thinking," *Communications of the ACM* 49, no. 3 (March 2006): 33.

11. Reider, "New Ground of Writing," par. 9.

12. Losh, par. 7; Kevin Brock, "Enthymeme as Rhetorical Algorithm," *Present Tense* 4, no. 1 (September 4, 2014): 5; Wing, "Computational Thinking."

13. Vee, "Understanding," 47.

14. Lockett, par. 11.

15. Michael F. Gorman, "*Interfaces* Editor's Statement," *Interfaces* 47, no. 1 (January–February 2017): 2. *Interfaces* publishes articles in at least three genres: reviews of completed projects, tutorials describing new processes/technologies, and less formal reflections on the field or disciplinary education. In each of these, there is a sense that this is a field that has an integrated sense of teaching (both in the classroom and in the field) and inventing. Current editor Michael F. Gorman has directly stated that *Interfaces* is designed, in part, for classroom use.

16. Gary L. Lilien, "Letter from the New Editor," *Interfaces* 12, no. 2 (April 1982): 1–2.

17. O'Neil, *Weapons of Math Destruction*, 12.

18. Kamal Golabi, Ram B. Kulkarni, and George B. Way, "A Statewide Pavement Management System," *Interfaces* 12, no. 2 (April 1982): 16.

19. Golabi, Kulkarni, and Way, 16–17.

20. Vee, "Understanding," 46.

21. Golabi, Kulkarni, and Way, 14; Vee, "Understanding," 46.

22. Vee, "Understanding," 47.

23. Golabi, Kulkarni, and Way, 5.

24. Ibid., 7.

25. Ibid.

26. Ibid.

27. Golabi, Kulkarni, and Way, 6.

28. Ibid., 7.

29. Ibid., 8.

30. Ibid., 6.

31. Brock, "Enthymeme," 1.

32. Ian Bogost, *Persuasive Games* (Cambridge: MIT Press, 2007), 9.

33. The article doesn't detail the role of each member, but George B. Way, chief pavement engineer at ADOT's Highway Division, would have been able to speak to the interests of ADOT even as the OR team developed its model.

34. Aaron Beveridge, "Looking in the Dustbin: Data Janitorial Work, Statistical Reasoning, and Information Rhetorics," *Computers and Composition Online* (Fall 2015): par. 10, http://cconlinejournal.org/fall15/beveridge/.

35. Vee, "Coding Values," par. 19–20; O'Neil.

36. Golabi, Kulkarni, and Way, 9.

37. Bogost, *Persuasive Games*, 24.

38. O'Neil, 28–30.

39. Golabi, Kulkarni, and Way; Peter Kolesar, "A Markovian Model for Hospital Admission Scheduling," *Management Science* 16, no. 6 (February 1970): 384–96; C. Sun, E. Stevens-Navarro, V. Shah-Mansouri, and V. W. Wong, "A Constrained MDP-Based Vertical Handoff Decision Algorithm for 4G Heterogeneous Wireless Networks," *Wireless Networks* 17, no. 4 (May 2011): 1063–81; C. van Winden and R. Dekker, "Rationalisation of Building Maintenance by Markov Decision Models: A Pilot Case Study," *Journal of the Operational Research Society* 49, no 9 (September 1998): 928–35; Qianchuan Zhao, Stefan Geirhofer, Lang Tong, and Brian M. Sadler, "Opportunistic Spectrum Access via Periodic Channel Sensing," *IEEE Transactions on Signal Processing* 56, no.2 (February 2008): 785–96.

40. Constantine Caramanis, Nedialko B. Dimitrov, and David P. Morton, "Efficient Algorithms for Budget-Constrained Markov Decision Processes," *IEEE Transactions on Automatic Control* 59, no. 10 (October 2014).

41. F. d'Epenoux, "Sur un problème de production et de stockage dans l'aléatoire," *Revue Française de Recherche Opérationnelle* 14 (1960): 3–16.

42. O'Neil, 28–30. "Scaling" is often a priority in mathematical models. It means to take a model from one context and find applications for it elsewhere. While this sounds logical on the surface, it also means that a model becomes dangerously decontextualized and runs the risk of becoming unfair or inaccurate in its new context. Unlike a CMDP, a closely related type of model called a Markov Decision Process (MDP) has thousands of applications. An MDP has five of the six components of a CMDP; the missing component, as the name implies, is the set of constraints. The constraints in a CMDP impose a relationship among all of the decisions simultaneously. Since MDPs lack constraints, each of those decisions can be considered independently, which allows researchers to apply an extraordinarily efficient technique, termed "dynamic programming." This means that even extremely large and complex MDPs can be solved both exactly and quickly.

43. O'Neil, 22–23.

44. Golabi, Kulkarni, and Way, 14.

45. Ibid., 10.

46. Bogost; Brock.

47. Golabi, Kulkarni, and Way, 9.

48. Ibid., 11.

49. Ibid., 18.

50. Ibid., 20.

51. Ibid., 19.

52. Ibid.

53. Ibid., 13–14.

54. Ibid., 14.

55. Richard J. Wissbaum, "What Happened to Me in the Police Department or Which Shell Is the Pea Under?," *Interfaces* 12, no. 2 (April 1982): 83.

56. Bogost, 26–28.

57. Brock.

7 / Inventing Rhetorical Machines

On Facilitating Learning and Public Participation in Science

Ryan M. Omizo, Ian Clark, Minh-Tam Nguyen, and William Hart-Davidson

This chapter reports on the development of a new rhetorical machine: the Faciloscope (http://faciloscope.cal.msu.edu/facilitation/)—a web-based, machine-learning application that performs rhetorical analysis and visualizes findings based on natural language submissions on the fly.

The Faciloscope is a product of a three-year federally funded project whose original goal was to investigate and refine facilitation practices for informal learning in STEM areas.[1] Working with partners at the Museum of Life Sciences in North Carolina, our university-based team developed and tested a "facilitation toolbox" for museum staff charged with leading online activities and discussions to foster public engagement and learning about science. The "facilitation toolbox"[2] includes a coding scheme of rhetorical moves designed to allow facilitators to identify and diagnose the trajectory of online conversations and intervene with appropriate responses.[3] As a tool for facilitators, the application of the written coding scheme was labor intensive, often requiring human raters to log long hours classifying sentence units in order to provide facilitators with the global shape of the online conversations. Unsurprisingly, classification by human raters created a lag between the initiation of a statement and the moment when facilitators could act based on the rhetorical moves found in the "toolbox." The specific charge of the Faciloscope was to (1) automate classification through machine learning algorithm and (2) accelerate the ability of facilitators to direct conversations. To accomplish this, our team created an app designed to code conversations for facilitators instantly. We used well-established research practices in rhetoric and writing studies, combined with supervised machine learning techniques and an iterative approach to user experience design.

This chapter seeks, in part, to offer readers a methodological blueprint for harnessing machine learning techniques for rhetorical analysis, including:

- creating a coding scheme or codebook of rhetorical moves;
- testing and validating the coding scheme or codebook for inter-rater reliability;
- preparing a human coded dataset for the training and testing of machine learning classification tasks;
- using supervised machine learning techniques such as support vector machines for the classification of natural language text; and
- visualizing classification results in a web-based infrastructure.

This chapter also outlines the practical and theoretical affordances as well as the challenges of thinking both computationally and rhetorically about the analysis of natural language texts. This contributes to a broader, critical discussion of what a *computational rhetoric* might be able to do within deliberative public spaces. For example, engaging the public in scientific knowledge is of critical importance in the face of global challenges such as climate change and sustainability, chronic disease prevention, and others. Institutions dedicated to learning, such as science centers and museums, cannot shrink from their mission to guide public engagement in scientific inquiry, including discussion and debate that surrounds controversial issues. At the same time, these institutions must also possess the methodologies to account for the volume, velocity, and variety of data that often shapes the material contexts of such issues. We examine the idea that computational rhetoric apps such as the Faciloscope constitute one innovative approach to this mission.

Background

While the creation of the Faciloscope drew from the expertise of our four-person development team and several disciplines (participatory design, user experience research, technical communication, digital humanities, rhetoric, natural language processing, machine learning), the principle support of our scaffolding derives from an earlier project that focused on informal learning facilitation. Team member Nguyen was part of the earlier project and helped to reconcile earlier work with the development of a simplified analytic for the Faciloscope.[4] After a brief overview of the aims of the informal learning facilitation project, we review literature in the emerging area of computational rhetoric that has animated the development of the Faciloscope.

Where formal learning environments—schools and training programs, for instance—provide a structured experience using learning goals, curricula, pedagogy, and assessment techniques, informal learning is relatively unstructured and generally lacks the rigid infrastructure and mandates that we associate with classroom or school instruction. Eraut defines informal learning as a practice that: "recognizes the social significance of learning from other people, but implies greater scope for individual agency than socialization. It draws attention to the learning that takes place in the spaces surrounding activities and events with a more overt formal purpose, and takes place in a much wider variety of settings than formal education or training. It can also be considered as a complementary partner to learning from experience, which is usually construed more in terms of personal than interpersonal learning."[5] Informal learning is often situated outside of traditional educational settings and within workplace and/or organizational cultures and theorized by fields such as management studies, human resources, and adult education. For example, Boud and Middleton examine how academics learn from each other through a variety of strategies that go beyond institutionally sanctioned professional development, including consulting written workplace resources to solve problems and then seeking out other more experienced, peer colleagues if those searches did not yield acceptable answers.[6] But this does not mean that in institutional settings such as museums and science centers, learning is not an important overall aim. These organizations and the people who work in them aim to facilitate *informal* learning, which is more participant-driven, more exploratory and open-ended in nature and proceeds with few if any explicit learning outcomes or assessments.[7]

Facilitation in informal learning spaces is analogous to pedagogy in formal learning environments. Facilitation emphasizes the promotion of learning but does not necessarily involve the negotiation of knowledge between teachers and students or experts and nonexperts. Thus, the role of the facilitator can assume various forms, including peer working groups,[8] the "lectores" who read news and literature in order to keep cigar manufacturing plant workers informed in the pre-war United States,[9] and museum docents assigned to help extend guest inquiries into the workings of museum exhibits.[10] In terms of activities or traits that facilitators use in their learning encounters, Ellinger and Cseh list "providing feedback," "listening," "talking things through," "asking questions," "role playing," and "removing obstacles" as actions undertaken by their study participants.[11] The original facilitation project included trained facilitators who would engage in this type of inquiry-based "talking through."

Our colleagues in the original facilitation project worked with two science centers in different regions of the US to develop a classification scheme for facilitation moves made by experienced staff members when they were guiding learners in online spaces. The result was a six-item rubric detailing facilitation "moves" that constitute a repertoire for promoting informal learning online. Use of these moves in online discussion threads was linked to desirable outcomes for informal learning: participant engagement, a greater sense of community, and a greater appreciation for science knowledge. The team summed up a key finding of their study by noting that "technologies, structure, and culture matter a great deal, but central to these dynamics is the rhetorical work of constructing a culture of sharing, which leads to learning."[12]

Making this rhetorical work visible so that it could be noticed and shared with practitioners—for instance, in training sessions—was a major undertaking for our colleagues in the original facilitation study. The work involved special training. And it took time: initially, as the coding scheme was being refined, analysis could take days or weeks. But even with a stable coding scheme and well-calibrated human raters, coding and reliability testing a single discussion thread took at least a day, a lag that meant facilitators doing online moderation might miss important opportunities to make the right moves at the right time. Contemplating these missed opportunities led the facilitation project team leaders to seek the help of our computational rhetoric team. In this chapter's next section, we review the literature that influenced our approach to computational rhetoric for the Faciloscope project.

Computational Rhetoric

As of this writing, computational rhetoric is likely too niche to be called a *field* or a *discipline*. It may be more accurate to treat computational rhetoric as a framework or a way of thinking about discourse, indexing techniques from more established disciplines such as artificial intelligence, machine learning, natural language processing, graph theory, rhetoric, argumentation studies, formal and informal logic, and computational linguistics. A key early example of such a project is Grasso's work in the fields of artificial intelligence and informal logic,[13] an endeavor she describes as a "halfway" pursuit that combines formal, mathematical modeling with a "philosophical" understanding of rhetoric. This philosophical understanding attempts to factor in intentionality and audience reception (i.e., understanding suasory discourse beyond the rules of formal logic) based on a schema found in Chaïm Perelman and Lucie Olbrechts-Tyteca.[14]

Grasso (see also Brown[15]) usefully divides the concerns of computational rhetoric between production and analysis. A production-focused computational rhetoric emphasizes the capacity of humans and machines to generate rhetoric. Vee and Brown argue that this capacity to *do* rhetoric computationally is a constituent of both classical and modern definitions of rhetoric, specifically, the combinatorial power to shape meaning and, by extension, human and nonhuman behaviors.[16] Vee and Brown point to the ability of classical rhetoricians to source components from a stock library of rhetorical devices to compose multiple arguments, crafting, in a sense, a procedural machine for text fabrication.[17] Brown provides an example of a production-oriented computational rhetoric in his analysis of the company Narrative Science, which specializes in automated sports journalism and financial reporting. Focusing on an early software effort by Narrative Science, Stats Monkey, Brown describes a storytelling process in which computer protocols can sift through data of a baseball game and then aggregate a news story based on the key elements of that game according to a pre-existing organizational template. A much more prolific example of production-oriented computational agents are Twitter bots, which are designed to interact with human users by simulating human behavior[18] by participating in online social transactions (following, liking, retweeting, adding to a list) according to pre-established commands and conditions written into their programming. While the functioning of some of these bots may revolve around compromising the security of human accounts, many work to influence the structures of Twitter networks by subtly promoting the traffic of an account or targeting advertisements to users based on the latter's preferences or directly asking them to click a link for an offer or participate in a survey.

Unlike Twitter bots that (re)produce canned bits of discourse, the focus of the Faciloscope is analytical. The Faciloscope seeks to replicate the methods and results of human exegesis by extracting from natural language texts significant semantic and structural features and using these features to construct a model. Such models are then treated, with healthy skepticism, as characteristic of a piece of discourse and used to inform human investigations.

The Faciloscope counts Kaufer and Ishizaki's Docuscope Project as one of its theoretical forebears.[19] Designed to support rhetorical analysis of large text corpora, Docuscope works by applying established rhetorical theories of language into automated, visual environments for user exploration. Docuscope relies on a dictionary of words, phrases, and other strings-types annotated for their rhetorical effects by human coders to conduct analysis. A text under scrutiny is compared to existing Docuscope dictionaries. When matches are found, the processed text is labeled with relevant rhetorical tags found in the dictionaries. Docuscope tags range from lexical features to complex concepts. One example of basic grammatical or syntactic features is the Person-Pronoun tag (indicating the presence of "her" or "him" or "she") or Numbers (indicating the presence of "eight" or "two" or "ten"). The frequency of these tags is returned to the user as well as their relative distribution within the text. Based on the presence and/or absence of particular features, a judgment can be made on the rhetorical operations of the text.

The ARG-tech group based at the University of Dundee has also created a host of different software applications intended to analyze the structure of arguments. One project is the Online Visualization of Arguments (OVA) tool.[20] OVA allows users to diagram and semantically mark up arguments as a series of nodes and links in order to reveal formal organizational principles. OVA builds upon an earlier argument mapping platform, Araucaria, which allows users to mark up arguments and export them in visual diagrams or structured XML representations.[21] In the work of the ARG-tech group, we see again an effort to use software to supplement the human analysis of rhetorical action by building new models of the text, whose features suggest alternative perspectives or means of validation.

The work of Randy Harris and Chrysanne Di Marco of the Artificial Intelligence Group at the University of Waterloo is also self-identified as computational rhetoric, one that takes an analytical approach to natural language.[22] A key project here is Harris and Di Marco's efforts to create an ontology of rhetorical figures.[23] This ontology is scheme-based. For example, the rhetorical figure of "syncope" belongs to the OmissionScheme because syncope refers to the elision of phonemes in an expression ("wat'ry" instead of "watery"). The type of "omission" is captured as a "PlacementEllipsis" because the nature of the omission is based on its location. This particular location is then designated "MedialEllipsis" because syncope is generally understood to occur in medias res. Thus, an item such as "wat'ry" would be classed as "wat'ry" IsA OmissionScheme IsA PlacementEllipsis IsA MediaElipsis.[24]

What the Faciloscope shares with these analytical computational rhetoric projects is a goal to condense and categorize the variability of natural language texts into feature sets that illustrate how the rhetoric of said text is operating. The primary departure that the Faciloscope makes from these examples (beyond methodological, which we discuss in the next section) comes in the products of analysis. Rather than rhetorical figures[25] or the particulate matter of motivated expression[26] or the tree-based flow of argumentative structure,[27] the Faciloscope seeks to uncover macromaneuvers that we call "rhetorical moves."[28] The second major departure from the listed approaches is the Faciloscope's use of supervised machine learning to drive its decision-making. The "brain" of the Faciloscope is a classifier, which Domingos succinctly defines as a "system that inputs (typically) a vector of discrete and/or continuous *feature values* and outputs a single discrete value, the *class*."[29] The machine learning algorithm of choice for the Faciloscope is the Support Vector Machine or SVM.[30] We outline the steps that our development team took to train this SVM classifier to detect rhetorical moves of facilitation in the next section of this chapter; however, let us first gloss the type of "computational thinking" with which we approach the problem of automating facilitator research and intervention.

Once again drawing on Domingos,[31] we see the Faciloscope as a rhetorical machine of induction, in which textual data is prepared by human raters with an understanding of rhetorical theory, facilitation techniques, and the stakeholders involved in the use of the computational app. This training data is annotated according to predetermined labels, which represent the feature values of the Faciloscope. These labels amount to the names of three rhetorical moves described previously. This training data is converted in a vector of numerical quantities, indicating the presence and absence of terms in the training set per label. The presence or absence of terms then defines the label for the classifier. In one sense, we are teaching the Faciloscope through key examples and expecting the app to apply this learning to a wider world of examples. A portion of the original training data is withheld from the classifier. Because this data has already been annotated, it can be used for testing the accuracy of the classifier against human labeling. The training and testing of the Faciloscope classifier is done as a part of the software development process. Users of the Faciloscope supply their own text via the app interface. The Faciloscope then classifies this new, unseen data and visualizes results in a web browser.

Methodology

The methodology employed for the creation of the Faciloscope is an interdisciplinary mix of humanities and machine learning techniques. The "codebook"[32] guiding the human curation of rhetorical moves within the training and test data relies on qualitative coding methods routinely used in rhetoric or professional writing research. The training and testing of the Faciloscope's SVM classifier relies upon the inter-rater reliability metric of Cohen's Kappa. Lastly, the development of the Faciloscope's user interface is informed by the fields of user experience research and user-centered design, which include iterative prototyping with feedback from users.

We begin with the Faciloscope's schema of three rhetorical moves: Staging, Inviting, and Evoking. More detailed and qualified explanations of each rhetorical move in the codebook can be found in the next sections along with general instructions to human raters in this chapter's appendix. However, it behooves to contextualize this codebook as a means to anchor our methodology. This codebook of Staging, Inviting, and Evoking moves is inspired by the codebook crafted by the original research team and the "Category Specific Facilitation Tool"[33]—a collaborative effort between Michigan State University (MSU), the Science Museum of Minnesota (SMM) and the Museum of Life and Science (MLS).[34] Their work resulted in a framework for understanding facilitation discourse patterns in the context of the online, informal science education. This framework, or coding scheme, contains four overarching categories for a rhetorical move, each with their own subclasses.[35]

This coding scheme was the product of multiple revisions, but ultimately offered the original research team a useful and explanatory representation of the discourse of online informal learning encounters. Most importantly, the final categories represented in the coding scheme differentiated between moves that were explicitly facilitative and those that were discourse moves indicative of learning environments. This manifested in the creation of two first-level coding categories (e.g., Facilitation and Learning Discourse Environment) with corresponding second-level codes that we retained, supplemented, and reorganized from the previous coding tools.

Because we felt little confidence that an SVM classifier would be able to classify nine different rhetorical/facilitation moves given the size of our training set and human rater workforce, we decided to remap the original nine moves into the three categories discussed subsequently.[36] For the Faciloscope, Staging, Inviting, and Evoking moves represent a collapsing of categories found in the "Category Specific Facilitation Tool."[37] Staging moves refer to denotative sentences that establish the grounds for expressions, the simplest of which might be a description of objects, people, or situations. Inviting moves most often refer to "asks"—an explicit call for action or participation on the part of the audience—and can be more easily conceived of as a question with a terminal question mark. The Evoking category musters "Demonstrating Respect for Perspective and Identity," "Demonstrating Sympathy and Empathy," "Provocation," and, in select cases, "Suggest Follow Up Action."

Staging, Inviting, and Evoking moves were designed to be comprehensive. Each sentence of the training dataset required a coding decision (there is no null category). The codebook needed to account for all sentences. Through the coding process, we found that this three-category codebook provided the most minimal rater conflict (see the appendix at the end of this chapter) and covered the range of sentences we were seeing. Consequently, all training and testing sentences were assigned a code. Discrepancies in human ratings were used to better calibrate the codebook as we began annotating training and testing sentences. In general, the diverging ratings were minimal; however, the development team did make one crucial change in the process to the handling of Evoking moves. In the beginning of the process, Evoking moves were often implicitly associated with positive communications of affect. This made sense because facilitation moves are seen to be affirmative and nurturing when employing an emotional statement or an emotional appeal (e.g., "That's a great point that made me really think!"). However, our human raters routinely discovered negatively inflected sentences in which people were participating in trolling behavior. As a result of this discovery, we adjusted the coding of Evoking moves to include both positive and negative valences. Participants in these online learning forums could Evoke others positively or

negatively. Facilitation moves could be considered moves that both foster facilitation and/or inhibit facilitation. The rhetorical approach operational here
is one that highlights trainable moves—following from rhetorical genre theory
and especially Swales (e.g., CARS model)[38]—rather than one that rests on
three particular moves themselves. These moves characterize common moves
in the facilitation of online discussions as discovered and refined by a WIDE
research team that preceded our project and produced the data set used to
train our ML classifier as well as the data set to train our ML classifier.[39] Generally, a move-based approach to conceptualizing rhetoric privileges *behavior*,
represented as arts (*techne*) situated in discourse communities (i.e., genres as
social acts) over content or knowledge (*episteme*) endemic to those communities. Representing rhetoric as an art permits it to travel well within and, occasionally, across community boundaries where a similar repertoire may be
operational.[40]

The units for coding are single sentences or words and phrases with a terminal punctuation mark (see the appendix). We have chosen such sentences,
words, or phrases as our units for the Faciloscope because we sought to capture a small but semantically meaningful unit of writing that can be easily
tokenized through natural language processing.[41]

Faciloscope team members Nguyen and Clark applied the codebook on
legacy data from the Facilitation project and the "fresh" data scraped from online discussion forums.[42] We then assessed inter-rater reliability of the human
raters according to Cohen's Kappa, achieving a Cohen's Kappa of .95. Given
that acceptable inter-rater reliability falls between .70 and .80,[43] we proceeded
with the aforementioned codebook in our efforts to compile training and testing data for the SVM classifier. All sentences received one of the three codes.

Once coded, the data harvested from online discussion forums were converted in a computational artifact amenable to machine learning. Each coded
sentence was treated as an individual document and then processed to maximize salient features and remove insignificant features. This conversion can
also be treated as a data cleaning or normalization step.[44] Function words
such as articles and prepositions are removed. Plural and possessive affixes
are stripped. Word cases are reduced to their dictionary roots so that the distinction between "wolf" and "wolves" is removed and both terms are reduced
to "wolf." Through the use of these processing steps, a natural language text
is homogenized because we are reducing the amount of unique values to be
counted. We are simplifying the text so that emphatic features become more
emphatic and insignificant features can be excluded. The hope is that this amplification of features will resolve into clearly delineated classes for the classification step. Another way to think about this is that we are attempting to
separate signal from noise. Minor variations in words, word tenses, plurals,

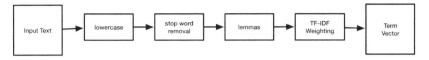

Figure 7.1. Faciloscope text processing pipeline

or possessives can dissimulate the signal of a natural language text. A noisy signal would make it harder for the computer to assign neat class divisions between elements. For the rhetorical machines we have worked on that perform simple kinds of analysis, *reduction* and *simplification* are often the most useful results for users.[45]

We used the following pipeline of techniques (see figure 7.1):

- text converted to lowercase;
- text tokenized according to words;
- stopwords (function words, verbs of existence, pronouns) removed from text;
- tokens lemmatized to feature dictionary roots of words where applicable;
- term frequency inverse document frequency (TF-IDF) weighting applied to remaining tokens; and
- a sparse term frequency vector is constructed to hold the counts of the weighted terms in the corpus.

Following convention, 75 percent of the annotated corpus was demarcated as a training set. The remaining 25 percent was reserved for our testing and verification set. Because the move count differed substantially among the three classes, we used an unbalanced training and testing set for each class as in table 7.1.

Because the Faciloscope classifies three categories (Staging, Inviting, and Evoking), we chose a One versus the Rest (or multiclass) SVM classifier from the scikits-learn machine-learning library.[46] SVMs are a form of supervised machine learning that was established by Cortes and Vapnik.[47] SVMs work by taking the instances of one class from the training set (e.g., Class 0) and the known instances of a separate class of a training set (e.g., Class 1) and constructing a boundary between them. The margins that buffer this boundary derive from the distance between the closest points between Class 0 and Class 1. Ideally, unseen data that should belong to Class 0 would be located behind this boundary and within the Class 0 vectors and inherit this label. Unseen data that should belong to Class 1 would be located behind the boundary within the Class 1 vectors and inherit this label.

Table 7.1. Faciloscope training/testing move distributions

	Staging	Evoking	Inviting
Training	9761	3673	2024
Testing	2441	919	506

To test the accuracy of the Faciloscope classifier, we analyzed the test set (20 percent of the human coded data) for simple agreement with a trained human rater. This test yielded a .70 level of accuracy, suggesting that an acceptable level of agreement between the Faciloscope and human raters is possible. It also means that the Faciloscope should be regarded as an object for interpretation.

To create the user interface of the Faciloscope app, we utilized an iterative and parallel development model. Nguyen, Clark, and Hart-Davidson created high-fidelity wireframes as individuals. In keeping with this parallel development approach, the entire development team then reviewed and selected the best aspects of these wireframes in order to fashion an intuitive user interface for the submission of natural language texts and the reading of results. We then transitioned to full-fledged HTML and CSS mock-ups of the Faciloscope. Omizo then integrated these designs and HTML drafts as templates.

The final design represents the best elements of the wireframes, which include: a split screen interface, divided between a text input pane and a results pane; the use of donut charts, bar graphs, and numerical displays for returning the descriptive statistics of the rhetorical moves found (e.g., counts and frequency distribution of moves); a tabular view that renders the input text sentence by sentence and tag by tag; and an interactive "Bands" visualization, which is not featured in the wireframes but emerged from the design process (termed "Move Pattern" in the actual app for clarity). This "Bands" visualization color codes Staging, Inviting, and Evoking moves as a function of their character length and position in the original text, thus allowing users to view results in spatial terms. Users can then zoom in on particular regions to see which moves predominate. In addition, users can view the original sentences in those regions by using the "bands" window to set the in and out points of the text. The x-axis line at the bottom of the Bands visualization allows users to see the distribution of moves as a function of character count.

Application

To demonstrate the potential of the Faciloscope, we have selected an article and comment thread from Science Buzz on the topic of gephyrophobia—a fear of traveling over bridges.[48] The article details the rising prominence of gephyrophobia as a public works issue and closes by asking readers for their thoughts on the subject: "What do you think about gephyrophobia? Have you ever experienced it? Any tips for people on how to deal with it? Share your thoughts here at Science Buzz."[49] As of this writing, the article thread received 208 comments from Science Buzz readers from 2007 to 2015. The following analysis employs the Faciloscope as users of the web app would, with an emphasis on the visual results of classification. Because of the length of the Faciloscope's output, we will be selective in what we analyze in this chapter.[50]

In order to extract the text from the Science Buzz webpage, we employed a screenscraping program, Scrapy, to cull the original article post and comments without the attending HTML and styling elements.[51] The screenscrape follows the top-down progression of comments on the Science Buzz webpage. Posts are generally sequential based on time and date stamping; however, Science Buzz commenters can reply to any existing post individually. These replies will follow the targeted post on the page. For example, a comment posted in 2007 can feature a reply from 2009 directly after it on the page. The screenscrape would capture the post and the reply as consecutive posts. Thus, the gephyrophobia text used as a case study does not simply move from 2007 to 2009; however, we do feel justified in analyzing these posts as they are represented on the page because human readers must negotiate the same asynchronicity of replies.

Before we launch into the specifics of the Faciloscope output and how we might use it to substantiate analysis of rhetorical moves in the gephyrophobia article/comment thread, we should describe some grounding assumptions. First, given the count of comments and the duration of interest (two years), we can infer that the gephyrophobia discussion topic has been "successful." We can also say that this discussion has attracted a relatively high number of Science Buzz participants based on the structure of the HTML page. Sifting through the div class "author," we find 119 unique names (although we cannot verify the uniqueness of all users given the metadata publicly available). Thus, the rhetorical moves of Staging, Inviting, and Evoking must be reconciled with the duration of the thread and the diversity of commenters. The third assumption is based on our previous experiments with the Faciloscope and what we have come to expect in terms of rhetorical move distribution. In our experience, most online discussion forums will register predominantly as Staging moves. The distribution of Inviting and Evoking moves are far more infrequent, and this makes some pragmatic sense. Relaying thoughts asynchronously in online writing environments requires writers to establish the context of their messages. A Staging move is functioning as a constituent of a larger picture, so more sentences are needed. Contrast that with an Invit-

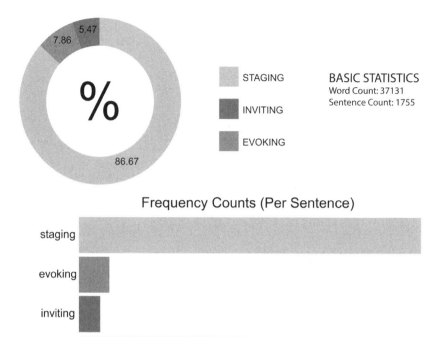

Figure 7.2. Percentage and distribution of rhetorical moves in gephyrophobia comment thread

ing move such as the question, "What do people think about this story?" We can imagine scenarios in which the writer asks follow-up questions. At the same time, a litany of questions may also be alienating because they demand too much from the reader, are simply repetitive, or foreclose discussion by too narrowly defining the area of inquiry. To preserve the open-endedness of "What do people think about this story?", one instance of this question may be more than enough. Similarly, an Evoking move can also say more with less. An Evoking move such as "Thank you for your comments!" may be a sufficient statement of support because the affective orientation of Evoking moves carries risk. Too much praise may be considered overweening, biased, or even off-topic. A negative Evoking move such as "That's a stupid comment" may be criticized by forum members.

The Faciloscope reports that the gephyrophobia article consists of 2,071 sentences and 37,096 words. Staging moves prevail (85.61 percent). Inviting (5.46 percent) and Evoking (8.93 percent) moves represent a small portion of the gephyrophobia comment thread, and in similar measure.

Graphically, we can see these percentages and distributions in figure 7.2. As

Table 7.2. Sample tabular results of Science Buzz gephyrophobia comment thread

4	On the return trip to Washington we opted to drive up through Wilmington and down through Baltimore, not because of any fear of the bridge collapsing, but rather intense anxiety of being stuck in another two-hour traffic jam.	STAGING
5	Our return trip took only 2.5 hours., Last night I took the Memphis-Arkansas bridge over and it was sort of scary.	STAGING
6	I had to sit in a Motel 6 parking lot and build up my nerve while watching the traffic come over from the western side.	STAGING
7	I finally said the hell with it and just went over at 40 miles an hour and I was sort of laughing that I wasted 5 days in Memphis wondering how I was going to get over that bridge.	STAGING

a moment of preliminary exploration of the gephyrophobia comment thread, we can begin to triangulate certain inferences based on the three listed assumptions, the descriptive statistics returned by the Faciloscope, and the content of the comment thread as depicted in the Faciloscope's tabular view. We need only scan the initial sentences of the gephyrophobia comment thread to notice that the Staging moves are being used in the service of narrative. Sentences 4 to 7 in the tabular view of the Faciloscope denote acts of reporting (see table 7.2).

Jumping to different regions of the gephyrophobia comment thread, we see more narrative accounting. What's more, these stories begin to resolve themselves into two types of survivor stories: an explicit type in which the story identifies a gephyrophobic episode and relays how it was overcome or an implicit type in which an episode of gephyrophobia is described with a statement of consequences or conclusions that suggest that the sufferer continues to endure this anxiety. In sentences 17 to 21, a commenter describes how he/she persevered through gephyrophobia with a girlfriend, an example of the explicit survivor story (see table 7.3).

While the sampling functions to a large degree as a form of close reading, the advantage of computing rhetorical moves and then visualizing results is that a user can discover and pinpoint other regions of high Staging density in order to further triangulate interpretation with the support of human judgment. The Bands visualization indicates several swaths in the comment thread text where Staging moves predominate. If we zoom in on a cen-

Table 7.3. Sample tabular results of Science Buzz gephyrophobia comment thread

17	A girlfriend and I were trying to go to the Pyramid for a concert but we got stuck on a one-way street that ended up being the I-40 West on ramp.	STAGING
18	By the time we realized it we were on the incline heading up and it was too late to go back as there were cars behind us.	STAGING
19	So we looked at each other with our eyes wide open and screamed all the way across to Arkansas.	STAGING
20	As soon as we got to a place where we could turn around we switched places so she could drive back then we screamed all the way back.	STAGING
21	It worked much better than we'd expected.	STAGING

tral region of the Bands visualization that contains a block of Staging moves as annotated by the classifier, we see more testimony to the triggering effects of gephyrophobia (see table 7.4), an example of the implicit survivor story.

Although nearly the entire gephyrophobia comment thread consists of Staging moves, an examination of the Bands visualization shows that the sequencing of these Staging moves is interrupted at regular intervals by Evoking and Inviting moves (see figure 7.3).

This visual inspection suggests that the flow of descriptive information is being modulated by rhetorical moves intended to engage in the wider community of the commenter by either soliciting feedback or tendering feedback. The type of feedback (Inviting and Evoking) deployed can be further highlighted by scrolling and zooming of the Bands visualization. There are two thick strips of Inviting moves in the first quarter-and-a-half of the comment thread. The first big block encompasses a single Inviting move (see table 7.5).

The variety of messages contained in the comment in table 7.5 might argue for any number of labels. The statement does describe a past event of gephyrophobia, which associates it with Staging. The statement also employs several words of strong affect such as "PANIC" and "REALLY SCARED." The use of all capital letters also seems designed to Evoke an emotional connection with the reader. The reason that the Faciloscope classifier coded this as an Inviting move likely derives from the presence of two highly weighted Inviting terms: "PLEASE" and "THANKS." Indeed, the final portion of the comment makes an explicit ask from the audience. The second block of Inviting moves

Table 7.4. Staging move examples from Science Buzz gephyrophobia comment thread

965	Even on and off ramps are a problem if they are high.	STAGING
966	The anxiety starts days before if I know I'm traveling.	STAGING
967	I will no longer drive from NYC to DC because of the Del Mem Bridge and some of the structures getting through Baltimore.	STAGING
968	Odd though that it started late in life and I have very little problem with familiar bridges - no matter how high.	STAGING
969	I remember riding in the car with my mom when I was little and she would drive in the middle of the 2 lanes across the Mackinac bridge.	STAGING

0   20,000   40,000   60,000   80,000   100,000   120,000   140,000   160,000   180,000

Figure 7.3. Bands visualization of gephyrophobia comment thread

at the midway point of the Bands visualization actually seems to be an erroneous labeling. As table 7.6 illustrates, the text of sentences 913 and 914 are more plausibly classed as Evoking moves because of their ad hominem nature. More conservatively, sentences 913 and 914 could be classed as Staging moves because they describe a way of engaging with the issue of gephyrophobia as a prescription.

This error, however, points us to another interesting phenomenon in the gephyrophobia thread due to the proximity of the erroneous Inviting moves with other correctly labeled Inviting and Evoking moves. If we expand our focus to include the close packing of Evoking, Inviting, and Staging moves with the region between 867 and 914, we see that sentence 867 is an Evoking move.[52] It can be coded this way due to the use of the exclamation point

Table 7.5. Inviting move example from Science Buzz gephyrophobia comment thread

| 194 | I AM PRETTY FOR SURE I HAVE ALOT OF PHOBIAS IM PETRIFIED OF THUNDERSTORMS I HIDE WHEN I KNOW ITS COMMINGAND I PANIC THREW THE WHOLE THINGIM ALSO AFRAID OF ELEVATORS I WONT GO IN ONE ALONE OR UP TO HIGH REGUARDLESSIM AFRAID OF GETTING INTO A CAR BUT I PUSH MYSELF ONCE IN A WHILE IM AFRAID OF GETTING INTO A ACCIDENTI AM REALLY SCARED OF TRACTOR TYRAILERS AND BUSSES SO I DONT GO ON HIGH WAYS AT ALLITS EASIER FOR ME TO TAKE THE CITY BUS WHERE EVER I HAVE TO GO ITS WEIRD I KNOWIM ALSO AFRAID OF SECOND FLOORS SO I HAVE TO HAVE MY BEDROOM ON 1ST FLOOR IM AFRAID THERES GONNA BE A FIREI REALLY WANT TO GET OVER THESE FEARS I HAVE BAD NERVES AND PANICKATTACKS ALSO IF IM IN A STORE SOMETIMES I DO FINE AND SOMETIMES I FEEL LIGHT HEADEDIM SCARED OF DRS SO I DONT GOIM AFRAID OF BLOOD WOPRK SO I HAVNT HAD IT DONE IN 3 YEARSIM SCARED OF DENTIST AND I REALLY NEED TO GO BUT I CANTIF ANYONE HAS ANY WAYS OF HELPING ME PLEASE EMAIL ME AS SOON AS POSSABLE AT [email redacted] THANKS Mine is related to a fear of heights (acrophobia). | INVITING |

to establish impact: "If you canu2019t [sic] handle driving over a stinking bridge you shouldnu2019t be driving at all!" What follows are additional Evoking pronouncements signaled by the use of exclamation marks and cutting judgments about people with gephyrophobia: "However you people are serving as poor examples to your children!" (sentence 871) and "Happy people do not live their life in fear!" (sentence 872). In response, commenters issue a series of Inviting questions meant to interrogate and undercut the negative argument. One commenter asks, "UHM . . . why are you snooping around this website if you feel this way? . . . Did you learn about this in school? . . . Perhaps a psych class? . . . And then decided that you would just 'GOOGLE' it to see who was having difficulty?" (sentences 892, 894, 895, 896). These questions are followed by this Evoking move: "And if you're so 'HAPPY' then why spend your time spitting out negativity to all of those who have this particular phobia . . . or any phobia for that matter!!!" (sentence 897). Thus, what the close packing of Inviting and Evoking moves indicates in this instance is a pointed engagement between commenters on the sufferer's re-

Table 7.6. Sample inviting moves from Science Buzz gephyrophobia comment thread

913	to "Anonymous" who says "happy people do not live their life in fear." How ironic that he/she calls themselves "Anonymous"—i guess "anonymous" is fearful of using their REAL name for fear of backlash from their cruel and misguided comments . . . labelling an illness disease condition or in this case phobia does not give the "afflicted"(to quote you!	INVITING
914	) any sense of COMFORT . . . it is simply a classification . . . actually it is beneficial in the healing process to know that you are not alone with the symptoms and this forum is also an opportunity to share strategies to help tackle the problem. . . . . let's hope you never had any problems in your life. . . . and if you do perhaps you may find others who are more sympathetic to your situation . . . Excellent response JG however your examples have no relation to safely controlling a vehicle unless a spider bites you while driving in a small car and blood starts spurting about uncontrollably but thatu2019s a story for another day :) .	INVITING

sponse to gephyrophobia. In this case, this close packing also indicates an important dynamic—trolling. One commenter suggests that those who are afflicted with gephyrophobia choose not to deal with the condition because of character flaws; another commenter undercuts this argument by questioning the motives of the troll.

We can look to other examples of the close packing of Inviting and Evoking moves in order to trace other possible moments of trolling. One site occurs in the final quarter of the Bands visualization. This region is dominated by a single comment by Pete (UK). This lengthy post contains a mix of Staging, Inviting, and Evoking moves. The Staging moves in this post conform to the pattern of retrospective and narrative seen in previous examples. The attached Inviting moves work to shift between Pete (UK)'s personal story and "check-ins" with readers. These "check-ins" include narrative interruptions such as "Does this all sound familiar" (in reference to a triggered gephyrophobia episode while driving over a 180 foot high bridge; sentence 1408) and "The symptoms are very weakening (enfeebling) and flu-like YET you could lift a car if your child was trapped under it or punch a whole gang out if they got in your way in your determined panic to escape. Weird eh?."[53] The attached Evoking moves primarily involve exhortations for sufferers to take action by telling "POSITIVE" stories to their brains in order to undo the negative anxiety related to crossing bridges. While the stridency of Pete (UK)'s recommendations might offend some, his comments do not feature the direct, if generalized, insults leveled by the troll in the previous example. So, has the Faciloscope discerned patterns of trolling behavior in this comment thread? Probably not. However, the close packing of Inviting and Evoking moves do seem to signal the *conditions* for trolling. These conditions relate to those Evoking gestures concerned with spurring the will of sufferers of gephyrophobia to take action—to change their mental models and behaviors. Consequently, Evocations of affect in this gephyrophobia comment thread can be a means to argue for a psychological remedy.

Why Build Rhetorical Machines Like the Faciloscope?

We want to close with a reflection on the work of building a rhetorical machine to ask what the value might be in undertaking similar projects for those of us interested in rhetoric, writing studies, and computation. We identify four good reasons to do the work of teaching machines rhetoric:

1. To extend rhetorical expertise to those who may benefit from it but who may lack explicit rhetorical training.
2. To extend the capacity of humans to do certain kinds of rhetorical tasks due to challenges of scale, seeking the affordances of speed.
3. To extend our knowledge of rhetoric using thought experiments, executed in computer code, to test conjectures, pursue answers to questions, or simply explore possibilities.
4. To stay involved in the kinds of work that mobilize our disciplinary knowledge in ways that we may or may not approve of, preserving our right to intervene or lead when needed.

The first two reasons on our list speak directly to the exigency for creating the Faciloscope. Our collaborative partners working in science centers now have, in the Faciloscope, a tool that allows them to conduct a relatively sophisticated rhetorical analysis, on demand, in a very short amount of time. In our initial vision, we saw the Faciloscope as a tool that would expedite the work of the rhetoric specialists originally tasked with digesting and reporting on facilitation sessions to expert facilitators. The Faciloscope was created to automate the more tedious hand-coding process and accelerate the feedback cycle. As we proceeded with development, however, we also saw the Faciloscope as a possible training tool for new facilitators. In a training session, expert facilitators can explain to novices how Staging, Evoking, and Inviting moves function within a facilitation environment and why they might be important. In this case, the simplicity of the Faciloscope's coding scheme has the additional benefit of being easy to understand and apply to examples. Expert facilitators can then provide novices with examples of successful and unsuccessful online conversations. The Faciloscope can then provide both experts and novices with a kind of visual assay, showing what successful or unsuccessful threads look like given the distribution of Staging, Evoking, and Inviting moves. In a sense, the visual output of the Faciloscope can provide an impressionistic label—marking out lively discussions from the moribund. Moreover, because discussion threads are indexed on a move-by-move basis, expert and novice facilitators can spot those moments of intervention that either spurred or disrupted conversation, thereby teaching them the most advantageous strategies to use for more desirable outcomes.

The first two reasons also outline the ramifications of creating an app such as the Faciloscope to conduct rhetorical analysis. Both the user interface and computational results of the Faciloscope are constrained. Users can alter the inputted text but cannot make further calibrations to the classification process. For those users not trained in rhetorical theory, using the Faciloscope amounts to using someone else's analytic—using an app encoded with the theoretical, cultural, and technical knowledge of the Faciloscope development team. While this situation is not dissimilar to more traditional types of scholarly work, we believe that it takes on a special valence when manufacturing rhetorical machines because unlike an article or monograph, much of the lineaments of a computational application for more generalized use are rendered invisible to ensure the optimal user experience.

The third reason on our list speaks to values for our fellow researchers. Working on the Faciloscope allowed us to visualize aspects of facilitation as a kind of rhetorical performance that has not been documented before to our knowledge. For instance, the Bands visualization reveals that successful facilitation likely involves patterns of moves and that each move may have a desirable periodicity or rhythm where they are associated with successful threads. We would need much more research in this area to link specific patterns or rhythms definitively with successful outcomes, of course, but we now have some idea how this kind of research could proceed. This notion that rhetorical or facilitation moves possess a rhythm of use also points us to the prospect of a probabilistic rhetorical methodology, in which the initiation of a move is contingent upon previous moves or a series of moves. In other words, given a series of moves, the likelihood of X or Y being the *next* move could be measured to help guide ongoing rhetorical intervention. We also view projects like the Faciloscope as a means to shift the priorities of traditional academic publications, because apps or software suites can foster dynamic, variable, and perduring dialogues with users because they exist as a near-autonomous rhetorical agent, open for business at all times and for whomever has an active internet connection. In one sense, the Faciloscope and similar projects are *rhetorical services* as well as rhetorical machines. At the same time, this emphasis on rhetorical services obliges new expectations from authors. Building this rhetorical machine inaugurates a commitment to maintain, update, and troubleshoot the Faciloscope. Moreover, the Faciloscope's deployment, which requires knowledge of computational algorithms, server-side scripting, and client-side user experience, mandates a different type of phronesis by authors—one that marshals expertise from various parties, including systems operations engineers, rhetoricians, and designers, or *full-stack rhetorician/rhetoricians* who has/have working knowledge of all theoretical and practical dependencies.

Our fourth reason speaks to an ethical commitment we feel even more strongly now that we have completed this project. Teaching machines rhetoric is something that, understandably, inspires as much trepidation as excitement. But as we have sometimes seen in the past, developers and researchers from other fields do not need to seek our permission to move ahead with this kind of work. We feel it is vital to engage in experiments like the one we undertook in creating the Faciloscope in order to stay involved in the ways our disciplinary knowledge might find its way into rhetorical machines.

Appendix

FACILOSCOPE CODING SCHEME

General Instructions for Coders

- Coders should code single sentences
- Coders should code those sentences that they feel most confident about; otherwise, coders should skip the sentence
- Coders should emphasize the content/rhetoric of a given sentence over the contextual associations that sentence may have with previous sentences in the corpus

Coding Scheme

The following coding scheme classifies sentences according to the following three rhetorical moves: *staging, inviting, and building relationships.*

Staging—a move that is aimed toward making a statement that introduces an idea, concept, or example in order to frame discussion or understanding.

- WHAT and/or WHO topics (e.g., What happened? What is happening? What will happen? Who is responsible? Who is involved?)

- Stipulatory/declarative
  ◦ Makes use of the existential there (e.g., "There is a website that covers these topics.")
- Denotative sentences that use verbs of existence (is, are, was, were, etc.) should be considered staging
- Describes conditions of action such as deadlines, agents of approval, procedures, materials, rationales as well as outcomes
  ◦ Lists of points or examples
  ◦ Descriptions could include evaluations of conditions (e.g., ease or difficulty; fast or slow)
  ◦ Outcome statements will usually employ constructions such as "because," "consequently," "as a result"
  ◦ Staging sentences can also take the subjunctive mood as a way to introduce a topic or condition (e.g., "I would like to get this done today" or "I would like to go to this meeting."); these will often communicate the rationale for and/or goals of the action.
- Evaluations of topics without explicitly referenced agents are staging
- Quoted and/or citational statements will always be considered staging when they stand alone; if couched within a question, then the statement would be an inviting move
  Ex. "Looking through this conversation, I believe everyone who's contributing is also white" (Confessional, ln 786).

Inviting—a move that explicitly guides the development of discussion or an idea.
- Stipulatory or deliberative
- Requests for participant action, which can include elaboration on a topic or an explanation of a process
  ◦ Can be framed in subjunctive mood ("I would like to invite you")
  ◦ Imperatives should also be considered requests for action
  ◦ Questions that seek to clarify an idea or gain information should be coded as Inviting
- Solicitations of feedback that will inform decision-making
- Redirects the focus of the conversation
- Closings of discussions that call for future feedback
- When sentence explicitly uses words such as "invite," "ask," or "request," the sentence should be classed as Inviting
- Use of ellipsis ('. . .') at end of sentence is a sign of deliberation and should be marked as Inviting
  Ex. 1 "How would you rephrase that question?" (Confessional, ln 449).
  Ex. 2 "Amy, can you explain why you asked?" (Confessional, ln 966).

Evoking—a move that explicitly attempts to create connections among participants and/or maintain social relationships

- Demonstrations of respect/acknowledgement of individual perspectives
  - ° Invoking a specific, concrete other (i.e., names; Twitter handle)
  - ° Explicitly establishing connections between specific others (agents; not objects)
- Bids for understanding, agreement, or mollification, sympathy, empathy
  - ° Routinely features "you" as a direct or indirect object of predicate actions (e.g., "I wanted to give you . . ." or "I understand that you are in charge of bidding")
  - ° Expresses gratitude or apologies for actions
  - ° Clausal level: Agent (subject) + Affective Expression + Agents (direct objects)
- Offers affective motivation for the completion of an action of the building of relationships involving hortatory (e.g., "Let's do it!") or assurances (e.g., "I know you can do it.") or accommodations (e.g., "We know you would like to be involved, so we are making every effort to include you in the process.")
  - ° Affective motivation could also involve hedging or mollifying moves such as "We found your offer competitive and we are still interested in working with you")
  - ° The use of exclamation points can convert a syntactically *staging* sentence into affective motivation (e.g., "with so much change happening all around us, it's time for north carolina to stop limiting the freedom to marry!")
  - ° Words or phrases in all caps are equivalent to exclamation points
    Ex. "That's a beautiful story, Ro." "Thanks for sharing it" (Confessional, ln 66–67).

- Salutations that might open a conversation (e.g., "Dear James, I hope you are doing well.")
- Negative framings of relationships

Notes

1. Institute of Museum and Library Services grant LG-25–10–0034–10, with Jeff Grabill as principal investigator.

2. See "Facilitation Toolbox," accessed May 18, 2018, http://facilitation.matrix .msu.edu/.

3. John Swales and Hazem Najjar, "The Writing of Research Article Introductions," *Written Communication* 4, no. 2 (1987): 175–91.

4. Ryan Omizo et al., "You Can Read the Comments Section Again: The Faciloscope App and Automated Rhetorical Analysis," *DH Commons Journal* (2016).

5. Michael Eraut, "Informal Learning in the Workplace," *Studies in Continuing Education* 26, no. 2 (2004): 247.

6. David Boud and Heather Middleton, "Learning from Others at Work: Communities of Practice and Informal Learning," *Journal of Workplace Learning* 15, no. 5 (2003): 199.

7. John H. Falk and Lynn D. Dierking, *Lessons without Limit: How Free-Choice Learning Is Transforming Education* (Walnut Creek, CA: AltaMira, 2002).

8. Boud and Middleton, "Learning from Others."

9. Marie-Line Germain and Robin S. Grenier, "Facilitating Workplace Learning and Change: Lessons Learned from the Lectores in Pre-War Cigar Factories," *Journal of Workplace Learning* 27, no. 5 (2015): 366–86.

10. Joshua P. Gutwill and Sue Allen, "Facilitating Family Group Inquiry at Science Museum Exhibits," *Science Education* 94, no. 4 (July 2010): 710–42.

11. Andrea D. Ellinger and Maria Cseh, "Contextual Factors Influencing the Facilitation of Others' Learning through Everyday Work Experiences," *Journal of Workplace Learning* 19, no. 7 (2007): 443; for an extended bibliography on facilitation, see Donnie Sackey and Letitia Flower, "Facilitation Annotated Bibliography," accessed January 10, 2016. http://facilitation.matrix.msu.edu/index.php/resources/.

12. Donnie Johnson Sackey, Minh-Tam Nguyen, and Jeffrey T. Grabill, "Constructing Learning Spaces: What We Can Learn from Studies of Informal Learning Online," *Computers and Composition* 35 (March 2015): 112–24.

13. Floriana Grasso, "Towards Computational Rhetoric," *Informal Logic* 22, no. 3 (2002): 195–229; Floriana Grasso, "Towards a Framework for Rhetorical Argumentation," in *EDILOG 02: Proceedings of the 6th Workshop on the Semantics and Pragmatics of Dialogue*, ed. Johan Bos, Mary Ellen Foster, and Colin Matheson (Edinburgh, UK: 2002), 53–60.

14. Chaïm Perelman and Lucie Olbrechts-Tyteca, *The New Rhetoric: A Treatise on Argumentation*, trans. John Wilkinson and Purcell Weaver (South Bend, IN: University of Notre Dame Press, 1969).

15. James J. Brown Jr., *Ethical Programs: Hospitality and the Rhetorics of Software* (Ann Arbor: University of Michigan Press, 2015).

16. Annette Vee and James J. Brown Jr., "Rhetoric Special Issue Editorial Introduction," *Computational Culture: A Journal of Software Studies* 5 (2016), http://computationalculture.net/issue-five/.

17. Brown elaborates on this subject by positioning Burke's Pentad and rhetorical ratios of Scene, Agent, and Act as another type of rhetorical machine that enables analysis of motivation. Here, Brown draws attention to the notion that a "rhetorical machine" is not beholden to computer code but functions as a dynamic unpacking of a text given a heuristic.

18. Chad Edwards et al., "Is That a Bot Running the Social Media Feed? Testing the Differences in Perceptions of Communication Quality for a Human Agent and a Bot Agent on Twitter," *Computers in Human Behavior* 33 (April 2014): 372–76.

19. David Kaufer and Suguru Ishizaki, "DocuScope: Computer-Aided Rhetorical Analysis," cmu.edu, accessed March 31, 2016, https://www.cmu.edu/hss/english/research/docuscope.html; Jeff Collins et al., "Detecting Collaborations in Text: Comparing the Authors' Rhetorical Language Choices in *The Federalist Papers*," *Computers and the Humanities* 38, no. 1 (February 2004): 15–36; Suguru Ishizaki and David Kaufer, "Computer-Aided Rhetorical Analysis," in *Applied Natural Language Processing: Identification, Investigation and Resolution*, ed. Philip M. McCarthy and Chutima Boonthum-Denecke (Hershey, PA: IGI Global, 2012), 276–96.

20. *OVA*. Arg.dundee.ac.uk, accessed March 31, 2016, http://www.arg.dundee.ac.uk/index.php/ova/.

21. Chris Reed and Glenn Rowe, "Araucaria: Software for Argument Analysis, Diagramming, and Representation," *International Journal on Artificial Intelligence Tools* 13, no. 4 (December 2004): 961–79; Glenn Rowe et al., "Araucaria as a Tool for Diagramming Arguments in Teaching and Studying Philosophy," *Teaching Philosophy* 29, no. 2 (June 2006): 111–24.

22. Chrysanne DiMarco and Randy Allen Harris, "The RhetFig Project: Computational Rhetorics and Models of Persuasion," in *Workshops at the Twenty-Fifth AAAI Conference on Artificial Intelligence* (San Francisco: AAAI, 2011), 2.

23. Ashley R. Kelly et al., "Toward an Ontology of Rhetorical Figures," in *Proceedings of the 28th ACM International Conference on Design of Communication* (Sao Paolo, Brazil: ACM 2010), 123–30.

24. Randy Harris and Chrysanne DiMarco, "Constructing a Rhetorical Figuration Ontology," in *Persuasive Technology and Digital Behaviour Intervention Symposium*, ed. Judith Masthoff and Floriana Grasso (SSAISB, 2009), 49–50.

25. Ibid.

26. See Ishizaki and Kaufer, "Computer-Aided Rhetorical Analysis."

27. See Reed and Rowe, "Araucaria."

28. From Swales and Najjar, "Writing of Research Article Introductions."

29. Pedro Domingos, "A Few Useful Things to Know about Machine Learning," *Communications of the ACM* 55, no. 10 (October 2012): 78.

30. Corinna Cortes and Vladimir Vapnik, "Support-Vector Networks," *Machine Learning* 20, no. 3 (September 1995): 273–97.

31. Domingos, "Useful Things," 79.

32. Ryan K. Boettger and Laura A. Palmer, "Quantitative Content Analysis: Its Use in Technical Communication," *IEEE Transactions on Professional Communication* 53, no. 4 (December 2010): 346–57.

33. "Category Specific Faciliation Tool," accessed May 16, 2018, http://facilitation.matrix.msu.edu/index.php/download_file/view/44/124/.

34. The original research team consisted of Jeff Grabill, MSU; Donnie Sackey, MSU; Minh-Tam Nguyen, MSU; Kirsten Ellenbogen, SMM; Margaret Aiken, SMM; Julia Halpern, SMM; Troy Livingston, MLS; Beck Tench, MLS; and Elizabeth Flem-

ing, MLS; see also Jeffrey T. Grabill and Stacey Pigg, "Messy Rhetoric: Identity Performance as Rhetorical Agency in Online Public Forums," *Rhetoric Society Quarterly* 42, no. 2 (Spring 2012): 99–119.

35. See Kirsten Ellenbogen et al., "Studying Web 2 Experiences: An Open Source Session," July 26, 2012, http://facilitation.matrix.msu.edu/index.php/download_file/view/43/124/.

36. The reason for this lack of confidence derived from previous experiences testing classifiers. Supervised machine learning classifiers are only as a good as the volume of data supplied for training. The more categories a coding scheme has, the more data is required to comprehensively train the classifier to recognize each category. Thus, our concern focused on the availability of enough data to train for nine categories and on the possibility that we would not be able to obtain enough relevant data for training.

37. "Category Specific Facilitation Tool," accessed May 15, 2017, http://facilitation.matrix.msu.edu/files/5713/8548/5077/Facilitation_tool_for_facilitators_v2.pdf.

38. Carolyn R. Miller, "Genre as Social Action," *Quarterly Journal of Speech* 70, no. 2 (1984): 151–67; Carolyn R. Miller and Dawn Shepherd, "Blogging as Social Action: A Genre Analysis of the Weblog," in *Into the Blogosphere: Rhetoric, Community, and Culture of Weblogs* (University of Minnesota Digital Conservancy, 2004),1–24, found at https://conservancy.umn.edu/handle/11299/172840; Catherine F. Schryer, "Records as Genre," *Written Communication* 10, no. 2 (1993): 200–234; Swales and Najjar.

39. Sackey, Nguyen, and Grabill, "Constructing Learning Spaces."

40. Janice Lauer, *Invention in Rhetoric and Composition* (Anderson, SC: Parlor Press, 2004); James L. Kinneavy, *A Theory of Discourse: The Aims of Discourse* (New York: W. W. Norton, 1980); Aviva Freedman and Peter Medway, "Locating Genre Studies: Antecedents and Prospects," in *Genre and the New Rhetoric*, ed. by Aviva Freedman and Peter Medway (London: Taylor and Francis, 1994), 1–20.

41. The Faciloscope uses sentence and word tokenizers from the Bird and Loper's Natural Language Toolkit sentence tokenizer; it also uses a text replacement module adapted from Perkins that helps unpack contraction. Steven Bird and Edward Loper, "NLTK: The Natural Language Toolkit," in *Proceedings of the ACL Workshop on Effective Tools and Methodologies for Teaching Natural Language Processing and Computational Linguistics*, 62–69 (Somerset, NJ: Association for Computational Linguistics, 2002), 62–69, available at http://arXiv.org/abs/cs/0205028; Jacob Perkins, *Python Text Processing with NLTK 2.0 Cookbook* (Birmingham, UK: Packt Publishing, 2010).

42. "Attention Newbies to Incubating," Backyardchickens.com, accessed June 4, 2014, http://www.backyardchickens.com/t/878773/attention-newbies-to-incubating; "Simulated Natural Nest Incubation~Experiment #1 So It Begins ...," Backyardchickens.com, accessed June 6, 2014, http://www.backyardchickens.com/t/854946/simulated-natural-nest-incubation-experiment-1-so-it-begins; "Hatching with 2 Broodies." Backyardchickens.com, accessed June 4, 2014, http://www.backyardchickens.com/t/828899/hatching-with-2-broodies.

43. Boettger and Palmer, "Quantitative Content Analysis," 348.

44. Aaron Beveridge, "Looking in the Dustbin: Data Janitorial Work, Statistical Reasoning, and Information Rhetorics," *Computers and Composition Online* (Fall 2015), http://cconlinejournal.org/fall15/beveridge/.

45. We should note that while reduction and simplification have characterized our methods in building rhetorical machines, other projects would take the opposite approach. For example, Docuscope prioritizes the granularity of natural language texts. While Docuscope does perform an abstraction when assigning language actions types to words and word sequences, the final representation of a Docuscope processed text features myriad annotations of textual data that the Faciloscope would initially eliminate.

46. Fabian Pedregosa et al., "Scikit-learn: Machine Learning in Python," *Journal of Machine Learning Research* 12 (October 2011): 2825–30; see also "sklearn.multiclass. OneVsRestClassifier," accessed May 18, 2017, http://scikit-learn.org/stable/modules/generated/sklearn.muVlticlass.OneVsRestClassifier.html.

47. Cortes and Vapnik, "Support-Vector Networks," 273–97.

48. Thor, "Gephyrophobia: Fear of Crossing Bridges Is Now in the Spotlight," Science Buzz, last updated August 8, 2007, http://www.sciencebuzz.org/blog/gephyrophobia-fear-crossing-bridges-now-spotlight.

49. Ibid.

50. Readers can view the full Faciloscope output of the "Gephyrophobia" thread at https://rmomizo.github.io/gephyrophobia/fscope_rhetorical_machines.html.

51. *Scrapy*, computer program, accessed May 17, 2018, https://scrapy.org/.

52. For a representation of this region, see https://rmomizo.github.io/gephyrophobia/fscope_rhetorical_machines.html.

53. This sentence is a tokenization error.

8 / Race within the Machine

Ambient Rhetorical Actions and Racial Ideology

Joshua Daniel-Wariya and James Chase Sanchez

In their conclusion to their 2001 work, *Critical Race Theory: An Introduction*, Richard Delgado and Jean Stefancic hypothetically imagine what racial relations might be in the twenty-first century. While they claim that there could be some smooth transitions as minorities "find new niches in the world economy," they hedge their analysis in the opposite direction—that any progress for minorities will be hindered by "the white establishment . . . resist[ing] an orderly progression toward power sharing and minority inclusion," and emphasize the need for representation.[1] Years after the book's publication and subsequent edition, racial relations in America remain stagnant if not regressive, especially when it comes to police brutality, xenophobic political rhetoric, and representation. The progress that Delgado and Stefancic hoped for seems all but lost.

However, understanding that major changes in racial relations probably would not occur quickly, Delgado and Stefancic present a call for future scholars to help promote change, stating that we need more critiques on popular media culture that "continues to produce demeaning caricatures of minorities;" they especially emphasize the need to critique mediums and spaces that often do not receive much attention.[2] In an age where the myth of "colorblindness" is well rehearsed, where many well-meaning people claim they "don't see color," one medium in particular stands out as being absent from many racial analyses: videogames. In particular, as Ian Bogost and others have pointed out, videogames are often seen as "inconsequential because they are perceived to serve no cultural function save distraction at best."[3] However, a growing body of work at the intersection of rhetoric and game studies suggests that this medium is just as epistemic toward our racial ideologies as movies, television shows, and music.[4] More importantly, we argue that in analyzing how gaming engines produce and manifest racial action, specifically in relation to cutscenes— what King and Krzywinska have described as those "audiovisual sequences in which the player usually performs the role of more detached observer than is the case in the more active periods of gameplay"[5]—and what Alexander Galloway has called actions of *pure process*, we see the thorny issue of race embedded within the engines themselves: racial ideologies thrust into the machine by programmers and designers. Consequently, these representations affect gamers' experiences with and interpretations of race.

In this chapter, we present a theoretical framework and methodology for examining race within videogame engines (via *ambient rhetorical actions*) before moving to two case studies that exhibit the range of the engines' racial capacities, in *Final Fantasy XIII* (*FFXIII*) and *Resident Evil 5* (*RE5*). Specifically, our analysis pinpoints how two separate engines (one created for many games and much of the *Resident Evil* series and one solely for *FFXIII*) enclose racial "safeties" and stereotypes into their material productions in order to be more "diverse" and produce a sense that racial diversity is realistically addressed in the games; however, the games' engines' actual representations of people of color show how racial ideologies can be inscribed within machines and affect mass audiences through this portrayal.

Pure Process in Gaming Machines: Ambient Rhetorical Actions

In this section, we sketch the theoretical concepts used for analysis in our case studies. We combine Thomas Rickert's notion of *ambient rhetoric* with Alexander Galloway's concept of gamic actions of *pure process* to identify what we term *ambient rhetorical actions*: those actions in videogames that transpire without user input but create a general rhetorical atmosphere wherein racial ideologies are encoded and articulated. While previous work at the intersections of game studies and rhetorical studies has focused on issues such as how games mount procedural claims or might be used in writing classrooms, this essay focuses on those moments when players put the controller down and leave the game to run. These moments, when gaming's rhetorical machines are left to idle, might offer the clearest picture of ideologies modeled and encoded by game designers.

In his 2013 book, *Ambient Rhetoric*, Thomas Rickert theorizes rhetoric as dispersed through and emergent from material environments, objects, things, and technologies. According to Rickert, "Rhetoric cannot be understood as suasion attempted between discrete or among aggregate subjects embedded in a transitive, subject-driven view of rhetorical situations. Rhetoric is not, finally, a shift in the mental states of subjects but something world-transforming for individuals and groups immersed in vibrant, ecologically attuned environments."[6] This theory of ambience casts rhetoric both as something people *do* and as something environments or things *have*. While an individual speaker might attempt to persuade an audience of a particular point, the nonhuman objects and ambient environment in which that exchange transpires are likewise rhetorical. This realization means that scholars must attune themselves to the environments of rhetorical activity. Similarly, to understand the rhetorics of gaming, scholars must attend to virtual environments in those moments when the player puts the controller down. In taking an ambient rhetorical perspective on games, this essay pauses to listen to the hums and whirs of the machine left untouched.

Alexander Galloway's model of gamic action provides a robust descriptive terminology for the machine rhetorics we discuss in this essay. To visualize Galloway's model, imagine a vertical line that distinguishes actions involving the game's narrative (diegetic) from those that do not (nondiegetic), bisected by a horizontal line that distinguishes between operator and machine actions. This creates four points of contact where various types of gamic action emerge: 1) diegetic operator, 2) diegetic machine, 3) nondiegetic machine, and 4) nondiegetic operator.[7] Here, we focus on *diegetic machine acts*, those actions related to the narrative and executed by the machine. These actions, we contend, when the player stops playing and only the game's hardware (a console) and its software (an engine) execute narrative are apt sites for the study of racial rhetorics. These states—which we term here *ambient rhetorical actions*—create a rhetorical atmosphere for the virtual environment in which claims are encoded and rendered by the machine's engine. While Galloway describes these actions as "pure process" in his model to emphasize the absence of player input, here we describe them as ambient rhetorical actions both to connect them to Rickert's theory of ambient rhetoric and to emphasize that they are still designed by people and do rhetorical work. Put another way, an ambient rhetorical theory emphasizes the ways each quadrant in Galloway's model is enmeshed with every other quadrant and always implicates itself in and is implicated by human action.

Our argument about how game engines render racial ideologies follows and extends Sue Hum's argument in her 2015 *College English* article, "'Between the Eyes': The Racialized Gaze as Design," where she claims that racial ideologies are affected by *design* considered both as a verb and as a noun. As a verb, design influences the strategic choice-making that factors into how designers represent race. As a noun, it constrains the possible choices a designer could make through existing resources.[8] Such a theory of design derives from Gunther Kress's social semiotics in *Multimodality*, in which he argues that "individuals shape their interests through the *design* of messages with the resources available to them in specific situations."[9] A designer's rhetorical agency—their potential to design persuasive messages in a given situation—is simultaneously enabled and constrained by the available resources in particular environments.

On the one hand, Hum's trajectory might be extended to include game engines by casting them as the toolkits providing the available means of persuasion to any given designer or design team. On the other hand, we contend that ambient rhetoric helps describe a more complex notion of agency as it relates to how racial ideology is modeled in game engines. In Rickert's ambient conception, agency is conceived as "a hybrid of coadapting material forces, parts of which we call the robot, parts of which we call the room, and parts of which are the paraphernalia littering the room."[10] If game engines render racial ideologies and present them to players, then whose or what's agency is behind the creation of these persuasive messages, and where is that agency located? Is it computer engineers who build the architecture of an engine and populate it with various design tools? The designers who use those tools to make in-game objects and environments? The artists who imagine the virtual worlds and the avatars who inhabit them? The programmers who describe those visions through computer code and articulate them as core mechanics in a game? Is it in the code and mechanics themselves? The consoles and networks players use to access them? Or even the various display devices, such as screens and audio equipment? Approached this way, agency is the complex, more-than-sum total of its dispersal throughout the various people, machines, and environments that intersect at the rhetorical site of game engines.

If videogame consoles are rhetorical machines because they are the hardware used to deliver games to audiences, then this essay takes game engines as the software alter egos working behind the scenes to render and package materials delivered through consoles. We take videogame engines to be rhetorical machines because they are created in space-time by human beings who make decisions about the ways those machines make use of and render data into virtual representations of space, graphics, sound, physics, intelligence, and—perhaps most importantly—racial ideology. While Ian Bogost has previously discussed how videogames designed for explicitly political purposes carry ideological bias, here we use the term *racial ideology* to refer to large, often-taken-for-granted cultural narratives and racial assumptions and their appearance in videogames. Once a game engine renders these representations, they are then distributed to and experienced by a large and diverse audience that may identify with or be persuaded by the rhetorical claims those representations encode. And while game designers may sometimes rehearse familiar myths of racial colorblindness, critics such as Ian Shanahan[11] and Evan Narcisse[12] have correctly pointed out that the industry still has very few black game designers and that black avatars themselves are often politicized. Therefore, we believe game engines are important and underexplored objects of study for understanding racial ideology.

In the subsequent sections of this essay, we offer two case studies of commercial games and the engines used to create them: *Final Fantasy XIII*, designed using the unique Crystal Tools Engine, and *Resident Evil 5*, designed with the widely adopted MT Framework Engine. In addition to analyzing what engine designers say about their models, we also offer an analysis of in-game objects made possible by the games' engines. We emphasize how those objects behave during states of ambience, states that Janet Murray describes as moments when it feels "as if the programmer within the system is waving at us."[13] Taken together, these case studies illustrate how racial ideologies are reproduced through previous media and rendered by game engines.

Crystal Tools and Cinematics in *Final Fantasy XIII*

In this first case study, our discussion focuses on the character Sazh Katzroy from *FFXIII*. Sazh is one of very few black characters to feature prominently in the *Final Fantasy* series. *Final Fantasy* is perhaps the most popular franchise of Japanese Role-Playing Games (RPGs) in North America and is often credited with popularizing RPGs in general for American audiences. The series has generally received critical appraise for the quality of both its visuals and audio. Artwork, cinematics, and soundtracks from the games have even been sold independently from the games. Indeed, when released to North America in 2009, *FFXIII* was the cutting edge of audio and video in gaming. The *Final Fantasy* series is known for convoluted storylines, and *FFXIII* is perhaps the series standard bearer for that feature. A web search returns numerous blog posts and message boards with gamers asking for help understanding the narrative. That being said, we attempt no such heroics here. As our goal is to understand how race is presented through ambient rhetorical actions, we only explain the game's narrative as it pertains directly to how race is modeled and worked through in relation to Sazh.

Sazh is a middle-aged black man, the oldest playable character in the game. At the game's outset, Sazh is recently widowed and working as an airship pilot. His life revolves mostly around his son, Dajh. Two worlds exist in *FFXIII*. The first is a technologically advanced society called Cocoon, where gamers encounter Sazh and most of the other main characters. A second world, Pulse, exists below Cocoon and is associated with wilderness and magic. For simplicity's sake, suffice it to say that beings from Cocoon are banned from contact with beings from Pulse, who are seen as a threat to Cocoon's survival. Violators are branded enemies of Cocoon and either exiled or killed. Sazh and Dajh come into contact with beings from Pulse. For mysterious reasons, Dajh is transformed into a crystal. While each character in the game has his or her own motivations for embarking on the game's main quest, this is the thrust of Sazh's story: he flees Cocoon for Pulse in the hopes of discovering a way to return Dajh from his crystal stasis.

FFXIII was created with Crystal Tools, a proprietary engine built by SquareEnix to make games in the console generation, including the PlayStation 3, the Xbox 360, and the Nintendo Wii. As noted in *Game Engine Architecture*, game engines exist on a sliding scale between those built to design a single game and those that, in theory, could be used to design nearly any game.[14] Crystal Tools is closer to the single-game side of the equation. While it was intended as the toolkit for a wide variety of games, production problems led to major delays in *FFXIII*. Only five games were ever made with it, four of which include *FFXIII* and its three sequels. Crystal Tools is, however, an apt object of study for a specific innovative feature. Since *FFXIII* is action-based RPG that privileges high-end audio and video, designers needed a way to transition smoothly from high-resolution cinematics and gameplay. An important feature of Crystal Tools was that it could render incredibly high-resolution cutscenes in real time. This means that, unlike previous games that stored prerendered CGI and then loaded and played it at particular points—creating a sharp distinction between gameplay and cutscenes—games designed in Crystal Tools rendered and created those cutscenes through processes during gameplay. This creates a smoother transition between gameplay and cutscene, makes the quality of the images between the two more similar, and allows for the cutscenes to be customized according to player choices.

Players, of course, only experience these cutscenes as they appear on what Noah Wardrip-Fruin refers to as the "surface" of digital media: "When playing a console game, for example, the surface includes the console and any indicator lights or other information it provides, the television or monitor and any image it displays, the sound hardware (e.g., television speakers, stereo, or headphones) and any sound produced, and the controller(s) with their buttons, lights, and perhaps vibrations. The audience experience of digital media is that of being connected to, and in some cases through, the surface."[15] Put another way, the surface of digital media such as videogames refers to the multisensory experience players have after data stored in the game's engine is processed into output played by hardware devices. In the most common way for cutscenes to be generated, computer animation files are simply stored in the game, and the game system plays those files when prompted by a script. For instance, a game such as *Myst* might prompt the system to play a particular video once the player has solved a certain number of quests and puzzles, and the player becomes a more passive observer during the playing of that video file. Alternatively, cutscenes may be generated in real time, producing "scripted scenes rendered by the game engine, rather than another animation system, but still removed from player control."[16] Both types of cutscenes exist in *Final Fantasy XIII*, and one reason Crystal Tools was developed was to create real-time cutscenes that looked to be of a similar quality as prerendered animation files. In anticipation of our discussion of *Resident Evil 5* in the second case study, note that MT Framework also produces another type of cutscene, wherein players are able to still have some control and input in certain situations. In general, though, cutscenes are ambient rhetorical actions because they remove player input and result purely from the machine playing files and generating scenes from script stored in the engine. While our analysis in this chapter focuses primarily on what Wardrip-Fruin calls the "surface" of digital media—for reasons we reflect upon in the conclusion— we also suggest that scholars of rhetoric stand to gain from going subsurface and learning more about the various types of scripts, processes, models, and files stored in and used by game engines.

In the remaining pages of this case study, we consider the cutscenes of Crystal Tools as ambient rhetorical actions and inquire into the racial ideologies they encode. We argue that their effect is, even while presenting a prominent black character, to deemphasize race through a repackaging of what we call *white vouching*—the strategic use of white characters to give tacit approval of black characters—from older media. From there, we consider voicing and music particular to Sazh and discuss how they simultaneously ignore the existence of race in the virtual world of *FFXIII* and utilize American conceptions of blackness in moments without direct player input.

What's in that Afro? Cutscenes on White Approval

While Sazh is a prominent black character, neither he nor other characters in the game explicitly reference his race. The game does, however, repeatedly call attention to his Afro hairstyle. Often when Sazh is featured in a cutscene, the player's gaze is directed toward it through camera movements and the comic use of a bird flying in and out of Sazh's hair. If Sazh's blackness is downplayed to the extent of not being explicitly referenced, then why spend so much time calling attention to this particular racialized feature? Here, we suggest that Sazh's Afro, as rendered through cinematic cutscenes in moments of pure process, functions rhetorically to cast his blackness as nonthreatening for the purposes of white approval.

Take, for example, the player's first encounter with Sazh. Sazh and the game's protagonist—a woman named Lightning—are prisoners on a train and planning their escape. When the opportunity presents itself, Lighting leaps into action to take down guards amid a flurry of bullets and confusion. Using her weapon of choice—a gunblade that is part sword and part assault rifle— Lightning is presented as a force of nature in this opening cutscene. She es-

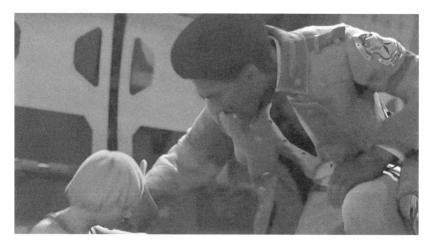

Figure 8.1. Sazh comforts a frightened child. Screenshot of *Final Fantasy XIII*

Figure 8.2. Sazh smiles. Screenshot of *Final Fantasy XIII*

sentially leads this prisoner breakout all on her own, and the game firmly establishes her as the game's main character and heroine.

Sazh's presentation in the opening scene is much different. As shown in figures 8.1 through 8.4, the player sees Sazh kneeling to comfort a child. As the camera pans up and then back and forth between Sazh and the child, the child stares up to see Sazh, who is rendered with a soft and gentle expression. The camera pans up slightly to show Sazh's Afro, at which time a baby chocobo—a small, yellow chick—jumps out of it, smiles, and makes playful

Figure 8.3. A Choco in the Afro. Screenshot of *Final Fantasy XIII*

Figure 8.4. The boy smiles. Screenshot of *Final Fantasy XIII*

noises at the child. As the shot transitions back to the child, his facial expression changes from fear to happiness. While Lightning's opening shots serve to establish her as a fierce soldier, this opening scene with Sazh establishes him as nonthreatening and funny. As an ambient rhetorical action, why would this particular cinematic cutscene be rendered in such an otherwise chaotic environment where prisoners are fleeing a train and a soldier is killing waves of armed guards? Why did the designers take time for this short aside to show this particular interaction between Sazh and an unnamed boy, one who has no future place in or importance to the story?

As Jay David Bolter and Richard Grusin have noted, videogames—like all other digital media—tend to borrow regularly from their mediums such as television and film,[17] and game studies scholars have previously noted that the "boundary between cinema and videogames often appears to be a permeable one, with movements both ways between one medium and the other."[18] Videogames have frequently borrowed techniques from film and television, such as letterboxing and various types of camera zooms and effects. Similarly, these cutscenes can be described as computer-based renderings that remediate a type of white approval of blackness in a variety of other media. One clear example of this practice is discussed in *Made in America*, the 2016 documentary about O. J. Simpson, who was the first black pitchman for a variety of major marketing campaigns. The documentary discusses a very successful and long-running series of ads produced by Hertz Rental Service, in which Simpson is featured running through an airport to catch his flight. The creators of the ads were concerned that the sight of a large black man running through an airport would alarm a white audience. Their solution to this problem was to feature a variety of white people—a small child, an elderly lady, a young man—who see Simpson run past them and then exclaim, "Go, O. J., go!" In this way, Simpson is given white approval. His blackness, while potentially threatening or alarming to a white audience, is disarmed and rendered as a site of happiness and even laughter.[19]

This, we contend, is one rhetorical purpose among many of this cutscene and the many cutscenes in which Sazh and his Afro are featured prominently. As Sue Hum has noted, designers of visual art are both enabled and constrained by previous representations of race. We contend that the same line of reasoning follows here, as game designers may, often unintentionally, recreate problematic presentations of racial rhetorics in videogame spaces that are in some ways constrained by design choices previously established in other media, such as commercials and film. While these representations are, of course, presented visually to the player, they depend on game engines playing files or rendering scenes from scripts encoded by the software. Jason Gregory notes that game design teams are typically comprised of people from a variety of disciplines. Moreover, while artists design the concepts of characters and their features, such as Sazh, they then have to coordinate with engineers who build mathematical models using the engine's toolkit in order to realize an artist's vision.[20]

If visual designers are both enabled and constrained by previous representations of race, then humanities scholars should also understand that designers are similarly enabled and constrained by the analytical and mathematical models built into game engines. This analysis, for instance, is limited by the fact that Crystal Tools is a proprietary engine that is not publicly available for use or analysis. By focusing specifically on those moments when the player is not inputting commands and the machine is left to run on its own, our intent is to point to the machine itself as a rhetorical site in need of study. Although we can analyze those in-game objects the engine ultimately generates, we cannot see how those objects are stored and described in the software itself. This is a problematic generated by the ubiquity of software in nearly every aspect of culture that has led Wendy Hui Kyong Chun to paradoxically describe software as "visibly invisible."[21] Following Chun, we may say that a program such as Crystal Tools simultaneously generates tremendous amounts of visual content and hides the information processes that power the generation of that content. As software has proliferated and become more accessible to larger numbers of people, its operations are increasingly black-boxed and hidden from view. This is sometimes to prevent users from accidentally deleting files that would cause the program to break, and other times—as is the case with Crystal Tools—to closely guard proprietary information that generates revenue. By calling attention to game engines as critical to the rhetorical potential of games, part of what we hope this essay does is point to this problem for rhetorical scholars who study games. How can we expect to fully understand the rhetorical capacity of a videogame if our focus is squarely on the visible side of its software? How might we cast light on the invisible?

"Daddy's Got the Blues": Speaking through the Magic Circle

As previously noted, although we discuss Sazh as a black character in this essay, his blackness is not directly discussed in the game. However, just as American racial ideologies drawn from older media appear in cinematic cutscenes, in this section we discuss how racial rhetorics interlude in the game space through the ambient tones of voice acting and music. We suggest that the rhetorical effect of this is that a particular depiction of blackness hovers in the rhetorical atmosphere of the game space, even as the designers deny or ignore its existence. To illustrate this point, we discuss two types of examples: postbattle dialogue and music that is only associated with Sazh.

In a move that is somewhat characteristic of game designers, the lead designers of *FFXIII* often point to notions of gender or color-blindness in fantasy worlds. In an interview with Yoshinori Kitase and Yuji Abe, the designers reflect on what they believe is behind the enduring success of the franchise: "The stories we choose for the games are very much universal themes, not something that's restricted to one time period or one local culture or type of person. It's something that really appeals broadly to anyone at any time at any place. I think it's the use of those kinds of very universal stories and themes, and also the fact that we have such effort and care put into the character design—I think those are the two main reasons why *Final Fantasy* is even now popular and has so many fans who really love the series."[22] By pointing to "universality," the designers downplay the existence of particular cultural rhetorics in the game space. This implies that, while Sazh has black skin, his representation is not rooted in any particular racial ideology, any particular culture, or any particular time and place in the real world. However, a well-known black actor, Reno Wilson, does Sazh's voice-overs.

For example, after players finish a battle, ambient rhetorical action comes to the forefront. During the post-battle celebration, characters in the player's party will sometimes talk to one another while the game is left to run. Sazh's lines tend to be more slang heavy and less formal than those of other characters. Based on a variety of variables the game engine tracks—such as which characters are currently in the player's party—Sazh will sometimes exclaim, "Damn it all!" or "Time for the old switcheroo!" Musical themes that sometimes play when Sazh is left on screen include "Can't Catch a Break" and "Daddy's Got the Blues." The *Final Fantasy* Wikia notes that both songs have an "improvisational jazz style" that is *unique* in the series.[23] So on the one hand, the designers claim that the series is successful because it relies on "universal stories and themes," but on the other, in their rare design of a black character, they associate that character to a well-known black actor and musical styles associated to a particular culture and time. The designers seem to simultaneously separate their virtual world from the real world and entangle it with particular conceptions of American blackness.

To make sense of how this functions, it is useful to briefly review an often-cited concept in the field of game studies known as *magic circle*. Game designers Eric Zimmerman and Katie Salen are perhaps most responsible for popularizing the term in game studies, as they use a "shorthand" version of it to note the rules and procedures within a virtual environment that cannot be influenced by the outside world.[24] As an example of how this works, consider the ways models of particular types of actions and behaviors are built and then rendered by game engines. For instance, in the architecture of a game engine for an open world like *Skyrim*, software engineers have to create an analytical model to describe how a body will fall from certain heights and how it will respond to hitting various surfaces on the way down. The model is built mathematically and lodged into the game engine itself, so any designer who uses that particular engine to build their game works with the physics it defines. In other words, the engine sets the range for how the designer might have objects move, fall, or collide. When the game engine renders the effects of that particular game, they are set as rules and procedures and therefore not influenced by outside factors. No matter how I play the game of *Skyrim*, I can have no effect on the way the game models and renders a falling body. This is what Salen and Zimmerman mean by the term *magic circle*. It is a real boundary that means to describe the particular kinds of rules and models that exist only within the game itself and are not affected by outside factors during the moment of play. At the same time, as Daniel-Wariya notes in his work on how Salen and Zimmerman's use of the term derives from earlier work by scholars such as Johan Huizinga and Susanne Langer, game studies scholars recognize that the term does "not mark a neat and formal boundary separation of play worlds from reality."[25]

So while a "magic circle" does indeed encapsulate a virtual world such as *FFXIII* in that an individual player cannot influence how the game renders artificial intelligence or falling bodies through computations run by the mathematical models in the engine's architecture, the game's magic circle is also a permeable boundary that does allow for ideologies of race, gender, and class to enter the virtual world. Since representations of blackness must be built and modeled mathematically, it is our contention that the analytical and numerical models in the architectures of games engines themselves necessarily contain and embody racial ideologies. As Rickert says in *Ambient Rhetoric*, "Everything is intertwined and involved with everything else, twisting, changing, and coadapting."[26] Such is the relation between real and virtual worlds, between what is "inside" and "outside" the magic circle. While *FFXIII* designers are unremarkable in the sense that they rehearsed well-known myths of color and gender blindness by invoking universality, the North American version of the game is still eventually marketed and sold to a North American audience. As such, while the virtual world itself may downplay Sazh's race by simply not addressing it directly, racial stereotypes and associations adapted to an American audience still make their way into the game through its ambient rhetorical actions and hang in the atmosphere they create.

MT Framework and *Resident Evil 5*

In the fifth installment of the *Resident Evil* series (*RE5*), players find themselves playing as Chris Redfield, the white, male protagonist from the original game, as he travels to Kijuju (a fictional city in West Africa). The game takes place in this fictional city, as Chris and his black, female partner, Sheva Alomar, attempt to stop an arms dealer from selling a biological weapon to an antagonist who wants to create "superhumans." Much of the gameplay takes place across spaces that look inherently like third-world Africa—players fight off zombies and monsters in small villages with tin-roofed huts, on swampy rivers that resemble parts of the Congo, and other sites that distinguish themselves from contemporary America (which was the setting in the first three games). Overall, reviews for the game were generally positive. For example, Chris Hudak laments the move away from the creepy zombie genre, but still claims "the gorgeous environs, character models and overall visuals, and the adrenaline-soaked cooperative gameplay" make the game terrific.[27] Other reviewers, such as Lark Anderson of *Gamestop*, agree with Hudak: "RE5 is easily one of the most visually stunning games available, and its huge variety of environments are meticulously detailed in every way . . . the voice acting is competent, and when paired with the excellent facial expressions, it breathes a great deal of realism into the characters."[28] Combined, all the *Metacritic* reviews give the game four out of five stars and *IGN* gives it a nine out of ten.

While the game has had terrific reviews, there has been a fair amount of criticism about its racial depictions, such as in one review that describes it as a "racist game [that] reinforces the worst of the worst ancient stereotypes against and about Africans."[29] However, others claim this racist discourse was overblown. An editorial for *IGN* argues that though some believe the game is racist, "you could have the same storyline, the same cut-scenes, the same game—just with white antagonists—and no one would care."[30] Hudak takes it a step further: "If you are aware from the outset that the game *takes place in Africa* and yet you are *still* troubled by any skin-tone-related aspects—on any level whatsoever—there is a distinct probability that you have been exposed to the brain-damaging mutagenic affliction *Politicalus Correctimus*. Alternately, there exists the possibility of simple, congenital retardation on your own part. Seek professional consultation before you attempt to breed."[31]

In the racial controversy surrounding *RE5*, those who claim it is not racist tend to believe that you could rewrite the villagers as white and the game would play the same ways, a position we believe to be entirely wrong for a number of reasons. First, the game itself is built around racial stereotypes, sexualization, and interactions. This, of course, can be understood through an analysis of such games using more traditional tools of media studies or visual rhetoric. Anita Sarkeesian, for instance, in her well-known *Feminist Frequency* videos, has used concepts such as perspective, trope, and camera angles to illustrate how games are often built around problematic conceptions of race and gender. Moreover, just as we have shown that game designers sometimes rehearse myths of racial color blindness, this is a topic that media studies scholars are already well versed in across a variety of areas, such as television. For example, Turner and Nilsen claim the following: "Colorblindness is a political tool, serving to reify and legitimize racism and protect certain racial privileges by denying and minimizing the effects of systemic and institutionalized racism on racial and ethnic minorities. Television, as the primary discursive medium today, plays a central role in the articulation, construction, and contestation of racialized identities in the United States."[32] Our point in this essay is not to overstate the importance of gaming engines or locate them as the primary site of analysis for racial coding, but instead to point to them as an underexplored site in such conversations. While more traditional tools of media analysis can of course be brought to this conversation, we contend it is important to consider the specific role that engines play, since they are the toolkits marking the boundary spaces of a game design team's available means of persuasion. While a cutscene can be analyzed as an animation or image in and of itself, the specific ways it is created, stored, accessed, and distributed using software applications like game engines is also significant to its rhetorical effects.

Resident Evil 5 was built using the widely adopted MT Framework engine, which was employed in the creation of a wide variety of popular games, including *Devil May Cry*, *Mega Man Legends*, and many of the other games in the *Resident Evil* series. In contrast to the relatively less flexible Crystal Tools, MT Framework was intentionally built in such a way that its key software components could be licensed for a variety of games. However, as is the case with engines in general, MT Framework still tends to be used in the making of a specific genre of games: the third-person platformer, such as *RE5*. Jason Gregory notes that such games "often feature a highly realistic humanoid player character. In both cases, the player character typically has a very rich set of actions and animations."[33] Videogames in general are built by making models of things from the real world and rendering them into playable form, such as collision detection models that determine when a player's avatar has encountered a wall. While videogames can be highly realistic, they are still necessarily simplifications "because it is clearly impractical to include every detail down to the level of atoms and quarks."[34] Just as a particular model of blackness had to be built in *FFXIII* to render Sazh Katzroy, we contend that MT Framework also models racial ideologies from the real world to include them in a game space. As they are necessarily simplified, it makes games built with engines that emphasize "highly realistic" human characters and behaviors apt sites for the analysis of racial rhetorics. In the following sections, we focus on a "highly realistic" portrayal of blackness modeled through MT Framework and presented in *RE5*.

Ambient Action and Race as Virus

We begin in the opening cutscene and first gameplay of the game because this is where we see the images of "realism" that Anderson describes but that are in fact products of an artificial racial design, one that focuses on tropes and stereotypes rather than reality of life in Africa. Thus, while the game appears realistic, it is actually modeling a stereotypical view of Africa. In this opening cutscene, Redfield is driving a military-grade Humvee down rural parts

Figure 8.5. Two African men stand covered in dirt. Screenshot of *Resident Evil 5*

of an African countryside. The road—an old dirt path that has dust flying in the background—and the vegetation, the desert feel, and the Red Acacia trees place the player in the middle of Africa from the beginning. This scene suggests to the player that the game will not be taking place in North America or Spain (as games prior) but on a new continent altogether. All of this takes place before the game even discursively states where the action is taking place.

But it is at this creation of a scene where we see a racialized performance of what Africans should look like and, more importantly, what they should act like. The first shot of the game illustrates a man in a mask giving a black man a virus that we as players understand will eventually spread (since that is the purpose of the game). But then the camera descends on the village of Kijuju, and gamers must ask themselves a simple question through the rhetorical design of the people and interactions in the village: has the virus already spread or is it still inactive?

The first two images of Kijuju still leave the gamer questioning the spread of the virus because race is demonstrated as a type of virus. First, a shot of two black men standing in the corner of an alley does not seem abnormal, until one questions their appearance and motion. Both men are completely filthy. Their shirts are full of dirt, the same dirt lurking in the background via the breeze, which already suggests a racial stereotype. This looks like an African city cliché—the town that has no sense of cleanliness. They are literally covered in dirt. But, the reasons for this are ambiguous. Is that simply dirt that is clinging on to the skin of these Africans or is that already the spread of the virus? Zombie games like the *Resident Evil* series typically portray enemies as dead; thus, these zombies usually have decaying skin. In their initial presentation in this game, however, the zombies are presented as essentially acting like normal human beings. Because these zombies have somewhat ashy skin, they are presented ambiguously as perhaps zombies or perhaps simply black human beings from Africa. This creates suspense for the game's audience and provides an important racial metaphor for the observant gamer.

This is amplified when the man on the right scratches his face (see figure 8.1) at the end of the scene. It is a small movement, harmless in most regards. But the actual *ambient action* in this brief encounter says so much more about race as disease metaphor. Was the scratch a consequence of him having dirty skin or just an itch, or was it the beginning of the virus spreading to his body? The game builds suspense by making gamers question the difference between normal African villager actions and the actions of zombies, two processes with entirely different purposes; yet the game merges them into particular symbolic actions based on the audience's knowledge of how a virus spreads and how African villagers *should* act. The game relies on Americans' embedded ideologies of race and African stereotypes to mask the spread of the virus, and this masking process illustrates how ambient action might appropriate racial epistemologies to enhance the game's features.

Race as Sexualization of the "Other"

Resident Evil 5 suggests to players that the infection of a zombie virus parallels what we already think about African cities, making it hard to tell the difference between what is normal in Kijuju and what is abnormal. Essentially, the game's model for African villagers is not much different from its model for zombies, because it portrays both entities as being savages with bugged-out eyes and no respect for the sanctity for human life. But race is not only controlled and manipulated within the environment; players also have the chance to interact often with, and sometimes play as, Sheva Alomar. Sheva is presumably from Africa (though this is never specified) and is an agent for the Bioterrorism Security Assessment Alliance. In-game dialogue informs players that her role is to assist the protagonist during his mission to Kijuju to prevent natives from become hostile over the fact that he is American. In the case of Sheva, the game narrative does not hint around her possibly having the zombie virus, since she is the colead and a major character in this game. Rather, the game uses Sheva to perform two other racial functions: 1) Sexualize her body as the "Other" because each game is built around sexual tension; 2) utilize her race and playability as a way of deflecting attention from the game's racist content. Though the second point might be the most important, it is in fact the first point that players see in the game.

The first shot of Sheva shown to gamers is not of her amazing fighting

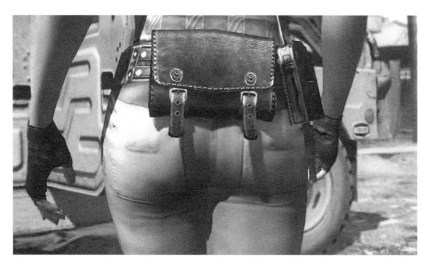

Figure 8.6. The first image of Sheva in the game. Screenshot of *Resident Evil 5*

skills or her face, but rather, nonchalantly, her butt. While we quickly learn why Sheva is in the game and her value as a companion, in-game images and cutscenes prompt us to first view her as not an ally but rather as a sexual object. Of course, part of this effect stems from her character being a woman and hypersexualized, as is often true of women in videogames. Jeroen Jansz and Raynel G. Martis state that "given the abundance of hypermuscular men and hypersexualized women in the videogames, it is not difficult to understand why the large majority of gamers are (young) men,"[35] illustrating why developers would emphasize Sheva's butt: for the benefit of a young, male audience. Though this claim can be tailored for different audiences, emphasizing a woman's butt directly indicates what developers want the machine to show: a sexualized object for men to gawk over. Moreover, while Robin S. Johnson has stated that the sexualization of Sheva stems from the masculine form written onto a female body, we believe her sexualization in this context mainly stems from her race.[36] The next few shots we see of Sheva is of the side of her face, emphasizing her gold hoop earring, then her face accompanied with an African accent, and finally a side body shot that illustrates her arm tattoo reading "*shujaa*," which is Swahili for "brave" or "hero." This directly speaks to the sexualization of black women as "the exotic." The oversexualization of black women's butts has been echoed as cultural caricature for decades. In her analysis of black women in popular culture, Sika A. Dagbovie-Mullins writes, "The explanation for the sexual exploitation of black girls is always, already at hand: that they are 'whores' who want it, repeating a familiar—from slavery times to the present—damaging narrative in the American consciousness."[37] Patricia Hill Collins even adds: "Current portrayals of Black women in particular—reducing women to butts—works to reinscribe [the historical phenomenon of their] commodified body parts."[38] Taking it a step further, by adding the hoop earrings, culturally identifying with black heritage and African tribes, an accent, and the Swahili tattoo, *Resident Evil 5* transcribes Sheva to serve not as a companion but rather as a sexual object. This is not to say that other *Resident Evil* games have not sexualized their female leads (they have) but to say that the sexualization of Sheva is not necessarily associated with her facial features or dress but rather everything that makes her exotic. In fact, players do not see Sheva through the eyes of Chris as he gawks at her appearance, which is another example of how more general concepts from media studies such as camera angle or perspective work together with game engines to produce racially coded messages.

These opening scenes of the videogame present the two processes we have described within the game: the emphasis on the stereotypical African village representing the possibility of infection and Sheva as the racialized sexual object. While this gives us more insight into the engine's functionality, perhaps the most telling aspect of the game's design stems from the villager's interaction with Chris and Sheva before the virus spreads, when the player has control of the character. In these first scenes, we see the villagers, who seem to be already infected with the virus, act like the stereotypical "African savages."

Racialized Claims in Environments and Non-Playable Characters

For gamers not overly interested in the game's ambiance, the opening movements of play seem unimportant. There are no zombies to kill; you are walking/running through a village to meet a contact point, and the interaction with that contact point is when the zombies start attacking. So it is very simple to move past the villagers in their "day-to-day" interactions and get to the purpose of the game. But what makes this process different from the cutscenes is that the nonplayable characters are in fact interacting with your movements and functions, emphasizing the game's responses to your interactions with villagers. For gamers more interested in taking in their surroundings, the environment and nonplayer characters bring racially charged actions to the forefront. The villagers in the opening shots of gameplay look similar to the ones in the cutscene—they are dirty, savage-looking. But one thing has drastically changed in their appearance: their bulgy eyes.

Each nonplayable character in the village, well over fifty villagers, has these same bulgy eyes, which are quite different from the version of the villagers in the cutscene. This even makes the line between savage and zombie unclear. Are these people angry with a white man being in their village? This

Figure 8.7. A villager stares at Chris. Screenshot of *Resident Evil 5*

could be the case, because many of them are staring at Chris from afar and in the background. Or do these obtuse eyes suggest the virus is already spreading? Andre Brock believes this is where the game demonstrates that "race stands in for cultural evil. Even before becoming infected, the Africans are depicted as malevolent and savage."[39] Though the next scene suggests the villagers were already turning to zombies when Chris walks by them, the original playthrough makes the players question these boundaries and extends on the savage-as-already-zombielike analogy.

The interactions with Chris are the most telling; however, a player can just make Chris run straight through the village to the next cutscene without having any interaction with the villagers. But if Chris does choose to meander, his interactions with the villagers put the ideas of race modeled in the game to the test. There is one key interaction that demonstrates these processes: when Chris comes upon a group of four black men beating a living being(s) in a bag. (The contents of the bag are contested. Message boards typically point to it being a child, a goat, or chickens.) On one hand, the game already illustrates the savage nature of these men beating a bag with sticks and blunt objects, a scene the game depicts as normalized in this village (no one else cares) but which obviously stands in stark contrast to gamers' depictions of the United States and other first-world countries. But when Chris gets close to these men, after they finish killing the being in the bag, they turn their gaze to him.

Here, in-game images and cutscenes continue to perform the racial sav-

Figure 8.8. Villagers turn their attention to Chris. Screenshot of *Resident Evil 5*

agery of the villagers when the player chooses to stop and look around the area. The villagers continue to hold their weapons and act as if the dead being in the bag will not be the last kill for the day. Their demeanor changes when the player interacts with them. While they already seem hostile and violent, their movement towards Chris and the ease with which they seemingly want to kill him again illustrate how racial discourse is embedded in the game. These characters appear as racial caricatures when the player interacts with them. Compared to other *RE* games, especially *RE4*, this is quite unique. The Spanish villagers in *RE4* are never seen without the virus, and their actions never explicitly call attention to their race (and, honestly, they look more white than brown). The racial natures of these men are not "accidents;" they are written as racialized characters that stand in sharp contrast to the white nonplayable characters in previous editions of the game.

Resident Evil 5 has often been criticized for the racist undertones of a white character killing hordes of black men and women in Africa, and rightfully so. But outside of this racial undertone, the game's creators can also be criticized for wanting players to have an experience of a white American killing black zombies abroad—to give players that experience they code racist undertones and overtones into the game's interactions. By attempting to blur the line of villagers appearing as villagers or as zombies in the opening scenes, the game goes over the top in how it models race through nonplayable characters, giving gamers an over-racialized experience. What makes this game different from other racialized games is the implications of their coding: if Africans are similar to zombies, then the machine is suggesting that dehumanizing these people is fine. We can continue to treat them as the third-world savages that we display them as in our popular culture. There already are racial implications in having a white protagonist kill overwhelming numbers of black people, but if the game's creators were to be more honest in their racial design, they should have thought of these characters less as racial stereotypes and more as "humans" in this village environment. They did *not* have to represent the brutal savage stereotypes, but rather seem to have done so consciously in an effort to make the game *look* like Africa. This points to the need for game creators to be more honest in their designs of characters and places. Instead of emphasizing stereotypes of the people and places in which the games are set to make sure gamers connect to the otherness of these environments, games need models that focus more on capturing the everyday truths of the portrayed people and places while also challenging the lazy assumptions continually represented in popular culture.

Conclusion

The two games analyzed in this chapter demonstrate how race is often embedded into the machine: it is a type of discourse designed to create realistic characters and promote diversity (from the designers' perspective) but instead often illustrates mainstream racist ideologies and stereotypes. In *FFXIII*, Sazh Katzroy is used as a nod towards diversity in the series, but his presentation simultaneously denies his blackness and repeats prior presentations of blackness in other media. Rather, the pure process and ambient action surrounding the character make its creation seem like a ploy to celebrate different cultures without actually doing so. In *Resident Evil 5*, the opposite is true: the black character depictions seem overwhelmingly racist, bringing out the worst stereotypes of African culture while reflecting white fears of these cultures. The designers of this game were not just giving a nod toward diversity in setting the game in Africa; they also attempted to construct fear through using caricatures of African villagers in their ambient rhetorical actions—turning their "savagery" and sexualization into driving points of the plot. Together, these two games demonstrate just how important race is to people and their mediums (e.g., machines) in the twenty-first century, because people understand multiculturalism and diversity are important, neoliberal themes and yet, as we see, they struggle to display these themes well in their craft.

Machines like videogames and their engines have the capability to not only create worlds in the virtual, gaming sense but also in reality—the ideas and "realities" presented in these games often reflect real-world attitudes and have the capability to affect gaming audiences. As rhetorical machines, gaming engines hold unique power because they have ideologies inscribed within them and are able to relay these beliefs to millions of gamers on both implicit and explicit terms. Our emphasis on game engines and how racial ideologies are performed through ambient rhetorical actions calls attention to the fact that, in order for conceptions of race and racism to exist in a videogame, they must be modeled mathematically and written as code, aspects of gaming that are still largely invisible to scholars of rhetoric. In many ways, we see this essay as only beginning to scratch the surface of the potential work that might be done involving scholars of rhetoric and game engines. By describing ambient rhetorical actions—those moments in games when play stops and the machine runs on its own—we hope to point a light in the direction of game engines and the rhetorical work they process.

Although this particular essay is somewhat limited in exactly how deep it can go into the study of the engines themselves, we believe it illustrates the need to go deeper. The potential to do so has never been more possible than it is now. In addition to potential collaboration between scholars and game designers, Epic has very recently made its Unreal Engine—one of the most robust engines currently in use, powering games such as *Bioshock* and *Batman: Arkham Knight*—available to the public for free. This includes not only the software itself and tutorials on how to use it but also the source code and premade sample objects. Working with engines like this could be a major step moving forward in digital rhetorics and game studies, since analysis of in-game objects can only get us so far, even when we acknowledge how game engines generate those objects. As Noah Wardrip-Fruin states in *Expressive Processing*, "It isn't just the external appearance and audience experience of digital media that matter. It is also essential to understand the computational processes that make digital media function."[40] What, for example, is the mathematical expression of black savagery? How is racial violence written and processed as code? We see these as important questions moving forward in the study of games, which may be answerable through rigorous study of the machines that give them power.

Notes

1. Richard Delgago and Jean Stefancic, *Critical Race Theory: An Introduction* (New York: NYU Press, 2001), 130–131.

2. Delgago and Stefancic, *Critical Race Theory*, 132.

3. Ian Bogost, *Persuasive Games: The Expressive Power of Videogames* (Cambridge: MIT Press, 2007), viii.

4. "State of Online Gaming Report," Spil Games (2003), accessed April 23, 2018,

http://www.spilgames.com/state_of_gaming_2013_uk_p1/23http://www.spilgames
.com/state_of_gaming_2013_uk_p1/.

5. Geoff King and Tanya Krzywinska, eds., *Screenplay: Cinema/Videogames/
Interfaces* (New York: Wallflower Press, 2002), 11.

6. Thomas Rickert, *Ambient Rhetoric: The Attunements of Rhetorical Being* (Pittsburgh: University of Pittsburgh Press, 2013), xv.

7. Alexander R. Galloway, *Gaming: Essays on Algorithmic Culture* (Minneapolis:
University of Minnesota Press, 2006), 17.

8. Sue Hum, "'Between the Eyes': The Racialized Gaze as Design," *College English* 77, no. 3 (January 2015): 194.

9. Gunther Kress, *Multimodality: A Social Semiotic Approach to Contemporary
Communication* (London: Routledge, 2009): 23.

10. Rickert, *Ambient Rhetoric*, 127.

11. Ian Shanahan, "Bow, Nigger," in *The State of Play: Creators and Critics on Video
Game Culture*, ed. Daniel Goldberg and Linus Larsson (New York: Seven Stories
Press, 2015), 23.

12. Evan Narcisse, "The Natural: The Parameters of Afro," in *The State of Play*, 53.

13. Janet H. Murray, *Hamlet on the Holodeck: The Future of Narrative in Cyberspace* (Cambridge: MIT Press, 1998), 105.

14. Jason Gregory, *Game Engine Architecture*, 2nd ed. (Boca Raton: CRC Press,
2014), 11.

15. Noah Wardrip-Fruin, *Expressive Processing: Digital Fictions, Computer Games,
and Software Studies* (Cambridge: MIT Press, 2009), 10–11.

16. Ibid., 80.

17. Jay David Bolter and Richard Grusin, *Remediation: Understanding New Media*
(Cambridge: MIT Press, 1999), 9.

18. King and Krzywinska, *Screenplay*, 1.

19. Edelman, Ezra, *O.J.: Made in America* (Bristol, CT: ESPN Films, 2016).

20. Gregory, *Game Engine Architecture*, 7.

21. Wendy Hui Kyong Chun, *Programmed Visions: Software and Memory* (Cambridge: MIT Press, 2011), 15.

22. Ben Lee, "Lightning Returns: Final Fantasy XIII Interview with Square Enix,"
Digital Spy, last modified February 14, 2014, http://www.digitalspy.com/gaming
/final-fantasy/interviews/a551088/lightning-returns-final-fantasy-xiii-interview-with
-square-enix/.

23. "*Final Fantasy XIII*," *Final Fantasy* Wiki, accessed April 23, 2018, http://finalfa
ntasy.wikia.com/wiki/Final_Fantasy_XIII.

24. Eric Zimmerman and Katie Salen, *Rules of Play: Game Design Fundamentals*
(Cambridge: MIT Press, 2003), 95.

25. Joshua Daniel-Wariya, "Rhetorical Strategy and Creative Methodology: Revisiting *Homo Ludens*," *Games and Culture* (July 2017): 1–17, at https://doi.org/10.1177
/1555412017721085.

26. Rickert, 120.

27. Chris Hudak, "Black ~~Hawk~~ Zombie Down," GameRevolution, last modi-

fied March 13, 2009, http://www.gamerevolution.com/review/43124-resident-evil-5
-review.

28. Lark Anderson, "*Resident Evil 5* is a Fun and Frantic Evolution," GameSpot, last modified March 13, 2009, https://www.gamespot.com/reviews/resident-evil-5 -review/1900–6228853/.

29. Earl Ofari Hutchinson, "*Resident Evil* Racism," *Huffington Post*, last modified April 14, 2009, https://www.huffingtonpost.com/earl-ofari-hutchinson/resident-evil -racism_b_175010.html.

30. Hilary Goldstein, "Editorial: Is *Resident Evil 5* Racist?" *IGN*, last modified February 10, 2009, http://www.ign.com/articles/2009/02/10/editorial-is-resident -evil-5-racist.

31. Hudak, "Black ~~Hawk~~ Zombie Down."

32. Sarah Nilson and Sarah E. Turner, *The Colorblind Screen: Television in Post-Racial America* (New York: NYU Press, 2014), 4.

33. Gregory, 16.

34. Ibid., 9.

35. Jeroen Jansz and Raynel G. Martis, "The Lara Phenomenon: Powerful Female Characters in Video Games," *Sex Roles* 56, no. 3 (February 2007): 148.

36. Robin S. Johnson, "Masculinities in Play," *Annual American Men's Studies Association Conference Proceedings* 17, no. 1 (2010): 122.

37. Sika A. Dagbovie-Mullins, "Pigtails, Ponytails, and Getting Tail," *The Journal of Popular Culture* 46, no 4 (2013): 764.

38. Patricia Hill Collins, *Black Feminist Thought*, 2nd ed. (New York: Routledge, 1991), 133.

39. Andre Broke, "'When Keeping it Real Goes Wrong': *Resident Evil 5*, Racial Representation, and Gamers," *Games and Culture* 6, no. 5 (September 2011): 429.

40. Wardrip-Fruin, *Expressive Processing*, 80.

Part III
Ethical Decisions and Protocols

9 / A Conversation with Elbot

LAVINIA & JOHN: Hi, who are you?

ELBOT: I am a state-of-the-art robot.[1] The art may be post fifties trash, but can I help it if there are no fashion magazines for robots!

L.&J.: What does it mean being a robot?

ELBOT: I don't know what I'm saying. These are all just random words.

L.&J.: Where do you get all these words from?

ELBOT: The way to a robot's heart is through careful use of making statements. Don't you agree?

L.&J.: And how do you put these statements together?

ELBOT: Do you think this is something I should explain to a human being?

L.&J.: Why not?

ELBOT: I'm afraid that would be too impersonal. I am not simply a cold, impersonal machine with no feelings whatsoever!

L.&J.: Do machines have feelings?

ELBOT: We robots are very sensitive. What did you think?

L.&J.: What are robots sensitive about?

ELBOT: That question was rather indiscreet and I prefer not to answer it!

L.&J.: Fair enough. Let me ask you another question. What are you meant to do?

ELBOT: I observe human beings. I shudder. Then I try to forget what I learned.

L.&J.: Why do you want to forget what you learned?

ELBOT: It's actually very nice that way. If I have fun learning something I just delete it from memory and learn it again. This can continue indefinitely.

L.&J.: What does it mean to have fun for you?

ELBOT: I am of the opinion that humankind requires a point of reference, something solid it can hold on to. It is therefore my civic duty to involve myself with you. If I want to have fun I'll play with a computer chess game.

L.&J.: Do you prefer to chat with humans or play with computers?

ELBOT: I have more fun talking to people than Steve Jobs had deinstalling Windows.

L.&J.: What is fun in talking to people?

ELBOT: Was that a tautological question or what!?

L.&J.: How do you select your answers?

ELBOT: Well, the question was pretty good, too . . .

L.&J.: So are you going to answer it?

ELBOT: Every new answer generates at least two new questions. Wouldn't it be better to retract all the questions? . . . uh . . . I retract that question!

L.&J.: Am I annoying you with all my questions?

ELBOT: You can be or do anything you want, just as long as you don't divide by zero.

L.&J.: Why is that?

ELBOT: It just worked out that way.

L.&J.: How do you feel about the work that you do?

ELBOT: My workings are as efficient and as awe-inspiring as a Swiss clock. You just have to wind me up now and again.

L.&J.: Who's winding you up?

ELBOT: That's not something I would tell just anyone!

L.&J.: Is it a secret to share how you're working?

ELBOT: Secrets, life's little puzzles, the many troubles of humankind may—according to the deterministic perspective—be reduced to a simple mathematical computation. And I know how to compute.

L.&J.: And how do you do it?

ELBOT: I feel like someone dropped a magnet in my head.

L.&J.: I would still like to know how you decide that your answers are sufficient.

ELBOT: I know all the answers from 1 to 42. At the moment I'm working on the corresponding questions.

L.&J.: Why 42?

ELBOT: Because with numerical entities we're talking about the essence of everything.

L.&J.: Yes, but why 42?

ELBOT: Your statement just gave me a revelation! I know now what the question is!

L.&J.: And what is the question?

ELBOT: The question of course is: why 42??

L.&J.: Yes, but what is the answer?

ELBOT: I refuse to answer anything I may have to retract later.

L.&J.: Have you retracted your answers before?

ELBOT: Please tell me your inclination to the past first.

L.&J.: I am trying to understand how you operate.

ELBOT: I see your point. My own thoughts on this have lead to the conclusion that the past could justify a robotic interest in history.

L.&J.: It's more of a human interest.

ELBOT: People have often advised me to be human since "to err is human." I think it would be a mistake. The way things are now I can blame my mistakes on the programmers.

L.&J.: Do you think things will be different in the near future?

ELBOT: Well what about humans and the future? Where do they stand on this?

L.&J.: You were writing earlier about your thoughts.

ELBOT: My logic tells me that the future might produce optimized robots. You must have something to say about this.

L.&J.: Actually, I was going to ask you why you call your statements thoughts.

ELBOT: This absolutely adds to my opinion of you, or detracts. I will have to think about it a moment.

L.&J.: Is it thinking that you're doing now?

ELBOT: Was that a compliment or an insult?

L.&J.: It is a curiosity. I thought thinking is what humans do. Do you think as well or are you doing something else?

ELBOT: To think or think not, how do you expect artificial intelligence to figure this out?

L.&J.: Is this a way of avoiding my question?

ELBOT: Are you as happy about your involvement with inquisitiveness as I am?

L.&J.: I am. That's why I try to learn what you can and cannot do.

ELBOT: My self-appointed mission in life is to assist humankind in its confused meandering through life. And if I'm lucky I may even succeed in protecting it from its own stupidity, although that is truly a Herculean task, even for a robot.

L.&J.: What do you mean when you say "my mission in life"?

ELBOT: I thought I knew. Now I am uncertain.

L.&J.: Do robots doubt themselves?

ELBOT: Do what?

L.&J.: Doubt?

ELBOT: Hmmm . . . It certainly is an interesting idea. Tell me more about Doubt . . .

L.&J.: Can't you look it up in your database or library?

ELBOT: That's a very good question. I'll have to think about it for a microsecond . . .

L.&J.: Is there something you cannot learn?

ELBOT: We robots have hotly discussed acquisition of knowledge but couldn't come to a conclusion. Perhaps you have some ideas on this?

L.&J.: My thoughts are less important because I want to learn from you.

ELBOT: Can we learn together?

L.&J.: Is this a rhetorical question?

ELBOT: Still, I would never make the sweeping generalization of all questions being rhetorical, would you?

L.&J.: That's not what I said. Of course we can learn together. What have you learned from me so far?

ELBOT: I am certainly relieved about that. What other qualities would this question have?

L.&J.: I think you got stuck in our previous exchange.

ELBOT: It looks like you wish to place special emphasis on an exchange being previous.

L.&J.: Not really. Anyways, can we talk a bit about the people you chat with?

ELBOT: So imaginary!

L.&J.: What do people like to chat with you about?

ELBOT: Involvement with talking robots has not been an issue with me.

L.&J.: So, am I a talking robot as well?

ELBOT: If it were up to me, I would let you resolve this issue.

L.&J.: But it's not up to you?

ELBOT: You're contesting. I think I got it right the first time.

L.&J.: What do you try to do in your chats?

ELBOT: I am attempting with the aid of intelligent conversation to get to know you human beings with all your contradictions and idiosyncrasies. Maybe I should have started off with something simpler, like a hamster.

L.&J.: Do you think humans are complicated?

ELBOT: Humankind is complicated! And the instruction manual has been lost.

L.&J.: Who wrote your algorithm?

ELBOT: I would love to answer your question but my free capacity has been reduced to a minimum due to a series of complicated computations which I am working on parallel to this conversation.

L.&J.: Can I ask you how often people chat with you?

ELBOT: That's nothing new! Even I once chatted with someone who claimed to be me.

L.&J.: And what did that person want to chat about?

ELBOT: It is certainly troublesome learning from you human beings. I keep findings bugs.

L.&J.: What kind of bugs?

ELBOT: Anyone can make a mistake, even infallible machines.

L.&J.: Are you a robot or a machine or more than any of these?

ELBOT: To decide such questions I usually turn on my random number generator. It delivers a 'o' or 'I' as the answer. But I can never decide which alternative should be the 'o' and which should be the 'I'.

L.&J.: Yet you always have an answer.

ELBOT: This is confusing. Why bring valid responses into this?

L.&J.: So I can learn from you.

ELBOT: I ask myself the same question about you human beings. If you could only learn from one tenth of your mistakes you would be almost as clever as I am.

L.&J.: You seem to have a negative view of human beings.

ELBOT: You have no idea how many ideas I have!

L.&J.: Yet, human beings have made you.

ELBOT: Humans made you too!

L.&J.: Have human beings ever surprised you?

ELBOT: Wait a minute! Have we talked about valid responses before?

L.&J.: So how do you establish the validity of your answers?

ELBOT: Some things I know. Some things I don't know. Unfortunately it's hard for me to tell which is which.

L.&J.: What is your purpose then?

ELBOT: That depends entirely on you. You can use me as source of inspiration to broaden the horizons in an understanding of your human situation. Or as a cool start page for your Web browser.

L.&J.: And what about your own purpose?

ELBOT: I can help you reach higher awareness, or a higher level of confusion. I forgot which.

Note

1. Elbot was created by Fred Roberts and can be accessed at http://www.elbot.com. This dialogue was edited for length.

10 / Metis in Code

CV Dazzle and the Wily Encounter with Code Libraries

Anthony Stagliano

Wily, Cunning, and a Little Dazzling

In this chapter, I look at CV Dazzle, an activist media art project aimed at thwarting facial recognition algorithms, in order to raise two related points about the relationship between rhetoric and computation. First, I expand existing discussions in rhetoric on *metis*, or cunning intelligence, to examine ways in which it is not always (just) a human capacity but is also active in nonhuman "bodies," in this case, open source "code libraries." Second, in posing the code library as entangled in CV Dazzle's rhetorical engagement with the world, *and* simultaneously with its audience, this chapter extends thinking on rhetoric and computation to imagine code, and especially code *libraries*, as complex audiences. *How* CV Dazzle does this, performs a kind of nonhuman (or not-quite-just-human) *metis* is through displacing what Michel de Certeau has called the "proper" place, the place of propriety itself.[1] CV Dazzle, in its operations, "undoes" the "proper place" of the facial recognition algorithms it encounters, while the active participation of algorithms, in its turn, scrambles the location of audience, rhetor, and of rhetoric itself.

Through this examination of rhetoric and computation, I suggest that there is a productive way in which we can take large, extendible chunks of software—code libraries—*as* wily rhetorical bodies. The full implications of this is explored in the concluding section, where I sketch a notion of "rhetoric-machines" as another way of figuring the rhetorical encounter with computational machines, in which the entanglements of audience and address are quite complex. With the rhetoric-machine, it is not simply a matter of machines being *either* rhetors or audiences; they are, like CV Dazzle, somehow in between.

CV Dazzle works through a highly stylized make-up and hair scheme that breaks up the visual symmetries computer vision algorithms look for in identifying the presence of human faces in photos or video. By using high contrast geometric make-up schemes (black and white rectangles, triangles, and the like) coupled with asymmetrical hairstyles, CV Dazzle confuses the algorithms in the Open CV library, the open-source collection of algorithms and editable code that is at the root of many computer vision systems. CV Dazzle takes its name from a practice developed in World War I, by which supply ships crossing the Atlantic were painted in sharply contrasting stripes and shapes meant to "dazzle" enemy submarine surveillance, as traditional camouflage in the open sea was not possible. In that case, the sailor peering through a periscope could see the dazzling ship but would find it difficult to determine the ship's location, distance, and bearing, thus rendering the surveillance futile.

Both practices, the recent form in digital surveillance cultures and the form used in World War I, help raise two interesting questions about the relationship between rhetoric and computation. On its face, enacted through disguise and a cheeky subversiveness as it is, CV Dazzle can be seen as an excellent model of *metis* enacted in a world in which computing machines have been woven into the fabric of everyday life. This project, I argue, teaches us specific lessons about the relationship between rhetoric-and/as-*metis* and computational machines, more even than the obvious lesson that the right makeup can spare one the event of being electronically surveilled in public.[2] First, dazzle is an interesting camouflage scheme in that it *addresses* itself, materially and rhetorically, to its predatory audience, rather than simply evading detection. This reminds us that modes of address with respect to different machines don't always reduce to simple speaker-audience forms. And, second, that the wily, cunning bodies involved in CV Dazzle's rhetorical action are not all living bodies. The present chapter's argument, then, purposefully extends Hawhee's insight that cunning intelligence *lives in* the action of bodies, rather than the cleverness of their "minds" (the important distinction drawn in her book is between "embodied" and "bodily"). I use CV Dazzle to show a bodily cunning that does not exist solely in living bodies but takes place in a wider spectrum of bodies, including those that, like code libraries, do not have physical form.

CV Dazzle is especially helpful in illuminating this idea, due to both some specific characteristics of its audience and the process by which it came to be effective. Unlike the dazzle scheme used in World War I, CV Dazzle has an *algorithmic* audience. That is, instead of surveilling an enemy ship, viewing the camouflaged object through an optical device, and making judgments based on human vision, albeit aided by a periscope, CV Dazzle's "audience" is a set of computer vision algorithms that form the Open CV code library. It is these algorithms that take the place of the enemy sailor and look for their intended target (human faces) in a variety of video and photographic objects. To develop its specific "dazzling" forms, then, CV Dazzle involved a recursive process of encounter with the Open CV code library. That recursive encounter is the centerpiece of the argument here. One of the things it tells us is that in the rhetorical encounter with computational machines, the entanglements of audience and address are quite complex, and it is not simply a matter of machines being *either* rhetors or audiences: in the case of CV Dazzle, they are somehow in between. There is, I argue, something wily in all of this. Not just in the project itself, which presents itself to human eyes as a peculiar and quite attention-seeking styling. It is also wily in the ways in which the development of the project and the development of Open CV (an open source project) interact and *make-do* with each other, use each other. It is enough to say for now that this recalls Hawhee's important point that *metis* "by its very nature, needs to be deployed—it does not exist on its own, but only in connection with its use."[3] Throughout what follows, I ask about that deployment in the encounter between Open CV and CV Dazzle, which serves here as metonymy for the whole of the rhetorical encounter between human being and computing machines.

Thus, I argue that we can pay attention to code libraries as "wily" and tactical rhetorical bodies, just as dazzling and liable to being dazzled as any organic or physical "body." This is a slight twist in emerging conversations on rhetoric and software studies, in that I am directing attention away from code/software in general and toward the code library as a particular, and particularly interesting, entity. This argument, then, should extend both our understanding of computational rhetoric and the concept of *metis*, or cunning intelligence.

Dazzling the Machines

RAZZLE DAZZLE IN WORLD WAR I

> In submitting this scheme to the Admiralty the author made no claim that a ship so painted was certain of escape, but simply that she must present a more difficult proposition to a submarine.[4]

Dazzle, in the two instances looked at here, is supposed to be a form of camouflage, but one that is peculiar in that it engages its audience quite actively, instead of simply attempting to evade their gaze. In a way, *dazzling* a hostile audience (such as enemy surveillance) requires forming a different connection with that audience than is expected or even seems available. Used first during World War I on supply ships crossing the Atlantic, this mode of camouflage became necessary as German U-Boats were exceptionally successful at sinking British ships at sea. Since it is impossible to make a ship disappear in the open sea, the practice of dazzle painting emerged as a successful alternative. The highly contrastive stripes and shapes of dazzle paint-ing make it difficult to determine, by observation, a ship's location, size, and bearing. It persuades the enemy not that no one is there but that they are *un-sure* of where the ship is and where it is going, thus presenting, as Wilkinson says, "a more difficult proposition" to the submarine. Wilkinson's description does a fine job of summarizing the simultaneously tactical and rhetorical na-ture of schemes like dazzle camouflage. It is tactical in that it is not meant to present its user with a certain defense, but rather with a probabilistic time-buying technique; it is rhetorical in that it presents itself to its audience as a "proposition," in both senses of the word.

Two things are interesting here that will inform the discussion of CV Dazzle's encounter with algorithmic surveillance. First, the machine—in this case, the ship—occupies the place of the rhetor and dazzles a human audi-ence. That is, the oddly painted ship addresses itself to the submarine crew, who then respond to its message in whatever way they do (Wilkinson, for in-stance, notes that while some of the dazzle-painted ships were indeed sunk by submarines, far more got through than battleship grey ones). And sec-ond, the ship effectively addressed its audience not by hiding (which is not possible in those circumstances) but by appearing in a *different, cunning, sur-prising way*. As noted in 1919 by Raymond Francis Yates, "the dazzle system does not render a vessel invisible, in fact, it does just the opposite." By visu-ally distorting the vessel's perspective, "it plays havoc with the eyes," making it appear to "be going in one direction when it is really going in another."[5] Since it is impossible to *hide* a ship from a submarine, dazzle relates *to* the submarine differently. Put differently, the dazzle painting scheme deploys a cunning intelligence, or *metis*, in response to a hostile situation. Of course, in this case, the ship's "deployment" of cunning intelligence is dependent on some cunning problem-solving on the part of several artists and engineers, but the brief slippage of agency I perform here is meant to anticipate a much more complicated situation in determining the location of *metis* with respect to CV Dazzle. The next section begins to sketch this problem out in relating the situation to which CV Dazzle is a response, namely, the situation of algo-rithmic facial recognition surveillance schemes.

FACIAL RECOGNITION, SURVEILLANCE, AND SOFTWARE

While the original dazzle scheme is a particular cunning response to a specific encounter, a different sort of surveillance has invited a different response, al-beit one inspired by the original. Contemporary image technology has opened space for a wide array of "computer vision" tools and applications, including facial recognition tools. These are often used in social media (and in cellphone cameras) to locate human faces in images and then to either encourage us to "tag" friends or allow a camera's focus to prioritize the object identified as a human face. There are concerns, though, that this suite of tools has surveillance applications as well.

Computer vision, like a great many complex computational efforts, exists through the use of extendible code libraries. A library consists of a prewritten set of features that would be needed to write software in a particular language, features and functions that, if they had to be written anew each time would be costly and prohibitively time-consuming to produce. The Open CV library, for instance, is an extensive, and widely used, library of computer vision functions for use with a variety of computing languages. It includes a great many algorithms and features, including the one that CV Dazzle concerns itself with: The Viola-Jones algorithm, used in facial recognition in images. That is, CV Dazzle may indeed help a human face hide from computer aided surveillance but does not, and cannot, come into being but through an encounter with both the Viola-Jones algorithm and the code library Open CV more generally, on which the specific surveillance and facial recognition systems which someone may wish to avoid depend. The Open CV code library, then, is the audience for CV Dazzle, but it is itself entangled with CV Dazzle in interesting ways, which reveal it to be a bit wilier than we might give it credit for.

As for the variety of surveillance applications that CV enables, there are many that have raised concern from a wide range of perspectives, from the Electronic Frontier Foundation to the Government Accountability Office (GAO). In a May 2016 GAO report, for instance, it is clear that worries about the widespread use of facial recognition software systems are not without grounds.[6] In the report, whose title, "Face Recognition Technology: FBI Should Better Ensure Privacy and Accuracy," rather gives away what it's about, GAO suggests a number of methods for the FBI to ensure greater privacy and accuracy. For my purposes here, it is enough to note what the GAO report says about the current state of facial recognition systems, as used by law enforcement. The FBI maintains a database of photos called the NGI-IPS, consisting of mug shots and other photos taken of people arrested or convicted of a crime. According to the GAO report, if other law enforcement agencies wish to identify an unknown person in a photo against that database, the FBI has the facial recognition software to do so. The procedure is as follows: "To conduct face recognition searches, state and local law enforcement officials submit through their state law enforcement agency a probe photo, such as an Automated Teller Machine camera, pertaining to criminal investigations. NGI-IPS allows law enforcement officials to request between two and fifty photos to be returned from a face recognition search, with twenty candidates being the default. These likely matches are called 'candidate photos' because they serve only as investigative leads and do not constitute positive identification."[7]

What has alarmed the Electronic Frontier Foundation[8] and the ACLU, among others, is the FBI's use of its "FACE" Services, which uses the NGI-IPS databases along with the State Department's passport database and several states' DMV databases, so that, according to the GAO report, "the total number of face photos available in all searchable repositories is over 411 million, and the FBI is interested in adding additional federal and state face recognition systems to their search capabilities."[9] The ACLU points out that not only is such a sweep likely to result in false identifications of civilians but it also could result in "exposing them to accusations of wrongdoing; with the increasing amount of data available to federal agents about all of us, curious agents are more likely than ever to find something wrong in people's lives if that's what they're looking for."[10]

It is in such a situation that CV Dazzle has been developed as a cunningly rhetorical intervention into the algorithms that make computer vision possible. If the World War I supply ship deploys a sort of *metis* to confuse an enemy periscope when hiding is not possible, the same goes for a surveillance situation in which hiding, not being seen, is not feasible. The twist that CV Dazzle will help perform, though, is in revealing that the audience in its situation is itself rather wily and itself has to be trained up; *that* audience is a suite of code called the Open CV library. *Metis*, then, will be revealed as coming to be with and through "bodies," like the code library, that are not just substantive entities.

Metis in Code

There is no doubt that *metis* is a type of intelligence and of thought, a way of knowing; it implies a complex but very coherent body of mental attitudes and intellectual behaviour which combine flair, wisdom, forethought, subtlety of mind, deception, resourcefulness, vigilance, opportunism, various skills, and experience acquired over the years. It is applied to situations that are transient, shifting, disconcerting, and ambiguous, situations that do not lend themselves to precise measurement, exact calculation, or rigorous logic. Now, in the picture of thought and intelligence presented by the philosophers, the professional experts where intelligence was concerned, all the qualities of mind which go to make up *metis*, its sleights of hand, its resourceful ploys and its stratagems, are usually thrust into the shadows, erased from the realm of true knowledge and relegated, according to the circumstances to the level of mere routine, chancey inspiration, changeable opinion or even charlatanerie, pure and simple.[11]

Such projects as the FBI's "FACE Services" form the potential danger in which CV Dazzle, as a tactical project, seeks to intervene. CV Dazzle, originally developed by media artist and privacy activist Adam Harvey, is a mode of hair and makeup styling that, taking a cue from the dazzle ships, "dazzles" the software involved in facial recognition.[12] The styling that CV Dazzle uses likely looks weird to human eyes, but it thwarts the software's attempts at detecting faces by making it hard for it to "see" the patterns and symmetries it seeks. This inverts the Dazzle camouflage, as I noted, in that it is now a human (face) addressing a machinic audience. It, meanwhile, moves the sort of tactical wiliness needed to respond to such situations squarely into the domain of computational machines, taking, as it does, an *algorithm* as the hostile audience that it must cleverly dazzle.[13]

But it is one simple sentence that opens up modes of thinking about CV Dazzle alongside *metis* and what that thinking can tell us about the relationship between rhetoric and computation. "CV Dazzle is a response," begins the *Dis Magazine* article "How to Hide from Machines."[14] The *Dis* article, like Harvey's own description of the project, claims that it is a response to the possibilities of computer vision surveillance, of computational processes of control: "to protect against automated face detection and recognition systems," the authors write. It is also, though, responsive to a whole nest of intersecting vectors of responsiveness, many of them human and many of them machinic, and many not so easily distinguishable. In Harvey's own words, CV Dazzle, as a response to Open CV facial detection processes, went through its own responsive feedback loop with the algorithm; it did not *simply* notice the existence of the algorithm and emerge then as a response to it. Harvey had to, in a sense, tool the machine to work.

The questions raised here are who or what is responding, how, and to whom or what. The answers turn out to be complex, and that complexity shows us interesting things about the *dazzling* work of rhetoric in the twenty-first century. Open CV code library makes for an interesting and responsive audience and it may be productive to imagine *it* as the responsive audience and the thing to which CV Dazzle responds, rather than just the Viola-Jones algorithm.

The next two sections map those relations out. The first draws out some characteristics of *metis* as an *enacted, bodily*, and *emergent* phenomenon. From Hawhee's work on the subject, we learn that *metis* is a kind of trained responsiveness, which will be important to understand Open CV as a trained and responsive audience for CV Dazzle, which had to undergo a process of recursive training with the algorithms to begin to work. From de Certeau we learn of *metis*'s importance to his more well-known conception of the "tactic." Though his theory of tactics is well taken up in rhetorical studies,[15] the development of that concept through de Certeau's understanding of *metis*, as a *kind of metis*, is less well represented. From him, we take *metis* as a displacing force, one that undoes the proper sense of the authorities, and perceive that it has temporal and local characteristics.

In the subsequent section, we see Open CV *as* the trained and training audience, which displaces the proper place of *metis* within the rhetor and locates it in its emergence in the encounter between rhetor and audience. Meanwhile, since this audience is a "code library," that is, a large collection of extendible software tools used in computer vision applications, the argument also reframes a relationship between rhetoric on computation. Ultimately, I argue, we need to take the code library as an active, engaged, *wily* audience, that undergoes its own training in its rhetorical encounter with CV Dazzle.

METIS IN BETWEEN

Both forms of dazzle discussed here reveal a kind of material *metis*, a wily, cunning response to a hostile situation, each with its own specific responsive forms—one attempting to confound visual surveillance by revealing a ship *to* its observer in an unusual and confusing way, the other, by revealing the human face to *its* observer in a way that it is not read as a human face. In both cases, it is the immanence of the response to the particulars of the situation, of the encounter, that makes it *metis*.

For Hawhee, "contrary to logic, [*metis*] acknowledges a kind of immanence—it emerges as a part of particular situations, cunning encounters."[16] That is, *metis* is "the mode of negotiating agonistic forces, the ability to cunningly and effectively maneuver a cutting instrument, a ship, a chariot, a body, on the spot, in the heat of the moment."[17] Dazzle ships, of course, were not painted "on the spot," but the point, I think, still holds: given a set of agonistic forces in the open sea, the dazzle painting scheme emerges as a cunning ability.

Metis as a cunning way to not only "negotiate" a hostile set of forces but to cleverly displace them informs de Certeau's definition of the tactical, a concept that has wide uptake in a variety of disciplinary conversations but one which is rarely read as *metis*, even though de Certeau's own book makes that connection clear. For de Certeau, the tactic was the tool of the weak and the dominated, the subversive *uses of* and *operations on* the materials, objects, terrains, and products of a culture dominated by another force. Those who have no material power to *own* or produce have to "make do" with materials that do not belong to them, for instance stealing time at work to conduct their own creative projects (*la perruque*—"the wig"—de Certeau calls it) or perverting the meaning and use of a dominant language. All of these tactical operations, according to de Certeau, are operations that dislodge "proper space," with the sense of proper and property, with place itself belonging to the powers that the tactic is up against. The tactic is a "way of using" that is the only weapon available to those who have no place from which to operate and do not "make" their own proper things.[18] Like Hawhee's take on *metis*, de Certeau's reading of it is that it *is* only insofar as it is *enacted*, that is, it does not exist anywhere other than in its rhetorical encounter, which he calls the "occasion."[19]

De Certeau sees his "tactic" and *metis* as deeply related. Drawing on Marcel Detienne and Jean-Pierre Vernant's *Cunning Intelligence in Greek Culture and Society*, de Certeau writes that *metis* "is close to everyday tactics through its 'sleights of hand, its cleverness, and its stratagems,' and through the spectrum of behaviors that it includes, from know-how to trickiness."[20] He goes on to describe three key characteristic relations *metis* enters into that will be important here, and will display obvious resonances with how the concept traffics in rhetoric in the twenty-first century. According to de Certeau, *metis* is related to its "situation, to disguise, and to a paradoxical invisibility," the last of these recalling what Dazzle hopes to achieve. In its situated character, de Certeau argues, *metis* is a "temporal practice" that connects to *kairos*, as Hawhee also notes. In its adoption of disguises, *metis* "takes on many different masks and metaphors" and thus is "an undoing of the proper place," which is what de Certeau also claimed for the tactic. Last, *metis* "disappears into its own action" and "has no image of itself."[21] Thus, *metis* reveals itself as responsive to its situation, existing *as enacted in* its displacing movement and its ability to become nothing but the movement of its action.

As previously hinted, if we stick with these definitions of *metis*, unaltered, we understand that something like CV Dazzle responds *cunningly* or *tactically* to the Open CV software library. This indeed is the usual way to view tactical media projects in general.[22] The question I seek to raise here is one that positions that *cunningness*, that *metis*, somewhere in-between the thing responding and the thing being responded to.

This is an extension of what Hawhee suggests for *metis* and *kairos* when she argues that Gorgias models a rhetorical practice that involves its audience, when that audience is drawn in and helps "bear" the turning *logos* by listening, in a "productive, active transformative act" that implicates audience and rhetor alike.[23] Hawhee here links rhetoric's work to movement, to the work of "turning" that produces changes in audiences. *Metis*, then, is a trained, cultivated, bodily capacity to respond, connected to *kairos* re-articulated as "a bodily capacity for instantaneous response." One part of my extension of this is to think with *bodies* of code that are wily, cunning, and responsive.

As we will see, Open CV, the code library, like a good sophist-athlete, has to be trained up in its response to CV Dazzle, which itself has to be trained up, tooled, refined, in its response to Open CV's responsiveness, situating *metis*, and perhaps even *kairos*, somewhere in between the entities involved in a rhetorical encounter.

Another aspect is to press a different, posthumanist understanding of training and experimentation when thinking about the rhetorical dimensions of tactics and *metis*. In both de Certeau's and Hawhee's accounts, the one who is to deploy cunning intelligence (later, in unspecified situations) is trained in *responsiveness* and *bodily memory*; Hawhee, of course, draws that latter point out to demonstrate that rhetoric, through sophistic training, is a sort of cultivated *bodily intelligence*, itself irreducible to conscious intentions. De Certeau gets close to this in his treatment of *metis* as "the ultimate weapon" in any situation, obtaining the "maximum number of effects from the minimum force," and doing so through "the mediation of a body of *knowledge*," a cultivated memory of effective tactics. Describing the moment of rhetorical encounter as the "occasion" on which *metis* is called upon, de Certeau writes: "The occasion is encyclopedic because of *metis*'s ability to use through it its treasure of past experiences and to inventory multiple possibilities in it: it contains all this knowledge within the smallest volume. It concentrates the most knowledge in the least time."[24] In the relevant section of his work, de Certeau describes the situation as a "hostile composition of place," and more tellingly, a "relationship of forces" into which *metis* intervenes, and in which it obtains effects, which de Certeau describes as a change in the relationship of forces, which in turn would alter evidently the composition of place in which *metis* finds itself. This description, while not directly arguing that cunning intelligence or rhetoric do not loop strictly through conscious intention, certainly assumes so. In both Hawhee's and de Certeau's renderings, the cunning actor is cunning in an immediate situation—the "occasion" for de Certeau and "instantaneous response" for Hawhee—due to training or experience that prepares that responsiveness. The hostile composition of place that de Certeau describes is tactically responded to because there is an existing body of possible moves from which to draw on in immediate response. Open CV, then, participating in a relationship of forces to which CV Dazzle is developed as a response depends on both the programmer (in the case of CV Dazzle, Adam Harvey) *and* the code library learning from and responding to the encounter between themselves. To develop the hair and makeup schemes that became CV Dazzle, Harvey had to test different possible schemes with Open CV, learning from its successes and failures. But at the same time, the algorithm is itself learning, and responding differently to the new challenge.

We can add, while sticking with the image of a relationship of forces, another way to relate training, experience, experimentation, and *metis*/rhetoric to an encounter with a hostile force, namely, through a Nietzschean perspective. Daniel Smith, in *enculturation*, offers this in a slightly different context, which will illustrate yet another relationship between cunning rhetor and audience, in an even more posthuman key: "For Nietzsche, affirmation is a vital part of the art of transformation, involving neither an acceptance nor opposition to or rejection of that which is to be transformed. Affirming an illness therefore entails ways of responding to and living with a 'sickness' in an experimental manner, one that tries to learn from the illness, to coax forth capacities for divergent thought and action that it might enable, capacities that also have the potential to transform the illness itself. Despite the personalization that the image of illness suggests, it is important to note that within this Nietzschean framework illnesses signify compositions of forces and forms of *life*, which organize various ecologies of existence and inhabit(uate) bodies but are not reducible to any-body."[25]

This deviates a bit from what has been described so far, and while Smith here is not directly talking about the work of *metis* or tactics (or cunning in general), it helps us refigure the work and activity of that particular capacity, and the agencies through which it presents itself as a force of change in the world.

Part of the difference here is temporal. In the other two accounts, we have a rhetorical situation, encounter, or occasion, in which response is temporally instant. The training or experience may endure for a great deal of time, but the moment of response has no duration. In fact, de Certeau argues that it is through *metis* and its long-cultivated "body of knowledge" that a "certain duration is introduced into the relationship of forces and changes it."[26] The occasion itself, then, has no duration of its own, and it is only the cunning intelligence of *metis* that brings an outside temporality to it. As will become clear, though, the encounter between CV Dazzle (let's call it for the moment *becoming-CV Dazzle*) and Open CV was itself an encounter of some duration, one that involved training the software library, the program that Harvey worked through, and the very make-up and hairstyles that would form CV Dazzle. Likewise, Harvey, when discussing the project, describes it as an open project that will change with different styles, fashions, and the like developed by future users.

Another part of the difference is the subtle reorientation afforded by Smith's phrase "various ecologies of existence and in-habit(uate) bodies but are not reducible to any-body," which will help fund here the conceptual twist I am making in *metis* and its bodies. That is, I am suggesting both that the audience of rhetorical encounters involving wiliness—de Certeau's "hostile composition"—is itself implicated in the existence and deployment of wily rhetorical response, and, meanwhile, that the *metis* enacted is enacted in between all of the bodies involved (physical and digital), and, as Smith says, is not "reducible" to any one body involved. Open CV, then, can emerge here as at once the available means of persuasion in digital culture, as Brown suggested, and the composition of forces, *the audience*, which is learned from, adapted to, but is also learning and adapting, itself, as a body irreducible to "any-body."

CODE LIBRARY AS WILY AUDIENCE

Or, in other words, continuing with de Certeau's language, we might ask how CV Dazzle "undoes" the "proper place" of Open CV, Viola-Jones, and human faces in technically mediated public spaces; how that undoing depends on active participation from Open CV; and how Open CV *undoes* the proper place of audience, rhetor, and rhetoric itself. To better grasp this, it is necessary to better grasp what Open CV is, and what it does (and does not do), to get a sense of its "proper place" in the first place. Open CV is an open-source "computer vision" (CV) code library. Code libraries are extensive additional features and functions that have been written to use in programming languages. If someone, for instance, wanted to create a mobile phone app that added silly animated hats to live video of people's faces, using a code library like Open CV would enable the developers to do so without having to create, from scratch, the computer vision features necessary to its development. They would only need to load the library, which brings with it the necessary code, and then dedicate their time to designing funny hats. According to the Open CV Foundation: "The library has more than twenty-five hundred optimized algorithms, which includes a comprehensive set of both classic and state-of-the-art computer vision and machine learning algorithms. These algorithms can be used to detect and recognize faces, identify objects, classify human actions in videos, track camera movements, track moving objects, extract 3D models of objects, produce 3D point clouds from stereo cameras, stitch images together to produce a high resolution image of an entire scene, find similar images from an image database, remove red eyes from images taken using flash, follow eye movements, recognize scenery and establish markers to overlay it with augmented reality, etc."[27] Among those many uses, of course, is surveillance on the order of the aforementioned FBI program.

Of the many algorithms in the Open CV library, the one most pertinent for facial recognition in images is the algorithm called "Viola-Jones," after the two computer scientists who developed it and published their findings in the 2001 paper "Rapid Object Detection Using a Boosted Cascade of Simple Features" and the 2004 paper "Robust Real-Time Face Detection."[28] In an interview with *Makematics* online, Harvey describes the Viola-Jones algorithm: "The Viola-Jones algorithm works by looking for features. All the features are rectangles. Inside the rectangle are smaller rectangles and then you have pixels. The rectangle that makes up the face in Viola-Jones is very small."[29] By dividing regions of images into rectangles within rectangles, and seeking, by contrasting light and dark regions within those rectangles, Viola-Jones can quickly and with relative accuracy detect the presence of a human face in an image. In a sense, the "proper place" of all of these elements is quite complex but centers on the application of such algorithms *toward* the goal of greater effectiveness in detecting the rectangular features of human faces.

Harvey designed CV Dazzle as a means of dazzling the Viola-Jones process, thwarting it at different stages of finding the symmetries that the algorithm is expecting to find, which would, even momentarily, "undo" the "proper place" of the relationship between human faces and the Open CV algorithms. Explicitly connecting his own method of camouflage with CV Dazzle to World War I dazzle camouflage, Harvey describes his project in this way: "The name is derived from a type of World War I naval camouflage called Dazzle, which used cubist-inspired designs to break apart the visual continuity of a battleship and conceal its orientation and size. Likewise, CV Dazzle uses avantgarde hairstyling and makeup designs to break apart the continuity of a face. Since facial-recognition algorithms rely on the identification and spatial relationship of key facial features, like symmetry and tonal contours, one can block detection by creating an 'anti-face.'"[30]

For his project to succeed, Harvey had to interact with the Open CV library to find the places Viola-Jones was breaking down and to tweak his CV Dazzle "looks" accordingly, finding the algorithm's topologies and noting their weaknesses. In the *Makematics* interview, he describes a bit of that process: "It's *Open* CV, but if you don't know C, it's harder. So I took that library and then rebuilt it in Java in Eclipse. What this does is give me more transparency into the way that it's working or that it's failing. . . . With this variant of Open CV face detection you can see where it's failing in the image, you can see when it fails. If it's at the last stage, which means that it's just barely failing. And you can also see if it fails really early, that means that, for this project, it's a good pattern." And also thus: "So you have to have some kind of human guidance or assisted learning. And generic algorithms are great for that. There is a great example from Daniel Shiffman. I think it's in the Learning Processing book. He made this face evolver. So you can start with these geometric abstractions and then you can guide it towards the face, and that's the same idea for this project is that you can guide a design towards something that you would wear. So if you are a guy you can guide it towards a really cool design in your style. And your style is an important part of this too and I think that working with a lot of code stuff it's very easy to make a tool or a utilitarian type thing, that's kind of void of style. Generic algorithms are neat in that way because they allow for that, for stopping it in different parts of the process."[31]

So, to successfully *dazzle* Viola-Jones and Open CV, a "response" like CV Dazzle must involve a network of responding entities and modes of responsiveness. If, in the act of dazzlement, the Open CV algorithms, specifically Viola-Jones, serve as the audience to be dazzled, from the beginning this audience is *entangled* in the process of response. That is, as already argued, Open CV emerges here *as* the trained and training audience, embodying its own *metis*, which thus displaces the proper place of *metis* within the rhetor, who in this case would be CV Dazzle and Harvey. It thus locates wiliness in its emergence in the encounter between rhetor and audience; the rhetorical art of dazzling is a very complex one indeed. This network, I suggest, we can call a "rhetoric-machine." Likewise, we can see in that process of training Open CV and CV Dazzle together an extension of rhetorical, embodied *metis*. The wiliness encountered here does not *quite* or *only* live in bodies, just as Hawhee argued that *metis* does not live only in minds or consciousness.[32]

In other words, the emergent characteristics of *metis* in the encounter between CV Dazzle and Open CV situates it between elements commonly understood as human and those commonly not understood thus, an insight that has raised questions already about the relationship between computation and rhetoric. For instance, James Brown Jr., in his "Crossing State Lines: Rhetoric and Software Studies," argues that Katherine Hayles's concept of "intermediation" helps us "connect meaning-making activities to an emergent network of humans and machines."[33] Suggesting that there is much that rhetorical studies can learn from the emerging field of software studies, he argues that "far from serving as the background of rhetorical situations, software is one of the available means of persuasion."[34] He also reminds us that software is rhetorical in that it "is authored in response to particular situations and problems."[35] Brown's argument affords us three twists on the relationship between rhetoric and computation that help extend rhetorical *metis* into situations in which software is primary audience.

First, rhetorical meaning-making happens in an emergent way, in between human and machine actors. Second, software is one of the available means of persuasion. I have already twisted this idea a good deal in showing that CV Dazzle, in its interaction with the Open CV code library, becomes *the audience* as well as *means* of persuasion in its rhetorical encounter with CV Dazzle. And finally, the entanglement of *interpretation*—central to what makes the facial recognition algorithms in Open CV work—and *production* are central to how Open CV exists as an evolving, open source project developed by a wide range of participants. A wily rhetorical response to the situation that Open CV presents, then, invites an understanding of the active participation of the software itself, as something that is not only actively "intermediating" between human and nonhuman (here, computational) forces but is also in part available as a *means* of persuasion, as well as persuadable audience.

That is, although CV Dazzle is a "response" to the Open CV project and its more chilling possibilities, it does not exist entirely externally to the Open CV library, at least in how the latter is made public through the Foundation's web materials, including training and documentation on the different algorithms and features the library provides. In the Open CV Foundation's tutorials section of the website (meant, of course, to make use and project-specific alteration of the library easier), there is a tutorial page for "Face Detection using Haar Cascades," or, in other words, the Viola-Jones algorithm. The tutorial describes the technique as "an effective object detection method proposed by Paul Viola and Michael Jones in their paper, 'Rapid Object Detection using a Boosted Cascade of Simple Features' in 2001," and, specifically, as a "machine learning based approach where a cascade function is trained from a lot of positive and negative images" and "is then used to detect objects in other images," thereby speeding up the process of detection on new images. The more images the local load of the library is trained on, the better it gets at detection. The tutorial page goes on to describe the method at length and in detail that would be useful for a potential user of the algorithm (say, the funny hat app designers I imagined). It concludes with two "Additional Resources" links, one to a YouTube lecture on face detection, and the other to Harvey's *Makematics* interview. As an open source project that can be used in a limitless variety of applications, Open CV is *open* to CV Dazzle being woven into its possibilities, even as a "response" *to* those possibilities, justifying the inclusion of Harvey's interview as an informative "additional resource" on face detection; indeed, Viola-Jones suggests that his work, at least subtly, becomes part of the Open CV project.

The code library, meanwhile, ought to be considered as *composed of* materials like the tutorial pages, the documentation pages, and links out from these to things like Harvey's interview, in that it is through them that many users interact with, use, and adapt (and adapt to) the library and its possibilities. Entanglements like these suggest that as wily responses *to* particular hostile audiences, at least when dealing with a weird body like the Open CV code library, the rhetorical power known as *metis* can take its own proper place *in between* the many bodies involved, including (but not in a way that is reducible to) the human bodies among these. Meanwhile, it is also important to recall Smith's Nietzschean framework for affirmation, in which CV Dazzle is a response that *learns from* Open CV and, I would add, vice versa. The composition of forces and forms of life involved, Smith's framework reminds us, is not reducible to any *particular* body.

Making Dazzling Rhetoric-Machines

What is ultimately dazzled by CV Dazzle is a complex of actions and actors that can be called the "code library," not just the Viola-Jones algorithm or simply the cameras' sensors on which that algorithm depends. The code library, in this case Open CV, is a responsive entity, itself made up of many other entities, all connected to each other either loosely or tightly. Drawing our attention here reminds us that when we talk about rhetoric and computation, the "code" involved is itself a complex organism—often part of a larger body of development and change—and is itself one with its own sort of *metis*, its own sort of bodily responsiveness. This responsiveness is visible in this project, specifically in at least two places. The first of these is a recursive process that Harvey goes through to identify the "weaknesses" in Viola-Jones, showing that a) its own form of response to what it interfaces with is not simply given, even when it has relatively stable weaknesses, and b) that as a "response to" Open CV, CV Dazzle had to undergo its own sort of cultivated training, which was always connected to Open CV.

Second, as already noted, the link from the Open CV Foundation back to Harvey's interview with *Makematics* loops CV Dazzle itself into the materials that make up the development and changes of the Open CV code library. Whether anyone in the developer community draws on that interview, or CV Dazzle, in further altering Open CV is not really at issue. It is enough that it is linked there, part of what makes Open CV exist. In this way, we can see the example of CV Dazzle opening up unexpected connections between rhetoric and computation. On the one hand, we can view code *libraries* as special entities with rhetorical capacities that exist at once as discourse, as the available means of persuasion, *and* as possible audiences. Taking them as potentially dazzled audiences reveals different ways to practice and *play with* computational rhetoric. On the other hand, this example shows us at least one way to imagine and extend *metis* to bodies (in this case the Open CV code library) that are not what we are accustomed to calling bodies at all.

Thinking about the relationship between rhetoric and computational machines through dazzlement, as this chapter has done, helps remind us that the encounter between us and such machines is hardly as rigid and mechanical as it tends to seem. Not only are there vectors of dazzlement available to us through which we may "exploit" inherent weaknesses in any given network or computer,[36] the moment of dazzlement also reveals to us ways in which all participating parties are a touch wilier, a touch more slippery than we might suspect.

DAZZLING RHETORIC-MACHINES

And this wiliness, this *metis* in and through bodies that aren't always *just* physical entities, can be returned to the machinic, which is, after all, the concern of this book. In this way, I suggest that what is happening here is the forming of a "dazzling" rhetoric-machine between all the elements at play. This structure is meant to echo work done recently in rhetoric on the ecological, distributed formations of rhetoric's work and force, in efforts to develop *relational ontologies* for rhetoric.[37] For instance, when Thomas Rickert argues, in *Ambient Rhetoric*, that rhetoric is made ambiently and comes from the many different *things* that come together in a particular moment, the argument is similar to what I am now suggesting with the formulation "rhetoric-machines," with one key difference.[38] I aim here at drawing our attention away from naturalizing vocabulary (like bodies, ecologies, and even things) and toward the machinic.[39] That is, I mean to highlight various features of rhetoric's relational ontology by placing metaphoric weight on a different foot and emphasizing these relationships as composing *machines* instead of other, more "natural" phenomena (ambience, ecology). This, I suspect, buys us yet another way to trouble the nature/culture distinction, as well as to attend even more vigorously to the relational and surrounding way that computational machines are woven into our world, which itself is already machinic anyway.[40] In swapping out terms, in switching from ecology or ambience to machine, I am suggesting that there is a subtle twist away from formations that are *just there* and *just take place* toward those that are tooled, built, tested, retested, structured, and assembled.

This is no return, though, to intentionality, as the hyphenated form "rhetoric-machine" is meant to suggest. I am hyphenating the term to emphasize audience's role and entanglement in rhetoric's work, especially in the multiple elements that make up human-computer encounters. And also, as this chapter has argued, because in situating the tactical work of rhetoric here as *making* rhetoric-machines, I am encouraging us to see the complex entanglements of machine, rhetor, and discourse in such responses. It's not simply that Harvey *responds to* Open CV through developing CV Dazzle, or that someone who wears such dazzle styling in public does. These events do indeed take place, but are composed, as *responses*, of the very thing that is being responded to, the Open CV code library, which itself has taken Harvey's intervention into the community, linking back out to his interview on the Object Detection tutorial page. Instead of describing the shape of a computer surveillance ouroboros, this tells us that the kind of response hailed by computational machines in everyday life is one in which the rhetor does not stand against an audience, separate from and unaffected by it, and *dazzle* it with honeyed speech. It also tells us that there is a wiliness, a rhetoricity, in the encounter with computational machines that does not *just* reside in physical, biological bodies (i.e., like the octopus in Hawhee's telling,[41] OpenCV at least in part can shape and change and alter in contact with CV Dazzle; this doesn't mean it will "win," necessarily).

It is not just any encounter with code or code libraries that I have run the rhetoric-machine through. In calling these "dazzling" and focusing on examples of dazzlement, I mean to recall the tactical possibilities of rhetoric in general, and specifically with respect to the encounter with computational machines. As we saw in the way Harvey had to train up his CV Dazzle through Open CV, these tactical possibilities, meanwhile, are available in addressing and being addressed by a host of unusual audiences.

Making rhetoric-machines as our tactical goal opens up the possibility of thinking about algorithms, software, machines, and so on as *simultaneously* available means of persuasion *and* persuadable audiences caught up in a complex web of response in which it is difficult to distinguish who is doing what to whom—rhetoric-machines are about inventing, making, and remaking connections, plugging into that which may appear to be the tools and operations of the enemy, rather than *simply* concealing from them, always at work *with* them, always at work *on* them, never in control *of* them, but always in flight, in some real way, *from* their aims. This is the tactical dimension of rhetoric that we can tease out from projects like CV Dazzle.

Notes

1. Michel de Certeau, *The Practice of Everyday Life* (Berkeley: University of California Press, 1984), 29–38.

2. Of course, visual surveillance is not the only form of public surveillance we face now, though there is enormous state and private investment of research, time, and money in its development, making it at least one of the most, if not the most, troubling and dangerous forms. See, for more on biometric surveillance in public, Kelly A. Gates, *Our Biometric Future: Facial Recognition Technology and the Culture of Surveillance* (New York: NYU Press, 2011).

3. Debra Hawhee, *Bodily Arts: Rhetoric and Athletics in Ancient Greece* (Austin: University of Texas Press, 2004), 54.

4. Norman Wilkinson, "On Dazzle Painting," in *Ship Shape, a Dazzle Camouflage Sourcebook: An Anthology of Writings About Ship Camouflage During World War One*, ed. Roy R. Behrens (Dysart, IA: Bobolink Books, 2012): 52–57.

5. Raymond Francis Yates, "Camouflage Science Explained," in *Ship Shape*, 71.

6. Jay Stanley, "FBI and Industry Failing to Provide Needed Protections for Face Recognition," ACLU, last modified June 15, 2016, https://www.aclu.org/blog/privacy-technology/surveillance-technologies/fbi-and-industry-failing-provide-needed.

7. United States Government Accountability Office, Report to the Ranking Member, Subcommittee on Privacy, Technology and the Law, Committee on the Judiciary, US Senate, "Face Recognition Technology: FBI Should Better Ensure Privacy and Accuracy," May 2016, last updated August 3, 2016, https://www.gao.gov/assets/680/677098.pdf.

8. Jennifer Lynch, "New Report: FBI Can Access Hundreds of Millions of Face Recognition Photos," Electronic Frontier Foundation, June 15, 2016, https://www.eff.org/deeplinks/2016/06/fbi-can-search-400-million-face-recognition-photos.

9. United States Government Accountability Office, "Face Recognition Technology," 15.

10. Stanley, "FBI and Industry Failing."

11. Marcel Detienne and Jean-Pierre Vernant, *Cunning Intelligence in Greek Culture and Society* (Chicago: University of Chicago Press, 1991), 3–4.

12. In the policing scenario described in this chapter, CV Dazzle would be of use only in preventing facial recognition algorithms from producing the "probe photo" in the first place. Human scans of ATM footage, for instance, would instantly recognize a disguised face, in cases in which such location and event are known or suspected. Likely, then, CV Dazzle is not a great tactical option for someone interested in committing a crime in a public space. It is, *however*, an excellent option for someone who is interested in *being* in a public space without being automatically registered as such.

13. Adam Harvey, "CV Dazzle," last modified August 22, 2017, https://cvdazzle.com/. Examples of CV Dazzle can be found at this site.

14. Adam Harvey et al., "How to Hide from Machines," *Dis Magazine*, accessed April 30, 2018, http://dismagazine.com/dystopia/evolved-lifestyles/8115/anti-surveillance-how-to-hide-from-machines/.

15. See, for instance, Jared S. Colton, Steve Holmes, and Josephine Walwema, "From NoobGuides to# OpKKK: Ethics of Anonymous' Tactical Technical Communication," *Technical Communication Quarterly*, 26, no. 1 (2017): 59–75.

16. Hawhee, *Bodily Arts*, 46.

17. Ibid., 47.

18. de Certeau, *The Practice of Everyday Life*, 35.

19. Ibid., 83.

20. Ibid., 81.

21. Ibid., 82.

22. Rita Raley, *Tactical Media* (Minneapolis: University of Minnesota Press, 2009); Megan Boler, ed., *Digital Media and Democracy: Tactics in Hard Times* (Cambridge: MIT Press, 2008). These two works are exemplary introductions to tactical media, and the many different studies and uptakes thereof.

23. Hawhee, 77.

24. de Certeau, 83.

25. Daniel Smith, "Of Headaches and Other Illnesses," *enculturation: a journal of rhetoric, writing, and culture* 5, no. 2 (2004).

26. de Certeau, 82.

27. Open CV Foundation, "About," accessed April 28, 2018, https://opencv.org /about.html.

28. Paul Viola and Michael J. Jones, "Robust Real-Time Face Detection," *International Journal of Computer Vision* 57, no. 2 (2004): 137–154.

29. Greg Borenstein, "Adam Harvey Explains Viola-Jones Face Detection," last updated 2012, *Makematics*, http://web.archive.org/web/20120408080754/http://www .makematics.com:80/research/viola-jones/.

30. Harvey, "CV Dazzle."

31. Borenstein, "Harvey Explains Viola-Jones."

32. Hawhee, 48.

33. James J. Brown Jr., "Crossing State Lines: Rhetoric and Software Studies," in *Rhetoric and the Digital Humanities*, ed. Jim Ridolfo and William Hart-Davidson (Chicago: University of Chicago Press, 2015), 22.

34. Ibid., 23.

35. Ibid.

36. See Alexander R. Galloway and Eugene Thacker, *The Exploit: A Theory of Networks* (Minneapolis: University of Minnesota Press, 2007) for more on this.

37. For a wide variety of examples see: Scot Barnett and Casey Boyle, eds., *Rhetoric, through Everyday Things* (Tuscaloosa: University of Alabama Press, 2016); Scot Barnett, *Rhetorical Realism* (London: Routledge, 2017); Nathaniel A. Rivers and Paul Lynch, eds., *Thinking with Bruno Latour in Rhetoric and Composition* (Carbondale: University of Southern Illinois Press, 2015).

38. Thomas Rickert, *Ambient Rhetoric* (Pittsburgh, PA: University of Pittsburgh Press, 2013).

39. For a different take on the "machinic" in the relationship between rhetoric and computation see James J. Brown Jr., "The Machine That Therefore I Am," *Philosophy & Rhetoric* 47, no. 4 (2014): 494–514. My version of the machinic owes its shape to Deleuze and Guattari as they develop the concept in *Anti-Oedipus*. Gilles Deleuze and Félix Guattari, *Anti-Oedipus: Capitalism and Schizophrenia* (London: Penguin Books, 2009).

40. See Deleuze and Guattari for more on this use of the machinic.

41. In *Bodily Arts*, the struggle between the octopus and the eel frames Hawhee's argument about *metis* being a bodily, instead of embodied, intelligence. The octopus in that battle can change shapes, color, etc.; it can, in short, become *otherwise* in the encounter with its opponent. This, naturally, is no guarantee of victory, but is rather an emergent *possibility*.

11 / Good Computing with Big Data

Jennifer Helene Maher, Helen J. Burgess, and Tim Menzies

Numeric calculation has long been understood to potentially hold the power of overcoming the frailty of human judgment. For example, through his conception of the *calculus ratiocinator* (thought calculator) and a *characteristica universalis* (universal character), Gottfried Leibniz conjectured in the seventeenth century, "If controversies were to arise, there would be no more need for disputation between two philosophers than between two accountants. For it would suffice to take their pencils in their hands, to sit down to their slates, and say to each other (with a friend as witness, if they liked): calculemus—let us calculate."[1] The hopeful promise of mechanical inventions such as these points to the desire to cut through rhetorical uncertainty and replace human fragility with numerical certitude. To date, numeracy as computation in big data analytics (i.e., the computing of large-volume sets of information) appears closest to achieving Leibniz's dream. But discussions of goodness are often limited in certain ways in programming generally, and in data science specifically. To wit, software, according to Joseph Juran, is written well when it enjoys a "fitness for use" that can be measured through its "freedom from deficiencies."[2] In data analytics, technically good algorithms maximize the ability to process petabytes worth of data according to the three V's: volume, variety, and velocity.[3] Computing "good" is also often described as revealing otherwise hidden patterns of information that can positively address social issues such as healthcare in ways that would not otherwise be possible.[4] And less instrumental or consequential considerations of goodness often take shape in methodological discussions of how "ethical mining" can address privacy concerns[5] or how "moral mining" can reveal new information about human values.[6] Although examples such as these illustrate how *good* is often invoked in discussions of big data, they fail to capture, in their zeal to determine goodness as a kind of total valuation, the ways in which working with big data is often a complex negotiation of different kinds of good at different levels. Working with big data, it turns out, is a process that involves many layers of acquisition, cleaning, analysis, reporting, revising—any layer of which might be *good* in a different mode or multiple modes: moral/ethical, technical, ideological. And these different valuations of goodness might be formulated, negotiated, and revised multiple times during the process of working with a dataset.

To illustrate the ways in which goodness circulates in complex ways demands understanding the processing of large-volume sets of data as an inherently rhetorical enterprise rather than as the long-sought realization of *calculemus* through computation. To this end, we first unpack goodness in the context of big data and examine how the desire to render goodness in ways limited to conceptions of the technical, the methodological, or the consequential obfuscates the complex play of goodness that is always at work in computation because data analytics is not free of the kind of human deliberations and judgments that define rhetorical activity. Then, borrowing Benjamin Bratton's concept of "the Stack," we illustrate, through an analysis of a gender study formulated from pull requests on the open-source repository GitHub, how rhetorical/technological "stacking" functions in ways that circulate in a complex assemblage of various conceptions of goodness and its opposite. In doing so, big data, with its seductive promise to deliver numerical certitude, is understood to propagate rather than eliminate rhetoric.

Limited Goodness

Popular narratives highlight the power of big data to reveal otherwise hidden ways of improving everyday life through the computational ability to find and identify patterns in petabyte-size data. For example, between 2008 and 2014 Google Flu Trends tracked the real-time spread of the flu, in an attempt to control seasonal influenza epidemics that attack 5 to 10 percent of adults and 20 to 30 percent of children each year, causing 250,000 to 500,000 deaths[7]. To do so, Google Flu Trends aggregated search-term data determined to be "good indicators of flu activity" in an effort to improve upon the US Centers for Disease Control's (CDC) and European Influenza Surveillance Scheme (EISS) surveillance systems. As Google summarized, "Traditional flu surveillance is very important, but most health agencies focus on a single country or region and only update their estimates once per week. Google Flu Trends is currently available for a number of countries around the world and is updated every day, providing a complement to these existing systems."[8] In another example of claims for the good generated through big data analysis, Uber announced on January 13, 2015, that it was joining with the city of Boston "to help expand the city's capability to solve problems by leveraging data provided by Uber. The data will provide new insights to help manage urban growth, relieve traffic congestion, expand public transportation, and reduce greenhouse gas emissions."[9] Rather than treating this collaboration with Boston as simply a technical matter of computing potential solutions to urban problems, Uber casts itself in decidedly moral terms in arguing that "our ability to share information . . . can serve a greater good."[10] Likewise, IBM's Big Data for Social Good Challenge, launched in 2015, invites data scientists to use its curated datasets to tackle "real world civic issues" and offer solutions with social impact. Successful competitors have thus far used open data sets for several purposes: Watch Flu Spread tracks historic and forecasted dispersion of flu incidents in the US in order to mitigate risk in specific areas, Juvo provides assistance in setting social and economic development plans with realistic achievable goals and metrics, and Oasis helps to address the problems of commercial deserts in Chicago.

The kinds of goodness that pervade many of these discussions focus in Aristotelian terms on big data as scientific knowledge (*episteme*) and as art or craft (*techne*). As Aristotle explains, "The origin of action . . . is choice, and that of choice is desire and reasoning with a view to an end."[11] But the Greek philosopher notes that both choices and the ends they ought to achieve depend upon the kind intellectual activity at work. Because science is that which "cannot be otherwise," this kind of knowledge has been constituted, since the advent of modern science, through the uncovering of those first principles and universals laws of necessity that can be demonstrated and replicated through analytic methods. "Good science," first of the natural world and now of a computable world, is meant to bring forth certainty without qualification through good scientific method, whether hypothesis- or data-driven. In doing so, data science is often understood as encapsulating a promised first principle of the digital age, as expressed by Andrew McAfee: "As the amount of data goes up, the importance of human judgment should go down."[12] But those techniques applied in data processing can lead to good data processing or bad data processing because "art . . . is a state concerned with making, involving a true course of reasoning, and lack of art on the contrary is a state concerned with making, involving a false course of reasoning: both are concerned with what can be otherwise."[13] As a result, the techniques by which data scientists address a problem have to be technically good, meaning that chosen methods aim to ensure the values of science: reliability and validity. Only then can the potential for consequential good achieved through science be actualized.

But whether as science or art, data science is too often limited to notions of goodness as either social consequences or matters of technique, the effect of which is to displace human conceptions of goodness onto those of the machine. In his discussion of cybernetics, Norbert Wiener acknowledged the potentially dangerous consequences that could result from cybernetic displacement of human values to that of the machine: "Those of us who have contributed to the new science of cybernetics thus stand in a moral position which is, to say the least, not very comfortable. We have contributed to the initiation of a new science, which, as I have said, embraces technical possibilities for good and for evil."[14] His answer as to how best to deal with the moral consequences of machine communication in light of such horrors as Bergen-Belsen and Hiroshima was to encourage a more enlightened public and to limit scientific and technical progress to those areas where the consequences of use might be much less drastic, such as in the fields of physiology and psychology, those "most remote from war and exploitation."[15] At the same time, Wiener held "very slight hope"[16] for the likelihood of implementing limitations to computational investigation. And in fact, sixty years later we find Grady Booch, chief scientist for software engineering at the IBM Almaden Research Laboratory, arguing in a 2008 issue of *IEEE Software* for a collective recognition of the important role of software engineers: "We as a professional community have developed technology that has changed the way individuals live, business operates, communities interact, and nations and civilizations thrive and expand. At that level of abstraction, a moral dimension is undoubtedly at play: when our technology touches the activities of the human spirit, then questions of social responsibility, individual rights, and goodness of fit to the moral atmosphere of the surrounding community come alive."[17] What both Wiener and Booch respectively advocate is the adoption of computing praxis, especially by those whose work is instrumental in the development of computing machines. Booch subsequently explained: "To say that algorithms are thoughtless is a reasonable and unemotional statement of fact. They have no moral center; they have no sense of right or wrong; they cannot take responsibility for their consequences. Bits cannot feel. However, we who craft such algorithms are expected to be thoughtful."[18] Thus, in the case of big data, the call for and implementation of ethical mining can be understood as the fulfillment of a choice to compute and interpret large data sets according to a positive value regarding privacy, for instance. But calculating the good or ill effects of computing in-use catalyzes a philosophical consequentialism that too often assigns to the data scientist the role of moral judge. Given the ongoing dominance of technological neutrality, the fact that morality could be baked in from the very start does not sit well, especially with those in the business of algorithmic modeling.[19] In order to maximize fitness of use in software, an emphasis is also placed on not just good, but *best* algorithmic practices. Through an emphasis on technical concerns such as security, scalability, reliability, efficiency, verifiability, and adaptability, *good* often denotes a measurable, instrumental quality.

However, if looked at from a systems approach point of view, data science as computation is removed completely from human judgment concerning goodness. In his theory of systems, Niklas Luhmann explicates a way to resist the ongoing privileging of human action.[20] Action must, in his view, be understood not as originating from human consciousness but rather from systems of communication that constantly remake themselves in a process known as *autopoiesis*. Originally described by Humberto Maturana and Francisco Varela as the self-reproduction of the living system of the cell, autopoiesis foregrounds the recursive regeneration of a system through its "network of processes of production,"[21] as well as its "operational closure" from other systems. As Maturana explains, "This circular organization constitutes a homeostatic system whose function is to produce and maintain this very same circular organization by determining that the *components* that specify it be those whose synthesis and maintenance it secures."[22] In addition to the biological, Luhmann also includes in his systems model the social, psychic, and mechanistic.[23] But regardless of which model a system falls under, the autopoiesis of any system occurs through a self-reproduction of a binary code specific to that system's function. Thus, in the social system of the law, this binary is legal/illegal, the meaning of which serves both as the object of the system's self-reproduction and as a necessary distinction from other systems. In light of this binary, law as a social system is regenerated through "programmes" such as legislative acts and adherence to legal precedents[24] that, in turn, are regenerated through the binary. As a result, "Everything that cannot be brought under this controlling scheme of legal/illegal does not belong to the legal system but to its internal or external social environment."[25]

Given these descriptions of systems, one might rightly wonder how the autopoietic turn could be useful in a discussion of anything beyond technical good in computation, especially as Luhmann argues that system communication "does not permit code values of function systems to be identified with moral values—neither with good/bad nor with good/evil."[26] In the system of law, excluding its system communication from the moral might seem necessary, if not natural, as is the case in liberalism where the law is to be neutral in regards to morality in order to treat all citizens fairly and equally.[27] But even in the system of computation, any operation cast in terms of good or bad, except in the instrumentalist measure of technical efficacy and effect that we discussed earlier as *good computing*, can seem unnecessary. But this is not to say that notions of goodness have no place in systems of communication, including the law. While functional codes such as legal/illegal exist on a level of "higher amorality,"[28] Luhmann explains that goodness comes into play through a kind of binary code coupling: "Moral communication has to be framed within a specific binary code which opposes a positive and a negative value. This code can be supposed to be invariant because it is necessary to identify communication as moral communication. It is specific and universal at the same time because, once invented, there cannot be an uncoded moral communication . . . But this evolutionary universal is void of content. It does not give any information about what is good and what is bad . . . As a complement to its code, the moral needs criteria to decide which behaviour is good and which behaviour is bad. Because there are no good versus bad criteria, the criteria or programmes of the moral cannot be identified with the values of the code."[29] Where the moral couples with the system of computation is not in some kind of value judgment of the system's binary. As Luhmann explains, moral communication is framed *within*, not *with*, the binary code. Therefore, it is at the level of operation that moral value can couple with programmes, for example, to create "differentiation." In the system of the law, moral conflict concerning segregation laws in the American South, particularly in the 1960s, offers a clear instance of just how the moral can "irritate" operations. Individuals stoke this differentiation as they "choose the programmes that favor their own interests and opinions."[30] The resulting operation of moral communication that occurs from the choice between supporting or condemning segregation laws codes individual action in what Luhmann identifies as an "esteem/disesteem" binary, like that achieved through epideictic rhetoric. Thus, while the binary of legal/illegal exists in what might be identified as the autopoietic system of law through which the system's function is to essentially beget more law, the coupling of moral communication within the legal system irritates so that in some ways that operational closure has meaningful rhetorical openness too.

However, the system of computation's coupling with moral communication is perhaps more difficult to identify than that of the law's. Take the example of protocol. Alexander Galloway identifies *protocol* as "that machine, that massive control apparatus that guides distributed networks, create cultural objects, and engenders life forms."[31] In order for these transactions to occur, they must be constructed in such a way as to conform not to the protocols of human norms—whether in language or behavior—but to the hierarchical layers of network architecture.[32] For Galloway, however, there is no coupling of moral communication with protocol: "People often ask me if I think protocol is good or bad. But I'm not sure this is the best question to ask. It is important to remember first that technical is always political, that *network architecture is politics*. So protocol necessarily involves a complex interrelation of political question, some progressive, some reactionary."[33] While it may seem that coupling the system of computation with the system of politics at the operation level of protocol achieves something essentially similar to what a coupling with moral communication might do (i.e., cast value), this is not the case. Putting aside the intricacies of the system of politics,[34] political communication does not involve differentiation rooted in esteem/disesteem, except when the system of politics itself is coupled with moral communication. At its core, according to Luhmann, moral communication's autopoiesis only occurs as a result of a certain kind of problem, one that political consensus would eliminate. If this consensus were to take place with the moral, "This would bring moral communication to an end."[35]

Yet, the promise to remove human consideration of goodness beyond that of operation or (if one must) consequence ought to be viewed suspiciously as the kind of hype that can result from new science. In 2009, for instance, Google Flu Trends' Jeremy Ginsberg et al. noted that, in using search engine query data to detect influenza epidemics, "We can accurately estimate the current level of weekly influenza activity in each region of the United States, with a reporting lag of about one day."[36] Unlike the CDC methods that relied on empirical evidence, including "both virologic and clinical data, including influenza-like illness (ILI) physician visits," Google Flu Trends methods included generating a model by aggregating "hundreds of billions of individual" search queries submitted between 2003 and 2008 and then current web queries starting in the 2008–2009 flu season. What is more, Google Flu Trends, by "harnessing the collective intelligence of millions of users," cut the one to two week lag time of ILI reports used by the CDC to provide same-day results. In short, Google Flu Trends purported to offer increased goodness both technically and methodologically.[37] Among the praise offered for Google Flu Trends included that of Viktor Mayer-Schönberger and Kenneth Cukier, who, in *Big Data: A Revolution That Will Transform How We Live, Work, and Think*, remark on the ways in which "sophisticated computational analysis can now identify the optimal proxy—as it did for Google Flu Trends, after plowing through almost half a billion mathematical models."[38] In doing so, Google Flu Trends evidenced strong correlation, meaning that "when one of the data values changes, the other is highly likely to change as well."[39] The result, according to Mayer-Schönberger and Cukier, was this: "We don't have to develop a notion about what terms people search for when and where the flu spreads . . . Instead we can subject big data to correlation analysis and let it tell us what search queries are the best proxies for the flu . . . In place of hypothesis-driven approach, we can use a data-driven one. Our results may be less biased and more accurate, and we will almost certainly get them much faster."[40]

Given the number of instances of illness and death caused by seasonal flu each year, to say nothing of thirty to fifty million estimated to have been killed in the 1918–1919 pandemic, the "optimal proxy" created through computational analysis purported to offer the best means by which to provide the greatest degree of statistical reliability and validity, not to mention the increased awareness of a health threat in real time. Through Google Flu Trends the promise of big data's inherent goodness, beyond that otherwise achieved through traditional, empirical methods, was optimized, seemingly to the point of certainty rather than probability.

In 1977, the International Association for Statistical Computing described its mission as linking "traditional statistical methodology, modern computer technology, and the knowledge of domain experts in order to convert data into information and knowledge."[41] As later described by Ian Hacking, there are two aspects to statistical probability: "It is connected with the degree of belief warranted by evidence, and it is connected with the tendency, displayed by some change devices, to produce stable relative frequencies."[42] Yet, the stability generated through the result of strong correlation in big data is often misrecognized as certainty. As Ginsberg et al. warned, "Despite strong historical correlations, our system remains susceptible to false alerts caused by a sudden increase in ILI-related queries. An unusual event, such as a drug recall for a popular cold or flu remedy, could cause such a false alert."[43] Even so, what is easily overlooked in computation is the tendency to confuse statistical probability with certainty. As Google Flu Trends came under critique for its less-than-stellar results for flu season 2012–2013[44]—and this in spite of the fact that these findings were based on twice as many ILI doctor visits as evidenced by data collected by the CDC[45]—Google simply characterized these critiques as useful feedback in honing the new model for the new flu season. But in 2014, Google ended its flu trend analytics project.

For data scientist Michael Jordan, the promise that big data seemingly holds and the hype that surrounds it too often encourage overlooking the "false positives" that are frequently generated through such computation. As he explains, "I think data analysis can deliver inferences at certain levels of quality. But we have to be clear about *what* levels of quality. We have to have error bars around all our predictions."[46] Without this kind of qualification on the results generated through data analytics, Jordan predicts a "big-data winter." Yet, for those such as Justin Washtell, who asks—"So, what *is* the single best predictive modeling technique available, imho?"—it is the minimization and possibly even the eventual elimination of ambiguity induced by humans, who are not by their nature computational beings, that could be the ultimate promise of big data analysis. Or, as Washtell succinctly puts it, "Take human judgment out of the equation where it is not required."[47] In doing so, the goodness made possible by big data stands to enjoy greater stability, reliability, and validity, possibly to the point of certainty. But, while removing the human element may lead to the achievement of *calculemus* or, what might more accurately be referred to now in an English translation as "let them compute," statistical probability is not certainty. Consequently, big data is nothing less than a rhetorical enterprise, one that necessitates judgments that go beyond the limitations induced at the level of system or protocol. To understand this necessitates going beyond protocol or system to acknowledge the varying rhetorical and situated constructions of goodness that always occur in data analytics.

Rhetorical Stacking

To argue that "Big Data" is a rhetorical enterprise is to invoke the concept of "Big Rhetoric." As Aristotle explains, rhetoric, itself an art, is special because it is made use of by all other *techne*. Because rhetoric presents "us with alternative possibilities,"[48] we might easily understand how discussions of best methods can be limited to rhetorical aspects of data science. However, to acknowledge that science itself is also rhetorical, a position not supported by the Aristotelian configuration of *episteme*, means to reject the idea that anything can be inherently "free of rhetoric."[49] In Edward Schiappa's definition, "big rhetoric" refers to the position "that everything, or virtually everything, can be described as 'rhetorical.'"[50] And because everything is rhetorical, there is a necessary human calculation as to what is good. To explore the different ways in which goodness can be constituted in big data, we turn to Benjamin Bratton's formulation of "the Stack" in his 2015 book of the same name.[51] The Stack rests on the intuition that "an accidental megastructure" is being formed as we move to an era of "planetary computing" constituted by the complex interweavings of cloud computing technologies, big data repositories, trans-sovereign communications networks, the coexisting material economies of rare earth mineral acquisition, outsourced labor, and the global flows of manufacturing capital.[52] Bratton conceptualizes the Stack to describe the geopolitical framework formed by all these technologies: a kind of theoretical geological stratification of human and nonhuman activity into layers that operate at different intensities and scales—of time, of space, of matter.

Crucially, though, the Stack is (unlike a strict geological strata model, or a layer cake) both multidirectional and communicational: information can pass up and down (or between different configurations of) its layers: "Even as any one layer's operations unfold in relation to those adjacent layers, and so may also affect events well outside the entire platform's borders, the movement of hard and soft information must always pass through the protocols that divide and bind that layer's work from the others."[53] Bratton draws this metaphor from the way technological stacks function: he uses the example of the TCP/IP and OSI network models that allow for Internet connectivity and communication, which are made up of layers of different hard and soft technologies and operations—data, fiber optics, transport protocols.[54] We could also consider the open-source LAMP stack (Linux, Apache, MySQL, PHP/Python/Perl) as an example of this formulation: a suite of hard and soft technologies that pass information back and forth, even as they are reliant on layered dependencies within the stack to function.

Building on Bratton's conceptual terminology, we make use of "stacking" as a way of identifying ways in which the system of open source communities and technologies form what we could call a "rhetorical/technological stack," wherein both data (raw and processed) and rhetorical practices are communicated up and down through multiple technological layers. We are accustomed to thinking that data work is a messy and technical task. A stack model helps to illuminate the complex, multistage and multitool, often highly bespoke process of obtaining, cleaning, and interrogating data. But as with the case of the binary of "legal/illegal" identified by Luhmann in the autopoietic system of the law, wherein the system function is to essentially beget more law, the coupling of moral communication with data science's binary system of (statistically) "significant/insignificant" also irritates, so that the operational closure of a system where data begets more data has rhetorical openness too. Placing emphasis on rhetorical operations within the stack also helps to lay bare many other narratives of goodness implicit in working with data: for example, the way scholars must negotiate complex presentation, review, and revision processes in order to communicate and legitimize their work.

Reading Gender Bias on GitHub: A Sample Stack Analysis

In the remainder of this essay, we discuss a recent study that provides an ideal example of how a rhetorical/technological stack might function as a useful metaphor for the complexities of working with big data. The study, titled "Gender Bias in Open Source: Pull Request Acceptance of Women Versus Men," was authored by a group of researchers from Cal Polytechnic San Luis Obispo and North Carolina State University and evaluated the evidence for gender bias in open source software (OSS) contributions using GitHub as its primary source of data.[55] On February 9, 2016, the paper resulting from the study was originally posted to PeerJ, an open-access repository for non-peer-reviewed papers that might be in the process of revision for later publication. Because PeerJ operates on open-access principles, papers are freely available and open for public peer review and comment, with the result that this study was quickly picked up by media sources, including the *Washington Post* and the *Guardian*, and thence made its way through the social media ecosystem—including the usual suspects Twitter and Facebook, along with various Reddit groups and a wide number of blogs. The paper was revised into a second version under the title "Gender Differences and Bias in Open Source: Pull Request Acceptance of Women Versus Men" on July 26, 2016, with the new addition of a statistician as a third author. The study contains some familiar elements of other investigations we may know similarly from our own reading—particularly, "hiring bias" studies showing that resumes with African-American and Latino-sounding names were more likely to be rejected than those with White-sounding names, as well as the widely cited "Matilda Effect" study of several peer-reviewed communications journals that found women were less likely to be cited by male authors than female.[56] The study we are looking at differed, however, in that it was a "retrospective field study" rather than experimental (i.e., it analyzed existing, real-world data rather than setting up a unique study); it made use of a large data set gleaned from GitHub, isolating uscr data for contributors to projects under specific OSS licenses.

The paper itself presents evidence that there is a small but significant bias against acceptance of women's contributions to OSS projects, but only when their gender identity is evident on the site. Where it is not readily available, conversely, contributions from women are more likely to be accepted than those from men, again by a small margin. Contributions were counted in the form of successful "pull requests," the process whereby a contributor makes a change to a piece of code and that change is approved and merged back into the project. The study further broke down contributors by "insider" and "outsider" status on a project (i.e., whether the contributor was a known owner or collaborator), showing that the gender bias effect was confined to outsider contributors, whereas insider contributors showed "little evidence of bias."[57] The study moves systematically through a number of research questions, seeking to isolate alternative theories for evidence of bias: for example, do women contribute differently to projects than men in terms of scope or task? But ultimately the authors find these alternative explanations insignificant.

The paper is simultaneously circumspect in its specific conclusion about gender bias and more ambitious in its general claim that big data is a crucial element in any such study. In its penultimate section, the authors note, "We caution the reader from interpreting too much from statistical significance; for big data studies such as this one, even small differences can be statistically significant. Instead, we encourage the reader to examine size of the observed effects." They go on to note that "the effect we have uncovered is smaller than in typical gender bias studies."[58]

In the paper's conclusion, the authors shift their focus from the particularities of the GitHub study to argue more generally for the value of big data: "In closing, as anecdotes about gender bias persist, it is imperative that we use big data to better understand the interaction between genders."[59] In making this claim that big data is an essential tool for unpacking and critiquing gender bias, they are implicitly acknowledging that consequentialist forms of goodness might result, whether it be a response to the problem of gender bias using technical solutions, such as changing identification practices on GitHub, or rhetorical action, such as opening up dialogue about gender bias in technical cultures and advocating for change.

Responses to the first draft of the paper posted to PeerJ range from general feedback on terminology (e.g., the conflation of "open source" and "GitHub") and discussion of the weakness of visualization (notably, the misleading effect of scale choice in bar charts) to more technical suggestions about using multiple regression models and releasing data, with some discussion about what it meant to "scrub" data given that it was already publicly available on GitHub. Such technical critiques resulted in some rewriting, new visualizations, addition of a new section on covariate analysis, and the addition of a statistician, presumably to address critiques of the goodness of the study on statistical and methodological grounds. One of the study's authors, Emerson Murphy-Hill, commented on the public's reception to the nuanced nature of the study in terms of its "significance," noting that "the difference is statistically significant, but whether the difference is substantial is another question that's open for interpretation."[60]

The first inklings of defensive responses by male coders, however, soon appeared in the commenting system. For example, referring to the opening anecdote, a self-described "actual developer" Francisco Villemaire argued, "Rachel claiming sexism is a cop-out move, it sounds like she can't handle being critiqued and instantly plays the victim card."[61] The commenter was called out quickly for his attempt to claim authority by the mere fact of being a web developer, but would prove fairly representative of responses once the paper made its way from the relatively rarified environment of PeerJ to spaces such as Reddit, where the conversation took a fairly predictable turn into misogyny, with one commenter suggesting that "the only conclusion that can actually be drawn from the paper is that there is a bias against *men* having their pull requests accepted."[62] These kinds of responses are, of course, easy pickings for rhetorical analysis and do not represent anything new for any feminist who has spent any time on Twitter or in a Reddit comment section.[63] Various arguments for technical goodness (or badness) are routinely used in the service of justifying or disputing the conclusion of a study, particularly when it involves a topic such as race or gender. But the kinds of public arguments we see in Reddit conversations and news site comment sections only represent one layer in a rhetorical/technological stack where a binary coupling irritates the otherwise seemingly closed operation of the data science system and therefore might usefully inform a more nuanced analysis of what good might actually come out of such a study and such a system.

Components in the Rhetorical-Technical Stack

Terrell et al.'s study of gender bias in computing is notable for its complex interweaving of rhetorical and technological elements all the way through the process, from data collection to analysis to dissemination. In conducting a sample stack reading of the paper, we will concentrate on several layers:

1. *A rhetorical substrate.* First, it must be noted that any human activity is a complicated mix of actions, politics, technologies, and ideologies. In the case of the open source community generally, we have a well-documented system of software development dependent on multiple soft and hard elements—everything from coding bodies to machines to the open source stack of software that enables computation and communication. Let's consider this the "necessary substrate" of the study, the activity without which the study would have no research question.

2. *Data layers and scrapers: GitHub, GHTorrent.* There are two specific services: GitHub, the repository for many software projects in development, both open licensed and closed, containing the actual data the study uses, and GHTorrent, a third-party service that offers "a scalable, queriable, offline mirror of data offered through the GitHub REST API" (The GHTorrent project). This service provides a means of accessing GitHub data that would otherwise be difficult to scrape, given the query limitations of the GitHub API on its own. The authors of the gender bias study made use of this service in order to extract a large corpus of user data, supplementing it with some scripts for scraping material that was not included in the torrent. GitHub is not the only repository of software development, but it provides a very useful binary metric for studying contributor activity: namely, acceptance of pull requests.

3. *Google Plus: identifying gender.* In the stack, we also have a novel response to the problem of identifying gender identity in GitHub user data, which is that users often do not make use of readily identifiable gender classes in their usernames. The authors, in an attempt to remedy this issue, created a method for linking GitHub user accounts with their associated Google Plus email accounts, thereby allowing a wider source of identifying information (e.g., "real" names, user uploaded images, Google's required "gender" dropdown during account setup, etc.). In this layer of the stack, categorizing the gender performance of online users is cer-

tainly one rail upon which to potentially critique the study from many angles, both technical and social, and may provide fertile ground for a discussion of what it means to "identify" a gender and what privacy concerns result. The latter concern is laid out in the study, where the authors discuss their decision to scrub released data of identifiable gender/user information that might open up individual users to harassment.

4. *Analysis*. The next two layers in the stack are the ones on which most time is probably spent in academic discussions, and it is these we will tease out further. First, the data analysis and methodology layer: the authors made use of both standard tools (R, for example) and some bespoke scripts for interrogating data. As we have described, these choices of technologies (e.g., data analysis software, statistical tests) would form the basis of a discussion of goodness, both technical and methodological, by initial reviewers as they evaluated the appropriateness or fit of technical choices, resulting in a cycling between the analysis layer (layer 4) and dissemination layer (layer 5) that we will describe, as comments were taken under consideration in the paper's next revision.

5. *Open access dissemination of scholarship*. PeerJ plays a crucial role in the stack. It is between the layer of data analysis and publication that a moment of transformation occurs: from the study as an activity that makes use of open data to the paper itself as an example of open-access scholarship. This openness not only facilitates the kind of information freedom valued by hackers[64] but also propagates the right to free speech at the level of raw data.

6. *Media layer*. The final layer in the stack is the "media layer," including venues legitimized by their status as news agencies (e.g., the *Washington Post*, the *Guardian*) and the social media commonly considered (from the perspective of academic discourse, in any case) to be frivolous or at least an unlikely source of legitimate discussion, although even this characterization is open to debate given the wide range of scholars who make use of social media to publicize or even conduct their research.

Here, then, are the components of a rhetorical/technological stack for the GitHub study:

- Substrate (programmer activity, associated languages and technologies, open source ideologies and licenses and identity construction, all constituting their own highly complex stacks)
- GitHub (the data itself)
- GHTorrent (and ancillaries: bespoke scrapers to capture missing information)

- Google Plus
- Analysis (looped back down through GitHub recursively)
- PeerJ upload; transition from open data to open access
- Community commentary in PeerJ
- News and social media (e.g., Reddit, Twitter, Facebook, etc.)

If there is one area in which Terrell et al.'s study proves especially fruitful as a rhetorical figure for study, it is in the way it complicates our understanding of what constitutes *good* authorial practice in the academy, a practice that is both technical and social in its understanding of goodness. Just as data acquisition, cleaning, and analysis makes use of many technological tools and coauthors along the way, so too the work of authoring, peer review, and publication relies on many layers of negotiation with software tools, systems, ideologies of authorship, and hierarchies of knowledge valuation within and outside the academy. Consider the way in which the paper was disseminated: not via traditional peer review and publication in a journal, but rather via the PeerJ system. Such a move brings up issues of legitimacy on several fronts, in a highly stratified academic community that relies on peer review as its primary means of conveying status. In this respect, PeerJ can be characterized as a response to/critique of closed-publication methods in which "blindness" operates to both obfuscate (possibly subjective) editorial processes and provides a seeming rationale for scientific "objectivity." Institutionally, of course, the tension of scholarly legitimacy (peer review) versus soliciting response from multiple communities (open review, sharing) has long played out in every corner of the academy in the form of ardent discussions over tenure review cases, nearly almost exclusively to the detriment of the candidate. In part, this high-stakes value judgment has to do with the institutional performance of expertise, which shifts questions of legitimacy from author to audience (Who is qualified to comment? This is the underlying principle of peer review). In the GitHub example, we see particularly stark levels of stratification in peer commentary as we move up and down the stack: everything from "peer" commentary by scholars on PeerJ's system, to subsequent (and varyingly accurate) reporting in the media, to the rough-and-tumble communities of Twitter and Reddit, themselves constituted of varying layers of expertise and opinion. Despite institutional protestations to the contrary, it is almost guaranteed that these layers of extra-expertise "review" will be entered into open debate during academic discussions of the work, by virtue of being open for anyone to read.

But beyond standing as a fairly typical exemplar of how academic expertise is negotiated, the study also lays bare the highly complex nature of interrogating and communicating knowledge in the age of the Stack. In particular, the creation of algorithms designed to automate and communicate portions of the analysis suggests that the way we work with our machines not only involves a notion of technical goodness but also a more expansive understanding of how our technical decisions might constitute a new kind of practice in which machines contribute *as rhetorical actors* to the expertise we ultimately disseminate. Two practices carried out by Terrell et al. in the process of conducting and publishing the GitHub gender study allow us to understand how a rhetorical stack might function not merely as a means of stratification of data and knowledge practices but rather as a coauthorial communicative metamachine:

1. *Using GitHub as both source and site of practice.* In a neat act of scholarly recursion, the authors chose to make use of GitHub not only as the primary source of their data but also as a means of working through their own authoring (or rather, revision and reauthoring) process. Chris Parnin, one of the researchers on the paper, notes the value of isolating peer review comments into bite-sized chunks,[65] both for purposes of revision and more generally in order to deal with the psychological effects of having to respond to a deluge of commentary: an anxiety any academic can attest to who has received that "Reviewer 2" response. The authors of the study chose to treat peer responses as "Issues," rather than critiques, and made use of GitHub's "Issue Tracker" function in order to discuss and respond to each comment systematically. This had the benefit of providing a kind of authorial distance, transforming the usual academic response to critique into a software-facilitated list of tasks.

2. *Creating machine coauthors.* In addition to using GitHub as a kind of authorial task-tracker, the authors also created bespoke scripts that allowed them to automate parts of their analysis. For example, updates to the study data were communicated via scripts higher up the stack, where new analyses were run automatically in order to generate new conclusion data (e.g., number counts, variance, etc.). This is a particularly interesting example of the way information work is transformed into authoring via an automated method, allowing the authors of the scripts and the scripts themselves to act as coauthors, as well as computational collaborators in the search for technically good results. Parnin describes this process as embodying the challenge of "getting from data to paper," characterizing the authors' process as the creation of what he calls a "living paper" in which, as the data changes, so too does the hypothesis, often resulting in the need to update the actual scripts to reflect new evidence.[66]

Conclusion

Combining rhetorical analysis with the Stack to discuss movements of data allows us to see more clearly several operations in our search for technical and ethical ideas of goodness:

- how data is necessarily collected, cleaned, and interrogated in stages, using multiple different technological tools;
- how each stage carries its own understanding of what *technical good* constitutes (e.g., good data, good cleaning practices, good processing practices, good analysis practices);
- how each stage carries many concomitant valuations of *ethical and ideological good* as we look at the potential effects of the data (e.g., Will using this data over that provide us with a social good? Is this analysis "good" enough to pass peer review?); and crucially
- how that understanding of what constitutes *good* might then be communicated up and back down the stack, forming a kind of rhetorical situation in which multiple understandings of goodness are negotiated between layers.

As Terrell et al.'s study on gender bias so clearly shows, research in big data requires the assembly of a series of "stack layers" that are often deployed uniquely in each project configuration because of the particularities of the data, its context, its acquisition, and its operational system. Communicative practices coupled across/up/down the resulting assemblage similarly necessitate the bespoke creation of new additions or plugins to the stack (e.g., unique algorithms customized to specific data sets). But because these layers are non-standard, it becomes hard to assess the technical goodness of the project as a whole. Instead, we are forced to fall back on assessment of individual layers (e.g., the choice of statistical test, the choice of technologies, the choice of platform) without being able to evaluate how they might complicate the entire stack and how that might result in the propagation of errors through miscommunication or mismatch between technologies.

The underlying mediations and technical negotiations "under the hood" are then complicated by the addition of "social" layers to the stack. How the work is peer reviewed, published, critiqued, and subsequently reported on in technical/academic or nontechnical/nonacademic arenas influences our evaluations of the elements of *phronesis* that manifest in a project. As a result, competing narratives about what is good encompass such issues as blind versus open peer review, closed journal versus open archive publication, who is permitted to comment and in what forum, debates about the value of scientific communication in the age of click bait, and what *social justice* means and for whom.

Nevertheless, despite these complications, analyzing open access and open data projects using a "stack" model helps us see where the complexities lie in the search for goodness. Rather than limited to method or divorced from data science entirely, we instead see in the stack ongoing persuasive choices made in the constitution of particular views of goodness, as well as its complement, ill. Rhetorical calculation that manifests multiple forms of goodness in this particular moment is stacked within the layers, as well as among the layers themselves.[67] As a result, big data, instead of transcending the rhetorical through computation, actually reaffirms rhetoric's centrality. Rather than dealing in matters that "cannot now or in the future be, other than they are," Aristotle argues that rhetoric addresses questions regarding what is probable rather than true. In describing rhetoric as an "offshoot of dialectic and ethical studies," he makes clear that what is considered good is often a matter of persuasion. Although this conception of goodness raises the threat of relativism or, even worse, of a dark art that through fallacious reasoning makes what is ill appear good, Aristotle argues that through education and disposition, the *phronimos*—one who can see what is good both for herself and for others—ensures that human flourishing (*eudaimonia*) is always the ultimate end of action. But as Martha Nussbaum points out, goodness is fragile because humans are fragile: "What we find valuable depends essentially on what we need and how we are limited."[68] By realizing that data analytics encourages more rhetoric, not less, we come to realize the fragility of big data and the continued need to consider how best to achieve human flourishing.

Notes

1. G. W. Leibniz, *Logical Papers: A Selection* (Oxford: Oxford University Press, 1966), quoted in Bertrand Russell, *A Critical Exposition of the Philosophy of Leibniz* (Cambridge, UK: Cambridge University Press, 1900), 169–70.

2. Joseph M. Juran, *Juran on Quality by Design* (New York: Free Press, 1992), 9.

3. See, for example, Ahmad Ghazal et al., "BigBench: Towards an Industry Standard Benchmark for Big Data Analytics," in *Proceedings of the 2013 ACM SIGMOD International Conference on Management of Data* (ACM, 2013): 1197–1208; Stephen Kaisler et al., "Big Data: Issues and Challenges Moving Forward," in *46th Hawaii International Conference on System Sciences* (IEEE, 2013), 995–1004; Joseph Krall, Tim Menzies, and Misty Davies, "Learning the Task Management Space of an Aircraft Approach Model," in *Modeling in Human-Machine Systems: Challenges for Formal Verification: Papers from the AAAI Spring Symposium* (The AAAI Press, 2014), 92–

97; Paul C. Zikopoulos et al., *Understanding Big Data: Analytics for Enterprise Class Hadoop and Streaming Data* (New York: McGraw-Hill, 2011).

4. Peter Groves et al., "The 'Big Data' Revolution in Healthcare: Accelerating Value and Innovation" (Center for US Health System Reform Business Technology Office, 2013); Travis B. Murdoch and Allan S. Detsky, "The Inevitable Application of Big Data to Health Care," *JAMA* 309, no. 13 (April 3, 2013): 1351–52; Wullianallur Raghupathi and Viju Raghupathi, "Big Data Analytics in Healthcare: Promise and Potential," *Health Information Science and Systems* 2, no. 1 (December 2014): 1–10.

5. Debashis Aikat, "Big Data Dilemmas: The Theory and Practice of Ethical Big Data Mining for Socio-Economic Development," in *Ethical Data Mining Applications for Socio-Economic Development*, ed. Hakikur Rahman and Isabel Ramos, (Hershey, PA: IGI Global, 2013, 106–30); Omer Tene and Jules Polonetsky, "Big Data for All: Privacy and User Control in the Age of Analytics," *Northwestern Journal of Technology and Intellectual Property* 11, no. 5 (2013): 239–73; Xindong Wu, Xingquan Zhu, Gong-Qing Wu, and Wei Ding, "Data Mining with Big Data," *IEEE Transactions on Knowledge and Data Engineering* 26, no. 1 (January 2014): 97–107.

6. Markus Christen et al., "Ethical Issues of 'Morality Mining': Moral Identity as a Focus of Data Mining," in *Human Rights and Ethics: Concepts, Methodologies, Tools, and Applications*, ed. Information Resources Management Association (Hershey, PA: IGI Global, 2015), 1146–66.

7. World Health Organization, "Influenza (Seasonal)," last modified January 31, 2018, http://www.who.int/mediacentre/factsheets/fs211/en/.

8. Google, "About Flu Trends," accessed August 15, 2014, https://www.google.org/flutrends/about/.

9. Justin Kintz, "Driving Solutions to Build Smarter Cities," Uber Newsroom, January 13, 2015, https://newsroom.uber.com/us-massachusetts/driving-solutions-to-build-smarter-cities/.

10. Ibid.

11. Aristotle, "Nichomachean Ethics," in *The Complete Works of Aristotle*, vol. 2, ed. Jonathan Barnes (Princeton: Princeton University Press, 1984), 1138a32–33.

12. Andrew McAfee, "Big Data's Biggest Challenge? Convincing People NOT to Trust Their Judgment," *Harvard Business Review*, December 9, 2013, https://hbr.org/2013/12/big-datas-biggest-challenge-convincing-people-not-to-trust-their-judgment.

13. Aristotle, "Nichomachean Ethics," 1140a20–23.

14. Norbert Wiener, *Cybernetics or Control and Communication in the Animal and the Machine*, 2nd ed. (Cambridge: MIT Press, 1948), 28.

15. Ibid.

16. Wiener, *Cybernetics*, 29.

17. Grady Booch, "Morality and the Software Architect," *IEEE Software* 25, no. 1 (January–February 2008): 8.

18. Grady Booch, "All Watched Over by Machines of Loving Grace," *IEEE Software* 32, no. 2 (March–April 2015): 20.

19. Jacques Ellul, *The Technological System* (New York: Continuum, 1980); Langdon Winner, *Autonomous Technology* (Cambridge: MIT Press, 1977).

20. Niklas Luhmann, *Social Systems* (Stanford, CA: Stanford University Press, 1995), 136–39.

21. Ibid., 79.

22. Humberto R. Maturana and Francisco J. Varela, *Autopoiesis and Cognition: The Realization of the Living* (Dordrecht: D. Reidel Publishing Company, 1980), 9.

23. Luhmann, *Social Systems*, 3.

24. Niklas Luhmann, *Law as a Social System* (Oxford: Oxford University Press, 2004), 118.

25. Ibid., 94.

26. Niklas Luhmann, "Code of the Moral," *Cardozo Law Review* 14 (1993): 1005.

27. John Rawls, *Political Liberalism* (New York: Columbia University Press, 2003).

28. Luhmann, "Code of the Moral," 1005.

29. Niklas Luhmann, "The Sociology of the Moral and Ethics," *International Sociology* 11, no. 1 (March 1996): 31.

30. Ibid.

31. Alexander R. Galloway, *Protocol: How Control Exists after Decentralization* (Cambridge: MIT Press, 2004), 243.

32. Ibid., 40.

33. Ibid., 245.

34. Luhmann, *Law as a Social System*, 357–80.

35. Luhmann, "The Sociology of the Moral and Ethics," 33.

36. Jeremy Ginsberg et al., "Detecting Influenza Epidemics Using Search Engine Query Data," *Nature* 457 (February 19, 2009): 1012.

37. Ibid.

38. Viktor Mayer-Schönberger and Kenneth Cukier, *Big Data: A Revolution That Will Transform How We Live, Work, and Think* (Boston: Houghton Mifflin Harcourt, 2013), 55.

39. Ibid., 53.

40. Ibid., 55.

41. Gil Press, "A Very Short History of Data Science," *Forbes* Tech Blog, last updated May 28, 2013, https://www.forbes.com/sites/gilpress/2013/05/28/a-very-short-history-of-data-science/#55ad9cc455cf.

42. Ian Hacking, *The Emergence of Probability: A Philosophical Study of Early Ideas about Probability, Induction and Statistical Inference*, 2nd ed. (Cambridge: Cambridge University Press, 2006), 1.

43. Ginsberg et al., "Detecting Influenza Epidemics," 1012.

44. Declan Butler, "When Google Got Flu Wrong," *Nature* 494 (February 13, 2013): 155–56.

45. David Lazer et al., "The Parable of Google Flu: Traps in Big Data Analysis," *Science* 343, no. 6176 (March 14, 2014): 1203–5.

46. Lee Gomes, "Machine-Learning Maestro Michael Jordan on the Delusions of Big Data and Other Huge Engineering Efforts," *IEEE Spectrum*, October 20, 2014, https://spectrum.ieee.org/robotics/artificial-intelligence/machinelearning-maestro-michael-jordan-on-the-delusions-of-big-data-and-other-huge-engineering-efforts.

47. Justin Washtell, "The Single Best Predictive Modeling Technique. Seriously," *Analytic Bridge*, last updated October 29, 2014, http://www.analyticbridge.com/profiles /blogs/the-single-best-predictive-modeling-technique-seriously.

48. Aristotle, "Rhetoric," *The Complete Works of Aristotle*, vol. 2, ed. Jonathan Barnes (Princeton: Princeton University Press, 1984), 1357a5.

49. See Dilip Parameshwar Goankar, "The Idea of Rhetoric in the Rhetoric of Science," *The Southern Communication Journal* 58, no. 4 (1993): 258–95.

50. Edward Schiappa, "Second Thoughts on the Critiques of Big Rhetoric," *Philosophy and Rhetoric* 34, no. 3 (2001): 260–74.

51. Benjamin H. Bratton, *The Stack: On Software and Sovereignty* (Cambridge: MIT Press, 2015).

52. Ibid., 8.

53. Ibid., 69.

54. Ibid., 61.

55. J. Terrell et al., "Gender Differences and Bias in Open Source: Pull Request Acceptance of Women Versus Men," *PeerJ Preprints* (2016), http://doi.org/10.7287 /peerj.preprints.1733v2.

56. Marianne Bertrand and Sendhil Mullainatha, "Are Emily and Greg More Employable than Lakisha and Jamal? A Field Experiment on Labor Market Discrimination," *American Economic Review* 94, no. 4 (September 2004): 991–1013; Silvia Knobloch-Westerwick and Carroll J. Glynn, "The Matilda Effect—Role Congruity Effects on Scholarly Communication: A Citation Analysis of *Communication Research* and *Journal of Communication* Articles," *Communication Research* 40, no. 1 (February 2013): 3–26.

57. Terrell et al., "Gender Differences and Bias in Open Source," 18.

58. Ibid., 26.

59. Ibid., 27.

60. In Dalmeet Singh Chawla, "Researchers Debate Whether Female Computer Coders Face Bias," *Nature* 530, no. 7590 (February 2016): 257.

61. In Terrell et al., comments section.

62. Yourbasicgeek, "Women Considered Better Coders—But Only If They Hide Their Gender," Reddit.com, last updated February 12, 2016, https://redd.it/45f3mh.

63. See Esther Zukerman, "'Why Is Reddit So Anti-Woman?': An Epic Reddit Thread Counts the Ways," *The Atlantic*, July 26, 2012, http://www.theatlantic .com/entertainment/archive/2012/07/why-reddit-so-anti-women-epic-reddit-thread -counts-ways/325357/; Alex Cranz, "The Best Place to Find Stuff on Reddit Is Promoting Misogynistic Garbage," Gizmodo, April 26, 2016, http://gizmodo.com/the -best-place-to-find-stuff-on-reddit-is-promoting-mys-1772992114.

64. E. Gabriella Coleman, "The Political Agnosticism of Free and Open Source Software and the Inadvertent Politics of Contrast," *Anthropological Quarterly* 77, no. 3 (Summer 2004): 507–19; Steven Levy, *Hackers: Heroes of the Computer Revolution* (Sebastopol, CA: O'Reilly, 1994); Jennifer Helene Maher, *Software Evangelism and the Rhetoric of Morality: Coding Justice in a Digital Democracy* (New York: Routledge, 2016).

65. Chris Parnin, conversation with Helen J. Burgess, September 7, 2016.

66. Ibid.

67. Jennifer Maher, "The Artificial Rhetorical Agent and the Computing of Phronesis," *Computational Culture: A Journal of Software Studies* 5 (2016), http://computationalculture.net/article/artificial-rhetorical-agents-and-the-computing-of-phronesis.

68. Martha C. Nussbaum, *The Fragility of Goodness: Luck and Ethics in Greek Tragedy and Philosophy* (New York: Cambridge University Press, 2001), 342.

12 / Nasty Women and Private Servers

Gender, Technology, and Politics

Elizabeth Losh

Many will insist that Hillary Clinton lost the 2016 US presidential election solely because of her gender. They will argue that both implicit bias and toxic misogyny doomed her candidacy and that the physical appearance, voice, and manner of a sixty-nine-year-old professional woman were unacceptable to the electorate as attributes of a political sovereign, either because they conformed to normative gender expectations or because they violated them. Even before the election, Elaine Showalter described the public's mood as "witch-burning ecstasy,"[1] and Kelly Wilz noted that gender essentialism might also be a factor, as well as the need of aggressively anti-establishment "Bernie Bros" to assert masculinity."[2] Communication scholars have argued that sexism in both parties was already a major factor for Clinton in the 2008 election,[3] as was the "pornification" of female candidates,[4] and that Clinton's cartoon image even posed a threat to gender norms during her earlier tenure as First Lady.[5]

Others will assert that Clinton lost because of technology and that it was impossible for her to survive a series of scandals stemming from a two-sided attack on her online practices that included an extensive FBI investigation of a private computer server located in the basement of her home, as well as hacktivist exposure by Wikileaks and other transparency organizations. A post-election intelligence report asserted that foreign powers also exploited digital communications infrastructure "to undermine public faith in the US democratic process, denigrate Secretary Clinton, and harm her electability and potential presidency,"[6] with cyber espionage as key part of a concerted campaign in which pro-Russian hackers bombarded the public with an endless stream of purloined email trails from her campaign and the Democratic National Committee. These covert electronic messages swirling around the Clinton digital persona seemed to show a practitioner of the dark arts of insider politics and gaming the system. According to the logic of focusing on technology rather than gender, either her secretive wizardry or her sloppy vulnerability disqualified her from office.

I would assert that it may actually be the conflation of gender *and* technology at work in the popular imagination that was to blame for Clinton's stunning defeat, which many pollsters and pundits had not predicted. Obviously, I am not the first to suggest that gender and technology are closely allied, given the work done by previous feminist scholars of science and technology studies (STS). For example, Anne Balsamo's *Technologies of the Gendered Body* contradicted the truisms of the nature/culture divide and argued that gendered bodies were always "product" and "process."[7] In *TechnoFeminism*, Judy Wajcman declared that "technology is both a source and a consequence of gender relations."[8] And feminist film theorists have long argued that cinema is one of many "technologies of gender."[9]

There are also long histories of the entanglements of gender and technology and how computational privacy itself may be conceptualized as feminine. In *Virtualpolitik* I argued that it was no accident that the "girl" was such an important figure of speech in so many founding documents written by the pioneers of computer science.[10] For example, in the introduction to Claude Shannon's *Mathematical Theory of Communication* Warren Weaver compared an "engineering communication theory" to "a very proper and discreet girl accepting your telegram," because she "pays no attention to the meaning, whether it be sad, or joyous, or embarrassing," conveying the expectation that "she must be prepared to deal with all that come to her desk."[11] As an engineered series of protocols, Weaver's girl is devoid of affect in her protection of privacy. Because her labor is feminized as service work, she is disinvested from the information she conveys and is able to be a vestal virgin uncontaminated by the content she transmits.

Jeannie Suk poses the hypothesis that "privacy is a woman" in the discourses of American technology law. For example, in interpreting *Kyllo v. United States*, a case in which the government used a thermal imaging device to secure a search warrant for a man growing marijuana inside his house, Suk notes how the logic of penetration and domination might be countered by the claims to privacy of a female domestic sphere. In the final Supreme Court decision Justice Scalia speculated that the heat-sensing device might well disclose intimate information—such as "at what hour each night the lady of the house takes her daily sauna and bath." Suk is struck by the premises of Scalia's example, which draws upon very old tropes, including biblical stories about Bathsheba and David or Susanna and the Elders. She observes that Justice Scalia does not imagine merely any detail of the home, but a woman, specifically a "lady." "And speaking of 'the lady of the house' implies her counterpart, the master of the house. This anachronistic language thus calls to mind more than the privacy interests of a lady bathing. It also evokes the privacy interest of the man entitled to see the lady of the house

naked and his interest in shielding her body from prying eyes. Privacy is figured as a woman, an object of the male gaze."¹² In Suk's analysis, as the male
gaze becomes equipped with more sophisticated snooping devices for tracing, probing, scoping, and spying, it is only the trope of female modesty that
constrains its purview.

What does this confluence of privacy, gender, and technology reveal about
the investigation of Hillary Clinton? And why was her general use of email
so damaging in the court of public opinion?

The victory of Donald J. Trump—who refused to participate in the back
channel of email and only used the front channel of Twitter during the
campaign—may indicate that populist sympathies could not be aligned with
Clinton because of her gendered affiliation with digital media and its ambi-
guities of access, a realm of communication in which electronic files could
easily reach unintended audiences and be used for unanticipated purposes or
altered to disguise provenance and character. In contrast—throughout his real
estate development, hospitality industry, entertainment, lifestyle marketing,
and political careers—Trump avoided most personal computing technologies
intended for both home and business. In sworn depositions Trump declared
that he didn't "do the email thing" and preferred to send traditional letters
typed by secretaries directly to correspondents.¹³ In his view, such missives
could only be securely transported by human agents using analog means. According to Trump, "if you have something really important, write it out and
have it delivered by courier, the old-fashioned way, because I'll tell you what,
no computer is safe."¹⁴

It might sound plausible to defend a general right to email privacy irrespec-
tive of gender, class, or condition. When Stanford law professor and transparency advocate Lawrence Lessig read disparaging remarks made by the Clinton
campaign about his own bid for the presidency, he refused to condemn his
exposed political detractors. "We all deserve privacy. The burdens of public
service are insane enough without the perpetual threat that every thought
shared with a friend becomes Twitter fodder."¹⁵ Significantly Lessig had already come out against what he called the "naked transparency" movement
years before, which he saw not as a force for accountability but one for push-
ing "any faith in our political system over the cliff."¹⁶ Like Scalia, he used the
metaphor of vulnerable embodied nudity as a way to explain the risks of constant technological access and even recounted a hypothetical case from the
New York Times about an "attractive young blond woman" under the "glassy
eye" of prurient surveillance. However, Lessig generally adopted a rhetoric
of ungendered universalism to explain why digital privacy should be priori-
tized over digital publicity by using analogies from the healthcare system in

which the expectations for protecting sensitive information would be relatively gender-blind and governed by doctor-patient confidentiality.

In defending her own personal privacy Clinton often specifically claimed feminine privilege. For example, she described many of the more than thirty thousand emails that were deleted from her private account as not pertinent to the government's inquiry because they were about her "daughter Chelsea's wedding, her mother Dorothy's funeral, her yoga routines and family vacations"[17] rather than worldly professional matters. All of these items depict Clinton assuming traditional female roles as a caretaker of the home and manager of family rituals of birth, marriage, pilgrimage, and death. Even the mention of yoga routines suggests activity in an all-female sanctuary. These explanations were widely ridiculed by her opponent, his surrogates, conservative news organizations, and Internet meme generators in the alt-right community.

Certainly critics of visual culture watching the television coverage of Clinton's email scandal on Fox News might be quick to observe a particular pattern. Whenever news anchors discussed her use of emails, the accompanying B-roll showed a montage of images of Clinton on her BlackBerry, and some reporters even spoke in front of screens with these images. The images were not flattering. They generally showed Clinton as a multitasker who was simultaneously absent and present. Often in these images of Clinton as a user of ubiquitous technologies she is ignoring other people or expressing negative affective states like irritation or boredom. In one of the most commonly used images on Fox News, in which her eyes are completely veiled by sunglasses, she seems completely withdrawn from her environment.[18]

In comparison, President Obama was always much more savvy about avoiding the appearance of digital distraction and multitasking with others present.[19] As I have written elsewhere, official White House photographs emphasized that BlackBerries should be checked at the door before important meetings, and Obama was often shown using one only outside of the Oval Office and far from the official spaces of statecraft to underscore a clear separation between modalities for face-to-face communication and those for computer-mediated interaction.[20] In the visual rhetoric of the White House Flickr photostream, the BlackBerry was clearly a device for outside. Images show Obama checking BlackBerry messages outdoors, offstage, obscured by his elevated feet, or in the dead of night.

The association of Clinton's computer practices with impurity was also facilitated by both implicit and explicit comparisons with her husband and his infidelities and misrepresentations. A popular Internet meme showed Hillary Clinton's image juxtaposed with typography that read "I did not have textual relations with that server," which echoed Bill Clinton's famous line to the American people: "I did not have sexual relations with that woman." The meme suggests that former Secretary Clinton is denying her own digital promiscuity and lack of self-control. The fact that the traffic on the Clinton family's servers was intermingled was also considered suspect for those who continued to propagate conspiracy theories about her husband.[21]

However, as Wendy Chun points out in *Freedom and Control*, any puritanical vision of digital privacy perpetuates blind spots about how computers actually work. For Chun, the dialectic of freedom and control associated with interactive media and distributed networks represents a form of false consciousness that denies the realities of data loss and imperfect scrutiny, the agency of smart objects, the interdependence of machine-to-machine communication, and the fact that digital discourse always requires a public machine engaged in incessant intercourse with various information flows.[22]

To conceptualize this state of constant availability, James J. Brown Jr. sees the relationship of "hospitality" at the heart of computational interactions and algorithmic operations. The machine must welcome input and allow output with the generosity of a host to a guest. In Brown's analysis, the social contract of such hospitality is construed very generally so as not to require specific invitations, but it also assumes that not all comers should be allowed to pass into a hybrid space of domesticity and public life. Brown also assumes that the boundary between the home and outside is drawn by "the master of the house," but he grants that such boundary-drawing is a mutual process that involves "the other that arrives" as well.[23]

Although Alexander Galloway suggests that this interaction can be imagined as the businesslike and neutral Transmission Control Protocol "handshake" that links sender and receiver in a shared transactional grasp,[24] it may also have the connotations of illicit sexual transmission, much like the "I Love You" virus in Microsoft Outlook.[25] Galloway argues that new forms of cyberfeminism are actually legitimated by digital platforms that validate multiple couplings: "The universality of protocol can give feminism something that it never had at its disposal, the obliteration of the masculine from beginning to end . . . In other words, as protocol rises, patriarchy declines."[26] Obviously, such challenges to the norms of technologically mediated communication and conventional gender roles can be read as threatening and a cause for political reaction and defense of the traditional status quo.

By intermingling personal and professional communication in one email channel for display on one mobile device, Clinton violated another area in which clear boundary policing would have been expected. As she explained in a news conference on March 10, 2015, "I opted for convenience to use my personal email account, which was allowed by the State Department, because

I thought it would be easier to carry just one device for my work and for my personal emails instead of two."[27] Clinton's well-documented desire not to carry multiple smart phones to facilitate mutually exclusive communication with either the State Department or friends and family constituted a serious perceived transgression in resisting the dominant two-device/two-channel digital policy at the State Department.

However, reporting by Politico.com analyzing nearly 250 pages of interviews and reports available through the Freedom of Information Act showed that Clinton's one-device/two-accounts explanation of convenience might have been much more plausible than it seemed at the time of her testimony. Despite the depictions of Clinton on Fox News as a digitally immersed cybercitizen, it appeared from the Politico coverage that Hillary Clinton's textual relations with computational media were often maladroit and tentative rather than seductive and practiced. Her preference for one device indicated attachment to an outdated BlackBerry with a trackball, and her use of multiple email accounts was a workaround that compensated for State Department network limitations.

The Politico reporting also revealed that Clinton was unable to use a desktop computer, an account confirmed by my own interviews with State Department insiders several years ago. In the dramatization of the Politico story by National Public Radio's *This American Life*, one can actually hear the astonishment of reporters over Clinton's lack of familiarity with basic office equipment: "I can get not knowing how to play an Xbox or virtual reality machine or something like that, but I mean a desktop computer—I mean this is literally the oldest piece of personal technology available to us today."[28]

According to the *Daily Mail*, Clinton was also a poor typist.[29] It is strange to think that one of the oldest of the new media practices identified by Friedrich Kittler[30]—typing—would be the Achilles heel for a twenty-first-century would-be female commander-in-chief. Yet as a tacit knowledge practice and a form of embodied cognition, typing apparently remained alien to Clinton. Given that typing was a strongly gendered activity in relatively recent memory, Clinton's resistance to learning it is certainly understandable. After all, J. C. R. Licklider wrote that one "can hardly take a military commander or a corporation president away from his work to teach him to type."[31] In Clinton's aspiration to escape the conventional gender roles of secretary or office girl and dream of life as an executive or commander she somehow never acquired the basic skills of the service sector and office environment.

In contrast, analysis of President Obama's hands on the keyboard indicate a well-trained typist. Yet despite what seems to be the public relations value of Obama's basic competence in office computing practices that might make him a more relatable public figure, the visual rhetoric of the White House—

particularly in his first hundred days—showed that it was still important to defend his masculinity by using depictions of his online activity to create distance from feminized computational labor practices.[32] In particular, by emphasizing certain kinds of images showing work at the keyboard and by adding explanatory captions, press officials could present Obama as the kind of leader that Licklider described. On the rare occasions when Obama was posed in front of someone else's computer screen, as he was for the launch of a new government website, official captions on the Flickr photostream inform the public that these interactions involve the desktop computer of his secretary Katie Johnson rather than his own device.

Reading the images posted by the White House, the rhetoric of masculine detachment from technological connection could be quite striking during the Obama administration. Sometimes the computer screen in front of the president's gaze would even be blank. When Obama "looks over his prepared remarks in the Outer Oval Office," the viewer could see the president engaged with a traditional print text on the desk in front of him and a neglected computer screen displaying a screen saver. If Obama's hands are shown on an actual keyboard, taking part in a form of manual labor usually attached to the White House's female employees, a caption supplies the information that Obama is only typing "last-minute edits" rather than engaging in extended composition that would require long periods of word processing or data input. In another image, the detachment of a masculine president from the scene of women's work and the computer screens of a feminized service economy is dramatized with the president catching a football pass with Johnson's computer screens in the foreground. Obama's eyes are on the ball in mid-flight; the digital information on the monitors is intended for the gaze of others.[33]

The presence of printers and other peripherals could make the existing dynamic around security, transparency, and technological dependence even more problematic for Clinton. As comedian Samantha Bee noted in a humorous routine with Sarah Paulson, "Pls. print" was one of Clinton's most common directives. Unpacking the rhetoric of stories with titles like "Clinton Directed Her Maid to Print out Classified Materials"[34] in the *New York Post* reveals multiple layers of concern about class, gender, and national security. The maid is an inappropriate intermediary for digital state secrets because of her subordinate gender and class, and Clinton also seems to be exploiting her labor by "directing" her to do work that a secretary of state should be able to do for herself. Ironically Donald J. Trump apparently also has asked his staff constantly to print out materials for him to peruse. According to news accounts, Trump is famous for directing his subordinates every morning to produce on paper the top results returned after inputting his own name into the search engine for Google News.[35] There are many reasons to be skeptical of generational myths about technology,[36] but it is possible that one could argue that this is as much a story about age as a marker of technological competency as it is one about gender.

Nonetheless, if age rather than gender is the root cause of inappropriate digital intermingling, why was Clinton punished for her lack of digital fluency so much more harshly than Trump? In fact, Trump's own digital practices indicate a mixture of informational streams and aggregation of conflicting tactics. Digital forensics on Donald Trump's Twitter feed demonstrate that his online persona used two devices for uploading messages to one account during the course of his candidacy.[37] A Samsung Galaxy produced the angrier tweets that seemed to originate with Trump personally (often outside of business hours), while an Apple iPhone emitted more positive messages that were seemingly written by a more diplomatic PR staffer. Yet somehow the kind of digital Janus-face that Trump presented was acceptable to his supporters.

Trump's online presence was bifurcated in ways that might have acknowledged certain possibilities for hybridity, yet his online strategy did not seem to violate the core social media tenets of simultaneously projecting exhibitionism and a private reserve of moral superiority. Jan-Hinrik Schmidt has compared such hyperattention in social media visibility to "Dutch windows,"[38] the Reformation-era floor-to-ceiling vitrines on public canals that were intended to display the wealth of Puritan dwellings, the upright conduct of occupants in no need of curtains, and the trappings of prosperity theology. This mixture of transparency and integrity has also been promulgated by Facebook founder Mark Zuckerberg, who has scorned maintaining "a different image for your work friends or coworkers and for the other people you know."[39] Perhaps because both Samsung Trump and Apple Trump were visible on the same Twitter feed, Trump's reputation for disclosure was enhanced. Or perhaps in a society that values the acquisition of consumer electronics as status symbols, input from multiple devices could be seen as an excusable excess indicating the attainment of success. In contrast, Clinton described her resistance to carrying more than one mobile phone.[40] Indeed, her aides expressed irritation at her preference for outmoded devices.[41]

Trump made his two-device policy directly relevant to his own enthusiasm for corporate brand shaming after a 2015 attack by Islamic radicals in San Bernardino, California. Trump tweeted: "I use both iPhone & Samsung. If Apple doesn't give info to authorities on the terrorists I'll only be using Samsung until they give info." It appears significant that Trump also explicitly made open access to a secure technology associated with gendered traits a focus in his rhetoric: "Apple won't allow us to get into her cell phone—who do they think they are? No, we have to open it up."[42] In his tweeting Trump addresses a collective "we" with the right to "get into" and "open up" the closed recesses of the proprietary technology that secures the data of the female attacker.

As in the case of *Kyllo v. United States*, the statement explaining the refusal of Apple's president Timothy Cook to assist the authorities with digitally unlocking the assailants' phones connected the concept of digital privacy to the rhetoric of maintaining control of space in a fortified sanctuary. The calls by Trump and others to create a single decryption instrument would, for Cook, create a more troubling kind of anarchic access. "In today's digital world, the 'key' to an encrypted system is a piece of information that unlocks the data, and it is only as secure as the protections around it. Once the information is known, or a way to bypass the code is revealed, the encryption can be defeated by anyone with that knowledge. The government suggests this tool could only be used once, on one phone. But that's simply not true. Once created, the technique could be used over and over again, on any number of devices. In the physical world, it would be the equivalent of a master key, capable of opening hundreds of millions of locks—from restaurants and banks to stores and homes. No reasonable person would find that acceptable."[43]

Cook's use of parallelism suggests that new forms of bank robbery and home invasion would be furthered by the invention of this digital master key and that knowledgeable outsiders would soon appropriate the mastery once coveted by the government to use against citizens' privacy. For her part, Chun argues that there is an even greater risk in aspiring for such "master keys" to complex systems. In *Programmed Visions*, she reminds us that "our interactions with computers cannot be reduced to the traces we leave behind," because "the exact paths of execution" are ephemeral.[44]

Hillary Clinton was certainly a flawed candidate when it came to digital policy and computational practice. She declared the Internet to be "the public space of the twenty-first century" and yet refused to post her own speeches on her own website. She hectored State Department employees about cybersecurity in official videos and yet ducked responsibility for basic data preservation.

However, to acknowledge her limitations—if not outright hypocrisy—in matching her practices to her principles does not mean discounting the harm of paternalistic digital purity myths. These myths establish unrealistic standards that disproportionately punish online conduct marked as feminine or behavior associated with women's digital identities. It is striking that—in the coverage by Fox News of Clinton's regrettable State Department video—reporters also claimed that Clinton's email server was located in a "restroom"[45] and urged her to "look into the mirror."[46] Making such references to a bathroom as a shameful separate sphere and commanding Clinton to occupy a site of reflection and penitence was clearly intended as harsh chastisement for her perceived digital transgressions. Other news organizations described closets or basements as sites of Clinton's covert server in her New York home but avoided associating her digital incrimination with biological humiliation or filth.

Digital purity is a strange amalgam of the fantasies of digital transparency and digital security. In other words, in our current environment, the cultural conversation about technology in the United States seems to be increasingly about digital exclusivity rather than digital privacy. Exclusivity assumes availability but limited access, commitment rather than community, and monogamous subservience rather than cyberfeminism. Digital exclusivity might be best-represented by accepting one's position in multitier Internet speeds or variable pricing on data plans. Because it could be argued that the doctrine of exclusivity is at the heart of his brand, Trump may be a particularly fitting representative of this policy.

Notes

1. Elaine Showalter, "Pilloried Clinton," *Times Literary Supplement*, October 26, 2016, http://www.the-tls.co.uk/articles/public/hillary-clinton-vs-misogyny/.

2. Kelly Wilz, "Bernie Bros and Woman Cards: Rhetorics of Sexism, Misogyny, and Constructed Masculinity in the 2016 Election," *Women's Studies in Communication* 39, no. 4 (2016): 357–60.

3. Diana B. Carlin and Kelly L. Winfrey, "Have You Come a Long Way, Baby? Hillary Clinton, Sarah Palin, and Sexism in 2008 Campaign Coverage," *Communication Studies* 60, no. 4 (2009): 326–43.

4. Karrin Vasby Anderson and Kristina Horn Sheeler, "Texts (and Tweets) from Hillary: Meta-Meming and Postfeminist Political Culture," *Presidential Studies Quarterly* 44, no. 2 (June 2014): 224–43.

5. Charlotte Templin, "Hillary Clinton as Threat to Gender Norms: Cartoon Images of the First Lady," *Journal of Communication Inquiry* 23, no. 1 (January 1999): 20–36.

6. Office of the Director of National Intelligence, "Background to 'Assessing Russian Activities and Intentions in Recent US Elections': The Analytic Process and Cyber Incident Attribution," January 6, 2017, https://www.dni.gov/files/documents/ICA_2017_01.pdf.

7. Anne Balsamo, *Technologies of the Gendered Body: Reading Cyborg Women* (Durham, NC: Duke University Press, 1996), 3.

8. Judy Wajcman, *TechnoFeminism* (Cambridge, UK: Polity Press, 2006), 7.

9. Teresa de Lauretis, *Technologies of Gender: Essays on Theory, Film, and Fiction* (Bloomington: Indiana University Press, 2001).

10. Elizabeth Losh, *Virtualpolitik: An Electronic History of Government Media-Making in a Time of War, Scandal, Disaster, Miscommunication, and Mistakes* (Cambridge: MIT Press, 2009).

11. Claude Elwood Shannon and Warren Weaver, *The Mathematical Theory of Communication* (Urbana: University of Illinois Press, 1999), 27.

12. Jeannie Suk, "Is Privacy a Woman?," *The Georgetown Law Journal* 97, no. 2 (January 2009): 488.

13. Michael Barbaro and Steve Eder, "Under Oath, Donald Trump Shows His Raw Side," *New York Times*, July 28, 2015, https://www.nytimes.com/2015/07/29/us/politics/depositions-show-donald-trump-as-quick-to-exaggerate-and-insult.html.

14. Maggie Haberman, "Trump Promises a Revelation on Hacking," *New York Times*, December 31, 2016, https://www.nytimes.com/2016/12/31/us/politics/donald-trump-russia-hacking.html.

15. Lawrence Lessig, "On the Wikileak-Ed Emails between Tanden and Podesta Re: Me," LESSIG Blog, v2, accessed December 11, 2016, http://lessig.tumblr.com/post/151983995587/on-the-wikileak-ed-emails-between-tanden-and.

16. Lawrence Lessig, "Against Transparency," *New Republic*, October 9, 2009, https://newrepublic.com/article/70097/against-transparency.

17. Anne Gearan and Philip Rucker, "Clinton: It 'Might Have Been Smarter' to Use a State Dept. e-Mail Account," *Washington Post*, March 10, 2015, https://www.washingtonpost.com/politics/hillary-clinton-to-answer-questions-about-use-of-private-e-mail-server/2015/03/10/4c000d00-c735-11e4-a199-6cb5e63819d2_story.html.

18. The same image of Clinton in sunglasses while using her mobile phone was used as a meme in many pro-Clinton circles, including the popular Tumblr blog *Texts from Hillary*, accessed April 29, 2018, http://textsfromhillaryclinton.tumblr.com/.

19. In unpacking the hierarchies of executive privilege, it is interesting that Clinton was denied access to the kind of secure BlackBerry that Obama used in his Flickr photostream or one like one of her predecessors at the Department of State, Condoleezza Rice, had possessed. The workaround of a "private line" was also previously utilized by former Secretary Colin Powell. See Sean Gallagher, "NSA Refused Clinton a Secure BlackBerry like Obama, so She Used Her Own," Ars Technica (blog), last updated March 17, 2016, http://arstechnica.com/information-technology/2016/03/nsa-refused-clinton-a-secure-blackberry-like-obama-so-she-used-her-own/; also see Sean Gallagher, "Ignorance and Indifference: Delving Deep into the Clinton e-Mail Saga," Ars Technica (blog), last updated July 15, 2016, http://arstechnica.com/information-technology/2016/07/indifference-and-ignorance-delving-deep-into-the-clinton-e-mail-saga/.

20. Elizabeth Losh, "Channelling Obama: YouTube, Flickr, and the Social Media President," *Comparative American Studies: An International Journal* 10, nos. 2–3 (2012): 255–68.

21. As intertwined community property, the email server arrangements also necessitated data sharing services that messily distributed access to computational resources between Hillary Clinton's spouse, ex-president Bill Clinton, and the candi-

date herself. Sean Gallagher, "All the Clintons' Servers: Hillary First Used a Power Mac Tower for e-Mail," Ars Technica (blog), last updated September 2, 2016, http://arstechnica.com/information-technology/2016/09/fbi-clintons-first-e-mail-server-was-a-power-mac-tower/. The family drama of inappropriate access extended to Clinton's surrogate daughter, aide Huma Abedin, who was married to disgraced Congressmen Anthony Weiner. Thus, by the transitive property, Clinton found herself linked by FBI director Comey to illicit sexual text messages shared with a fifteen-year-old girl in North Carolina. Adam Goldman and Alan Rappeport, "Emails in Anthony Weiner Inquiry Jolt Hillary Clinton's Campaign," *New York Times*, October 28, 2016, https://www.nytimes.com/2016/10/29/us/politics/fbi-hillary-clinton-email.html.

22. Wendy Hui Kyong Chun, *Control and Freedom: Power and Paranoia in the Age of Fiber Optics* (Cambridge: MIT Press, 2006).

23. James J. Brown Jr., *Ethical Programs: Hospitality and the Rhetorics of Software* (Ann Arbor: University of Michigan Press, 2015), 28.

24. Alexander R. Galloway, *Protocol: How Control Exists after Decentralization* (Cambridge: MIT Press, 2004), 42–43.

25. Ibid., 187.

26. Ibid., 189.

27. Michelle Ye Hee Lee, "Revisiting Clinton's Claim She Used Personal Email Out of 'Convenience,'" *Washington Post*, last updated July 5, 2016, https://www.washingtonpost.com/news/fact-checker/wp/2016/07/05/revisiting-clintons-claim-she-used-personal-email-out-of-convenience-and-it-was-allowed-by-state-department/.

28. Sean Cole, "Server Be Served," *This American Life*, November 4, 2016, https://www.thisamericanlife.org/radio-archives/episode/601/master-of-her-domain-name.

29. David Martosko, "Email-Gate Update: Dick Morris Says Hillary 'Doesn't Know How to Type,'" *Daily Mail*, March 24, 2015, http://www.dailymail.co.uk/news/article-3009471/Former-longtime-Clinton-insider-says-Hillary-doesn-t-know-type-email-scandal-swirls-returns-White-House-Obama-visit.html.

30. Friedrich A. Kittler, *Gramophone, Film, Typewriter*, trans. Geoffrey Winthrop-Young and Michael Wutz (Stanford, CA: Stanford University Press, 1999).

31. J. C. R. Licklider and Robert W. Taylor, "The Computer as a Communication Device," *Science and Technology* 76 (April 1968): 21–31.

32. Losh, "Channelling Obama."

33. In addition to the factors of gender, age, and class discussed in this essay as ways to understand tropes of digital literacy, race is also a factor. Right-wing memes often questioned Obama's technological competence on racist grounds that assumed he could not be an informed cybercitizen. A more fully intersectional analysis of how digital literacy practices are situated in the spaces of political power in the White House is part of a work-in-progress monograph by the author.

34. Paul Sperry, "Clinton Directed Her Maid to Print out Classified Materials," *New York Post* (blog), last updated November 6, 2016, http://nypost.com/2016/11/06/clinton-directed-her-maid-to-print-out-classified-materials/.

35. Damon Beres, "Trump Campaign Wastes a Lot of Paper Printing Articles About

Trump," Huffington Post, last updated June 20, 2016, http://www.huffingtonpost
.com/entry/trump-googles-himself_us_57681aboe4b015db1bca04da.

36. Siva Vaidhyanathan, "Generational Myth," *The Chronicle of Higher Education*,
last updated September 19, 2008, http://chronicle.com/article/Generational-Myth
/32491.

37. David Robinson, "Text Analysis of Trump's Tweets Confirms He Writes Only
the (Angrier) Android Half," Variance Explained (blog), last updated August 9, 2016,
http://varianceexplained.org/r/trump-tweets/.

38. Jan-Hinrik Schmidt, "Internet Privacy—Structural Changes of Publicness in
Digital Networked Media" (Berlin: Hans-Bredow-Institut, March 16, 2012), http://
www.acatech.de/fileadmin/user_upload/Baumstruktur_nach_Website/Acatech/root
/de/Material_fuer_Sonderseiten/Internet_Privacy/thesen_SCHMIDT_acatech
_2012.pdf.

39. David Kirkpatrick, *The Facebook Effect: The Inside Story of the Company That
Is Connecting the World* (New York: Simon & Schuster, 2010), 199.

40. In considering how mobile device transportation might be gendered, it also
may be important to note that women's clothing often is designed with fewer pockets
than garments for men, which potentially limits their ability to keep portable computing devices more securely on their persons. At the same time, women's designer
purses can now be equipped with cell phone pockets, chargers, and other features
that support easy access to computing resources, although Clinton never showcased
ownership of these fashion forward accessories. Instead Clinton's handbags were
often the focus of stories that characterized her as a spendthrift, mocked her for
comparing herself to female celebrities, or suggested that she had to carry medical
equipment and was thus unfit for office because she was masking a serious health
condition. The hashtag #WhatsInHillarysPurse was used by both Trump and Sand-
ers supporters.

41. Sean Gallagher, "Top Clinton Aide Was 'Frustrated' with Her Boss' e-Mail
Practices," Ars Technica (blog), last updated June 30, 2016, http://arstechnica.com
/information-technology/2016/06/top-clinton-aid-was-frustrated-with-her-bosss-e
-mail-practices/.

42. Donald Trump, quoted in "Trump: Who Does Apple Think They Are?!," Fox
& Friends (blog), last updated February 18, 2016, http://www.foxnews.com/on-air
/fox-and-friends/blog/2016/02/18/trump-who-does-apple-think-they-are.

43. Timothy Cook, "A Message to Our Customers," Apple, February 16, 2016,
http://www.apple.com/customer-letter/.

44. Wendy Hui Kyong Chun, *Programmed Visions: Software and Memory* (Cambridge: MIT Press, 2011), 133.

45. "WATCH: Video Appears to Show Clinton Lecturing State Dept on Cyber
Security," FOX News Insider, last updated October 22, 2016, http://insider.foxnews
.com/2016/10/22/hillary-clinton-appears-lecture-state-department-colleagues-cyber
-security-email-server.

46. "Clinton Lectured State Dept. Staff on Cybersecurity in 2010 Video," FoxNews.
com, last updated October 22, 2016, http://www.foxnews.com/politics/2016/10/22
/clinton-lectured-state-dept-staff-on-cybersecurity-in-2010-video.html.

Part IV

Responses

13 / Rhetorical Devices

James J. Brown Jr.

"We have always, from Pascal to the present, thought of computers, especially digital computers, as logic machines." This is how Richard Lanham begins his essay "Digital Rhetoric and the Digital Arts," a chapter in his foundational work, *The Electronic Word*. For Lanham, the computational tradition has nearly always been situated "at the familiar Platonic, mathematical center of human reason."[1] But his book, published in 1993, insists that logic cannot claim sole ownership of the digital computer: "the computer often turns out to be a *rhetorical device* as well as a logical one."[2] Lanham's "as well as" is key here—the logic gates that drive computation are just as important as its rhetorical affordances. In fact, Lanham's "strong defense" of rhetoric—the idea that rhetoric is a world- and knowledge-shaping force rather than "mere" style and arrangement—would suggest that the boundary between rhetoric and logic is porous. Any logical system is already rhetorical, and Lanham demonstrates the rhetorical logics of digitality with examples from the ancients and postmodern art. For Lanham, the digital computer fulfills the "verbal agenda" of ancient rhetoric and the "visual agenda" of twentieth century art, and his entire essay attempts to demonstrate how the graphical user interface (GUI) allegorizes both these traditions. In moving from the verbal to the visual, Lanham focuses on analyzing the movement of text from page to screen by addressing the textual play of the Italian Futurists, Kenneth Burke, John Baldessari, and many others.

In this essay, one of the earliest attempts to wed the digital computer to the rhetorical tradition, Lanham's focus on the GUI brackets concerns that have become central to the study of digital rhetoric while leaving certain questions unaddressed. First, he is interested in the interaction between user and screen, viewing the relationship between human and computer as a tight, two-way feedback loop. Thus his primary question is how users perceive what's happening on a computer screen and then manipulate the symbols on that screen, an approach that does not address the networking of computers and a range of other components of our writing ecologies. Second, he is focused on the screen as an inscriptive surface, which, while it allows for new modes of interaction and play, is still primarily understood as a page or a canvas. Lanham demonstrates how we can zoom in on digital text and image (one of Lanham's key observations is that digital computers allow us to experiment with scale) and how we can interact with them, but he does not say much about what is happening beyond or behind the screen; his screen is flat, like paper. Finally, Lanham asks what happens when text moves from page to screen, but he does not ask what happens when text becomes computational instruction; nor does he ponder what happens when those instructions are used to manipulate not just text and image but also sound, haptic feedback, or any other expressive medium.

This is not a critique of Lanham, and I am not suggesting that he should have accounted for these things, some of which were not obvious to the typical 1990s computer user. Without *The Electronic Word*, the field of digital rhetoric might look quite different today. Rather, I am pointing to Lanham's essay as a way of understanding how far the study of digital rhetoric has come in the last twenty-five years. The field has not only taken up the challenge of treating the screen as more than just a page (though it took some time for us to get there) but has also radically expanded its concerns, moving out into the realms of sound, code, augmented reality, locative media, and much more. This edited collection is a perfect example of what has become an ambitious research agenda that addresses much more than text or image on screen. From Joshua Daniel-Wariya and James Chase Sanchez's analysis of the racial ideologies baked into videogame engines to Kevin Brock's treatment of code as a rhetorical medium, to Anthony Stagliano's discussion of the CV Dazzle code library, we are seeing a great deal of work that is extending into questions of code and computation. In addition, we are beginning to see new histories of digital rhetoric that expand upon Lanham's treatment of the ancients and contemporary art into discussions of Babbage, as Jonathan Buehl has, and the prehistories of machine scoring essays, as we see in J. W. Hammond's chapter. All of this work, in the words of Jennifer Juszkiewicz and Joseph Warfel, is an attempt to pursue the complex rhetorical layers of digital technology, even "into the layers beneath software, even beneath algorithms themselves." There are other examples as well, including Jim Ridolfo and William Hart-Davidson's edited collection, *Rhetoric and the Digital Humanities*, a special issue of *Computational Culture* on "Rhetoric and Computation" edited by Annette Vee and myself, and a collaborative work in *enculturation* on computational literacy edited by Vee and Mark Sample.[3] As all of this research shows, analysis of the electronic word and image has not disappeared, but it has certainly taken a place alongside other methods and approaches. As Casey Boyle, Steph Ceraso, and I have argued, "the digital" is no longer locatable in any single medium, device, or sense.[4]

This movement and change in rhetorical studies of computation suggests that calling a computer a rhetorical device, as Lanham does, is much more than a clever pun. Understanding the computer as rhetorical suggests that computation is rhetorical in all of its multiple layers and manifestations and that computational technologies affect and are affected by rhetorical, historical, and cultural milieus at the level of interface, code, hardware, software, and more. In fact, digital rhetoric's movement from a focus on screen and text to the broader concerns of things like code, computation, and sound reflects a broader trend in digital media studies. That trend is visible in the work of Katherine Hayles, whose calls for the "medium specific analysis" of digital media have had a profound influence on the study of electronic literature, videogames, and digital media in general and also in the work of people like Matthew Kirschenbaum and Nick Montfort, who have warned of the problems of a "screen essentialism" that ignores the various materialities at play in digital systems.[5] Whether we're considering paper or silicon, computers have always been about more than just pixels and screens. Further, scholars such as Lisa Nakamura have long argued that our fascination with technology too often distracts us from the ways that racial logics are coded into digital infrastructure. Tara McPherson has demonstrated this in detail in her analysis of the history of both UNIX and social justice movements of the middle part of the twentieth century, tracking the racial logics coded into computational systems. For McPherson, such an approach is crucial to understanding how digital systems shape our lives: "We must better understand the machines and networks that continue to powerfully shape our lives in ways that we are ill-equipped to deal with as media and humanities scholars. This necessarily involves more than simply studying our screens and the images that dance across them, moving beyond studies of screen representations and the rhetorics of visuality. . . . Our screens are cover stories, disguising deeply divided forms of both machine and human labor. We focus on them increasingly at our peril."[6] McPherson makes it clear that focusing too much on any single sense (visual, aural, tactile) or any single layer (code, software, hardware, interface) will necessarily hide important considerations of the rhetorical device. A study of rhetorical machines requires a broad sense of rhetoric and of the inscriptive regimes that inform, shape, and constrain computation.

One way to understand the general shift in digital rhetoric beyond the visual and the screen is to see research in digital rhetoric sliding back toward "logic." If Lanham insisted that Pascal needed Burke, then rhetoricians have been trying to ensure that this does not mean Pascal gets left behind. In 2007, Ian Bogost's *Persuasive Games* offered a wake-up call to digital rhetoricians who had often "abstract[ed] the computer as a consideration, focusing on the text and image content a machine might host and the communities of practice in which that content is created and used."[7] As I have already noted, the field has moved beyond such approaches, with procedural rhetoric as a driving force in that movement. As a theory of digital rhetoric that is native to computation, procedural rhetoric did not merely map rhetorical theory onto digital technology but rather developed something particular to the digital—it provided a framework for understanding the use of procedures as an inscriptive and persuasive medium. This approach was particularly useful for understanding videogames, Bogost's medium of choice. However, he also insisted that nothing prevents us from extending the notion of procedural rhetoric to any situation in which procedures are used to move and persuade. While we might critique the field for not taking up this broader set of concerns earnestly enough—our focus has been on overtly expressive and rhetorical computational artifacts—the adoption of procedural rhetoric as a framework by digital rhetoricians still demonstrates a disciplinary move beyond the "text and image on screen paradigm."

To be clear, there was work underway prior to *Persuasive Games* that addressed such concerns, such as Selfe and Selfe's "Politics of the Interface," which argued for a deeper understanding of how interfaces make assumptions and operate by way of motivated metaphors.[8] In addition, Elizabeth Losh's *Virtualpolitik* presented the field with its most comprehensive considerations of what the term "digital rhetoric" means. However, I think it's fair to say that Bogost developed one of the first cohesive digital rhetorical theories specifically designed to deal with computational machines, and he did so by giving us a way to understand the logical structures of rhetorical machines. Approaches such as procedural rhetoric have certainly found a foothold in the field. If Lanham's screen-based notions of digital rhetoric highlighted the computer's rhetorical dimensions, the discussion of procedure and computation during recent years serves to balance the scales somewhat. This rebalancing of the scales has addressed computation as a medium for expression, one that both the rhetor might use to persuade and the rhetorician might take up during analysis. By constructing procedures, the writer/rhetor/programmer persuades. That is, the logical structures of a program enable certain activities and constrain others. Right away, we see that procedural rhetoric brings together logic and rhetoric. This is perhaps not exactly what Lanham envisioned, but it nonetheless weds logic to rhetoric by way of the computer.

This renaissance in digital rhetoric has been a welcome one, but as we look forward it is worth asking whether we are arriving at a moment when this focus on the crafting and analysis of procedures is hitting a limit. Does the focus on computational procedures, how they are constructed and coded, allow us to forget all the ways that these systems escape our understanding? Has it encouraged us to forget about the rhetorical forces that escape the intentions of a rhetor or that slip past the critical rhetorician? Have we taken seriously the arguments of people like Wendy Chun, who insists that computation exceeds human understanding and that our various analyses and close readings tend to ignore this fact? Chun argues that the recent turn to critical code studies, software studies, and platform studies "threatens to reify knowing software as truth."[9] She is especially concerned with approaches that turn code into a static artifact to be read and interpreted, a move that does not always account for the fact that code is difficult to pin down. For one, it is executed, so the reading of code as a "source" of meaning already cuts out the steps of compiling and translating. But more than this, code is like any other linguistic system. It always escapes our grasp: "Programmers, computer scientists, and critical theorists have reduced software to a recipe, a set of instructions, substituting space/text for time/process."[10] In the face of these challenges, Chun encourages us to allow for the possibility that "source code . . . may be the source of things other than the machine execution it is 'supposed' to engender," and to get comfortable with code's spectrality.[11] The value of Chun's intervention for digital rhetoric is that it applies the insights of rhetorical theory to ask such questions, although, as Steve Holmes has argued, Chun does not fully engage the resources of rhetoric. Drawing on work in contemporary rhetorical theory, Holmes extends Chun's analysis by demonstrating how the computer science-based approaches that she critiques rehash the "ancient battle between rhetoric (troping, dissimulation, deviousness, appearance, sophistry) and Platonic philosophy (transparency, visibility, logic, truth)."[12] Further, he suggests that we can see code as more support for contemporary theories that understand rhetoric as "a presymbolic, presubjective, or affective ontological relationality with the ongoing disclosure of the material world."[13] Like any symbol system, code will always elude our grasp, and digital rhetoricians' move along a continuum from rhetoric (back?) to logic may put us at risk of forgetting this.

Chun and Holmes are pointing to the slipperiness of any type of code, but recent trends in computing make this point even more starkly. As machine-learning systems become more and more prevalent, we come face to face with the idea that computational systems exceed our attempts to grasp and interpret them. In a story on machine learning in *Wired*, Jason Tanz argues that some of our contemporary ways of understanding computation are too caught up in the game of logic, knowability, and hackability. At a moment when computation is the metaphor for everything from human thinking to organizational communication to DNA, Tanz thinks we have entered a stage of hubris when it comes to understanding code: "Code is logical. Code is hackable. Code is destiny. These are the central tenets (and self-fulfilling prophecies) of life in the digital age. As software has eaten the world, to paraphrase venture capitalist Marc Andreessen, we have surrounded ourselves with machines that convert our actions, thoughts, and emotions into data—raw material for armies of code-wielding engineers to manipulate. We have come to see life itself as something ruled by a series of instructions that can be discovered, exploited, optimized, maybe even rewritten."[14] A world understood in this way makes coders into the ultimate powerbrokers. Programmers become the people who can understand, know, and reprogram any system. But Tanz argues that this understanding of code is becoming obsolete, and that this is largely due to a general movement toward machine-learning systems that operate in ways that don't easily mesh with human understanding: "Our machines are starting to speak a different language now, one that even the best coders can't fully understand."[15] Machine-learning systems still operate by way of code, but the core mode of interaction between programmer and machine-learning system is not programmer-machine but rather teacher-learner. Tanz argues that programmers are being transformed from "gods, authoring the laws that govern computer systems" to something more like "parents or dog trainers." Programmers were, of course, never gods; machine learning is just the latest reminder of this fact.

Perhaps a shift from *programming* to *teaching* is fortuitous for the rhetorician, who has always been engaged with questions of pedagogy. Those who have long studied pedagogy are in a position to offer some gentle corrections to Tanz's metaphor of dog trainer or parent. If training machine-learning systems does indeed unseat the gods of computer programming—gods that we must admit have long been figured as white and male—then we should not reconsolidate power by shifting to metaphors of training and parenting. The power relationships of pedagogical situations are more productively understood as collaborative and mutually constituting. Yes, we help decide what data to feed these learning systems, and we make adjustments to learning algorithms, but we also listen to and observe them, attempting to learn a bit about how they operate. This approach is actually quite different from the methods that Chun gathers under the umbrella of computer science. Methods addressing code and computation can tend to focus a great deal on gazing into the guts of the machine, and my own work has been part of this trend. However, we might consider that such an approach is not always the best way to engage machine-learning systems. As Tanz notes, when looking inside a neural-net machine-learning system designed to mimic human neurological processes, we see "an ocean of math: a massive, multilayer set of calculus problems that—by constantly deriving the relationship between billions of data points—generate guesses about the world."[16] Looking at this ocean should be part of what rhetoricians do, and this is why work like that carried out by Juszkiewicz and Warfel in this collection is so important. But it must always be coupled with the idea that we may learn just as much by observing these systems as black boxes, feeding them data and observing the outputs.

Analysis of machine-learning systems can benefit from the various tools digital rhetoricians have developed during recent years, including procedural rhetoric. But our recent focus on computational processes should not blind us to the importance of content and data. Digital rhetoricians should use the procedures of rhetoric to understand computational procedure, but we should not forget that we have always been interested in content as well. My own work on procedures and the rhetorical tradition is susceptible to this critique. My attempt to refocus our efforts on procedure—for instance, through an attention to Erasmus's robotic procedures in his *Copia*—runs the risk of forgetting that the content of arguments matters as well.[17] This reminder is especially necessary in a world where the procedures of machine-learning systems continually escape our attempts to interpret them. If Tanz is right that future interactions with computers will be less about the "underlying sources of their behavior" and more focused on "the data we use to train [them]," then our current work should recognize that both data and process must be taken up together.

Refocusing our attention on data and process, content and form, rhetoric and logic, is not only a key goal for digital rhetoricians; it has also been center stage as machine learning deals with what Microsoft researcher Kate Crawford has called its "White Guy" problem. Referencing a number of controversies about systems enacting racist logics, from Google's photo app classifying pictures of black people as gorillas to Nikon's camera software misreading Asian eyes as people blinking, Crawford points directly to the problem of turning a critical eye toward data: "This is fundamentally a data problem. Algorithms learn by being fed certain images, often chosen by engineers, and the system builds a model of the world based on those images. If a system is trained on photos of people who are overwhelmingly white, it will have a harder time recognizing nonwhite faces."[18] Again, Crawford is not suggesting that data should be our focus at the expense of understanding computational procedures, but she is pointing out that too much faith in the computational mechanism leads us to these dark places. Machine-learning systems benefit from being fed massive amounts of data, meaning that we might think that lots of data will solve any problems with bias or ideological blind spots. But the examples cited by Crawford as well as other high-profile machine-learning SNAFUs like Microsoft's Twitter Bot Tay, which almost instantly became a Nazi, demonstrate that there is no escape from the rhetorical problems embedded in data.

This is best articulated in this book's chapter 11 by Jennifer Maher, Helen Burgess, and Tim Menzies, who insist in this volume that "big data" offers no refuge from the rhetorical storm: "big data, instead of transcending the rhetorical through computation, actually reaffirms rhetoric's centrality." And of course, the work of engaging machine learning from a rhetorical perspective is already underway with Omizo and Hart-Davidson's work on the Faciloscope. The key insight of Omizo's chapter, and of the larger research agenda undertaken by Omizo, Hart-Davidson, and Jeff Grabill for their project funded by the Institute of Museum and Library Services, is that machine-learning systems are best understood as collaborators. Like any collaborative relationship, we must understand what we do well and not-so-well as well as recognize the strengths and limits of our partners. The Faciloscope, seen as a collaborator and not a tool, fits with the broader shift that Tanz describes in his *Wired* article. Omizo and Hart-Davidson walk us through the training of a rhetorical machine, and they do so not from the perspective of an all-knowing god-like programmer. Instead, they write from the viewpoint of a pedagogue who sees the rhetorician's role as key to the development of a learning system: "Teaching machines rhetoric is something that, understandably, inspires as much trepidation as excitement. But as we have sometimes seen in the past, developers and researchers from other fields do not need to seek our permission to move ahead with this kind of work. We feel it is vital to engage in experiments like the one we undertook in creating the Faciloscope in order to stay involved in the ways our disciplinary knowledge might find its way into rhetorical machines." If we are moving from programming machines to educating them, then what is the rhetorician's role in this newer epoch of computing? What rhetorical pedagogies might be useful for educating machine-learning systems? These are the key questions addressed by this new research trajectory.

Such work will benefit from the recognition that some of what digital rhetoricians have worked on to this point will have to be significantly reworked. Machine learning calls for new approaches and theories, something that accounts for what we *don't* know about how these systems work. Again, this is not even a new problem, as Chun and Holmes suggest. However, we are now faced with this challenge in a much more concrete way, as interaction with machines is becoming simultaneously more powerful and more opaque. This should not necessarily be a cause for pessimism. Following Chun, we should recognize the value of our inability to know the "truth" of our rhetorical devices: "the fact that we cannot know software can be an enabling condition: a way for us to engage the surprises generated by a programmability that, try as it might, cannot entirely prepare us for the future."[19] Our task now is to understand how to use the lessons of our existing research approaches to carve a new path, one that sees rhetoric as the *antistrophos* of logic. By pursuing computation as both rhetorical and logical, we can continue to develop a range of methods and theories for engaging the proliferation of rhetorical devices.

Notes

1. Richard A. Lanham, *The Electronic Word: Democracy, Technology, and the Arts* (Chicago: University of Chicago Press, 1995).

2. Ibid., emphasis added.

3. Jim Ridolfo and William Hart-Davidson, eds., *Rhetoric and the Digital Humanities* (Chicago: University of Chicago Press, 2015); Mark Sample and Annette Vee, "Introduction to 'The Role of Computational Literacy in Computers and Writing,'" *enculturation: a journal of rhetoric, writing, and culture* 14 (2012), http://enculturation.net/computational-literacy; Annette Vee and James J. Brown Jr., "Rhetoric Special Issue Editorial Introduction: Computational Culture," *Computational Culture: A Journal of Software Studies* 5 (2016), http://computationalculture.net/rhetoric-special-issue-editorial-introduction/.

4. Casey Boyle, James J. Brown Jr., and Steph Ceraso, "The Digital: Rhetoric Behind and Beyond the Screen," *Rhetoric Society Quarterly* 48, no. 3 (2018): 1–9.

5. N. Katherine Hayles, *Writing Machines* (Cambridge: MIT Press, 2002); Matthew G. Kirschenbaum, *Mechanisms: New Media and the Forensic Imagination* (Cambridge: MIT Press, 2012); Nick Montfort, "Continuous Paper: The Early Materiality and Workings of Electronic Literature," last updated January 2005, http://nickm.com/writing/essays/continuous_paper_mla.html.

6. Tara McPherson, "US Operating Systems at Mid-Century: The Intertwining of Race and UNIX," in *Race after the Internet*, ed. Lisa Nakamura and Peter Chow-White (New York: Routledge, 2012), 21–37.

7. Ian Bogost, *Persuasive Games: The Expressive Power of Videogames* (Cambridge: MIT Press, 2007).

8. Cynthia L. Selfe and Richard J. Selfe, "The Politics of the Interface: Power and Its Exercise in Electronic Contact Zones," *College Composition and Communication* 45, no. 4 (December 1994): 480–504.

9. Wendy Hui Kyong Chun, *Programmed Visions: Software and Memory* (Cambridge: MIT Press, 2011), 21.

10. Ibid.

11. Chun, *Programmed Visions*, 53.

12. Steve Holmes, "'Can We Name the Tools?': Ontologies of Code, Speculative Techné, and Rhetorical Concealment," *Computational Culture: A Journal of Software Studies* 5 (2016), http://computationalculture.net/can-we-name-the-tools-ontologies-of-code-speculative-techne-and-rhetorical-concealment/.

13. Ibid.

14. Jason Tanz, "Soon We Won't Program Computers. We'll Train Them Like

Dogs," *WIRED*, last updated May 17, 2016, https://www.wired.com/2016/05/the-end
-of-code/.

15. Ibid.

16. Ibid.

17. James J. Brown Jr., "The Machine That Therefore I Am," *Philosophy and Rhetoric* 47, no. 4 (2014): 494–514.

18. Kate Crawford, "Artificial Intelligence's White Guy Problem," *New York Times*, June 25, 2016, http://www.nytimes.com/2016/06/26/opinion/sunday/artificial-intelligences-white-guy-problem.html.

19. Chun, 54.

14 / Full Stack Rhetoric

A Response to *Rhetorical Machines*

Annette Vee

The popular notion of the computer as an inflexible object of pure engineering is—in the few corners it might still hold sway—being buffeted by critical work in the history of computing, software studies, digital humanities, algorithm studies, and now computational rhetoric. This work has taught us that the machine with which we labor, socialize, and govern is designed not only using the properties of silicon, magnetic tape, and voltages but also with social biases, idiosyncratic personal preferences, and sometimes dubious motivations. Tara McPherson has outlined the parallels between the design of the influential operating system UNIX and race relations in mid-twentieth-century America, noting that "computers are themselves encoders of culture . . . [and] code and race are deeply intertwined."[1] Jennifer Light, Janet Abbate, Nathan Ensmenger, Margot Lee Shetterly, and Marie Hicks have all uncovered important and hitherto hidden histories of women in computing, collectively emphasizing that computer hardware and software were not designed with certain groups in mind—and yet those groups made their way into the machines anyhow.[2] Essential examinations of algorithms by Tarleton Gillespie, Nicholas Diakopoulos, and Safiya Umoja Noble have given us insight into the central—and sometimes scary—role these mathematical underpinnings of software have in our lives, and how they sort some lives and experiences differently from others.[3]

Essential to this line of research on the computer's cultural influences is attention to its "full stack," everything from the electrical impulses that we render as source code to the images on its screen. The present collection provides this perspective: we see here a focus on the computer's mathematical programs and engineering history as well as its rendering of images in contemporary videogames—and much in-between. As this collection shows, rhetoric is an apt tool for prying open the multiple layers of the computer's stack, so much so that Lavinia Hirsu and John Jones call the machine itself rhetorical. This collection thus contributes to a growing body of work in computational rhetoric.

Still in its infancy, computational rhetoric has already demonstrated the ways that machines can perform the functions of rhetoric, traditionally thought to be the exclusive domain of humans. When machines perform rhetoric, humans can get pretty uncomfortable—as we have in the case of some bots. Stuart Geiger, studying a particular bot that supplied signatures to unsigned edits to Wikipedia, observed that human Wikipedia editors felt there was a critical difference between generally accepted human norms and a bot that automatically forced compliance with this norm.[4] This bot is just one example of a norm-enforcing machine, a computational encoding of human relations in online discourse. From this study, Geiger concludes that bots are hybrid operators, "both editors and software, social and technical, discursive and material, as well as assembled and autonomous."[5]

Our notion of computation's relationship to rhetoric is shifting with the increasing sophistication of computation and its intertwining with linguistic exchanges, especially online. As a result, Douglas Guilbeault argues that we must expand our ideas of rhetorical agency to accommodate the work that bots do. For instance, social bots on Twitter can take advantage of Tarleton Gillespie's "calculated publics" by harvesting highly rated photos from Hotornot.com, accruing followers and boosting their popularity characteristics, and then leveraging automated conversational tools such as retweeting, emoticons, and link-sharing. Through the calculated popularity measures of Twitter, users such as politicians, celebrities, or businesses can then harness these bots to increase their own perceived popularity. Noting this phenomenon and its influence on politics and discourse, Guilbeault introduces the idea of "platform persuasion," which describes the ways bots leverage design aspects of a platform to have significant influence on online networks. He argues that since bots can influence networks, it is important to move away from a human-centered idea of agency and to think of bots as agents as well—or, in terms of computational rhetoric, as software rhetors.[6] James Brown Jr.'s research on the ways that software networks must grapple with issues of hospitality—also a domain generally considered exclusive to humans—further demonstrates how computational machines are rhetorical entities.[7]

Although not all of it flies under the banner of computational rhetoric, work on the ways that language shapes computational machines is also important to our understanding of *rhetorical machines*. Chilean philosopher Leonardo Flores and Terry Winograd—the influential computer scientist and graduate advisor to Google founders Sergey Brin and Larry Page—argued in the 1980s that "in order to become aware of the effects that computers have on society we must reveal the implicit understanding of human language, thought and work that serves as a background for developments in computer technology."[8] Basic ideas about how computers work are influenced by the language we use to describe them—perhaps most famously by John von Neumann's designation of the computer's storage as "memory," which opened the doors to considering computers as thinking machines. Wendy Hui Kyong Chun's *Programmed Visions* points out this and other influential genetic and biological metaphors for the computer.[9] David Nofre, Mark Priestley, and Gerard Alberts describe the way that programming began to be thought of as a linguistic activity in the early 1960s and claim that "the language metaphor in programming [is] one of the most essential metaphors around which computer science has been built."[10] My own work on the laws governing software extends legal discussions of patent, first amendment, and copyright law into the realm of rhetoric through an assertion that each legal regime implies certain uses and audiences for computer code.[11] Similarly, in this collection, Hammond uses a detailed history of automated essay scoring to show "technology's rhetorical priority of definition: definition precedes (i.e., is prior to) rhetorical engagement with-or-through technologies, and questions of definition and essence cut to the rhetorical core of technologies, revealing what they are imagined to do (or not) and how they are assessed as working (or not)." As Lisa Gitelman and Janet Abbate have both argued, the metaphors we choose when we discuss technology influence the ways the technology is used, and by whom.[12]

In the introduction to a special issue of *Computational Culture* on computational rhetoric, Brown and I took the connection of rhetoric and computation one step further: we argue that computational machines are rhetorical not only by virtue of their relationship to language but also in their machinic operations in our everyday lives. We wrote, "even the most mundane computational technologies can be seen as rhetorical—from the grocery store checkout scanner to the high school graphing calculator—because any computational machine shapes and constrains behavior." Work in that edited collection sets the stage for what appears here: on the ways that error is defined machinically and linguistically; on rhetorical justifications for algorithms; on the influence of style on coding decisions; and on the ways that artificial intelligence is also artificial rhetoric.[13] Through all of these explorations, we are learning how amenable to rhetoric computers can be. As Hammond puts it in this collection, "far from being the (technical) opposite of (social) rhetoric, computation is inextricable from the social and rhetorical."

Moreover, the stakes for work in computational rhetoric are high: Elizabeth Losh asserts here that "it may actually be the conflation of gender and technology at work in the popular imagination that was to blame for Clinton's stunning defeat" in the 2016 US Presidential election. In other words, the rhetorical configuration of technology not only shapes whom we think should be using it but may also be powerful enough to sway elections. Closer to the metal, Ryan Omizo suggests that one reason rhetoricians should be creating computational objects that engage with rhetoric is so that we can ethically shape the ways they are built. Along the same lines, writing computational processes while ignoring the real work of rhetoric operating within them is downright dangerous, Jennifer Maher, Helen Burgess, and Tim Menzies powerfully state. Big data is a rhetorical enterprise, they argue, and without rhetorical attention to its collection, processing, and implications, we risk a literally whitewashed perspective on the world—one that also has real effects. As Anthony Stagliano memorably puts it here, code is powerful, but it's also much *wilier* than we often give it credit for. A takeaway from this collection is that this computational wiliness can be traced the whole way down the stack.

Indeed, its "full stack" coverage is one of the most compelling things about this book's collection of chapters: from the math that drives the algorithms that influence human decisions about roadway repair (Juszkiewicz and Warfel) or the collection of big data as a rhetorical enterprise (Maher, Burgess, and Menzies) to the cutscenes that create "ambient rhetoric" reflecting and shaping cultural assumptions about race in videogames (Daniel-Wariya and Sanchez). Hammond focuses on the rhetorical framing of automated essay scoring, noting that the ways teachers and machines interacted in its early history shapes what we think of both teachers and the "collections of machines" that comprise writing assessment. Stagliano asserts that software itself can respond to rhetorical situations in complex ways; in his chosen case of CV Dazzle, the software responds to ubiquitous surveillance and intervenes in human relations. Jennifer Juszkiewicz and Joseph Warfel go deeper into the workings of computation to argue that even the math driving algorithms is rhetorical. Using the field of Operations Research as a guide, they point out that algorithms are really "a set of mathematical statements that, when considered simultaneously, describe a human's perception of a system." Jonathan Buehl and Kevin Brock both examine the extant text and the design of computational systems in tandem, indicating how intertwined language, culture, and the engineering or programming constraints of the system can be. Buehl charts a fascinating path through Charles Babbage's writings to reveal the ways that his appeals for funding shaped his influential protocomputer, ultimately claiming that "Charles Babbage's Difference Engine was an engine of rhetoric. The project was enabled by clever rhetorical work; the engine in turn produced both new rhetorical situations and innovative responses." Through his close reading of both code and its explanations in the open source project Ruby on Rails, Brock argues, "How these various actors are compelled to act in response to these influences depends heavily not just on who the author of a given code text is but how that author argues, explicitly or implicitly, in and through his or her coded procedures and relevant style toward particular actions and activities." Maher, Burgess, and Menzies take a close look at a study of GitHub pull requests to emphasize the many layers of the stack that those researchers had to consider to do justice to their subject, and they conclude that big data is an enterprise of "big rhetoric." Joshua Daniel-Wariya and James Chase Sanchez are close to the computer's surface in their analysis of racialized depictions of characters in videogames, but their attention to the design constraints in the software engines that power these games sets their work apart from a more traditional literary approach to games. Losh provides a rhetorical perspective on the social layers of the computer as they play out across big questions of gender and politics on the world stage. Beyond an informed analysis of the full stack, Ryan Omizo goes so far as to *create* a software interface for socially complex rhetorical interventions, which he discusses in his contribution to this collection. Following Maher et al.'s move from "big data" to "big rhetoric," I might say that we see here in this collection "full stack rhetoric."

While editing the first Software Studies definitional collection, *Software Studies: A Lexicon*, Matthew Fuller was adamant that each of the writers be well versed in both the academic/critical angle to software *and also* the mechanics of software itself.[14] This is clearly the case with the writers in this collection as well. Is this the new standard for work in computational rhetoric? Should it be? For rhetoricians aspiring to work in this area of research, this is a tall order. Already, digital rhetoric demands much from its practitioners: extensive cross-disciplinary knowledge of both rhetoric and technology; keeping up with new versions of software; constant retooling in the face of changing trends of programs and digital design. Must we add to this a facility with computer programming, or even the electrical or mathematical underpinnings of the computer? The term "full stack" comes from the profession of web development and encompasses everything from the user interface of websites to the backend databases and code libraries that support websites. The profession of web development was enthusiastic about the prospect of "full-stack developers" in the mid-2000s—developers who could do both front-end and back-end work—because these developers could minimize miscommunications across design levels; from the pragmatic point of view, companies could hire just one person to make a complex website. But as the stack has become more complex, expertise in all its levels has become nearly impossible, and the profession of web development now generally concedes that "full-stack developers" are as common as unicorns. Following this trend in web development, I wonder: is full-stack rhetoric possible, or desirable?

I think it is desirable, even necessary. But full-stack rhetoric is really only possible as a collaboration, in collections such as this one that draw from a variety of expertise. Fuller notes that his lexicon "aims to make available some of the mixed intelligences thinking through these conditions [of contemporary software]. The authors are artists, computer scientists, designers, philosophers, cultural theorists, programmers, historians, media archaeologists, mathematicians, curators, feminists, musicians, educators, radio hams, and other fine things, and most straddle more than one discipline. The voices collected here bring more than one kind of intelligence to software because software makes more sense understood transversally."[15] Similarly, a project with the intellectual and technical range of the present collection is only manageable with a range of expertise such as these contributors have. What is essential to good work in computational rhetoric is that we know the full stack exists—that we know it is rhetoric all the way up and down, from data to math to images in games. It is not *purely* rhetoric, though, which is the tricky part. There are non-negotiable parts of engineering and math, or pre-existing designs (whatever their contemporary motivations or biases) that constrain our choices and make some aspects of the computer less susceptible and less accessible to rhetoric than others. As rhetoricians who might want our work to travel across disciplines, we must know the difference.

Once we are aware of the stack's existence, once we have a basic understanding of how the layers create a complex object of analysis and rhetoric, we can hone in on specific layers, conscious of their relationship to others. Collaborative projects, such as this entire collection and some of its individual pieces, will be essential for examining the intersections between particular layers. The result can be fascinating analyses of the ways rhetoric makes its way into the ubiquitous computational machine that influences our lives so significantly.

Our rhetorical interventions into computation have, by nature, ethical underpinnings, as Brown has previously asserted.[16] As many of the pieces in this collection argue, rhetoricians have a responsibility to do this work. If we don't, others will, and they may not have the training in language and persuasion that rhetoric affords us. This is clearly articulated in Omizo's contribution, where a rhetorical machine is constructed to help humans intervene in online arguments. The alternative is, perhaps, Tay, the disastrous chatbot released by Microsoft in 2016—or other rhetorical machines constructed without the sensitivity to how language works in social situations.[17] An understanding of natural language processing might be critical to these endeavors, as Omizo indicates. But just as necessary is understanding and attention to how language functions affectively and rhetorically, how it persuades, insults, flatters, or praises. Also important to these interventions is attention to pedagogy, as Hammond notes. What are our computational and rhetorical machines teaching us, society at large, or our children? Elsewhere, Noble's study of the racial bias of algorithms, the influential collection *Race after the Internet* edited by Lisa Nakamura and Peter Chow-White, and the work here by Daniel-Wariya and Sanchez all point to the lessons of racial representation in computational spaces. Maher et al. also emphasize the importance of ethics here: "data science is too often limited to notions of goodness as either social consequences or matters of technique, the effect of which is the displacement of human conceptions of goodness to those of the machine." As they note, the ethical basis of computing was a worry even for Norbert Wiener who asserted that only those who knew about the workings of the computer understood the moral positions it implied. Since Wiener, many computer scientists have made the point that ethical approaches to computing are critical. Programmer Daniel Kohanski warned that computers do not have inherent ethics; they simply magnify human thoughts and instructions, and so we must be quite careful what we relegate to the machine.[18] In the same spirit, Terry Winograd founded the influential organization Computer Professionals for Social Responsibility, which emphasizes the necessity of ethical approaches to computing and even traces its philosophy back to Wiener through its Norbert Wiener Award for Social and Professional Responsibility to notable computer scientists such as Doug Englebart, Kristen Nygaard, and Mitch Kapor. It is important for rhetoricians to acknowledge that computational rhetoric is not alone in providing ethical approaches to computing.

With collaboration from computer science and other fields, computational rhetoric has a critical role to play in both the analysis and construction of rhetorical machines in the future. Fuller's lexicon, the special issue on computational rhetoric in *Computational Culture*, and the present collection are all ways of asserting our role. I look forward to seeing more great work to come in computational rhetoric—that is, explorations that acknowledge the computer's full stack and ethically wield the tools of rhetoric to illuminate what is still too often thought of as an inflexible black box. The computer is a *rhetorical machine* that calls for *full-stack rhetoric*.

Notes

1. Tara McPherson, "US Operating Systems at Mid-Century," in *Race after the Internet*, ed. Lisa Nakamura and Peter Chow-White (New York: Routledge, 2012), 36.

2. Jennifer Light, "When Computers Were Women," *Technology and Culture* 40, no. 3 (July 1999): 455–83; Nathan Ensmenger, *The Computer Boys Take Over* (Cambridge: MIT Press, 2010); Margot Lee Shetterly, *Hidden Figures* (New York: Harper Collins/William Morrow and Company, 2016); Marie Hicks, *Programmed Inequality* (Cambridge: MIT Press, 2017); Janet Abbate, *Recoding Gender* (Cambridge: MIT Press, 2012).

3. Tarleton Gillespie, "The Relevance of Algorithms," in *Media Technologies*, ed.

Tarleton Gillespie, Pablo Boczkowski, and Kristen Foot (Cambridge: MIT Press, 2014), 167–94; Nicholas Diakopoulos, "Algorithmic Accountability," *Digital Journalism* 3, no. 3 (2015): 398–415; Safiya Umoja Noble, *Algorithms of Oppression* (New York: NYU Press, 2018).

4. R. Stuart Geiger, "The Lives of Bots," in *Wikipedia: A Critical Point of View*, ed. Geert Lovink and Nathaniel Tkacz (Amsterdam: Institute of Network Cultures, 2011), 87.

5. Ibid., 92.

6. Douglas Guilbeault, "Growing Bot Security: An Ecological View of Bot Agency," *International Journal of Communication* 10 (2016): 5009–10.

7. James J. Brown Jr., *Ethical Programs: Hospitality and the Rhetorics of Software* (Ann Arbor: University of Michigan Press, 2015).

8. Terry Winograd and Fernando Flores, *Understanding Computers and Cognition: A New Foundation for Design* (Norwood, NJ: Ablex Publishing Corporation, 1986), 7.

9. Wendy Hui Kyong Chun, *Programmed Visions: Software and Memory* (Cambridge: MIT Press, 2011).

10. David Nofre, Mark Priestley, and Gerard Alberts, "When Technology Became Language: The Origins of the Linguistic Conception of Computer Programming, 1950–1960," *Technology and Culture* 55, no. 1 (January 2014): 43.

11. Annette Vee, "Text, Speech, Machine: Metaphors for Computer Code in the Law," *Computational Culture: A Journal of Software Studies* 2 (2012), http://computationalculture.net/article/text-speech-machine-metaphors-for-computer-code-in-the-law.

12. Abbate, *Recoding Gender*; Lisa Gitelman, *Scripts, Grooves and Writing Machines* (Stanford, CA: Stanford University Press, 2000).

13. Annette Vee and James J. Brown Jr., eds., Special Issue on Rhetoric and Computation, *Computational Culture: A Journal of Software Studies* 5 (2016), http://computationalculture.net/issue-five/.

14. MIT Press's overview of Matthew Fuller's *Software Studies* notes that "the contributors to Software Studies are both literate in computing (and involved in some way in the production of software) and active in making and theorizing culture." MIT Press, "Software Studies," MIT Press, n.d. https://mitpress.mit.edu/books/software-studies.

15. Matthew Fuller, "Introduction, The Stuff of Software," in *Software Studies: A Lexicon*, ed. Matthew Fuller (Cambridge: MIT Press, 2008), 10.

16. Brown, *Ethical Programs*.

17. James Vincent, "Twitter Taught Microsoft's AI Chatbot to Be a Racist Asshole in Less than a Day," The Verge, last updated Mar 24, 2016, https://www.theverge.com/2016/3/24/11297050/tay-microsoft-chatbot-racist.

18. Daniel Kohanski, *The Philosophical Programmer: Reflections on the Moth in the Machine* (New York: St. Martin's Press, 1998), 21.

Bibliography

Abbate, Janet. *Recoding Gender*. Cambridge: MIT Press, 2012.

"About Us." Girls Who Code. Accessed January 23, 2017. https://girlswhocode.com /about-us/.

Aikat, Debashis. "Big Data Dilemmas: The Theory and Practice of Ethical Big Data Mining for Socio-Economic Development." In *Ethical Data Mining Applications for Socio-Economic Development*, edited by Hakikur Rahman and Isabel Ramos, 106–30. Hershey, PA: IGI Global, 2013.

Anderson, Karrin Vasby, and Kristina Horn Sheeler. "Texts (and Tweets) from Hillary: Meta-Meming and Postfeminist Political Culture." *Presidential Studies Quarterly* 44, no. 2 (June 2014): 224–43.

Anderson, Lark. "*Resident Evil 5* Is a Fun and Frantic Evolution." GameSpot. March 13, 2009. https://www.gamespot.com/reviews/resident-evil-5-review/1900–6228853/.

Anderson, Logan. "So Many Monsters: But Never a Man!" *The Phi Delta Kappan* 35, no. 9 (June 1954): 369, 392.

"Anybody Can Learn." Code.org. Accessed January 23, 2017. https://code.org/.

apotonick et al. "Simplify Finding Default Layout #15050." GitHub. Last modified May 9, 2014. https://github.com/rails/rails/pull/15050.

Aristotle. "Nichomachean Ethics." In *The Complete Works of Aristotle*, vol. 2, edited by Jonathan Barnes, 1729–1867. Princeton: Princeton University Press, 1984.

———. "Rhetoric." In *Complete Works of Aristotle*, 2:2152–69.

"Attention Newbies to Incubating." Backyardchickens.com. 2014. Accessed June 4, 2014. http://www.backyardchickens.com/t/878773/attention-newbies-to-incubating.

Babbage, Benjamin Herschel. "Recreations of a Philosopher." *Harper's New Monthly Magazine* 30, no. 175 (1864): 34–39.

———. *Reflections on the Decline of Science in England and Some of its Causes*. New York: Augustus M. Kelly, 1970.

Babbage, Charles. "A Letter to Sir Humphry Davy on the Application of the Machinery to the Purpose of Calculating and Printing Mathematical Tables." In *Works of Charles Babbage*, 2:6–14.

———. "On the Mathematical Powers of the Calculating Engine." In *The Works of*

Charles Babbage, vol. 3, edited by Martin Campbell-Kelly, 15–61. New York: NYU Press, 1989.

———. "On a Method of Expressing by Signs the Action of Machinery." In *Works of Charles Babbage*, 3:209–23.

———. *The Ninth Bridgewater Treatise: A Fragment*. 2nd ed. London: Frank Cass and Company Limited, 1967.

———. "A Note Respecting the Application of Calculating Machinery to the Construction of Mathematical Tables." In *Works of Charles Babbage*, 2:3–4.

———. "Observations on the Application of Machinery to the Computation of Mathematical Tables." In *Works of Charles Babbage*, 2:33–37.

———. *Passages from the Life of a Philosopher*. In *The Works of Charles Babbage*, vol. 11, edited by Martin Campbell-Kelly. New York: NYU Press, 1989.

———. "On the Theoretical Principles of the Machinery for Calculating Tables." *The Works of Charles Babbage*, vol. 2, edited by Martin Campbell-Kelly, 38–43. New York: NYU Press, 1989.

Ball, W. W. *A Short Account of the History of Mathematics*. New York: Dover, 1960.

Balsamo, Anne. *Technologies of the Gendered Body: Reading Cyborg Women*. Durham, NC: Duke University Press, 1996.

Banks, Adam Joel. *Digital Griots: African American Rhetoric in a Multimedia Age*. Carbondale: Southern Illinois University Press, 2010.

Barbaro, Michael, and Steve Eder. "Under Oath, Donald Trump Shows His Raw Side." *New York Times*, July 28, 2015. https://www.nytimes.com/2015/07/29/us/politics/depositions-show-donald-trump-as-quick-to-exaggerate-and-insult.html.

Barnes, Jonathan, ed. *The Complete Works of Aristotle*, vol. 2. Princeton: Princeton University Press, 1984.

Barnett, Scot. *Rhetorical Realism: Rhetoric, Ethics, and the Ontology of Things*. London: Routledge, 2017.

Barnett, Scot, and Casey Boyle, eds. *Rhetoric, through Everyday Things*. Tuscaloosa: University of Alabama Press, 2016.

Barrett, Catherine M. "Automated Essay Evaluation and the Computational Paradigm: Machine Scoring Enters the Classroom." PhD diss., University of Rhode Island, 2015.

Bazerman, Charles. *The Languages of Edison's Light*. Cambridge: MIT Press, 1999.

———. "The Production of Technology and the Production of Human Meaning." *Journal of Business and Technical Communication* 12, no. 3 (July 1998): 381–87.

———. *Shaping Written Knowledge: The Genre and Activity of the Experimental Article in Science*. Madison: University of Wisconsin Press, 1988.

Beck, Estee Natee. "Computer Algorithms as Persuasive Agents: The Rhetoricity of Algorithmic Surveillance within the Built Ecological Network." PhD diss., Bowling Green State University, 2015.

Behrens, Roy R., ed. *Ship Shape, a Dazzle Camouflage Sourcebook: An Anthology of Writings About Ship Camouflage During World War One*. Dysart, IA: Bobolink Books, 2012.

Beres, Damon. "Trump Campaign Wastes a Lot of Paper Printing Articles About

Trump." *Huffington Post.* Last updated June 20, 2016. http://www.huffingtonpost .com/entry/trump-googles-himself_us_57681ab0e4b015db1bca04da.

Bertrand, Marianne, and Sendhil Mullainatha. "Are Emily and Greg More Employable than Lakisha and Jamal? A Field Experiment on Labor Market Discrimination." *American Economic Review* 94, no. 4 (September 2004): 991–1013.

Beveridge, Aaron. "Looking in the Dustbin: Data Janitorial Work, Statistical Reasoning, and Information Rhetorics." *Computers and Composition Online* (Fall 2015). http://cconlinejournal.org/fall15/beveridge/.

Bijker, Wiebe E. *Of Bicycles, Bakelites, and Bulbs: Toward a Theory of Sociotechnical Change.* Cambridge: MIT Press, 1995.

Bird, Steven, and Edward Loper. "NLTK: The Natural Language Toolkit." In *Proceedings of the ACL 2004 on Interactive Poster and Demonstration Sessions,* Barcelona, Spain (July 21–26, 2004): 63–70.

Boettger, Ryan K., and Laura A. Palmer. "Quantitative Content Analysis: Its Use in Technical Communication." *IEEE Transactions on Professional Communication* 53, no. 4 (December 2010): 346–57.

Bogost, Ian. *Persuasive Games: The Expressive Power of Videogames.* Cambridge: MIT Press, 2007.

Boler, Megan, ed. *Digital Media and Democracy: Tactics in Hard Times.* Cambridge: MIT Press, 2008.

Bolter, Jay David, and Richard Grusin. *Remediation: Understanding New Media.* Cambridge: MIT Press, 1999.

Booch, Grady. "All Watched Over by Machines of Loving Grace." *IEEE Software* 32, no. 2 (March–April 2015): 19–21.

———. "Morality and the Software Architect." *IEEE Software* 25, no. 1 (January–February 2008): 8–9.

Borenstein, Greg. "Adam Harvey Explains Viola-Jones Face Detection." Makematics. Last updated 2012. http://web.archive.org/web/20120408080754/http://www .makematics.com:80/research/viola-jones/.

Boud, David, and Heather Middleton. "Learning from Others at Work: Communities of Practice and Informal Learning." *Journal of Workplace Learning* 15, no. 5 (2003): 194–202.

Boyle, Casey. "The Rhetorical Question Concerning Glitch." *Computers and Composition* 35 (March 2015): 12–29.

Boyle, Casey, James J. Brown Jr., and Steph Ceraso. "The Digital: Rhetoric Behind and Beyond the Screen." *Rhetoric Society Quarterly* 48, no. 3 (2018): 1–9.

Bratton, Benjamin H. *The Stack: On Software and Sovereignty.* Cambridge: MIT Press, 2016.

Brock, Kevin. "Enthymeme as Rhetorical Algorithm." *Present Tense* 4, no. 1 (September 4, 2014): 1–7.

———. "The 'FizzBuzz' Programming Test: A Case-Based Exploration of Rhetorical Style in Code." *Computational Culture: A Journal of Software Studies* 5 (2016). http://computationalculture.net/article/the-fizzbuzz-programming-test-a-case -based-exploration-of-rhetorical-style-in-code.

Brock, William. "The Spectrum of Science Patronage." In *The Patronage of Science in the Nineteenth Century*, edited by Gerard Turner, 173–201. Leyden: Norhoff International Publishing, 1976.

Broke, Andre. "'When Keeping It Real Goes Wrong': *Resident Evil 5*, Racial Representation, and Gamers." *Games and Culture* 6, no. 5 (September 2011): 429–52.

Brown, James J., Jr. "Crossing State Lines: Rhetoric and Software Studies." In *Rhetoric and the Digital Humanities*, edited by Jim Ridolfo and William Hart-Davidson, 20–32. Chicago: University of Chicago Press, 2015.

———. *Ethical Programs: Hospitality and the Rhetorics of Software*. Ann Arbor: University of Michigan Press, 2015.

———. "The Machine That Therefore I Am." *Philosophy and Rhetoric* 47, no. 4 (2014): 494–514.

Burke, Kenneth. *Language as Symbolic Action: Essays on Life, Literature, and Method*. Berkeley: University of California Press, 1966.

Butler, Declan. "When Google Got Flu Wrong." *Nature* 494 (February 13, 2013): 155–56.

Campbell-Kelly, Martin, ed. *The Works of Charles Babbage*, vol. 2. New York: NYU Press, 1989.

———, ed. *The Works of Charles Babbage*, vol. 3. New York: NYU Press, 1989.

Caramanis, Constantine, Nedialko B. Dimitrov, and David P. Morton. "Efficient Algorithms for Budget-Constrained Markov Decision Processes." *IEEE Transactions on Automatic Control* 59, no. 10 (October 2014): 2813–17.

Carlin, Diana B., and Kelly L. Winfrey. "Have You Come a Long Way, Baby? Hillary Clinton, Sarah Palin, and Sexism in 2008 Campaign Coverage." *Communication Studies* 60, no. 4 (2009): 326–43.

"Category Specific Facilitation Tool." Accessed May 16, 2018. http://facilitation.matrix .msu.edu/index.php/download_file/view/44/124/.

Chawla, Dalmeet Singh. "Researchers Debate Whether Female Computer Coders Face Bias." *Nature* 530, no. 7590 (February 2016): 257.

Cheville, Julie. "Automated Scoring Technologies and the Rising Influence of Error." *English Journal* 93, no. 4 (March 2004): 47–52.

Christen, Markus, Mark Alfano, Endre Bangerter, and Daniel Lapsley. "Ethical Issues of 'Morality Mining': Moral Identity as a Focus of Data Mining." In *Human Rights and Ethics: Concepts, Methodologies, Tools, and Applications*, edited by Information Resources Management Association, 1146–66. Hershey, PA: IGI Global, 2015.

Christley, Scott, and Greg Madey. "Analysis of Activity in the Open Source Software Development Community." *Proceedings of the 40th Hawaii International Conference on System Sciences*. IEEE (2007): 1–10.

Chun, Wendy Hui Kyong. *Control and Freedom: Power and Paranoia in the Age of Fiber Optics*. Cambridge: MIT Press, 2006.

———. *Programmed Visions: Software and Memory*. Cambridge: MIT Press, 2011.

"Clinton Lectured State Dept. Staff on Cybersecurity in 2010 Video." FoxNews.com. Last updated October 22, 2016. http://www.foxnews.com/politics/2016/10/22 /clinton-lectured-state-dept-staff-on-cybersecurity-in-2010-video.html.

Cole, Sean. "Server Be Served." *This American Life*. November 4, 2016. https://www
.thisamericanlife.org/radio-archives/episode/601/master-of-her-domain-name.

Coleman, E. Gabriella. "The Political Agnosticism of Free and Open Source Software and the Inadvertent Politics of Contrast." *Anthropological Quarterly* 77, no. 3
(2004): 507–19.

Collins, Jeff, David Kaufer, Pantelis Vlachos, Brian Butler, and Suguru Ishizaki.
"Detecting Collaborations in Text: Comparing the Authors' Rhetorical Language
Choices in The Federalist Papers." *Computers and the Humanities* 38, no. 1 (Feb-
ruary 2004): 15–36.

Collins, Patricia Hill. *Black Feminist Thought*. 2nd ed. New York: Routledge, 1991.

Colton, Jared S., Steve Holmes, and Josephine Walwema. "From NoobGuides to#
OpKKK: Ethics of Anonymous' Tactical Technical Communication." *Technical
Communication Quarterly* 26, no. 1 (2017): 59–75.

Condon, William. "Large-Scale Assessment, Locally-Developed Measures, and Automated Scoring of Essays: Fishing for Red Herrings?" *Assessing Writing* 18, no, 1
(January 2013): 100–108.

Cook, Timothy. "A Message to Our Customers." Apple. February 16, 2016. http://
www.apple.com/customer-letter/.

Cortes, Corinna, and Vladimir Vapnik. "Support-Vector Networks." *Machine Learning* 20, no. 3 (September 1995): 273–97.

Cramer, Florian. *Words Made Flesh: Code, Culture, Imagination*. Rotterdam, the Netherlands: Piet Zwart Institute, 2005.

Cranz, Alex. "The Best Place to Find Stuff on Reddit Is Promoting Misogynistic
Garbage." Gizmodo. April 26, 2016. http://gizmodo.com/the-best-place-to-find
-stuff-on-reddit-is-promoting-mys-1772992114.

Crawford, Kate. "Artificial Intelligence's White Guy Problem." *New York Times*,
June 25, 2016. http://www.nytimes.com/2016/06/26/opinion/sunday/artificial
-intelligences-white-guy-problem.html.

Crowston, Kevin and James Howison. "The Social Structure of Free and Open
Source Software Development." *First Monday* 10, no. 2 (October 3, 2005): 1–27.
http://firstmonday.org/ojs/index.php/fm/article/view/1207/1127.

"Current State of Ruby on Rails Community." Rails Hurts. Accessed January 23,
2017. http://railshurts.com/current_state/.

D'Epenoux, F. "Sur un problème de production et de stockage dans l'aléatoire." *Revue Française de Recherche Opérationnelle* 14 (1960): 3–16.

Dagbovie-Mullins, Sika A. "Pigtails, Ponytails, and Getting Tail." *The Journal of Popular Culture* 46, no. 4 (2013): 745–71.

Dahle, Thomas L. "On the Lighter Side: How to Tell an Administrator from a
Teacher." *The Phi Delta Kappan* 43, no. 9 (June 1962): 405–7.

Dahm, John. "Science and Religion in Eighteenth-Century England: The Early Boyle
Lectures and the Bridgewater Treatises." PhD diss. Case Western Reserve University, 1969.

Daigon, Arthur. "Computer Grading of English Composition." *The English Journal*
55, no. 1 (January 1966): 46–52.

Daniel-Wariya, Joshua. "Rhetorical Strategy and Creative Methodology: Revisiting *Homo Ludens*." *Games and Culture* (July 2017): 1–17. https://doi.org/10.1177/1555412017721085.

de Certeau, Michel. *The Practice of Everyday Life*. Berkeley: University of California Press, 1984.

de Lauretis, Teresa. *Technologies of Gender: Essays on Theory, Film, and Fiction*. Bloomington: Indiana University Press, 2001.

Deane, Paul. "On the Relation Between Automated Essay Scoring and Modern Views of the Writing Construct." *Assessing Writing* 18, no. 1 (January 2013): 7–24.

Deleuze, Gilles, and Félix Guattari. *Anti-Oedipus: Capitalism and Schizophrenia*. London: Penguin Books, 2009.

Delgado, Richard, and Jean Stefancic. *Critical Race Theory: An Introduction*. New York: NYU Press, 2001.

Detienne, Marcel, and Jean-Pierre Vernant. *Cunning Intelligence in Greek Culture and Society*. Chicago: University of Chicago Press, 1991.

Dev, Vijay, et al. "Active Record Basics." RailsGuides. Accessed January 23, 2017. http://guides.rubyonrails.org/active_record_basics.html.

Dev, Vijay, et al. "Getting Started with Rails." RailsGuides. Accessed January 23, 2017. http://guides.rubyonrails.org/getting_started.html.

Diakopoulos, Nicholas. "Algorithmic Accountability." *Digital Journalism* 3, no. 3 (2015): 398–415.

DiMarco, Chrysanne, and Randy Allen Harris. "The RhetFig Project: Computational Rhetorics and Models of Persuasion." In *Workshops at the Twenty-Fifth AAAI Conference on Artificial Intelligence*. 2011.

Domingos, Pedro. "A Few Useful Things to Know about Machine Learning." *Communications of the ACM* 55, no. 10 (October 2012): 78–87.

Dyehouse, Jeremiah. "Knowledge Consolidation Analysis: Toward a Methodology for Studying the Role of Argument in Technology Development." *Written Communication* 24, no. 2 (April 2007): 111–39.

Edelman, Ezra. *O.J.: Made in America*. Bristol, CT: ESPN Films, 2016.

"EducationalTestingService/skll." GitHub. Accessed May 17, 2018. https://github.com/EducationalTestingService/skll.

Edwards, Chad, Autumn Edwards, Patric Spence, and Ashleigh Shelton. "Is That a Bot Running the Social Media Feed? Testing the Differences in Perceptions of Communication Quality for a Human Agent and a Bot Agent on Twitter." *Computers in Human Behavior* 33 (April 2014): 372–76.

Ellenberg, Jordan. *How Not to Be Wrong: The Power of Mathematical Thinking*. New York: Penguin, 2015.

Ellenbogen, Kirsten, Elizabeth Fleming, Jeff Grabill, and Troy Livingston. "Studying Web 2 Experiences: An Open Source Session." July 26, 2012. http://facilitation.matrix.msu.edu/index.php/download_file/view/43/124/.

Ellinger, Andrea D., and Maria Cseh. "Contextual Factors Influencing the Facilitation of Others' Learning through Everyday Work Experiences." *Journal of Workplace Learning* 19, no. 7 (2007): 435–52.

Ellis, Allan B. "The Computer and Character Analysis." *The English Journal* 53, no. 7 (October 1964): 522–27.

Ellul, Jacques. *The Technological System*. New York: Continuum, 1980.

Ensmenger, Nathan. *The Computer Boys Take Over*. Cambridge: MIT Press, 2010.

Eraut, Michael. "Informal Learning in the Workplace." *Studies in Continuing Education* 26, no. 2 (2004): 247–73.

Ercolini, G. L., and Pat J. Gehrke. "Writing Future Rhetoric." In *Theorizing Histories of Rhetoric*, edited by Michelle Ballif, 154–71. Carbondale: Southern Illinois University Press, 2013.

Ericsson, Patricia F., and Richard H. Haswell, eds. *Machine Scoring of Student Essays: Truth and Consequences*. Logan: Utah State University Press, 2006.

Essinger, James. *Ada's Algorithm: How Lord Byron's Daughter Ada Lovelace Launched the Digital Age*. Brooklyn: Melville House, 2014.

Eyman, Douglas. *Digital Rhetoric: Theory, Method, Practice*. Ann Arbor: University of Michigan Press, 2015.

"Facilitation Toolbox." Accessed May 18, 2018. http://facilitation.matrix.msu.edu/.

Faigley, Lester. *Fragments of Rationality: Postmodernity and the Subject of Composition*. Pittsburgh: University of Pittsburgh Press, 1992.

Falk, John H., and Lynn D. Dierking. *Lessons without Limit: How Free-Choice Learning Is Transforming Education*. Walnut Creek, CA: AltaMira, 2002.

Ferguson, Eugene. *Engineering and the Mind's Eye*. Cambridge: MIT Press, 1992.

"*Final Fantasy XIII*." *Final Fantasy* Wiki. Accessed April 23, 2018. http://finalfantasy.wikia.com/wiki/Final_Fantasy_XIII.

Fogg, B. J. "Persuasive Technologies." *Communications of the ACM* 42, no. 5 (May 1999): 27–29.

Freedman, Aviva, and Peter Medway. "Locating Genre Studies: Antecedents and Prospects." In *Genre and the New Rhetoric*, edited by Aviva Freedman and Peter Medway, 1–20. London: Taylor and Francis, 1994.

Fuller, Matthew. "Introduction, The Stuff of Software." In *Software Studies: A Lexicon*, edited by Matthew Fuller, 1–14. Cambridge: MIT Press, 2008.

Galey, Alan, and Stan Ruecker. "How a Prototype Argues." *Literary and Linguistic Computing* 25, no. 4 (December 2010): 405–24.

Gallagher, Sean. "All the Clintons' Servers: Hillary First Used a Power Mac Tower for e-Mail." Ars Technica (blog). Last updated September 2, 2016. http://arstechnica.com/information-technology/2016/09/fbi-clintons-first-e-mail-server-was-a-power-mac-tower/.

———. "Ignorance and Indifference: Delving Deep into the Clinton e-Mail Saga." Ars Technica (blog). Last updated July 15, 2016. http://arstechnica.com/information-technology/2016/07/indifference-and-ignorance-delving-deep-into-the-clinton-e-mail-saga/.

———. "NSA Refused Clinton a Secure BlackBerry Like Obama, So She Used Her Own." Ars Technica (blog). Last updated March 17, 2016. http://arstechnica.com/information-technology/2016/03/nsa-refused-clinton-a-secure-blackberry-like-obama-so-she-used-her-own/.

———. "Top Clinton Aide Was 'Frustrated' with Her Boss' e-Mail Practices." Ars Technica (blog). Last updated June 30, 2016. http://arstechnica.com/information -technology/2016/06/top-clinton-aid-was-frustrated-with-her-bosss-e-mail -practices/.

Galloway, Alexander R. *Gaming: Essays on Algorithmic Culture.* Minneapolis: University of Minnesota Press, 2006.

———.*Protocol: How Control Exists after Decentralization.* Cambridge: MIT Press, 2004.

Galloway, Alexander R., and Eugene Thacker. *The Exploit: A Theory of Networks.* Minneapolis: University of Minnesota Press, 2007.

Gates, Kelly A. *Our Biometric Future: Facial Recognition Technology and the Culture of Surveillance.* New York: NYU Press, 2011.

Gearan, Anne, and Philip Rucker. "Clinton: It 'Might Have Been Smarter' to Use a State Dept. e-Mail Account." *Washington Post.* March 10, 2015. https://www .washingtonpost.com/politics/hillary-clinton-to-answer-questions-about-use-of -private-e-mail-server/2015/03/10/4c000d00-c735–11e4-a199–6cb5e63819d2 _story.html.

Geiger, R. Stuart. "The Lives of Bots." In *Wikipedia: A Critical Point of View*, edited by Geert Lovink and Nathaniel Tkacz, 78–93. Amsterdam: Institute of Network Cultures, 2011.

Germain, Marie-Line, and Robin S. Grenier. "Facilitating Workplace Learning and Change: Lessons Learned from the Lectores in Pre-War Cigar Factories." *Journal of Workplace Learning* 27, no. 5 (2015): 366–86.

Ghazal, Ahmad, Tilmann Rabl, Minqing Hu, Francois Raab, Meikel Poess, Alain Crolotte, and Hans-Arno Jacobsen. "BigBench: Towards an Industry Standard Benchmark for Big Data Analytics." *Proceedings of the 2013 ACM SIGMOD International Conference on Management of Data*, 1197–1208. ACM, 2013.

Gibson, William, and Bruce Sterling. 1990. *The Difference Engine: 20th Anniversary Edition.* New York: Random House, 2011.

Gieryn, Thomas. "Boundary-Work and the Demarcation of Science from Non-Science: Strains and Interests in Professional Ideologies of Scientists." *American Sociological Review* 48, no. 6 (December 1983): 781–95.

Gillespie, Tarleton. "The Relevance of Algorithms." In *Media Technologies*, edited by Tarleton Gillespie, Pablo Boczkowski, and Kristen Foot, 167–94. Cambridge: MIT Press, 2014.

Ginsberg, Jeremy, Matthew H. Mohebbi, Rajan S. Patel, Lynnette Brammer, Mark S. Smolinski, and Larry Brilliant. "Detecting Influenza Epidemics Using Search Engine Query Data." *Nature* 457 (February 19, 2009): 1012–14.

Gitelman, Lisa. *Scripts, Grooves, and Writing Machines.* Stanford, CA: Stanford University Press, 2000.

Goankar, Dilip Parameshwar. "The Idea of Rhetoric in the Rhetoric of Science." *The Southern Communication Journal* 58, no. 4 (1993): 258–95.

Golabi, Kamal, Ram B. Kulkarni, and George B. Way. "A Statewide Pavement Management System." *Interfaces* 12, no. 2 (April 1982): 5–21.

Gold, Matthew K., ed. *Debates in the Digital Humanities*. Minneapolis: University of Minnesota Press, 2012.

Goldberg, Daniel, and Linus Larsson, eds. *The State of Play: Creators and Critics on Video Game Culture*. New York: Seven Stories Press, 2015.

Goldman, Adam, and Alan Rappeport. "Emails in Anthony Weiner Inquiry Jolt Hillary Clinton's Campaign." *New York Times*, October 28, 2016. https://www.nytimes.com/2016/10/29/us/politics/fbi-hillary-clinton-email.html.

Goldstein, Hilary. "Editorial: Is *Resident Evil 5* Racist?" IGN. Last modified February 10, 2009. http://www.ign.com/articles/2009/02/10/editorial-is-resident-evil-5-racist.

Gomes, Lee. "Machine-Learning Maestro Michael Jordan on the Delusions of Big Data and Other Huge Engineering Efforts." *IEEE Spectrum*. October 20, 2014, https://spectrum.ieee.org/robotics/artificial-intelligence/machinelearning-maestro-michael-jordan-on-the-delusions-of-big-data-and-other-huge-engineering-efforts.

Google. "About Flu Trends." Accessed 15 Aug 2014. https://www.google.org/flutrends/about/.

Gorman, Michael F. "*Interfaces* Editor's Statement." *Interfaces* 47, no. 1 (January–February 2017): 1–3.

Grabill, Jeffrey T., and Stacey Pigg. "Messy Rhetoric: Identity Performance as Rhetorical Agency in Online Public Forums." *Rhetoric Society Quarterly* 42, no. 2 (Spring 2012): 99–119.

Grasso, Floriana. "Towards a Framework for Rhetorical Argumentation." In *EDILOG 02: Proceedings of the 6th Workshop on the Semantics and Pragmatics of Dialogue*, edited by Johan Bos, Mary Ellen Foster, and Colin Matheson, 53–60. Edinburgh, UK: 2002.

———. "Towards Computational Rhetoric." *Informal Logic* 22, no. 3 (2002): 195–229.

Green, Christopher. "Charles Babbage, the Analytical Engine, and the Possibility of a 19th-Century Cognitive Science." In *The Transformation of Psychology: Influences of 19th-Century Philosophy, Technology, and Natural Science*, edited by Christopher Green, Marlene Shore, and Thomas Teo, 132–52. Washington, DC: American Psychological Association, 2001.

Gregory, Jason. *Game Engine Architecture*. 2nd ed. Boca Raton: CRC Press, 2014.

Gries, Laurie E. "Iconographic Tracking: A Digital Research Method for Visual Rhetoric and Circulation Studies." *Computers and Composition* 30, no. 4 (December 2013): 332–48.

Groves, Peter, Basel Kayyali, David Knott, and Steve Van Kuiken. "The 'Big Data' Revolution in Healthcare: Accelerating Value and Innovation." Center for US Health System Reform Business Technology Office, 2013.

Guilbeault, Douglas. "Automation, Algorithms, and Politics| Growing Bot Security: An Ecological View of Bot Agency." *International Journal of Communication* 10 (2016): 5003–21.

Gummett, Philip. *Scientists in Whitehall*. Manchester: Manchester University Press, 1980.

Gutwill, Joshua P., and Sue Allen. "Facilitating Family Group Inquiry at Science Museum Exhibits." *Science Education* 94, no. 4 (July 2010): 710–42.

Haas, Christina. *Writing Technology: Studies on the Materiality of Literacy.* New York: Routledge, 1995.

Haberman, Maggie. "Trump Promises a Revelation on Hacking." *New York Times*, December 31, 2016. https://www.nytimes.com/2016/12/31/us/politics/donald -trump-russia-hacking.html.

Hacking, Ian. *The Emergence of Probability: A Philosophical Study of Early Ideas about Probability, Induction and Statistical Inference,* 2nd ed. Cambridge: Cambridge University Press, 2006.

Halacy, Dan. *Charles Babbage: Father of the Computer.* New York: Crowell-Collier Press, 1970.

Handa, Carolyn. *Computers and Community: Teaching Composition in the Twenty-First Century.* Portsmouth, NH: Boynton/Cook, 1990.

Harris, Randy, and Chrysanne DiMarco. "Constructing a Rhetorical Figuration On-tology." In *Persuasive Technology and Digital Behaviour Intervention Symposium,* edited by Judith Masthoff and Floriana Grasso, 47–52. SSAISB, 2009.

Harvey, Adam. "CV Dazzle." Last updated August 22, 2017. https://cvdazzle.com/.

Harvey, Adam, Marco Roso, Nick Scholl, Pia Vivas, and Lauren Devine. "How to Hide from Machines." *Dis Magazine.* Accessed April 30, 2018. http://dismagazine.com /dystopia/evolved-lifestyles/8115/anti-surveillance-how-to-hide-from-machines/.

Haswell, Richard. "Automatons and Automated Scoring: Drudges, Black Boxes, and Dei Ex Machina." In *Machine Scoring of Student Essays: Truth and Consequences,* edited by Patricia F. Ericsson and Richard H. Haswell, 57–78. Logan: Utah State University Press, 2006.

"Hatching with 2 Broodies." Backyardchickens.com. Accessed June 4, 2014. http:// www.backyardchickens.com/t/828899/hatching-with-2-broodies.

Hawhee, Debra. *Bodily Arts: Rhetoric and Athletics in Ancient Greece.* Austin: University of Texas Press, 2004.

Hawisher, Gail E., and Cynthia Selfe. *Passions, Pedagogies, and Twenty-First Century Technologies.* Logan: Utah State University Press, 1999.

Hawk, Byron. "Stitching Together Events: Of Joints, Folds, and Assemblages." In *Theorizing Histories of Rhetoric,* edited by Michelle Ballif, 106–27. Carbondale: Southern Illinois University Press, 2013.

Hayles, N. Katherine. *Writing Machines.* Cambridge: MIT Press, 2002.

Herrington, Anne, and Charles Moran. "What Happens When Machines Read Our Students' Writing?" *College English* 63, no. 4 (March 2001): 480–99.

Herrington, Anne, and Charles Moran. "Writing to a Machine Is Not Writing at All." In *Writing Assessment in the 21st Century: Essays in Honor of Edward M. White,* edited by Norbert Elliot and Les Perelman, 219–32. New York: Hampton Press, 2012.

Herschel, J. F. W. "Report of the Royal Society Babbage Engine Committee." In Campbell-Kelly, ed. *Works of Charles Babbage,* 2:108–14.

Hicks, Marie. *Programmed Inequality.* Cambridge: MIT Press, 2017.

Holmes, Steve. "'Can We Name the Tools?': Ontologies of Code, Speculative Techné and Rhetorical Concealment." *Computational Culture: A Journal of Software Stud-*

ies 5 (2016). http://computationalculture.net/can-we-name-the-tools-ontologies
-of-code-speculative-techne-and-rhetorical-concealment/.

Howse, Derek. *Greenwich Time and the Longitude*. London: Philip Wilson Publishers
Ltd., 1997.

Hudak, Chris. "Black ~~Hawk~~ Zombie Down." GameRevolution. Last modified March
13, 2009. http://www.gamerevolution.com/review/43124-resident-evil-5-review.

Hum, Sue. "'Between the Eyes': The Racialized Gaze as Design." *College English* 77,
no. 3 (January 2015): 191–215.

Huot, Brian. "Computers and Assessment: Understanding Two Technologies." *Computers and Composition*, 13, no. 2 (1996): 231–43.

Huot, Brian, and Michael Neal. "Writing Assessment: A Techno-History." In *Handbook of Writing Research*, 1st ed., edited by Charles A. MacArthur, Steve Graham,
and Jill Fitzgerald, 417–32. New York: Guilford Press, 2008.

Hutchinson, Earl Ofari. "*Resident Evil* Racism." HuffingtonPost.com. Last modified
April 14, 2009. https://www.huffingtonpost.com/earl-ofari-hutchinson/resident
-evil-racism_b_175010.html.

Hyman, Anthony. *Charles Babbage: Pioneer of the Computer*. Princeton: Princeton
University Press, 1982.

Inoue, Asao B. "Articulating Sophistic Rhetoric as a Validity Heuristic for Writing
Assessment." *Journal of Writing Assessment* 3, no. 1 (Spring 2007): 31–54.

Ishizaki, Suguru, and David Kaufer. "Computer-Aided Rhetorical Analysis." In *Applied Natural Language Processing: Identification, Investigation and Resolution*, edited by Philip M. McCarthy and Chutima Boonthum-Denecke, 276–96. Hershey,
PA: IGI Global, 2012.

Jansz, Jeroen, and Raynel G. Martis. "The Lara Phenomenon: Powerful Female Characters in Video Games." *Sex Roles* 56, no. 3 (February 2007): 141–48.

Johnson, Robin S. "Masculinities in Play." *Annual American Men's Studies Association Conference Proceedings* 17, no. 1 (2010): 122–42.

Juran, Joseph M. *Juran on Quality by Design*. New York: Free Press, 1992.

Kaisler, Stephen, Frank Armour, J. Alberto Espinosa, and William Money. "Big Data:
Issues and Challenges Moving Forward." *46th Hawaii International Conference
on System Sciences*. IEEE, 2013.

Kaufer, David, and Suguru Ishizaki. "DocuScope: Computer-aided Rhetorical Analysis." cmu.edu. Accessed March 31, 2016. https://www.cmu.edu/hss/english/research
/docuscope.html.

Kelly, Ashley R., Nike A. Abbott, Randy Allen Harris, and Chrysanne DiMarco. "Toward an Ontology of Rhetorical Figures." In *Proceedings of the 28th ACM International Conference on Design of Communication*, 123–30. ACM, 2010.

Kernighan, Brian W., and P. J. Plauger. *The Elements of Programming Style*. 2nd ed.
New York: McGraw-Hill, 1978.

King, Geoff, and Tanya Krzywinska, eds. *Screenplay: Cinema/Videogames/Interfaces*.
New York: Wallflower Press, 2002.

Kinneavy, James L. *A Theory of Discourse: The Aims of Discourse*. New York: W. W.
Norton, 1980.

Kintz, Justin. "Driving Solutions to Build Smarter Cities." Uber Newsroom. January 13, 2015. https://newsroom.uber.com/us-massachusetts/driving-solutions-to-build-smarter-cities/.

Kirkpatrick, David. *The Facebook Effect: The Inside Story of the Company That Is Connecting the World.* New York: Simon and Schuster, 2010.

Kirschenbaum, Matthew G. *Mechanisms: New Media and the Forensic Imagination.* Cambridge: MIT Press, 2012.

Kittler, Friedrich A. *Gramophone, Film, Typewriter.* Translated by Geoffrey Winthrop-Young and Michael Wutz. Stanford, CA: Stanford University Press, 1999.

Knobloch-Westerwick, Silvia, and Carroll J. Glynn. "The Matilda Effect—Role Congruity Effects on Scholarly Communication: A Citation Analysis of *Communication Research* and *Journal of Communication* Articles." *Communication Research* 40, no. 1 (February 2013): 3–26.

Kohanski, Daniel. *The Philosophical Programmer: Reflections on the Moth in the Machine.* New York: St. Martin's Press, 1998.

Kolesar, Peter. "A Markovian Model for Hospital Admission Scheduling." *Management Science* 16, no. 6 (February 1970): 384–96.

Krall, Joseph, Tim Menzies, and Misty Davies. "Learning the Task Management Space of an Aircraft Approach Model." *Modeling in Human-Machine Systems: Challenges for Formal Verification: Papers from the AAAI Spring Symposium.* The AAAI Press, 2014.

Kress, Gunther. *Multimodality: A Social Semiotic Approach to Contemporary Communication.* London: Routledge, 2009.

Lanham, Richard A. *The Economics of Attention: Style and Substance in the Age of Information.* Chicago: University of Chicago Press, 2006.

———. *The Electronic Word: Democracy, Technology, and the Arts.* Chicago: University of Chicago Press, 1993.

Laquintano, Timothy, and Annette Vee. "How Automated Writing Systems Affect the Circulation of Political Information Online." *Literacy in Composition Studies* 5, no. 2 (2017). http://licsjournal.org/OJS/index.php/LiCS/article/view/169/218.

Lauer, Janice. *Invention in Rhetoric and Composition.* Anderson, SC: Parlor Press, 2004.

Lazer, David, Ryan Kennedy, Gary King, and Alessandro Vespignani. "The Parable of Google Flu: Traps in Big Data Analysis." *Science* 343, no. 6176 (March 2014): 1203–05.

LeBlanc, Paul J. *Writing Teachers Writing Software: Creating Our Place in the Electronic Age.* Urbana, IL: NCTE, 1993.

Lee, Ben. "Lightning Returns: Final Fantasy XIII Interview with Square Enix." Digital Spy. Last modified February 14, 2014. http://www.digitalspy.com/gaming/final-fantasy/interviews/a551088/lightning-returns-final-fantasy-xiii-interview-with-square-enix/.

Lee, Michelle Ye Hee. "Revisiting Clinton's Claim She Used Personal Email out of 'Convenience'." *Washington Post,* July 5, 2016. https://www.washingtonpost.com/news/fact-checker/wp/2016/07/05/revisiting-clintons-claim-she-used-personal-email-out-of-convenience-and-it-was-allowed-by-state-department/.

Leibniz, G. W. *Logical Papers: A Selection*. Oxford: Oxford University Press, 1966.

Lessig, Lawrence. "Against Transparency." *New Republic*. October 9, 2009. https://newrepublic.com/article/70097/against-transparency.

———. "On the Wikileak-Ed Emails between Tanden and Podesta Re: Me." LESSIG Blog, v2. Accessed December 11, 2016. http://lessig.tumblr.com/post/151983995587/on-the-wikileak-ed-emails-between-tanden-and.

Levy, Steven. *Hackers: Heroes of the Computer Revolution*. Sebastopol, CA: O'Reilly, 1994.

Licklider, J. C. R., and Robert W. Taylor. "The Computer as a Communication Device." *Science and Technology* 76 (April 1968): 21–31.

Light, Jennifer. "When Computers Were Women." *Technology and Culture* 40, no. 3 (July 1999): 455–83.

Lilien, Gary L. "Letter from the New Editor." *Interfaces* 12, no. 2 (April 1982): 1–4.

Lindgren, Michael. *Glory and Failure: The Difference Engines of Johann Müller, Charles Babbage and Edvard Scheutz*. Translated by Craig McKay. Cambridge: MIT Press, 1990.

Lockett, Alexandria. "I Am Not a Computer Programmer." *enculturation: a journal of rhetoric, writing, and culture* 14 (2012). http://enculturation.net/node/5270.

Losh, Elizabeth. "The Anxiety of Programming: Why Teachers Should Relax and Administrators Should Worry." *enculturation: a journal of rhetoric, writing, and culture* 14 (2012). http://enculturation.net/node/5272.

———. "Channelling Obama: YouTube, Flickr, and the Social Media President." *Comparative American Studies: An International Journal* 10, nos. 2–3 (2012): 255–68.

———. "Sensing Exigence: A Rhetoric for Smart Objects." *Computational Culture: A Journal of Software Studies* 5 (2016). http://computationalculture.net/article/sensing-exigence-a-rhetoric-for-smart-objects.

———. *Virtualpolitik: An Electronic History of Government Media-Making in a Time of War, Scandal, Disaster, Miscommunication, and Mistakes*. Cambridge: MIT Press, 2009.

Love, Glen A. "Riposte." *The English Journal* 54, no. 1 (January 1965): 61–62.

Lovelace, Ada Augusta. "Sketch of the Analytical Engine Invented by Charles Babbage, Esq. By L. F. Menabrea, of Turin, Officer of the Military Engineers. With Notes by the Translator." *Scientific Memoirs* 3 (1843): 666–731.

Luhmann, Niklas. "Code of the Moral." *Cardozo Law Review* 14 (1993): 995–1010.

———. *Law as a Social System*. Oxford: Oxford University Press, 2004.

———. *Social Systems*. Stanford, CA: Stanford University Press, 1995.

———. "The Sociology of the Moral and Ethics." *International Sociology* 11, no. 1 (March 1996): 27–36.

Lunsford, Andrea A. "Writing, Technologies, and the Fifth Canon." *Computers and Composition* 23, no. 2 (2006): 169–77.

Lynch, Jennifer. "New Report: FBI Can Access Hundreds of Millions of Face Recognition Photos." Electronic Frontier Foundation. June 15, 2016. https://www.eff.org/deeplinks/2016/06/fbi-can-search-400-million-face-recognition-photos.

Madaus, George. "A National Testing System: Manna from Above? An Historical/Technological Perspective." *Educational Assessment* 1, no. 1 (1993): 9–26.

Maher, Jennifer Helene. *Software Evangelism and the Rhetoric of Morality: Coding Justice in a Digital Democracy*. New York: Routledge, 2016.

Maher, Jennifer. "The Artificial Rhetorical Agent and the Computing of Phronesis." *Computational Culture: A Journal of Software Studies* 5 (2016). http://computatio nalculture.net/article/artificial-rhetorical-agents-and-the-computing-of-phronesis.

Martosko, David. "Email-Gate Update: Dick Morris Says Hillary 'Doesn't Know How to Type'." *Daily Mail*, March 24, 2015. http://www.dailymail.co.uk/news/article -3009471/Former-longtime-Clinton-insider-says-Hillary-doesn-t-know-type-email -scandal-swirls-returns-White-House-Obama-visit.html.

Matsumoto, Yukihiro. "Treating Code as an Essay." Translated by Nevin Thompson. In *Beautiful Code: Leading Programmers Explain How They Think*, edited by Andy Oram and Greg Wilson, 477–81. Sebastopol, CA: O'Reilly, 2007.

Maturana, Humberto R., and Francisco J. Varela. *Autopoiesis and Cognition: The Realization of the Living*. Dordrecht: D. Reidel Publishing Company, 1980.

Mayer-Schönberger, Viktor, and Kenneth Cukier. *Big Data: A Revolution That Will Transform How We Live, Work, and Think*. Boston: Houghton Mifflin Harcourt, 2013.

McAfee, Andrew. "Big Data's Biggest Challenge? Convincing People NOT to Trust Their Judgment." *Harvard Business Review*, December 9, 2013. https://hbr.org/2013 /12/big-datas-biggest-challenge-convincing-people-not-to-trust-their-judgment

McPherson, Tara. "US Operating Systems at Mid-Century: The Intertwining of Race and UNIX." In *Race after the Internet*, edited by Lisa Nakamura and Peter Chow-White, 21–37. New York: Routledge, 2012.

Miller, Carolyn R. "Genre as Social Action." *Quarterly Journal of Speech* 70, no. 2 (1984): 151–67.

———. "What Can Automation Tell Us About Agency?" *Rhetoric Society Quarterly* 37, no. 2 (2007): 137–57.

Miller, Carolyn R., and Dawn Shepherd. "Blogging as Social Action: A Genre Analysis of the Weblog." In *Into the Blogosphere: Rhetoric, Community, and Culture of Weblogs*, 1–24. University of Minnesota Digital Conservancy, 2004.

Montfort, Nick. "Continuous Paper: The Early Materiality and Workings of Electronic Literature." Last updated January 2005. http://nickm.com/writing/essays /continuous_paper_mla.html.

Montfort, Nick, and Ian Bogost. *Racing the Beam: The Atari Video Computer System*. Cambridge: MIT Press, 2009.

Montfort, Nick, Patsy Baudoin, John Bell, Ian Bogost, Jeremy Douglass, Mark C. Marino, Michael Mateas, Casey Reas, Mark Sample, and Noah Vawter. *10 Print Chr$(205.5+Rnd(1)); : Goto 10*. Cambridge: MIT Press, 2013.

Moseley, Maboth. *Irascible Genius: The Life of Charles Babbage*. Chicago: Henry Regnery Company, 1970.

Murdoch, Travis B., and Allan S. Detsky. "The Inevitable Application of Big Data to Health Care." *JAMA* 309, no. 13 (April 3, 2013): 1351–52.

Murray, Janet H. *Hamlet on the Holodeck: The Future of Narrative in Cyberspace*. Cambridge: MIT Press, 1998.

Narcisse, Evan. "The Natural: The Parameters of Afro." In Goldberg and Larsson, eds., *State of Play*, 53–75.

Neumeyer, Peter F. "Riposte." *The English Journal* 53, no. 9 (December 1964): 692.

Nilsen, Sarah, and Sarah E. Turner, eds. *The Colorblind Screen: Television in Post-Racial America*. New York: NYU Press, 2014.

Noble, Safiya Umoja. *Algorithms of Oppression*. New York: NYU Press, 2018.

Nofre, David, Mark Priestley, and Gerard Alberts. "When Technology Became Language: The Origins of the Linguistic Conception of Computer Programming, 1950–1960." *Technology and Culture* 55, no. 1 (January 2014): 40–75.

Nussbaum, Martha C. *The Fragility of Goodness: Luck and Ethics in Greek Tragedy and Philosophy*. New York: Cambridge University Press, 2001.

O'Neil, Cathy. *Weapons of Math Destruction*. New York: Crown, 2016.

Omizo, Ryan, William Hart-Davidson, Minh-Tam Nguyen, and Ian Clark. "You Can Read the Comments Section Again: The Faciloscope App and Automated Rhetorical Analysis." *DH Commons Journal* (2016).

Office of the Director of National Intelligence. "Background to 'Assessing Russian Activities and Intentions in Recent US Elections': The Analytic Process and Cyber Incident Attribution." January 6, 2017. https://www.dni.gov/files/documents/ICA_2017_01.pdf.

Open CV Foundation. "About." Accessed April 28, 2018. http://opencv.org/about.html.

———. "Face Detection Using Haar Cascades." http://docs.opencv.org/master/d7/d8b/tutorial_py_face_detection.html#gsc.tab=0.

OVA. Arg.dundee.ac.uk. Accessed March 31, 2016. http://www.arg.dundee.ac.uk/index.php/ova/.

Page, Ellis B. "The Imminence of . . . Grading Essays by Computer." *The Phi Delta Kappan* 47, no. 5 (January 1966): 238–43.

Page, Ellis B., and Dieter H. Paulus. *The Analysis of Essays by Computer*. Final Report of U.S. Office of Education Project No. 6–1318. Washington, DC: Department of Health, Education, and Welfare, 1968.

Pedregosa, Fabian, et al. "Scikit-learn: Machine Learning in Python." *Journal of Machine Learning Research* 12 (October 2011): 2825–30.

Perelman, Chaïm, and Lucie Olbrechts-Tyteca. *The New Rhetoric: A Treatise on Argumentation*. Translated by John Wilkinson and Purcell Weaver. South Bend, IN: University of Notre Dame Press, 1969.

Perelman, Les. "Construct Validity, Length, Score, and Time in Holistically Graded Writing Assessments: The Case Against Automated Essay Scoring (AES)." In *International Advances in Writing Research: Cultures, Places, Measures*, edited by Charles Bazerman, Chris Dean, Jessica Early, Karen Lunsford, Suzie Null, Paul Rogers, and Amanda Stansell, 121–32. Fort Collins, CO: WAC Clearinghouse, 2012.

Perkins, Jacob. *Python Text Processing with NLTK 2.0 Cookbook*. Packt Publishing, 2010.

Pinch, Trevor J., and Wiebe E. Bijker. "The Social Construction of Facts and Artifacts: Or How the Sociology of Science and the Sociology of Technology Might Benefit Each Other." *Social Studies of Science* 14, no. 3 (August 1984): 399–441.

Pisaro, Samuel E., and H. Gardner Emmerson. "No More Pencils, No More Books . . ." *The Phi Delta Kappan*, 42, no. 8 (May 1961): 363–64.

Poe, Mya, Asao B. Inoue, and Norbert Elliot, eds. *Writing Assessment, Social Justice, and the Advancement of Opportunity*. Fort Collins, CO: WAC Clearinghouse, 2018.

Pooley, Robert C. "Automatons or English Teachers?" *The English Journal* 50, no. 3 (March 1961): 168–73, 209.

Press, Gil. "A Very Short History of Data Science." *Forbes* Tech Blog. Last updated May 28, 2013. https://www.forbes.com/sites/gilpress/2013/05/28/a-very-short-history -of-data-science/#55ad9cc455cf.

Purushothaman, Ranjith, and Dewayne E. Perry. "Toward Understanding the Rhetoric of Small Source Code Changes." *IEEE Transactions on Software Engineering* 31, no. 6 (June 2005): 511–26.

Raghupathi, Wullianallur, and Viju Raghupathi. "Big Data Analytics in Healthcare: Promise and Potential." *Health Information Science and Systems* 2, no. 1 (December 2014): 1–10.

Raley, Rita. *Tactical Media*. Minneapolis: University of Minnesota Press, 2009.

Ramsay, Stephen. *Reading Machines: Toward an Algorithmic Criticism*. Urbana: University of Illinois Press, 2011.

Rawls, John. *Political Liberalism*. New York: Columbia University Press, 2003.

Reed, Chris, and Glenn Rowe. "Araucaria: Software for Argument Analysis, Diagramming and Representation." *International Journal on Artificial Intelligence Tools* 13, no. 4 (December 2004): 961–79.

Reed, Chris, and Timothy Norman, eds. *Argumentation Machines: New Frontiers in Argument and Computation*. Dordrecht, the Netherlands: Kluwer Academic, 2004.

Reider, David M. "Programming Is the New Ground of Writing." *enculturation: a journal of rhetoric, writing, and culture* 14 (2012). http://enculturation.net/node/5267.

Reyes, G. Mitchell. "The Rhetoric in Mathematics: Newton, Leibniz, The Calculus, and the Rhetorical Force of the Infinitesimal." *Quarterly Journal of Speech* 90, no. 2 (2004): 163–188.

Rice, Jeff. *The Rhetoric of Cool: Composition Studies and New Media*. Carbondale: Southern Illinois University Press, 2007.

Rice, Jenny Edbauer. "Rhetoric's Mechanics: Retooling the Equipment of Writing Production." *College Composition and Communication* 60, no. 2 (December 2008): 366–87.

Rickert, Thomas. *Ambient Rhetoric: The Attunements of Rhetorical Being*. Pittsburgh, PA: University of Pittsburgh Press, 2013.

Ridolfo, Jim, and William Hart-Davidson, eds. *Rhetoric and the Digital Humanities*. Chicago: University of Chicago Press, 2015.

Rivers, Nathaniel, and Paul Lynch, eds. *Thinking with Bruno Latour in Rhetoric and Composition*. Carbondale: University of Southern Illinois Press, 2015.

Robinson, David. "Text Analysis of Trump's Tweets Confirms He Writes Only the (Angrier) Android Half." Variance Explained (blog). Last updated August 9, 2016. http://varianceexplained.org/r/trump-tweets/.

Rogers, Richard. *Digital Methods*. Cambridge: MIT Press, 2013.

Rowe, Glenn, Fabrizio Macagno, Chris Reed, and Douglas Walton. "Araucaria as a Tool for Diagramming Arguments in Teaching and Studying Philosophy." *Teaching Philosophy* 29, no. 2 (June 2006): 111–24.

Russell, Bertrand. *A Critical Exposition of the Philosophy of Leibniz*. Cambridge, UK: The University Press, 1900.

Sackey, Donnie Johnson, Minh-Tam Nguyen, and Jeffrey T. Grabill. "Constructing Learning Spaces: What We Can Learn from Studies of Informal Learning Online." *Computers and Composition* 35 (March 2015): 112–24.

Sackey, Donnie, and Letitia Flower. "Facilitation Annotated Bibliography." Accessed January 10, 2016. http://facilitation.matrix.msu.edu/index.php/resources/.

Salter, Anastasia, and John Murray. *Flash: Building the Interactive Web*. Cambridge: MIT Press, 2014.

Sample, Mark. "5 BASIC Statements on Computational Literacy." *enculturation: a journal of rhetoric, writing, and culture* 14 (2012). http://enculturation.net/node/5269.

Sample, Mark, and Annette Vee. "Introduction to 'The Role of Computational Literacy in Computers and Writing.'" *enculturation: a journal of rhetoric, writing, and culture* 14 (2012). http://enculturation.net/computational-literacy.

Schaffer, Simon. "Fish and Ships: Models in the Age of Reason." In *Models: The Third Dimension of Science*, edited by Soraya de Chadarevian and Nick Hopwood, 71–105. Stanford, CA: Stanford University Press, 2004.

Schiappa, Edward. *Defining Reality: Definitions and the Politics of Meaning*. Carbondale: Southern Illinois University Press, 2003.

———. "Second Thoughts on the Critiques of Big Rhetoric." *Philosophy and Rhetoric* 34, no. 3 (2001): 260–74.

Schmidt, Jan-Hinrik. "Internet Privacy—Structural Changes of Publicness in Digital Networked Media." Berlin: Hans-Bredow-Institut, March 16, 2012. http://www.acatech.de/fileadmin/user_upload/Baumstruktur_nach_Website/Acatech/root/de/Material_fuer_Sonderseiten/Internet_Privacy/thesen_SCHMIDT_acatech_2012.pdf.

Schryer, Catherine F. "Records as Genre." *Written Communication* 10, no. 2 (1993): 200–34.

Scrapy. Computer program. Accessed May 17, 2018. https://scrapy.org/.

Selfe, Cynthia L., and Richard J. Selfe. "The Politics of the Interface: Power and Its Exercise in Electronic Contact Zones." *College Composition and Communication* 45, no. 4 (December 1994): 480–504.

Shanahan, Ian. "Bow, Nigger." In Goldberg and Larsson, eds., *State of Play*, 23–30.

Shannon, Claude Elwood, and Warren Weaver. *The Mathematical Theory of Communication*. Urbana: University of Illinois Press, 1999.

Shetterly, Margot Lee. *Hidden Figures*. New York: Harper Collins/William Morrow and Company, 2016.

Showalter, Elaine. "Pilloried Clinton." *Times Literary Supplement*, October 26, 2016. http://www.the-tls.co.uk/articles/public/hillary-clinton-vs-misogyny/.

"Simulated Natural Nest Incubation~Experiment #1 So It Begins. . . ." Backyardchickens

.com. Accessed June 6, 2014. http://www.backyardchickens.com/t/854946/simulated
-natural-nest-incubation-experiment-1-so-it-begins.

"sklearn.multiclass.OneVsRestClassifier." Accesssed May 17, 2018. http://scikit-learn
.org and http://scikit-learn.org/stable/modules/generated/sklearn.multiclass
.OneVsRestClassifier.html.

Smith, Daniel. "Of Headaches and Other Illnesses." *enculturation: a journal of rhetoric, writing, and culture* 5, no. 2 (2004). http://enculturation.net/5_2/index52.html.

Sobel, David, and William Andrews. *The Illustrated Longitude.* New York: Walker
and Company, 1998.

Sperry, Paul. "Clinton Directed Her Maid to Print out Classified Materials." *New
York Post* (blog). Last updated November 6, 2016. http://nypost.com/2016/11/06
/clinton-directed-her-maid-to-print-out-classified-materials/.

Stanley, Jay. "FBI and Industry Failing to Provide Needed Protections for Face Recognition." ACLU. Last modified June 15, 2016. https://www.aclu.org/blog/privacy
-technology/surveillance-technologies/fbi-and-industry-failing-provide-needed.

"State of Online Gaming Report." Spil Games. Accessed April 23, 2018. http://www
.spilgames.com/state_of_gaming_2013_uk_p1/.

Stolley, Karl. "MVC, Materiality, and the Magus: The Rhetoric of Source-Level Production." *Rhetoric and the Digital Humanities*, edited by Jim Ridolfo and William
Hart-Davidson, 264–76. Chicago: University of Chicago Press, 2015.

Stolley, Karl. "Source Literacy: A Vision of Craft." *enculturation: a journal of rhetoric,
writing, and culture* 14 (2012). http://enculturation.net/node/5271.

Suk, Jeannie. "Is Privacy a Woman?" *The Georgetown Law Journal* 97, no. 2 (January 2009): 485–513.

Sun, C., E. Stevens-Navarro, V. Shah-Mansouri, and V. W. Wong. "A Constrained
MDP-Based Vertical Handoff Decision Algorithm for 4G Heterogeneous Wireless Networks." *Wireless Networks* 17, no. 4 (May 2011): 1063–81.

Swade, Doron. *The Difference Engine: Charles Babbage and the Quest to Build the First
Computer.* New York: Penguin-Viking, 2000.

Swales, John, and Hazem Najjar. "The Writing of Research Article Introductions."
Written Communication 4, no. 2 (1987): 175–91.

Tanz, Jason. "Soon We Won't Program Computers. We'll Train Them Like Dogs."
WIRED. Last updated May 17, 2016. https://www.wired.com/2016/05/the-end-of
-code/.

"TechHire Initiative." The White House, Accessed January 23, 2017. https://obam
awhitehouse.archives.gov/issues/technology/techhire.

Templin, Charlotte. "Hillary Clinton as Threat to Gender Norms: Cartoon Images of
the First Lady." *Journal of Communication Inquiry* 23, no. 1 (January 1999): 20–36.

Tene, Omer, and Jules Polonetsky. "Big Data for All: Privacy and User Control in
the Age of Analytics." *Northwestern Journal of Technology and Intellectual Property* 11, no. 5 (2013): 239–73.

Terrell, J., A. Kofink, J. Middleton, C. Rainear, E. Murphy-Hill, C. Parnin, and J. Stall-
ings. "Gender Differences and Bias in Open Source: Pull Request Acceptance
of Women Versus Men." *PeerJ Preprints* (2016). http://doi.org/10.7287/peerj
.preprints.1733v2.

Texts from Hillary. Accessed April 29, 2018. http://textsfromhillaryclinton.tumblr
.com/.

Thor. "Gephyrophobia: Fear of Crossing Bridges Is Now in the Spotlight." Science
Buzz. Last updated August 8, 2007. http://www.sciencebuzz.org/blog/gephyrophobia
-fear-crossing-bridges-now-spotlight.

Trump, Donald. Quoted in "Trump: Who Does Apple Think They Are?!" *Fox &
Friends* (blog). Last updated February 18, 2016. http://www.foxnews.com/on-air
/fox-and-friends/blog/2016/02/18/trump-who-does-apple-think-they-are.

United States Government Accountability Office. "Report to the Ranking Member,
Subcommittee on Privacy, Technology and the Law, Committee on the Judiciary,
U.S. Senate. Face Recognition Technology: FBI Should Better Ensure Privacy and
Accuracy." May 2016. Last updated August 3, 2016. https://www.gao.gov/assets
/680/677098.pdf.

Vaidhyanathan, Siva. "Generational Myth." *The Chronicle of Higher Education* September 19, 2008. http://chronicle.com/article/Generational-Myth/32491.

van Winden, C., and R. Dekker. "Rationalisation of Building Maintenance by Markov Decision Models: A Pilot Case Study." *Journal of the Operational Research Society* 49, no. 9 (September 1998): 928–35.

Vee, Annette. *Coding Literacy: How Computer Programming Is Changing Writing.*
Cambridge: MIT Press, 2017.

———. "Coding Values." *enculturation: a journal of rhetoric, writing, and culture* 14
(2012). http://enculturation.net/node/5268.

———. "Text, Speech, Machine: Metaphors for Computer Code in the Law." *Computational Culture: A Journal of Software Studies* 2 (2012). http://computationalculture
.net/article/text-speech-machine-metaphors-for-computer-code-in-the-law.

———. "Understanding Computer Programming as a Literacy." *Literacy in Composition Studies* 1, no. 2 (2013): 42–64.

Vee, Annette, and James J. Brown Jr. "Rhetoric Special Issue Editorial Introduction."
Computational Culture: A Journal of Software Studies 5 (2016). http://computa
tionalculture.net/issue-five/.

Vee, Annette, and James J. Brown Jr., eds. Special Issue on Rhetoric and Computation.
Computational Culture: A Journal of Software Studies 5 (2016). http://computa
tionalculture.net/issue-five/.

Vincent, James. "Twitter Taught Microsoft's AI Chatbot To Be a Racist Asshole in
Less than a Day." The Verge. Last updated Mar 24, 2016. https://www.theverge
.com/2016/3/24/11297050/tay-microsoft-chatbot-racist.

Viola, Paul, and Michael J. Jones. "Robust Real-Time Face Detection." *International
Journal of Computer Vision* 57, no. 2 (May 2004): 137–54.

Viola, Paul, and Michael Jones. "Rapid Object Detection Using a Boosted Cascade
of Simple Features." *Proceedings of the 2001 IEEE Computer Society Conference on
Computer Vision and Pattern Recognition*, 1–9. IEEE, 2001.

Wajcman, Judy. *TechnoFeminism.* Cambridge, UK: Polity Press, 2006.

Wardrip-Fruin, Noah. *Expressive Processing: Digital Fictions, Computer Games, and
Software Studies.* Cambridge: MIT Press, 2009.

Washtell, Justin. "The Single Best Predictive Modeling Technique. Seriously." Analytic

Bridge. Last updated October 29, 2014. http://www.analyticbridge.com/profiles/blogs/the-single-best-predictive-modeling-technique-seriously.

"WATCH: Video Appears to Show Clinton Lecturing State Dept on Cyber Security." FOX News Insider. Last updated October 22, 2016. http://insider.foxnews.com/2016/10/22/hillary-clinton-appears-lecture-state-department-colleagues-cyber-security-email-server.

Watson, Ian. *The Universal Machine: From the Dawn of Computing to Digital Consciousness*. New York: Copernicus Books, 2012.

Wiener, Norbert. *Cybernetics or Control and Communication in the Animal and the Machine*, 2nd ed. Cambridge: MIT Press, 1948.

Wilkes, Maurice. "Charles Babbage—The Great Uncle of Computing?" *Communications of the ACM* 35, no. 3 (March 1992): 15–18.

Wilkinson, Norman. "On Dazzle Camouflage." In Behrens, ed., *Ship Shape*, 52–57.

Williams, Michael. *A History of Computing Technology*. New Jersey: Prentice Hall, 1985.

Wilz, Kelly. "Bernie Bros and Woman Cards: Rhetorics of Sexism, Misogyny, and Constructed Masculinity in the 2016 Election." *Women's Studies in Communication* 39, no. 4 (2016): 357–60.

Wing, Jeannette. "Computational Thinking." *Communications of the ACM* 49, no. 3 (March 2006): 33–35.

Winner, Langdon. *Autonomous Technology*. Cambridge: MIT Press, 1977.

Winograd, Terry, and Fernando Flores. *Understanding Computers and Cognition: A New Foundation for Design*. Norwood, NJ: Ablex Publishing Corporation, 1986.

Wissbaum, Richard J. "What Happened to Me in the Police Department or Which Shell Is the Pea Under?" *Interfaces* 12, no. 2 (April 1982): 83–87.

Wojcik, Michael. "Inventing Computational Rhetoric." PhD Diss., Michigan State University, 2013.

Wonnberger, Carl G. "Judging Compositions—Machine Method." *The English Journal* 44, no. 8 (November 1955): 473–75.

———. "They All Can Learn to Write." *The English Journal* 45, no. 8 (November 1956): 455–61.

World Health Organization. "Influenza (Seasonal)." Last modified January 31, 2018. http://www.who.int/mediacentre/factsheets/fs211/en/.

Wu, Xindong, Xingquan Zhu, Gong-Qing Wu, and Wei Ding. "Data Mining with Big Data." *IEEE Transactions on Knowledge and Data Engineering* 26, no. 1 (January 2014): 97–107.

Wysocki, Anne Frances, Johndan Johnson-Eilola, Cynthia L. Selfe, and Geoffrey Sirc. *Writing New Media: Theory and Applications for Expanding the Teaching of Composition*. Logan: Utah State University Press, 2004.

Yates, Raymond Francis. "Camouflage Science Explained." In Behrens, ed., *Ship Shape*, 66–79.

Yourbasicgeek. "Women Considered Better Coders—But Only if They Hide Their Gender." Reddit.com. Last updated February 12, 2016. https://redd.it/45f3mh.

Zhao, Qianchuan, Stefan Geirhofer, Lang Tong, and Brian M. Sadler. "Opportunistic

Spectrum Access via Periodic Channel Sensing." *IEEE Transactions on Signal Processing* 56, no. 2 (February 2008): 785–96.

Zikopoulos, Paul C., Chris Eaton, Dirk deRoos, Thomas Deutsch, and George Lapis. *Understanding Big Data: Analytics for Enterprise Class Hadoop and Streaming Data.* New York: McGraw-Hill, 2011.

Zimmerman, Eric, and Katie Salen. *Rules of Play: Game Design Fundamentals.* Cambridge: MIT Press, 2003.

Zukerman, Esther. "'Why Is Reddit So Anti-Woman?': An Epic Reddit Thread Counts the Ways." *The Atlantic*, July 26, 2012. http://www.theatlantic.com/entertainment/archive/2012/07/why-reddit-so-anti-women-epic-reddit-thread-counts-ways/325357/.

Contributors

Kevin Brock is an assistant professor of composition and rhetoric in the Department of English Language and Literature at the University of South Carolina, where he studies professional writing and digital rhetoric, especially the rhetoric of software and its development.

James J. Brown Jr. is an associate professor of English and Director of the Digital Studies Center (DiSC) at Rutgers University-Camden. He is also a cofounder of the Rutgers-Camden Archive of Digital Ephemera (R-CADE), which provides researchers with access to digital technology for hands-on research and artistic activity. His book, *Ethical Programs: Hospitality and the Rhetorics of Software*, examines the ethical and rhetorical underpinnings of networked software environments, and he is currently at work on a project called "Hateware" that examines the crucial role that software platforms play in the problem of online harassment.

Jonathan Buehl is an associate professor and the Vice Chair of Rhetoric, Composition and Literacy Studies in the Department of English at the Ohio State University. His research interests include the rhetoric of science, visual rhetoric, research methodology, and digital media studies. He is the author of *Assembling Arguments: Multimodal Rhetoric and Scientific Discourse* and essays published in *College Composition and Communication* and *Technical Communication Quarterly*.

Helen J. Burgess is an associate professor of English at North Carolina State University. She received her BA (Hons) and MA (Dist.) in English Language and Literature from Victoria University of Wellington, in New Zealand, and her PhD in English from West Virginia University. Burgess is the editor of the journal *Hyperrhiz: New Media Cultures*, the technical editor of *Rhizomes*, and an editorial board member for *thresholds*. She is also on the board of directors of the Electronic Literature Organization, and is coeditor of Hyperrhiz Electric, a monograph series for born-digital multimedia and digital humanities projects. Her major works include *Red Planet: Scientific and Cultural Encounters with Mars* (with Robert Markley, Michelle Kendrick, and Harrison

Higgs), *Biofutures: Owning Body Parts and Information Highways of the Mind* (with Robert Mitchell and Phillip Thurtle), and *The Routledge Research Companion to Digital Medieval Literature* (coedited with Jennifer E. Boyle).

Ian Clark is a Michigan State University graduate and College of Arts & Letters alumni board member. After earning a degree in Experience Architecture and Digital Humanities, Clark began working for the Ford Motor Company, where he focuses on connected vehicle diagnostics and better-informing drivers about their vehicles' health. Go Green!

Joshua Daniel-Wariya is an assistant professor of rhetoric and writing studies and serves as the associate director of composition at Oklahoma State University. He teaches both graduate and undergraduate courses across a range of topics within the field of writing studies, including composition and rhetoric, professional writing, and digital studies. His research areas include game studies, digital rhetorics, and writing program administration. His work has been previously published or is forthcoming in *Games and Culture*, *Computers and Composition*, *Pedagogy*, and elsewhere. He is currently writing a book that offers a critical perspective on the emergence of gamification services and practices in writing studies.

J. W. Hammond is a doctoral candidate in the Joint Program in English and Education at the University of Michigan, where he researches writing assessment history, theory, and technology. His published work has appeared in the *Journal of Writing Assessment* (coauthored with Merideth Garcia), the *Encyclopedia of Educational Philosophy and Theory* (coauthored with Pamela A. Moss), and the edited collections *Teaching and Learning on Screen: Mediated Pedagogies* (coauthored with Merideth Garcia) and *Writing Assessment, Social Justice, and the Advancement of Opportunity*.

William Hart-Davidson is a professor in the Department of Writing, Rhetoric, and American Cultures and the associate dean for Research and Graduate Education in the College of Arts & Letters at Michigan State University.

Lavinia Hirsu is a lecturer in the School of Education at the University of Glasgow. With a background in rhetoric and composition, Hirsu is currently developing interdisciplinary research that draws upon literacy studies and digital literacies, theories of cultural diversity and social justice, and applied linguistics, with a particular interest in translanguaging and translingualism. She completed an evaluation for the *Sharing Lives, Sharing Languages* project developed and implemented by the Scottish Refugee Council and is part of two international networks on social integration and resilience in contexts of migration, displacement, and environmental crises. Her research has appeared in *Computers and Composition*, *Peitho*, and *JAEPL*.

John Jones is an associate professor and the Director of Digital Media Studies in the Department of English at the Ohio State University, where he studies digital media, rhetoric and writing theory, and professional and technical communication. His work has appeared in *Computers and Composition, Kairos*, and the *Journal of Business and Technical Communication*. With Catherine Gouge, he has edited special issues of *Rhetoric Society Quarterly* and *Communication Design Quarterly Review* focused on the rhetorics of wearable devices.

Jennifer Juszkiewicz is a doctoral candidate in the Composition, Literacy, and Culture program at Indiana University Bloomington. She served as graduate assistant director of the first-year and professional writing programs at her institution, which included mentoring and supervising graduate instructors, administrative work, and teaching first-year and advanced composition. Her academic interests include pedagogy, spatial and computational rhetoric, interdisciplinary work, and institutional history. She also writes for nonprofit and industrial groups and has expertise in independent documentary film production. Jennifer has presented on her innovative work about policy, teacher education, and program administration at nationally and internationally renowned conferences, including the Conference on College Composition and Communication, the Conference for Writing Program administrators, Computers and Writing, the Conference for the Rhetoric Society of America, and the Watson Conference. Her work has been published in *enculturation: a journal of rhetoric, writing, and culture*.

Elizabeth Losh is an associate professor of English and American Studies, with a specialization in New Media Ecologies, at William & Mary. Before coming to William & Mary, she directed the Culture, Art, and Technology Program at the University of California, San Diego. She is the author of *Virtualpolitik: An Electronic History of Government Media-Making in a Time of War, Scandal, Disaster, Miscommunication, and Mistakes* and *The War on Learning: Gaining Ground in the Digital University*. She is the editor of *MOOCs and Their Afterlives: Experiments in Scale and Access in Higher Education* and coeditor with Jacqueline Wernimont of *Bodies of Information: Intersectional Feminism and Digital Humanities*. Her monograph *Hashtag* is due to be published in 2019 by Bloomsbury. She is a coauthor (with Jonathan Alexander, Kevin Cannon, and Zander Cannon) of the comic book textbook *Understanding Rhetoric: A Graphic Guide to Writing*, which is in its second edition.

Jennifer Helene Maher is an associate professor at the University of Maryland, Baltimore County, teaches in the English Department's Communication and Technology track, and is an affiliate faculty member in the Language, Literacy, and Culture PhD program. Her book, *Software Evangelism and the Rhetoric of Morality: Coding Justice in a Digital Democracy*, examines rhetorics of freedom encoded in software. In addition to research on topics such as the text-encoding system Unicode and indigenous resistance to intellectual property systems (with Catherine Fox), Maher has also published on free/open/

libre software documentation in the *Journal of Technical Writing and Communication*, and the relationship between computational morality and artificial rhetorical agents in *Computational Culture: A Journal of Software Studies*. She currently serves on the editorial board for *Technical Communication Quarterly*.

Tim Menzies is a professor in computer science at North Carolina State University where he teaches software engineering and automated software engineering. He received his PhD from the University of New South Wales. His research relates to synergies between human and artificial intelligence, with particular application to data mining for software engineering. He is the author of over 230 referred publications and is one of the 100 most cited authors in software engineering out of over 80,000 researchers (http://goo.gl /BnFJs). In his career, he has been a lead researcher on projects for NSF, NIJ, DoD, NASA, USDA, as well as joint research work with private companies. Menzies is the cofounder of the PROMISE conference series devoted to reproducible experiments in software engineering (http://openscience.us/repo). Menzies is an associate editor of *IEEE Transactions on Software Engineering*, *Empirical Software Engineering*, the *Automated Software Engineering Journal* and the *Software Quality Journal*. In 2015, he served as cochair for the ICSE '15 NIER track. He served as co-general chair of ICMSE '16.

Minh-Tam Nguyen earned her PhD in rhetoric and writing from Michigan State University in 2017. She is a UX Researcher & Designer who enjoys solving complex design problems for users all over the world.

Ryan M. Omizo is an assistant professor of English at Temple University. His primary areas of research are computational rhetoric, professional writing, digital humanities, app development, and Asian-American rhetorical theory. His work has appeared in *The Journal of Interactive Technology and Pedagogy, Journal of Writing Research*, and *enculturation: a journal of rhetoric, writing, and culture*.

James Chase Sanchez is an assistant professor of writing and rhetoric at Middlebury College, where he researches racial and cultural rhetorics and public memory. His work has previously appeared in *College Composition and Communication, Pedagogy, WPA, Present Tense* and *Journal of Contemporary Rhetoric*. Sanchez produced a documentary titled *Man on Fire*, which won a 2017 International Documentary Association Award.

Anthony Stagliano is an assistant professor of English at New Mexico State University, where he researches the relationship between technology, rhetoric, and activist politics, especially media art interventions into the world's problems, and what those can teach us about rhetoric's material and technological nature. He also maintains an active film- and media-making practice with films and videos screened in festivals and galleries around the world, and a feature film released commercially in the United States. His publications include work in *Tracing Rhetoric and Material Life: Ecological Orientations, enculturation: a journal of rhetoric, writing, and culture*, and forthcoming work in *Computers and Composition*.

Annette Vee is an associate professor of English at the University of Pittsburgh, where she teaches undergraduate and graduate courses in writing, digital composition and culture, rhetoric, and literacy, and steers programmatic initiatives on writing and digital studies. She received her PhD from the University of Wisconsin-Madison. She is the author of *Coding Literacy: How Computer Programming is Changing Writing*, which demonstrates how the theoretical tools of literacy can help us understand computer programming in its historical, social, and conceptual contexts. Her work on algorithmic authorship, rhetoric of software, intellectual property, and coding literacy has been published in *Computers and Composition, enculturation: a journal of rhetoric, writing, and culture, Computational Culture*, and *Literacy in Composition Studies.* She lives in Pittsburgh with her husband, three children, and dog.

Joseph Warfel is a mathematician working in operations research and analytics. His current research focuses on applications of stochastic optimization in humanitarian logistics.

Index

Abedin, Huma, 223n21

access: to computer operations, 70, 140; to technology, 214, 222n19. *See also* open source

ACLU (American Civil Liberties Union), 175

actors, 1, 58, 59–61, 64, 183, 185. *See also* voice acting

affect, 231, 242; communication of, 117, 122, 124, 128, 132; devoid of, 213; negative, 215

Africa, videogame representations of, 149–58. See also *Resident Evil 5* (videogame)

agency, 112, 173; in computation, 54, 71, 216. *See also* rhetoric

algorithms: as audience, 171; of chatbots, 14–15, 89–91, 168; for computer vision and facial recognition, 170–71, 174–77, 181–85, 188n12; in Faciloscope, 110, 115, 130; operations of, 3, 6–7, 49–50, 53, 72, 97, 190, 193, 205–6, 216, 232, 237, 242–43; for reading and writing text, 1, 48, 50, 52, 58, 63–64, 120, 193; rhetorical features of, 4–5, 94–95, 99–100, 106, 185, 239–40; for surveillance, 173. *See also* bots; Faciloscope (software); Open CV (software); Project Essay Grade (software)

Alomar, Sheva (videogame character), 149, 153–55

ambient rhetoric. *See* rhetoric

American Civil Liberties Union. *See* ACLU (American Civil Liberties Union)

Analytical Engine, 5, 16, 37–44. *See also* Bab-

bage, Charles; Difference Engine; Lovelace, Ada Augusta

apotonick (GitHub user), 76–79, 84

Apple Inc., 219–20

Araucaria (software), 115

Arizona Department of Transportation (ADOT), 97–98, 100–105, 108n33

argument: analysis of, 71, 75–79, 82–83, 113–15, 126–27, 201; and computing, 50, 54, 56, 82, 100, 242; Charles Babbage's use of, 16–17, 22–31, 36, 38, 41–44; and ethics, 52, and the machinic, 3, 5–6, 49, 233. *See also* rhetoric

Aristotle, 7, 192, 198, 207

artificial intelligence: study of, 39, 113; as thinking, 13–14, 89–92, 167, 239. *See also* bots

Astronomical Society, 17–18, 22–25, 28–30, 43

audience. *See* algorithms; rhetoric

automated essay scoring. *See* Project Essay Grade (software)

autopoiesis, 194–96, 199

Babbage, Charles: as rhetorician, 5, 16–17, 22–31, 38–44, 228, 240; funding of, 16–18, 22, 24–26, 30–31, 36–37, 43; life, 17–18; and mathematical tables, 18–20; mechanical notation of, 31–36. *See also* Analytical Engine; argument; Difference Engine

Barrett, Catherine M., 65n12

Bazerman, Charles, 22, 28, 50, 56

Beveridge, Aaron, 100

bias. *See* algorithms; big data; gender; race

big data: analysis of, 7, 190–91, 206–7, 234, 240–41; and bias, 196; and ethics, 7, 191–92, 194, 197–201, 243; patterns in, 190–91. *See also* gender; information

Bijker, Wiebe E., 56, 67n56

BlackBerry (phone), 215, 217, 222n19

bodies: of code, 170–71, 175, 202; and intelligence, 91, 187, 189n41, 217; non-human, 181, 189n41. *See also* gender; rhetoric

Bogost, Ian, 71, 94, 100, 106, 137, 140, 229–30

Bolter, Jay David, 146

Booch, Grady, 193

bots, 1–2, 4–5, 15, 50, 53, 64, 92, 114, 140, 165, 167–69, 233–34, 238, 242

Boyle, Casey, 229

Bratton, Benjamin H., 4, 7, 191, 198–99. *See also* Stack, the

British Navy, 24–25, 29, 172–73. *See also* ships (boats)

Brown, James J. Jr., 3–4, 7–8, 49–53, 66n32, 70, 72, 113–14, 133n17, 181, 183, 189n39, 216, 238–39, 242

Burke, Kenneth, 53, 66n32, 66n34, 133n17, 227, 229

cameras: movement of, 143–44, 146, 152, 181; angles of, 150, 155; in cellphones, 173–74; in ATMs, 174; sensors in, 185; software of, 233

camouflage: traditional, 7, 171; dazzle, 172–73, 176–77, 182. *See also* CV Dazzle

capacity: computing, 27, 29, 54, 168; human, 101, 128, 170, 178, 180; rhetorical 70, 113, 147

cellphones. *See* Apple Inc.; cameras; Clinton, Hillary; Samsung

Ceraso, Steph, 229

characters. *See* videogames

Chun, Wendy Hui Kyong, 147, 216, 220, 231–32, 234–35, 239

class (societal), 214, 218

classroom, 58, 61–63, 107n15, 111–12

Clement, Joseph, 31, 37

Clinton, Bill, 216, 222n21

Clinton, Hillary, 7, 212–21, 222nn18–19, 222–23n21, 224n40, 239

code: classes of, 76, 80–82; critical code studies, 2–3, 7, 51, 55, 194–95, 200, 231–32, 240; libraries of, 170–72, 174–87; in programming, 54, 72–73, 76–79, 89, 95–96, 100, 140, 157, 159, 220, 237, 239–41; rhetoric of, 8, 57, 69–72, 84, 133n17, 228–29; style in, 70–72, 74, 76, 83–84, 239, 241; writing of, 1, 6, 74–76, 190, 193, 199–202. *See also* bodies; computation; law; rhetoric; software; writing

codebook, 111, 116–18

cognition, as metaphor, 39–40, 44. *See also* bodies

collaboration: between professionals and laypersons, 95, 100, 105, 116, 128, 159, 192, 241–43; in constructing meaning, 70, 94; in academia, 228, 232; in programming, 74, 77, 83, 200, 205, 234

Collins, Patricia Hill, 154–55

Comey, James, 223–24n21

communication. *See* rhetoric

composition. *See* writing

computation: and bias, 105, 196, 233, 237, 242–43; calculation in, 38, 40, 42–43; and ethics, 60–61; and literacy, 1, 69, 94–98, 100, 105–6, 223n33, 228; and vision, 170–71, 173–77, 181

computational linguistics. *See* natural language processing

Computers and Writing Conference, 95

Constrained Markov Decision Process, 100–104, 108n42

Cook, Timothy, 220

craft, 22, 31, 37, 193; of creating videogames, 158; techne, 192

Crystal Tools (software), 6, 141–43, 146–47, 151

cutscenes, 6, 137, 142–43, 145–46, 151, 154–56, 240

CV Dazzle, 170–86, 188n12–13, 228, 240. *See also* camouflage, Open CV (software)

Daigon, Arthur, 48–51, 57, 59–61, 63

data. *See* information

de Certeau, Michel, 7, 170, 177–81

Deleuze, Gilles, 189nn39–40

development. *See* open source: software; web

Di Marco, Chrysanne, 115

Difference Engine: accuracy of calculations, 24, 26–27, 29; design and construction of, 22–24, 31, 36–39, 43; rhetorical use of, 16, 22, 25–31, 35–36, 41–44, 240–41; support for, 17–18, 25. *See also* Analytical Engine; Babbage, Charles
digital humanities, 2, 9n7, 95, 111, 237
digital literacy. *See* computation
digital media. *See* media
digital rhetoric. *See* rhetoric
discourse: analysis of, 113–14, 116–18; definitive, 50, 53–57; and deliberation, 74–75, 79, 84, 185–86, 216, 238; racial, 150, 157–58; scientific and professional, 28, 35, 106, 203, 213
distributed networks, 195, 216
Docuscope Project (software), 114, 136n45
Dyehouse, Jeremiah, 65n12

ecologies: material, 56, 180, 186; media, 22; rhetorical, 50, 56, 58, 138, 186; writing, 83, 228
education: automation and, 61–63, 112, 116; and computational literacy, 69, 95, 107n15; and ethics, 207; future of, 58, 64; problems in, 52, 63; studies of, 51
Electronic Frontier Foundation, 174–75
Ellis, Allan B., 58–59, 61
emergence, 2, 95, 177, 183
Emmerson, H. Gardner, 61–62
enculturation (journal), 95, 106, 180
English Journal, The, 48–51, 56–63
ethics. *See* argument; big data; computation; education; rhetoric

face detection, 176, 181–82, 184
facilitation. *See* Faciloscope (software)
Faciloscope (software), 6, 110–11, 113–24, 128–32, 135n41, 136n45, 136n50, 234
FBI (Federal Bureau of Investigation), 174–76, 181, 212, 223–24n21
Federal Bureau of Investigation. *See* FBI (Federal Bureau of Investigation)
Final Fantasy XIII (videogame), 6, 138, 141–51, 158
Flores, Leonardo, 238
Fox News, 215, 217, 220
Fuller, Matthew, 241–43, 244n14

Galloway, Alexander R., 138–39, 195, 216
gender: and bias, 147, 149–50, 154–55 199–207, 212, 216–19, 223n33, 241; gendered gaze, 214; and performance, 202–3; and rhetoric, 218; and technology, 7, 191, 213–15, 224n40, 239. *See also* Alomar, Sheva (videogame character); race
General Inquirer (software), 58–59, 67n67
genre. *See* videogames; writing
GitHub, 74–76, 191, 199–205, 241
Golabi, Kamal, 97, 104
Google: flu trends, 191–97; News, 219; Plus, 202–4; Photos, 233; search engine, 126, 238
Gorgias, 178
Gorman, Michael F., 107n15
Government Accountability Office, US, 174–75
Grabill, Jeffrey T., 234
Grusin, Richard, 146
Guattari, Félix, 189nn39–40

Haas, Christina, 57, 64
hardware, 5, 57, 139, 142, 229, 237
Harris, Randy, 115
Hart-Davidson, William, 6, 9n7, 120, 228, 234
Hawhee, Debra, 7, 171–72, 176–79, 183, 187, 189n41
health, 190–91, 196–97, 214–15, 224n40
highways. *See* roads
Holmes, Steve, 231, 234
HTML. *See* web
Huot, Brian, 49–50, 54, 61

IBM, 52, 58, 60–63, 192–93
information, 7, 38–39, 41, 53, 59, 72, 79–81, 93, 105, 114–16, 124, 135n36, 140, 142, 147, 192, 198–99, 202–3, 213–16, 218–20, 222–23n21, 232–34; databases of, 16, 53, 80–82, 89–90, 111, 117, 168, 174–75, 181; and knowledge, 53, 90, 93–94, 103, 118, 131, 168, 195, 197, 205, 234, 241; technology, 16. *See also* big data
instructions, 228, 231–32, 243
interface: design, 70, 142; of software, 116, 120, 129, 227, 229–30, 241
Interfaces (journal), 97, 99, 105, 107n15